A <u>NEW</u> PICTORIAL HISTORY OF THE

TALKIES

by DANIEL BLUM

Revised and Enlarged by John Kobal

G. P. PUTNAM'S SONS   New York

ACKNOWLEDGMENTS

Acknowledgments are due to the following for the loan of pictures and assistance in compiling this book:
Photoplay magazine, Ideal Publishing Corp., 20th Century-Fox, Warner Brothers, Paramount, Metro-Goldwyn-Mayer, Universal-International, Columbia, United Artists, Buena Vista, Republic, Walt Disney, Allied Artists, Rank, Gala, Royal Films International, Landau, Louis de Rochemont, Kingsley International, Lopert, Brandon Films, Joseph Burstyn, Distributing Corporation of America, Italian Film Export, Continental Distributing Corp., Janus, Embassy, Contemporary Films, British Lion, Avco-Ambassy, C.I.C., Cinema Centre, National General, Film Unifaree; also John Willis, Carl Raymund, Earl Forbes, William Thomas, Louis Melancon, Neal Graham, Dion McGregor, Ray Stuart, Richard Barthelmess, Clara Kimball Young, Gilbert Roland, Taylor Holmes, Pola Negri, and Lillian Gish.

SBN 399-11231-6

Library of Congress Catalog
Card Number 73-77887

Fourth Impression

PRINTED IN THE UNITED STATES OF AMERICA

JOAN CRAWFORD

EUGENIE BESSERER, AL JOLSON IN "THE JAZZ SINGER"
DIRECTED BY ALAN CROSLAND (1927 WARNER BROS.)

JOAN BENNETT, GEORGE ARLISS, FLORENCE ARLISS IN "DISRAELI" (1929
WARNER BROS.) MR. ARLISS WON AN ACADEMY AWARD
FOR HIS PORTRAYAL IN THIS FILM

CHARLES MORTON, JANET GAYNOR, NANCY
DREXEL, BARRY NORTON IN "FOUR DEVILS"
(1929 FOX) PART-TALKIE

THE EARLY TALKIES

Silence was no longer golden as far as the motion picture industry was concerned. In fact, by 1929 it was conceded, even by the most stubborn executives, that the sound film was here to stay. The novelty was over and motion pictures, heretofore affectionately called the "Movies," were now dubbed the "Talkies." It was the renaissance of pictures. The first talking pictures were very bad, but they indicated possibilities of this new medium. There was a tendency to hurl anything on the screen as long as it talked. The voice suddenly became of great concern. Incoming trains to Hollywood were bringing actors from the East who could speak! Among the silent screen stars, most of whom had little or no stage training or experience, there was a mad scramble for cultivation of the voice. Voice training became an important factor.

The amazingly rapid adaptation of sound by the industry, after Al Jolson sang to his mother in "The Jazz Singer," led to the erroneous belief that the talking picture was something new.

RAYMOND HACKETT, H. B. WARNER, NORMA
SHEARER IN "THE TRIAL OF MARY DUGAN"
DIRECTED BY BAYARD VEILLIER (1929 M-G-M)

CULLEN LANDIS, HELENE COSTELLO IN "LIGHTS OF NEW YORK"
DIRECTED BY BRYAN FOY (1929 WARNER BROS.)

RUTH CHATTERTON, RAYMOND HACKETT IN "MADAME X" DIRECTED BY LIONEL
BARRYMORE (1929 M-G-M) SCENARIST, WILLARD MACK, BASED ON
PLAY BY ALEXANDER BISSON

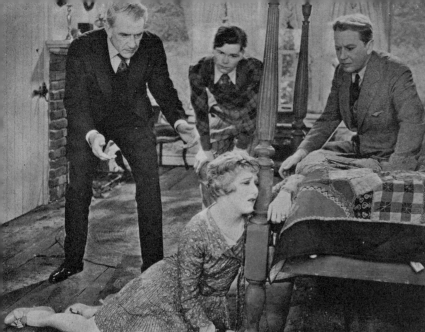

GEORGE IRVING, WILLIAM JANNEY, MARY PICKFORD (HER FIRST ALL-TALKING PICTURE), MATT MOORE IN "COQUETTE" (1929 UNITED ARTISTS) MISS PICKFORD WON AN ACADEMY AWARD FOR HER PERFORMANCE IN THIS FILM

HAROLD LLOYD (HIS FIRST TALKING PICTURE), CHARLES MIDDLETON IN "WELCOME DANGER" (1929 PARAMOUNT)

DOUGLAS FAIRBANKS IN "THE IRON MASK" (1929 UNITED ARTISTS) PART-TALKIE

JETTA GOUDAL, ALBERT CONTI, LUPE VELEZ, GEORGE FAWCETT, WILLIAM BOYD IN "LADY OF THE PAVEMENTS" DIRECTED BY D. W. GRIFFITH (1929 UNITED ARTISTS) PART-TALKIE

EMILY FITZROY, LAURA LA PLANTE, JOSEPH SCHILDKRAUT, OTIS HARLAN IN "SHOWBOAT" (1929 UNIVERSAL) PART-TALKIE

DANIEL HAYES, NINA MAY McKENNY IN "HALLELUJAH"
DIRECTED BY KING VIDOR (1929 M-G-M)

LOWELL SHERMAN, MARION NIXON, JOHN BARRYMORE
IN "GENERAL CRACK" (1929 WARNER BROS.)

THE EARLY TALKIES (Cont.)

The development of sound in relation to photographs had been in the developing stages over fifty years. There are instances of several experiments long before Edison's "Kinetoscope" in 1894. This was a crude device to synchronize sound with pictures by the use of ear tubes to catch the sound. Public demonstrations were held, but the reaction was negative and the demand for the first "Talkie" was nil, so the device was promptly withdrawn. In the years that followed, scientists continued their investigations. Several other devices appeared. One was called Synchroscope, imported by Carl Laemmle from his native Germany; another was the Cameraphone, later known as the Kinetophone, which was Thomas A. Edison's brain child; still another was the Phonofilm which Dr. Lee DeForest invented. None of these received acclaim. Exhibitors were skeptical and soon they were withdrawn. D. W. Griffith, who probably did more toward developing motion pictures as an art than any other one man, did not curb his pioneering spirit as far as sound film was concerned. Using a device known as the Photokinema, he showed his film "Dream Street" in 1921 at Town Hall in New York City with a sound accompaniment. The dialogue consumed about two hundred feet of the film. Griffith was praised for his effort, but the commercial talking picture was still in the future.

It was not until Sam Warner, of Warner Brothers, interested his three brothers, Harry, Albert and Jack, in a device emanating from the Bell Laboratories, and jointly owned by Western Electric and the American Telephone and Telegraph Company, that commercial talkies came into existence.

HELEN MORGAN IN "APPLAUSE"
(1929 PARAMOUNT)

GEORGE O'BRIEN IN "NOAH'S ARK"
(1929 WARNER BROS.) PART-TALKIE

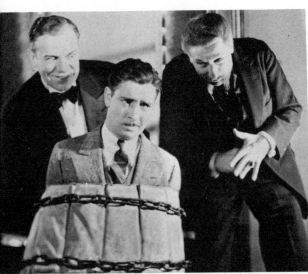

MONTAGU LOVE, RONALD COLMAN, LAWRENCE GRANT IN
"BULLDOG DRUMMOND" (1929 UNITED ARTISTS)
A SAMUEL GOLDWYN PRODUCTION

RUTH CHATTERTON

OTTO, BETTY COMPSON, ERIC VON STROHEIM IN "THE GREAT
GABBO" (1929 SONO ART-WORLD WIDE)

RICHARD ARLEN, GARY COOPER IN
"THE VIRGINIAN" (1929 PARAMOUNT)

CONRAD NAGEL, CHARLES BICKFORD, KAY JOHNSON
IN "DYNAMITE" (1929 M-G-M) CECIL B. DE
MILLE'S FIRST ALL-TALKING FILM

GEORGE DURYEA, SOPHIE TUCKER, LILA LEE
IN "HONKY TONK" (1929 WARNER BROS.)

ROBERT ELLIS, MERNA KENNEDY, GLENN TRYON
IN "BROADWAY" (1929 UNIVERSAL)

DOROTHY BURGESS, WARNER BAXTER IN "IN OLD ARIZONA" (1929 FOX)
MR. BAXTER WON AN ACADEMY AWARD FOR HIS PERFORMANCE IN THIS FILM

ZEPPO, CHICO, GROUCHO AND HARPO MARX, CYRIL RING, MARY
EATON, MARGARET DUMONT IN "THE COCOANUTS" (1929
PARAMOUNT) MARX BROTHERS FIRST ALL-TALKING FILM

AL JOLSON, DAVEY LEE IN
"THE SINGING FOOL" (1928
WARNER BROS.) PART-TALKIE

"SINGING IN THE RAIN" NUMBER FROM "HOLLYWOOD REVUE OF
1929" (M-G-M) BROX SISTERS, BUSTER KEATON, MARION DAVIES,
JOAN CRAWFORD, GEORGE K. ARTHUR

FANNY BRICE IN "MY MAN"
(1928 WARNER BROS.)

WILLIAM BAKEWELL, NANCY WELFORD IN "THE GOLD
DIGGERS OF BROADWAY" (1929 WARNER BROS.)

RALPH GRAVES, BELLE BAKER IN
"SONG OF LOVE" (1929 COLUMBIA)

CISSY FITZGERALD, BOBBY CLARK IN
"THE DIPLOMATS" (1929 FOX)

Audiences are saying it, Everywhere:—

WILLIAM DAVIDSON, TEXAS GUINAN IN
"QUEEN OF THE NIGHT CLUBS"
(1929 WARNER BROS.)

DAVID ROLLINS, SUE CAROL DOING
"THE BREAKAWAY" IN "FOX MOVIETONE
FOLLIES OF 1929"

At last, "PICTURES that TALK like LIVING PEOPLE!"

Vitaphone Talking Pictures are electrifying audiences the country over!

For *Vitaphone* brings to you the greatest of the world's great entertainers . . .

Screen stars! Stage stars! Opera stars! Famous orchestras! Master musicians!

Vitaphone recreates them *ALL* before your eyes. You see and hear them act, talk, sing and play—like human beings in the flesh!

Do not confuse *Vitaphone* with mere "sound effects."

Vitaphone is the *ONE* proved successful talking picture—exclusive product of Warner Bros.

Remember this—if it's not Warner Bros. *Vitaphone*, it's *NOT* the real, life-like talking picture.

Vitaphone climaxes all previous entertainment achievements. See and hear this marvel of the age—*Vitaphone*.

WARNER BROS. VITAPHONE TALKING PICTURES

If it's *Not* a WARNER PICTURE it's *Not* VITAPHONE

NORMA TERRIS, J. HAROLD MURRAY IN
"MARRIED IN HOLLYWOOD"
(1929 FOX)

MARIAN NIXON, SALLY O'NEIL, MYRNA LOY, PATSY RUTH
MILLER, LILA LEE, ALICE WHITE

SHIRLEY MASON, VIOLA DANA

SCENES FROM "SHOW OF SHOWS" (1929 WARNER BROS.)

BEN TURPIN, HEINIE CONKLIN, LUPINO LANE, LEE
MORAN, BERT ROACH, LLOYD HAMILTON

ANITA PAGE, CHARLES KING, BESSIE LOVE AND CHORUS IN "BROADWAY MELODY" DIRECTED BY
HARRY BEAUMONT (1929 M-G-M) THIS FILM WON AN ACADEMY AWARD
AS THE OUTSTANDING FILM OF THE YEAR.

JOHN BOLES, CARLOTTA KING
IN "THE DESERT SONG"
(1929 WARNER BROS.)

JOHN BOLES, BEBE DANIELS
IN "RIO RITA" DIRECTED BY
LUTHER REED (1929 RADIO)

IRENE BORDONI, JACK BUCHANAN
IN "PARIS"
(1929 FIRST NATIONAL)

THE EARLY TALKIES (Cont.)

In April of 1926, Warner Brothers were licensed by Western Electric Company to produce talking pictures under its system of patents. Warners decided to use the disc method, since abandoned, and called their device Vitaphone. "Don Juan," a silent film starring John Barrymore, was in production at the time. It was chosen to have a synchronized musical accompaniment by the New York Philharmonic Orchestra under the direction of Henry Hadley. With their own Warner Theatre in New York equipped for Vitaphone, on August 6, 1926, Vitaphone was premiered. In addition to the feature film, Will H. Hays made an introductory speech from the screen; Giovanni Martinelli, Marion Talley and Anna Case, assisted by the Metropolitan Opera Chorus, sang; and Micha Elman and Efrem Zimbalist played their violins. The event was a sensation. The industry was interested, but not convinced. The following year, October, 1927, Al Jolson not only sang but actually spoke from the screen in "The Jazz Singer." The success of this feature film was the signal for sound. Talkies were on their way. William Fox, with his Fox-Movietone, was the first to join the bandwagon. On July 15, 1928, Warners released "Lights of New York," the first all-talking feature film ever made. By the fall of 1929, nearly five thousand theatres in the United States were equipped with sound.

By 1930, with few exceptions, silent films were a thing of the past. The outstanding holdout was Charles Chaplin who released "City Lights" in 1931 and "Modern Times" in 1936 — both silent films with synchronized sound effects. It was not until 1940 that Chaplin bowed to the inevitable and made his first talking picture, "The Great Dictator." Except for the Chaplin films, the last silent film of any importance to be made was Garbo's "The Kiss," released in November of 1929. It was the last silent picture Metro-Goldwyn-Mayer ever made. The following year, billboards across the country were headlining the event in bold type: GARBO TALKS! Garbo was M-G-M's greatest box-office attraction. Garbo had a thick Swedish accent and a low throaty speaking voice. Could she conquer sound? There was a great deal of needless anxiety among the M-G-M higher-ups. Garbo's talkie debut in "Anna Christie" was a great success. The "Talkies" were not as kind to many of the other silent stars. John Gilbert was a glaring example. Prior to sound, he was the great lover of the screen. His high, squeaky voice was ludicrously alien to his strenuous love-making and the audiences laughed at him. Clara Bow, Corinne Griffith, William Haines, Norma Talmadge, Colleen Moore, Vilma Banky and Billie Dove were some of the other stellar lights who could not surmount the advent of the "Talkies," and, after valiant struggles, soon faded from the microphones.

(UNITED ARTISTS)

THE TAMING OF THE SHREW

Play by William Shakespeare; Additional Dialogue by Director, Samuel Taylor; Settings by William Cameron Menzies and Laurence Irving; Photography, Karl Struss; Film Editor, Allan McNeil. Released Oct. 26, 1929.

CAST

Katherine	Mary Pickford
Petruchio	Douglas Fairbanks
Baptista	Edwin Maxwell
Gremio	Joseph Cawthorn
Grumio	Clyde Cook
Hortensio	Geoffrey Wardwell
Bianca	Dorothy Jordan

JOSEPH CAWTHORNE, DOUGLAS FAIRBANKS, MARY PICKFORD
Top: DOUGLAS FAIRBANKS, MARY PICKFORD IN
"TAMING OF THE SHREW" (1929 UNITED ARTISTS)

LENORE ULRIC

PAUL MUNI

JEANNE EAGELS

HENRY KOLKER

NANCE O'NEIL

ROBERT EDESON

STAGE STARS APPEARING IN TALKIES

LOIS WILSON, BERT LYTELL, JASON ROBARDS
IN "ON TRIAL" (1928 WARNER BROS.)

CHARLES FARRELL, MARY DUNCAN
IN "THE RIVER"
(1928 FOX) PART-TALKIE

SALLY BLANE, RUDY VALLEE, DANNY O'SHEA, MARIE
DRESSLER, EDDIE NUGENT IN "THE VAGABOND
LOVER" (1929 RADIO) VALLEE'S FIRST FILM

JEANNE EAGELS, ANTHONY BUSHELL IN
"JEALOUSY" (1929 PARAMOUNT)

MARIE DRESSLER, POLLY MORAN IN
"DANGEROUS FEMALES" (1929 PARAMOUNT)

CHARLES FARRELL, JANET GAYNOR IN
"SUNNY SIDE UP" (1929 FOX)

JOHN LODER

BETTY COMPSON

LOWELL SHERMAN

PAULINE FREDERICK

KENNETH HARLAN

MARJORIE RAMBEAU

NICK STUART

LOUISE DRESSER

REGIS TOOMEY

MYRNA LOY

ALMA RUBENS

RUDY VALLEE

DOROTHY MACKAILL, BETTY COMPSON, MILTON SILLS, DOUGLAS FAIRBANKS, JR., SYLVIA ASHTON IN "THE BARKER" (1928 FIRST NATIONAL) PART-TALKIE

DON ALVARADO, LILI DAMITA IN "THE BRIDGE OF SAN LUIS REY" (1929 M-G-M) PART-TALKIE

HILDA VAUGHN, ROBERT MONTGOMERY, CHARLES McNAUGHTON, BERYL MERCER, CLAUDE ALLISTER IN "THREE LIVE GHOSTS" (1929 UNITED ARTISTS)

PAT O'MALLEY, CHESTER MORRIS IN "ALIBI" (1929 UNITED ARTISTS)

DOLORES DEL RIO, ROLAND DREW IN "EVANGELINE" (1929 UNITED ARTISTS) PART-TALKIE

PAUL MUNI, DON TERRY IN "THE VALIANT" (1929 FOX) MUNI'S FILM DEBUT

HARRISON FORD

SHARON LYNN

LANE CHANDLER

MOLLY O'DAY

RICHARD KEENE

DONALD CRISP

13

MYRNA LOY, ALICE JOYCE, CARROLL NYE
IN "THE SQUALL"
(1929 FIRST NATIONAL)

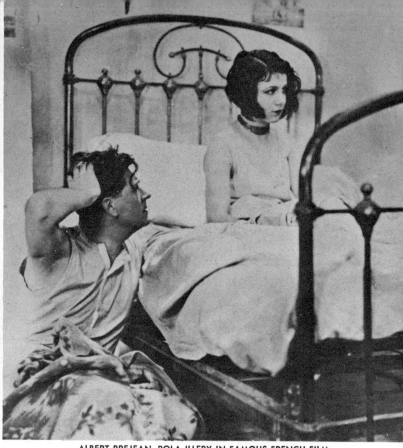

ALBERT PREJEAN, POLA ILLERY IN FAMOUS FRENCH FILM
"SOUS LES TOITS DE PARIS" ("UNDER THE ROOFS OF
PARIS") WRITTEN AND DIRECTED BY RENÉ CLAIRE.

EDWARD EVERETT HORTON
IN "THE HOTTENTOT"
(1929 WARNER BROS.)

MARGARET LIVINGSTON
IN "THE CHARLATAN"
(1929 UNIVERSAL)

JACK BENNY IN "HOLLYWOOD
REVUE OF 1929" (M-G-M)

ALBERTA VAUGHN IN
"NOISY NEIGHBORS"
(1929 PATHÉ)

GRANT WITHERS IN
"TIGER ROSE"
(1929 WARNER BROS.)

JOSEPH ALLEN, RICHARD DIX, MIRIAM SEEGAR,
NELLA WALKER IN "SEVEN KEYS
TO BALDPATE" (1929 RADIO)

JACK MULHALL IN THE FIRST DUAL ROLE
EVER ATTEMPTED IN THE TALKIES IN
"DARK STREET" (1929 FIRST NATIONAL)

OLIVE TELL, DORIS EATON, ALLEN KEARNS,
FRANK CRAVEN, THEODOR VON ELTZ
IN "THE VERY IDEA" (1929 RADIO)

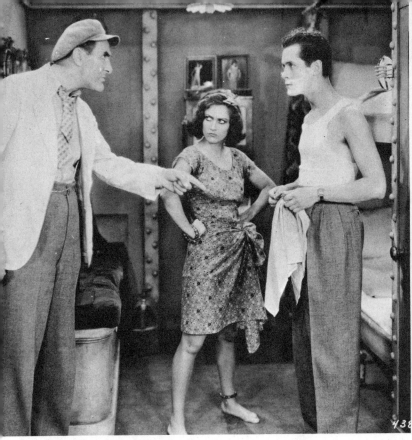

ERNEST TORRENCE, JOAN CRAWFORD, ROBERT MONTGOMERY IN "UNTAMED"
(JOAN CRAWFORD'S FIRST TALKIE) (1929 M-G-M)

VICTOR McLAGLEN, LILI DAMITA, EDMUND LOWE IN
"THE COCK-EYED WORLD" (1929 FOX)

LENORE ULRIC, ROBERT FRASER
Above: LOUIS WOLHEIM, LENORE ULRIC
IN "FROZEN JUSTICE" (1929 FOX)

GARY COOPER

MICKEY MOUSE IN HIS FIRST TALKING PICTURE, "STEAMBOAT WILLIE"
(1929 WALT DISNEY PRODUCTION)

DOROTHY JORDAN, MARION HARRIS, RAMON
NOVARRO IN "DEVIL MAY CARE"
(1929 M-G-M)

OWEN MOORE, DIANE ELLIS, PHILLIPS SMALLEY,
CAROLE LOMBARD, WILLIAM BEVAN, BILL BOYD
IN "HIGH VOLTAGE" (1929 PATHÉ)

THOMAS MEIGHAN, LILA LEE, GLADYS BROCKWELL,
H. B. WARNER IN "THE ARGYLE CASE"
(1929 WARNER BROS.)

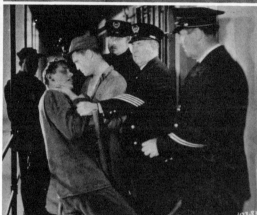

MARIE DRESSLER, WALLACE BEERY, DOROTHY JORDAN
Top: WALLACE BEERY, MARIE DRESSLER IN
"MIN AND BILL" DIRECTED BY GEORGE HILL (M-G-M)

CATHERINE DALE OWEN, JUDITH VOSSELI, LAWRENCE
TIBBETT (also top) IN "ROGUE SONG" DIRECTED BY
LIONEL BARRYMORE (M-G-M)

ROBERT MONTGOMERY, CHESTER MORRIS
Top: WALLACE BEERY, CHESTER MORRIS IN "THE
BIG HOUSE" DIRECTED BY GEORGE HILL (M-G-M)

GRACE MOORE IN HER FILM DEBUT AS JENNY
LIND IN "A LADY'S MORALS" (M-G-M)

ROLAND YOUNG, LILLIAN ROTH, KAY JOHNSON, REGINALD DENNY
IN "MADAM SATAN" (M-G-M) A CECIL B. DE MILLE PRODUCTION

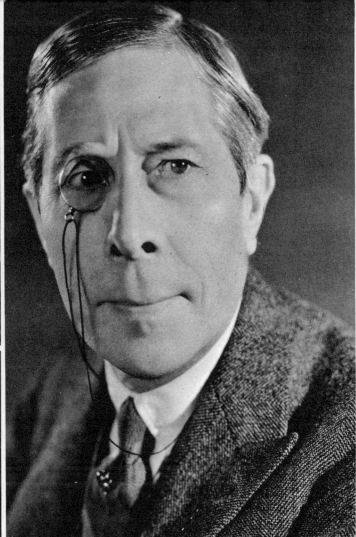

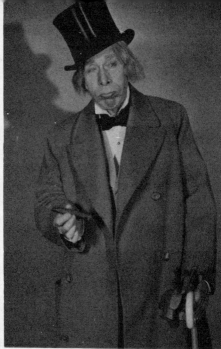

RALPH FORBES, H. B. WARNER, ALICE JOYCE,
GEORGE ARLISS (also top) IN "THE GREEN
GODDESS" (WARNER BROS.)

GEORGE ARLISS

GEORGE ARLISS (also top), BETTY LAWFORD,
REGINALD SHEFFIELD IN "OLD ENGLISH"
(WARNER BROS.)

GEORGE O'BRIEN IN
"ROUGH ROMANCE" (FOX)

1930 After the early chaotic period when sound was first introduced to the public, the industry settled down. Using its technical resources, it was developing better sound reproduction; the microphone was learning to move with the camera and a balance between sound and the image was established. The year's outstanding films included three war pictures: Academy Award winner "All Quiet on the Western Front," "Journey's End" and "Hell's Angels"; also, D. W. Griffith's "Abraham Lincoln," "Holiday," "Min and Bill," "The Big House," "With Byrd at the South Pole," "Old English," "The Divorcée" and "Anna Christie."

Among the new personalities to come to public attention were: Jean Harlow in "Hell's Angels," John Wayne in "The Big Trail," Spencer Tracy and Humphrey Bogart in "Up the River," Ginger Rogers in "Manhattan Mary," James Cagney in "Sinner's Holiday" and Edward G. Robinson in "Little Caesar." This latter picture was the beginning of a cycle of gangster films. Lon Chaney was in a remake of "The Unholy Three." It was his only talkie prior to his death on August 26, 1930. Marlene Dietrich, who created a furor in the German film "The Blue Angel," signed a contract with Paramount. "Morocco" was her first American film. Lillian Gish made her talkie debut in "One Romantic Night." Among the stage stars who re-created their famous roles were: Otis Skinner in "Kismet," Cyril Maude in "Grumpy," Charlotte Greenwood in "So Long, Letty," Dennis King in "The Vagabond King," Ed Wynn in "Manhattan Mary," Eddie Cantor in "Whoopee," and Joe Cook in "Rain or Shine." John Murray Anderson, famous stage director, was lured West for "King of Jazz," an elaborate revue which starred band leader Paul Whiteman.

RAMON NOVARRO IN "IN
GAY MADRID" (M-G-M)

BELLE BENNETT

GEORGE SIDNEY, VERA GORDON, KATE PRICE,
CHARLIE MURRAY IN "THE COHENS AND
KELLYS IN AFRICA" (UNIVERSAL)

MILTON SILLS

AMOS (FREEMAN GOSDEN), ANDY (CHARLES
CORRELL) IN "CHECK AND DOUBLE CHECK" (RADIO)

VILMA BANKY

LOUISE DRESSER, JOEL McCREA, WILL ROGERS IN "LIGHTNIN'" (FOX)

BLANCHE SWEET, TOM MOORE IN "THE WOMAN RACKET" (M-G-M)

MIRIAM HOPKINS, CHARLES STARRETT IN "FAST AND LOOSE" (PARAMOUNT)

MILTON SILLS, JANE KEITH, RAYMOND HACKETT IN "THE SEA WOLF" (FOX)

BEN LYON
Top: JEAN HARLOW, BEN LYON Center:
DOUGLAS GILMORE, JEAN HARLOW,
JAMES HALL, BEN LYON

JEAN HARLOW
SCENES FROM "HELL'S ANGELS" DIRECTED BY HOWARD HUGHES (UNITED ARTISTS)

JAMES HALL

WILLIAM COLLIER, SR., ELIZABETH PATTERSON, CHARLES EATON, REX BELL IN "HARMONY AT HOME" (FOX)

VICTOR MOORE, HELEN KANE IN "DANGEROUS NAN McGREW" (PARAMOUNT)

GEORGE BANCROFT, JESSIE ROYCE LANDIS IN "DERELICT" (PARAMOUNT)

LESLIE HOWARD, BERYL MERCER, ALEC B. FRANCIS, ALISON SKIPWORTH IN "OUTWARD BOUND" (WARNER BROS.)

LEW AYRES, LOUIS WOLHEIM
Right: LEW AYRES

LEW AYRES, RAYMOND GRIFFITH

(UNIVERSAL)

ALL QUIET ON THE WESTERN FRONT

Producer, Carl Laemmle, Jr.; Director, Lewis Milestone; Novel by Erich Maria Remarque; Adaptation by Maxwell Anderson; Scenario by George Abbott. Released April 27, 1930.

CAST

Katczinsky	Louis Wolheim
Paul Baumer	Lew Ayres
Himmelstoss	John Wray
Gerard Duval	Raymond Griffith
Tjaden	George "Slim" Summerville
Muller	Russell Gleason
Albert	William Bakewell
Leer	Scott Kolk
Behm	Walter Brown Rogers
Kemmerich	Ben Alexander
Peter	Owen Davis, Jr.
Detering	Harold Goodwin
Lieutenant Bertinck	Pat Collins
Westhus	Richard Alexander
Kantorek	Arnold Lucy
Hammacher	Heinie Conklin
Herr Meyer	Edmund Breese
Wachter	Bodil Rosing
Ginger	Bill Strong
Miss Baumer	Marion Clayton
Mrs. Baumer	Beryl Mercer
Mr. Baumer	Edwin Maxwell
Suzanne	Yola d'Avril
French Girls	Renée Damonde
	Poupee Andriot
Sister Libertine	Bertha Mann
Poster Girl	Joan Marsh

YOLA D'AVRIL, LEW AYRES, WILLIAM BAKEWELL, RENEE DAMONDE, POUPEE ANDRIOT, SCOTT KOLK
Above: (left) SCOTT KOLK (right) WILLIAM BAKEWELL

1930

SCOTT KOLK, WALTER ROGERS, SLIM SUMMERVILLE, WILLIAM BAKEWELL, LEW AYRES, RUSSELL GLEASON, OWEN DAVIS, JR.
Above: (left) LOUIS WOLHEIM (right) SLIM SUMMERVILLE

JAMES CAGNEY

IRENE DUNNE

BARBARA STANWYCK

HUMPHREY BOGART

DAVID MANNERS (also above), COLIN CLIVE
IN "JOURNEY'S END" DIRECTED
BY JAMES WHALE (TIFFANY)

JOAN PEERS, RICHARD CROMWELL (also above),
NOAH BEERY IN "TOL'ABLE DAVID" DIRECTED BY
JOHN BLYSTONE (COLUMBIA)

MARLENE DIETRICH
Above: EMIL JANNINGS IN "THE BLUE ANGEL"
DIRECTED BY JOSEF VON STERNBERG (PARAMOUNT)

EUGENE PALLETTE, CLIVE BROOK, HELEN WARE, HENRY
WADSWORTH, EVELYN BRENT IN
"SLIGHTLY SCARLET" (PARAMOUNT)

LUPE VELEZ, LEW AYRES, EDWARD G. ROBINSON
IN "EAST IS WEST" (UNIVERSAL)

JOBYNA HOWLAND, BERT WHEELER, ROBERT
WOOLSEY IN "DIXIANA" (RADIO)

GARBO TALKS!

Garbo made her debut in talkies in Eugene O'Neill's famous play, "Anna Christie," and was a success. The silent version, made in 1923, was equally successful for Blanche Sweet. Garbo followed this with another well-known play, Edward Sheldon's "Romance." Doris Keane had created the leading stage role and also appeared in the silent version in 1920.

(M-G-M)

ANNA CHRISTIE

Director	Clarence Brown
Author	Eugene O'Neill
Scenarist	Frances Marion
Dialoguer	Eugene O'Neill
Cameraman	William Daniels
Editor	Hugh Wynn
Recording Engineer	Douglas Shearer
Released	Feb. 21, 1930

CAST

Anna Christie	Garbo
Matt	Charles Bickford
Chris Christofsson	George Marion
Marthy	Marie Dressler
Larry	Lee Phelps
Johnny the Priest	James T. Mack

GRETA GARBO, MARIE DRESSLER Above: GEORGE MARION, GRETA GARBO, CHARLES BICKFORD Top: GRETA GARBO, GEORGE MARION IN "ANNA CHRISTIE" (M-G-M)

LEWIS STONE, GRETA GARBO, CLARA BLANDICK Above: GRETA GARBO, GAVIN GORDON Top: LEWIS STONE, GRETA GARBO IN "ROMANCE" (M-G-M)

CLAIRE LUCE, SPENCER TRACY, HUMPHREY BOGART IN "UP THE RIVER" (FOX)

MARIE DRESSLER IN "ANNA CHRISTIE" (M-G-M)

1930

LEE TRACY, CHARLES FARRELL, ROSE HOBART IN "LILIOM" (FOX)

ROD LA ROCQUE, HEDDA HOPPER, TYRELL DAVIS, RAYMOND HACKETT, SALLY EILERS, NORMA SHEARER, GILBERT EMERY, MARIE DRESSLER IN "LET US BE GAY" (M-G-M)

TYLER BROOKE, ROBERT MONTGOMERY, CHESTER MORRIS, NORMA SHEARER, FLORENCE ELDRIDGE, ROBERT ELLIOTT, MARY DORAN IN "THE DIVORCÉE" DIRECTED BY ROBERT Z. LEONARD (M-G-M)

CAROLE LOMBARD IN "SAFETY IN NUMBERS" (PARAMOUNT)

DENNIS KING IN "THE VAGABOND KING" (PARAMOUNT)

JEANETTE MacDONALD IN "THE VAGABOND KING" (PARAMOUNT)

GARY COOPER IN "SEVEN DAYS' LEAVE" (PARAMOUNT)

MARLENE DIETRICH IN "MOROCCO" (PARAMOUNT)

CYRIL MAUDE IN "GRUMPY" (PARAMOUNT)

GARY COOPER, BERYL MERCER IN "SEVEN DAYS' LEAVE" (PARAMOUNT)

WILLIAM (STAGE) BOYD, GARY COOPER IN "THE SPOILERS" DIRECTED BY EDWIN CAREWE (PARAMOUNT)

LILLIAN ROTH, DENNIS KING IN "THE VAGABOND KING" (PARAMOUNT)

22

A PRODUCTION SHOT FROM "ABRAHAM LINCOLN"
WITH D. W. GRIFFITH CENTER

IAN KEITH, KAY HAMMOND, WALTER HUSTON
IN "ABRAHAM LINCOLN"

A D. W. GRIFFITH PRODUCTION (UNITED ARTISTS RELEASE)

MARY ASTOR, ANN HARDING
IN "HOLIDAY"
(PATHÉ)

1929-30 AWARD WINNERS 1930-31

Left to right: George Arliss, who won for his performance in "Disraeli"; Marie Dressler's portrayal of Min in "Min and Bill" won her an Oscar; Norma Shearer won hers for "The Divorcée," and Lionel Barrymore's was won for his role in "A Free Soul."

BARBARA STANWYCK, ROD LA ROCQUE
IN "THE LOCKED DOOR"
(UNITED ARTISTS)

ETHEL WALES, CLARA BLANDICK, JACKIE COOGAN, JACKIE SEARLE
IN "TOM SAWYER"
(PARAMOUNT)

1930

MARY BRIAN, ARNOLD KORFF, INA CLAIRE, HENRIETTA CROSMAN,
FREDRIC MARCH IN "THE ROYAL FAMILY OF BROADWAY"
(PARAMOUNT)

JOHN WAYNE, MARGUERITE CHURCHILL

JOHN WAYNE, TYRONE POWER, SR., IAN KEITH
SCENES FROM "THE BIG TRAIL" DIRECTED BY RAOUL WALSH (FOX)

JOHN WAYNE

ARTHUR STONE, WALTER HUSTON, DOROTHY RENIER
IN "THE BAD MAN"
(FIRST NATIONAL)

EDWARD G. ROBINSON, ROBERT AMES, VILMA
BANKY IN "A LADY TO LOVE"
(M-G-M)

EMILY FITZROY, ANGELA MAWBY, JOHN BARRYMORE
IN "THE MAN FROM BLANKLEY'S"
(WARNER BROS.)

JOHN LODER, CORINNE GRIFFITH
IN "LILIES OF THE FIELD"
(FIRST NATIONAL)

MARILYN MILLER, LAWRENCE GRAY
IN "SUNNY"
(FIRST NATIONAL)

RIN-TIN-TIN, CHARLES DELANEY
IN "THE MAN HUNTER"
(WARNER BROS.)

SALLY EILERS, BUSTER KEATON
IN "DOUGH BOYS"
(M-G-M)

LON CHANEY

CLAIRE LUCE

CHARLIE MURRAY

HEDDA HOPPER

JOEL McCREA

JEAN ARTHUR

24

FARINA, CHUBBY CHANEY, DOROTHY DE BARBA, MARY ANN JACKSON, PETE, SHIRLEY JEAN RICKERT, WHEEZER, JACKIE COOPER, STYMIE MATHEW BEARD
IN "OUR GANG" (HAL ROACH COMEDIES)

HARPO, CHICO and GROUCHO MARX, MARGARET DUMONT
IN "ANIMAL CRACKERS"
(PARAMOUNT)

NOAH BEERY, ALICE GENTLE, ALEXANDER
GRAY, BERNICE CLAIRE IN "SONG
OF THE FLAME" (FIRST NATIONAL)

GINGER ROGERS, ED WYNN, LOU HOLTZ
IN "MANHATTAN MARY"
(PARAMOUNT)

ANN HARDING
IN "GIRL OF THE GOLDEN WEST"
(FIRST NATIONAL)

WINIFRED WESTOVER
IN "LUMMOX"
(UNITED ARTISTS)

RICHARD BARTHELMESS
IN "SON OF THE GODS"
(FIRST NATIONAL)

HAROLD LLOYD
IN "FEET FIRST"
(PARAMOUNT)

1930

AL JOLSON
IN "MAMMY"
(WARNER BROS.)

EDWARD G. ROBINSON
IN "LITTLE CAESAR"
(FIRST NATIONAL)

MICKEY McGUIRE
(MICKEY ROONEY)
(RADIO)

ALLAN PRIOR, WALTER PIDGEON, VIVIENNE SEGAL
IN "BRIDE OF THE REGIMENT"
(FIRST NATIONAL)

ALICE JOYCE, JOHN McCORMACK
IN "SONG O' MY HEART"
(FOX)

NORMA TALMADGE, WILLIAM FARNUM, EDWIN MAXWELL, HENRY KOLKER
IN "DU BARRY, WOMAN OF PASSION" (UNITED ARTISTS)
THIS WAS THE LAST FILM EVER MADE BY MISS TALMADGE

JOAN BENNETT, JOHN BARRYMORE
IN "MOBY DICK"
(WARNER BROS.)

MARLENE DIETRICH, GARY COOPER IN "MOROCCO"
DIRECTED BY JOSEF VON STERNBERG
(PARAMOUNT)

1930

GEORGES CARPENTIER (FORMER HEAVYWEIGHT CHAMPION OF FRANCE),
SALLY O'NEIL IN "HOLD EVERYTHING"
(WARNER BROS.)

JOHN BARRYMORE

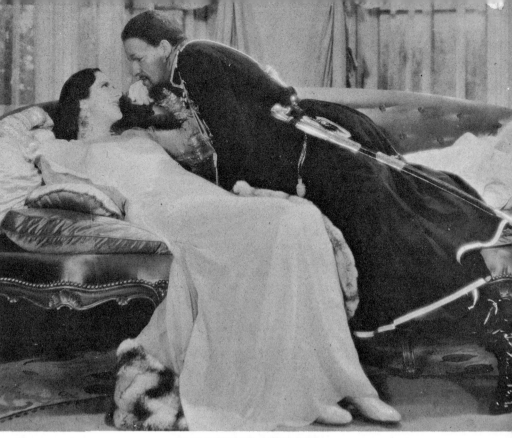

WILL ROGERS, FRANK ALBERTSON Top: MAUREEN O'SULLIVAN, WILLIAM FARNUM, WILL ROGERS IN "A CONNECTICUT YANKEE" DIRECTED BY DAVID BUTLER (FOX)

LYNN FONTANNE, ALFRED LUNT IN "THE GUARDSMAN" DIRECTED BY SIDNEY FRANKLIN (M-G-M)

DOUGLAS FAIRBANKS, EDWARD EVERETT HORTON IN "REACHING FOR THE MOON" (UNITED ARTISTS)

DOUGLAS FAIRBANKS IN "AROUND THE WORLD IN 80 MINUTES" (UNITED ARTISTS)

MARY PICKFORD IN "KIKI" (UNITED ARTISTS)

JOSEPH CAWTHORN, MARY PICKFORD, REGINALD DENNY IN "KIKI" (UNITED ARTISTS)

ELEANOR BOARDMAN, WARNER BAXTER, PAUL CAVANAGH IN "THE SQUAW MAN" (M-G-M)

DON ALVARADO IN "CAPTAIN THUNDER" (WARNER BROS.)

CONWAY TEARLE IN "THE LADY WHO DARED" (FIRST NATIONAL)

CHESTER MORRIS IN "CORSAIR" (UNITED ARTISTS)

REGINALD DENNY, BUSTER KEATON, DOROTHY CHRISTIE IN "PARLOR, BEDROOM AND BATH" (M-G-M)

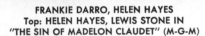

FRANKIE DARRO, HELEN HAYES
Top: HELEN HAYES, LEWIS STONE IN
"THE SIN OF MADELON CLAUDET" (M-G-M)

HELEN HAYES IN
"THE SIN OF MADELON CLAUDET"
DIRECTED BY EDGAR SELWYN (M-G-M)

HELEN HAYES, RONALD COLMAN Top: ALEC B.
FRANCIS, RONALD COLMAN, RICHARD BENNETT IN
"ARROWSMITH" DIRECTED BY JOHN FORD (UNITED ARTISTS)

BERT LAHR, CHARLOTTE GREENWOOD
IN "FLYING HIGH"
(M-G-M)

1931 The popularity of talkies continued to increase. Eighty-three per cent of the theatres in the United States were equipped for sound. England was not far behind with 75 per cent. "Cimarron," directed by Wesley Ruggles, was voted an Academy Award as the best picture of the year. Other Award winners were Helen Hayes, for her performance in her talking-film debut in "The Sin of Madelon Claudet"; Frances Marion, most famous of silent screen scenarists, for her original "The Champ"; Wallace Beery for his acting in the same film; and Norman Taurog for his direction of "Skippy," which made a star of Jackie Cooper. Walt Disney won the first of many Academy Awards with "Flowers and Trees," his first animated cartoon in Technicolor. Fine films included "Arrowsmith," "Street Scene," and "The Front Page." Among the famous pioneer stars of the silent days who were now heard on the screen were Mary Pickford, Lillian Gish, Clara Kimball Young, Alice Joyce, Norma Talmadge, Mae Marsh, Maurice Costello, Blanche Sweet, Antonio Moreno, Kathlyn Williams and Henry B. Walthall. New personalities bidding for favor were Clark Gable, Bette Davis and Bing Crosby. Gable, who had been an extra in silent pictures, had his first speaking part in "The Painted Desert." Bette Davis, who had appeared on the New York stage in "Broken Dishes," was signed by Universal and had minor roles in "Seed" and "Bad Sister." Bing Crosby had been singing with the Rhythm Boys. Mack Sennett spotted him and put him in two-reel comedies. Warner Brothers paid Constance Bennett the all-time high salary of $30,000 per week for emoting in an unimportant film, "Bought." Alfred Lunt and Lynn Fontanne, famous stage couple, made their first and only appearance in talkies when M-G-M persuaded them to film their stage success, "The Guardsman." Warner Oland, a character actor, made his first appearance as Charlie Chan, an oriental detective, a role he played in many films. Boris Karloff, an English actor who had been playing minor roles, was suddenly catapulted to fame in a horror film, "Frankenstein," which also had several sequels. Bela Lugosi, an Hungarian actor, met the same fate with "Dracula."

LEW AYRES IN
"THE IRON MAN"
(UNIVERSAL)

CLARK GABLE, MILDRED HARRIS, WALTER
McGRAIL, BARBARA STANWYCK IN
"NIGHT NURSE" (WARNER BROS.)

JACK HOLT, FAY WRAY
IN "DIRIGIBLE"
(COLUMBIA)

PHILLIPS HOLMES (center) IN
"AN AMERICAN TRAGEDY"
(PARAMOUNT)

ELEANOR BOARDMAN, JOHNNY MACK BROWN,
GAVIN GORDON IN "THE GREAT MEADOW"
DIRECTED BY CHARLES BRABIN (M-G-M)

CONSTANCE BENNETT with her father RICHARD
BENNETT IN "BOUGHT"
(WARNER BROS.)

CONSTANCE BENNETT, CLARK GABLE, ANITA
PAGE IN "THE EASIEST WAY"
(M-G-M)

NORMA SHEARER

NORMA SHEARER, LIONEL BARRYMORE
IN "A FREE SOUL" DIRECTED BY
ROBERT Z. LEONARD (M-G-M)

LUCY BEAUMONT, NORMA SHEARER, CLARK GABLE,
LESLIE HOWARD IN "A FREE SOUL"
(M-G-M)

EVELYN BRENT, CONRAD NAGEL
IN "THE PAGAN LADY"
(COLUMBIA)

MIRIAM HOPKINS, MAURICE CHEVALIER, CLAUDETTE
COLBERT IN "THE SMILING LIEUTENANT"
DIRECTED BY ERNST LUBITSCH (PARAMOUNT)

MARLENE DIETRICH, WARNER OLAND
IN "DISHONORED"
(PARAMOUNT)

ROBERT WILLIAMS, INA CLAIRE, ROBERT AMES,
MYRNA LOY IN "REBOUND"
(RKO)

JACKIE COOPER

RAY DOOLEY, EDDIE DOWLING
IN "HONEYMOON LANE"
(PARAMOUNT)

JACKIE COOPER, MITZI GREEN, JACKIE SEARL
IN "SKIPPY" DIRECTED BY
NORMAN TAUROG (PARAMOUNT)

JACKIE COOGAN, HELEN JEROME EDDY,
JACKIE COOPER IN "SOOKY"
(PARAMOUNT)

GENE RAYMOND   JUNE COLLYER   BARRY NORTON   VIRGINIA BRUCE   CHARLES STARRETT   DAVID TORRENCE

JOHN MILJAN, PURNELL PRATT, DOUGLASS MONTGOMERY, JOAN CRAWFORD IN "PAID" (M-G-M) Above: PAULINE FREDERICK, JOAN CRAWFORD IN "THIS MODERN AGE" (M-G-M)

CLARK GABLE, JOAN CRAWFORD IN "POSSESSED" (M-G-M)

LESTER VAIL, JOAN CRAWFORD Above: EARLE FOXE, JOAN CRAWFORD, CLARK GABLE IN "DANCE, FOOLS, DANCE" (M-G-M)

KEN MAYNARD, CHARLES KING, DONALD KEITH IN "BRANDED MEN" (TIFFANY)

EDWARD WOODS, JAMES CAGNEY IN "PUBLIC ENEMY" (WARNER BROS.)

SESSUE HAYAKAWA   RUTH ROLAND

32

GRETA GARBO

THE ONE AND ONLY GRETA GARBO IN THE ARMS OF FASCINATING CLARK GABLE! WHAT A PAIR OF SCREEN LOVERS THEY MAKE!

GRETA GARBO

magnificently thrilling in David Graham Phillips classic love story—

SUSAN LENOX

(HER FALL AND RISE)

with an all-star cast including

CLARK GABLE Jean Hersholt John Miljan

A ROBERT Z. LEONARD Production

Get ready for the supreme, exotic thrill of your picture-going days! Here truly is gorgeous Greta Garbo in the picture that will make you forget all her previous triumphs. Come and be thrilled.

METRO-GOLDWYN-MAYER

Sold by her father, she runs away.

The circus owner shows his true colors!

CECILE CUNNINGHAM, GRETA GARBO, CLARK GABLE
Above: GRETA GARBO, CLARK GABLE IN
"SUSAN LENOX" (M-G-M)

GRETA GARBO, ROBERT MONTGOMERY, OSCAR APFEL
Above: GRETA GARBO, LEWIS STONE IN
"INSPIRATION" DIRECTED BY CLARENCE BROWN
(M-G-M) FROM DAUDET'S "SAPHO"

RICHARD ARLEN, ZITA JOHANN, EDWARD G.
ROBINSON IN "TIGER SHARK"
(FIRST NATIONAL)

NORMAN KERRY

KATHLYN WILLIAMS

1931

DUNCAN RENALDO, EDWINA BOOTH, HARRY CAREY
IN "TRADER HORN" DIRECTED BY
W. S. VAN DYKE (M-G-M)

33

DOROTHY REVIER

ELLIOTT NUGENT

FIFI D'ORSAY

EDWARD NUGENT

ELSIE FERGUSON

CHARLES MORTON

DOROTHY SEBASTIAN

JOHN GARRICK, MARGUERITE CHURCHILL,
WARNER OLAND IN "CHARLIE CHAN
CARRIES ON" (FOX)

BETTE DAVIS, CONRAD NAGEL
IN "BAD SISTER"
(UNIVERSAL)

WALTER HUSTON, PHILLIPS HOLMES
IN "THE CRIMINAL CODE"
(COLUMBIA)

RICHARD DIX, IRENE DUNNE

RICHARD DIX, IRENE DUNNE
SCENES FROM "CIMARRON" DIRECTED BY WESLEY RUGGLES (RKO)
ACADEMY AWARD WINNER 1930-31

RICHARD DIX

LEW CODY, CONSTANCE BENNETT, JOEL McCREA,
HEDDA HOPPER, WALTER WALKER
IN "COMMON LAW" (PATHÉ)

ERIC LINDEN, ARLENE JUDGE
IN "ARE THESE OUR CHILDREN?"
(RKO)

W. C. FIELDS, MARILYN MILLER, LEON ERROL IN
"HER MAJESTY, LOVE"
(FIRST NATIONAL)

| SIDNEY BLACKMER | SYLVIA SIDNEY | JOHN GARRICK | LILA LEE | PAUL KELLY | LOIS WILSON | PAUL CAVANAGH |

HARPO, ZEPPO, CHICO and GROUCHO MARX
IN "MONKEY BUSINESS"
(PARAMOUNT)

| SPENCER TRACY | MARLENE DIETRICH | CLARK GABLE | BETTE DAVIS |

PROMISING PERSONALITIES

ALISON SKIPWORTH, MELVYN DOUGLAS, GLORIA
SWANSON IN "TONIGHT OR NEVER"
(UNITED ARTISTS)

1931

IVOR NOVELLO, RUTH CHATTERTON
IN "ONCE A LADY" DIRECTED BY
GUTHRIE McCLINTIC (PARAMOUNT)

DOROTHY MACKAILL, JOEL McCREA, CLARA
KIMBALL YOUNG, FREEMAN WOOD
IN "KEPT HUSBANDS" (RKO)

35

BORIS KARLOFF IN "FRANKENSTEIN"
DIRECTED BY JAMES WHALE (UNIVERSAL)

BORIS KARLOFF
IN "FRANKENSTEIN"
(UNIVERSAL)

BELA LUGOSI
IN "DRACULA"
(UNIVERSAL)

FRANCES DADE, BELA LUGOSI
IN "DRACULA"
(UNIVERSAL)

DOUGLASS MONTGOMERY, MAE CLARKE
IN "WATERLOO BRIDGE"
(UNIVERSAL)

MARIAN MARSH, BRAMWELL FLETCHER, JOHN BARRYMORE
IN "SVENGALI" DIRECTED BY ARCHIE MAYO
(WARNER BROS.)

MONTAGU LOVE, DORIS KENYON, LIONEL BELMORE,
GEORGE ARLISS, DUDLEY DIGGES IN "ALEXANDER
HAMILTON" (WARNER BROS.)

ELIZABETH PATTERSON, WARNER BAXTER, JANET
GAYNOR IN "DADDY LONG LEGS"
(FOX)

THE COX TWINS, LOIS WILSON, BETTE DAVIS,
RAYMOND HACKETT, DICK WINSLOW IN "SEED"
DIRECTED BY JOHN M. STAHL (UNIVERSAL)

LEON JANNEY
IN "PENROD AND SAM"
(FIRST NATIONAL)

BING CROSBY (also above) IN A
MACK SENNETT COMEDY
1931

NORA LANE, EDMUND LOWE, WARNER BAXTER
IN "THE CISCO KID" DIRECTED BY
IRVING CUMMINGS (FOX)

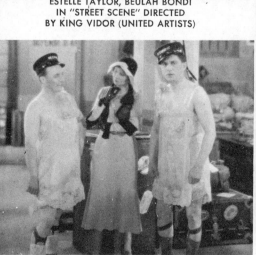

ESTELLE TAYLOR, BEULAH BONDI
IN "STREET SCENE" DIRECTED
BY KING VIDOR (UNITED ARTISTS)

CHIC JOHNSON, HELEN BRODERICK, OLE OLSEN
IN "FIFTY MILLION FRENCHMEN"
(WARNER BROS.)

ADOLPHE MENJOU, PAT O'BRIEN
IN "FRONT PAGE" DIRECTED BY LEWIS MILESTONE
(UNITED ARTISTS)

MADGE EVANS, JOAN BLONDELL, INA CLAIRE IN
"THE GREEKS HAD A WORD FOR THEM"
(UNITED ARTISTS)

MAE WEST MADE HER FILM DEBUT
WITH GEORGE RAFT IN "NIGHT AFTER NIGHT"
(PARAMOUNT)

HENRY STEPHENSON, MYRNA LOY, WILLIAM GARGAN,
LESLIE HOWARD IN "THE ANIMAL KINGDOM"
(RKO)

DOUGLAS FAIRBANKS IN
"MR. ROBINSON CRUSOE"
(UNITED ARTISTS)

1932 WAMPUS BABY STARS: Rear Row: TOSHIA MORI, BOOTS MALLORY, RUTH HALL, GLORIA STUART,
PATRICIA ELLIS, GINGER ROGERS, LILIAN BOND, EVALYN KNAPP, MARIAN SHOCKLEY Front Row:
DOROTHY WILSON, MARY CARLISLE, LONA ANDRE, ELEANOR HOLM, DOROTHY LAYTON

WILLARD ROBERTSON, LARRY STEERS, FRED SANTLEY, FRED
SULLIVAN, RICHARD BENNETT Above: W. C. FIELDS, ALISON
SKIPWORTH IN "IF I HAD A MILLION"
(PARAMOUNT)

JOAN CRAWFORD
IN "RAIN"
(UNITED ARTISTS)

JOAN CRAWFORD, WALTER HUSTON
Above: BEN HENDRICKS, WALTER CATLETT, JOAN CRAWFORD,
WILLIAM GARGAN, FREDERIC HOWARD IN "RAIN" DIRECTED
BY LEWIS MILESTONE (UNITED ARTISTS)

JOEL McCREA, DOLORES DEL RIO
IN "BIRD OF PARADISE"
(RKO)

GREGORY RATOFF, CONSTANCE BENNETT, NEIL
HAMILTON IN "WHAT PRICE HOLLYWOOD"
(RKO)

BILLIE DOVE, ROBERT MONTGOMERY, MARION DAVIES
IN "BLONDIE OF THE FOLLIES"
(M-G-M)

JOEL McCREA
IN "BIRD OF PARADISE"
(RKO)

1932 The most ambitious production was M-G-M's star-studded Academy Award winning "Grand Hotel," taken from Vicki Baum's best-selling novel and directed by Edmund Goulding. Fredric March received an award for his dual performance in "Dr. Jekyll and Mr. Hyde," and Walt Disney received a special citation as creator of Mickey Mouse. Among the best films were "A Farewell to Arms," "One Way Passage," "Scarface," "I Am a Fugitive from a Chain Gang," "Back Street," "Smilin' Through" and "The Man I Killed." Cecil B. De Mille made another Biblical spectacle, "The Sign of the Cross." Eugene O'Neill's play "Strange Interlude" was not too successfully transported to the screen. George M. Cohan, of stage fame, made his talkie debut in "The Phantom President." Mae West, who had great stage success with "Diamond Lil," made her film debut in "Night After Night." It was the beginning of her spectacular picture career. Katharine Hepburn, a young actress from the stage hit "The Warrior's Husband," appeared in "A Bill of Divorcement" and was promptly declared "the find of the year." Johnny Weissmuller, a former Olympic swimming champion, made "Tarzan, The Ape Man," the first of a series of Tarzan features. He became so identified with the role that he became the most famous of all the film Tarzans. Shirley Temple, at the age of three, was appearing in Educational two-reel comedies. Charles Laughton in "Payment Deferred" and George Raft in "Scarface" were two other newcomers to the Hollywood scene. For the first and only time in their long careers, Ethel, John and Lionel Barrymore appeared together in "Rasputin and the Empress." Joan Crawford played Sadie Thompson in "Rain"; Garbo, a prestige star, appeared in "Grand Hotel," "Mata Hari" and "As You Desire Me." Jesse L. Lasky, one of filmdom's pioneer producers, left Paramount to become an independent producer for Fox. Among the foreign imports to receive American acclaim were the German films "Maedchen in Uniform" and Eric Charell's "Congress Dances" which starred English Lilian Harvey; and the French trilogy "Marius," "Fanny" and "Cesar" which starred Raimu. Radio City Music Hall, largest theatre in the world devoted to the cinema, opened its doors on December 27, 1932.

BILLIE DOVE
IN "BLONDIE OF THE FOLLIES"
(M-G-M)

VINCE BARNETT, GEORGE RAFT, PAUL MUNI
Above: OSGOOD PERKINS, PAUL MUNI IN
"SCARFACE" DIRECTED BY HOWARD HAWKS
(UNITED ARTISTS)

PAUL MUNI
IN "SCARFACE"
(UNITED ARTISTS)

PAUL MUNI, EDWARD J. McNAMARA, DAVID LANDAU
Above: PAUL MUNI IN "I AM A FUGITIVE FROM
A CHAIN GANG" DIRECTED BY MERVYN LE ROY
(WARNER BROS.)

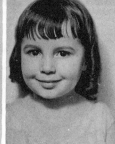

DOLORES COSTELLO　　**JUNIOR DURKIN**　　**CORA SUE COLLINS**

HARRY LANGDON
IN "THE HITCH HIKER"
(FIRST NATIONAL)

KATHARINE HEPBURN, BILLIE BURKE, JOHN BARRYMORE
IN "A BILL OF DIVORCEMENT" DIRECTED BY
GEORGE CUKOR (RKO)

KATHARINE HEPBURN, DAVID MANNERS IN
"A BILL OF DIVORCEMENT"
(RKO)

FREDRIC MARCH

VIVIAN TOBIN, FERDINAND GOTTSCHALK, ROBERT MANNING, FREDRIC MARCH, CLAUDETTE COLBERT
Above left: CLAUDETTE COLBERT, CHARLES LAUGHTON Above right: ELISSA LANDI, FREDRIC
MARCH IN CECIL B. DE MILLE'S PRODUCTION OF "THE SIGN OF THE CROSS" (PARAMOUNT)

CLAUDETTE COLBERT

SUSAN FLEMING, JACK OAKIE, LYDA ROBERTI
IN "MILLION DOLLAR LEGS"
(PARAMOUNT)

DAVID ROLLINS　　**1932**　　ANITA PAGE　　JOHN DARROW

MATTY KEMP, DOROTHY JORDAN,
WILL ROGERS, IRENE RICH IN
"DOWN TO EARTH" (FOX)

GILBERT ROLAND, CLARA BOW
IN "CALL HER SAVAGE"
(FOX)

KARL DANE

LILI DAMITA

REX LEASE

CHARLES "CHIC" SALES, JACKIE COOPER
IN "WHEN A FELLOW NEEDS A FRIEND"
(M-G-M)

JACK DEMPSEY, JUNE GALE IN "WIN,
LOSE OR DRAW," A VITAPHONE SHORT
(WARNER BROS.)

JEANETTE MacDONALD, MAURICE CHEVALIER,
GENEVIEVE TOBIN IN "ONE HOUR WITH YOU"
DIRECTED BY ERNST LUBITSCH (PARAMOUNT PICTURES)

PHILLIPS HOLMES, LOUISE CARTER, NANCY CARROLL,
LIONEL BARRYMORE IN "BROKEN LULLABY"
DIRECTED BY ERNST LUBITSCH

GARY COOPER, TALLULAH BANKHEAD, CHARLES LAUGHTON,
IN "DEVIL AND THE DEEP" Above: CHARLES BICKFORD,
TALLULAH BANKHEAD, PAUL LUKAS IN "THUNDER BELOW"

MIRIAM HOPKINS AS IVY
IN "DR. JEKYLL AND MR. HYDE" DIRECTED BY ROUBEN MAMOULIAN
(PARAMOUNT PRODUCTIONS)

MIRIAM HOPKINS, FREDRIC MARCH IN DUAL ROLE

DONALD DILLAWAY

CHESTER MORRIS, SYLVIA SIDNEY, JOHN
WRAY, NED SPARKS IN "THE MIRACLE MAN"
(PARAMOUNT)

RIN-TIN-TIN

1932

LUIS TRENKER, TALA BIRELL,
VICTOR VARCONI IN "THE DOOMED
BATTALION" (UNIVERSAL)

FRANK ALBERTSON

JOAN CRAWFORD, JOHN BARRYMORE, LIONEL BARRYMORE, LEWIS STONE Above: JOHN BARRYMORE, GRETA GARBO

(M-G-M)

GRAND HOTEL

From William A. Drake's American play version of "Menschen im Hotel" by Vicki Baum; Director, Edmund Goulding; Photographer, William Daniels; Film Editor, Blanche Sewell; Recording Engineer, Douglas Shearer; Gowns, Adrian; Art Director, Cedric Gibbons. Premiered at Astor Theatre, N.Y.C., April 12, 1932. Released September 10, 1932.

CAST

Grusinskaya	Garbo
The Baron	John Barrymore
Flaemmchen, the Stenographer	Joan Crawford
General Director of Preysing	Wallace Beery
Otto Kringlein	Lionel Barrymore
Doctor Otternschlag	Lewis Stone
Senf, the Porter	Jean Hersholt
Meierheim	Robert McWade
Zinnowitz	Purnell B. Pratt
Pimenov	Ferdinand Gottschalk
Suzette	Rafaela Ottiano
Chauffeur	Morgan Wallace
Gerstenkorn	Tully Marshall
Rohna	Frank Conroy
Schweimann	Murray Kinnell
Dr. Waltz	Edwin Maxwell

FERDINAND GOTTSCHALK, GRETA GARBO, RAFAELA OTTIANO Above: LIONEL BARRYMORE, JOAN CRAWFORD, WALLACE BEERY

RAMON NOVARRO, GRETA GARBO, LIONEL BARRYMORE Above HELEN JEROME EDDY, ALEC B. FRANCIS, BLANCHE FREDERICI, GRETA GARBO, RAMON NOVARRO IN "MATA HARI" (M-G-M)

GARY COOPER, ADOLPHE MENJOU, MARY PHILLIPS, HELEN HAYES Above: GARY COOPER, HELEN HAYES IN "A FAREWELL TO ARMS" (PARAMOUNT)

OWEN MOORE, ERIC VON STROHEIM, GRETA GARBO, MELVYN DOUGLAS, HEDDA HOPPER Above: OWEN MOORE, GRETA GARBO, ERIC VON STROHEIM IN "AS YOU DESIRE ME" (M-G-M)

GRETA GARBO

JOHNNY WEISSMULLER IN HIS FIRST TARZAN MOVIE,
"TARZAN, THE APE MAN"
(M-G-M)

JOHNNY WEISSMULLER Top: MAUREEN O'SULLIVAN, C. AUBREY
SMITH, NEIL HAMILTON, JOHNNY WEISSMULLER Center: MAUREEN
O'SULLIVAN, NEIL HAMILTON, JOHNNY WEISSMULLER

MARLENE DIETRICH, WARNER OLAND, CLIVE
BROOK IN "SHANGHAI EXPRESS"
(PARAMOUNT)

1932

PRESTON FOSTER
IN "THE LAST MILE"
(WORLD WIDE)

CHARLES FARRELL, JANET GAYNOR, ROBERT McWADE
IN "THE FIRST YEAR"
(FOX)

JOHN BOLES, IRENE DUNNE IN
"BACK STREET" DIRECTED BY
JOHN M. STAHL (UNIVERSAL)

LILIAN HARVEY, HENRY GARAT IN "CONGRESS
DANCES" AN ERICH POMMER PRODUCTION
DIRECTED BY ERIC CHARELL (UNITED ARTISTS)

MARIE DRESSLER, MYRNA LOY
IN "EMMA" (M-G-M)

LEO CARRILLO

LILIAN HARVEY IN
"CONGRESS DANCES"

OLGA BACLANOVA

OLGA BACLANOVA, WALLACE FORD
IN "FREAKS" (M-G-M)

CLARK GABLE, JEAN HARLOW
IN "RED DUST"
(M-G-M)

WILLIAM POWELL, KAY FRANCIS
IN "ONE WAY PASSAGE" DIRECTED BY
TAY GARNETT (WARNER BROS.)

DOROTHEA WIECK, HERTHA THIELE
IN "MAEDCHEN IN UNIFORM"
("GIRLS IN UNIFORM") DIRECTED BY
LEONTINE SAGAN

BETTE DAVIS, GEORGE ARLISS, VIOLET HEMING, LOUISE
CLOSSER HALE IN "THE MAN WHO PLAYED GOD"
(WARNER BROS.)

SHIRLEY TEMPLE, EUGENE BUTLER
IN "GLAD RAGS TO RICHES"
(EDUCATIONAL COMEDY)

RALPH MORGAN, TAD ALEXANDER, ETHEL BARRYMORE,
JOHN BARRYMORE IN "RASPUTIN AND THE EMPRESS"

CLAUDIA DELL, TOM MIX IN "DESTRY RIDES AGAIN" (UNIVERSAL)

JACK HOXIE, DYNAMITE, ALICE DAY IN "GOLD" (MAJESTIC)

TIM McCOY, ALBERTA VAUGHN, WALLACE MacDONALD IN "DARING DANGER" (COLUMBIA)

BOB STEELE IN "SON OF OKLAHOMA" (TREM CARR PRODUCTION)

COWBOY STARS

HOOT GIBSON IN "THE LONG, LONG TRAIL" (UNIVERSAL)

TOM MIX (UNIVERSAL)

BUCK JONES IN "SUNDOWN RIDER" (COLUMBIA)

TIM McCOY IN "CORNERED" (COLUMBIA)

RICHARD BARTHELMESS, BETTE DAVIS, BERTON CHURCHILL, VIRGINIA HAMMOND IN "THE CABIN IN THE COTTON" (FIRST NATIONAL)

ARTHUR BYRON, BETTE DAVIS, SPENCER TRACY IN "TWENTY THOUSAND YEARS IN SING SING" (FIRST NATIONAL)

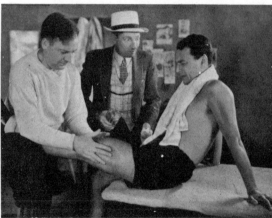

PAT O'MALLEY, LEE MORAN, WILLIAM COLLIER, JR. IN "THE FIGHTING GENTLEMAN" (MONARCH)

PEGGY SHANNON, CHARLES "BUDDY" ROGERS, FRANCES STARR, MAUDE EBURNE, RICHARD BENNETT IN "THIS RECKLESS AGE" (PARAMOUNT)

MARIAN NIXON IN "REBECCA OF SUNNYBROOK FARM" (FOX)

H. B. WARNER, HELEN HAYES, LEWIS STONE, RAMON NOVARRO IN "THE SON-DAUGHTER" (M-G-M)

MOLLY O'DAY, REED HOWES
IN "DEVIL ON DECK"
(SONO-ART)

BARBARA STANWYCK
IN "SO BIG"
(WARNER BROS.)

BING CROSBY, STUART ERWIN
IN "THE BIG BROADCAST"
(PARAMOUNT)

LESLIE HOWARD, NORMA SHEARER
IN "SMILIN' THROUGH"
(M-G-M)

EDWARD G. ROBINSON, BEBE
DANIELS IN "SILVER DOLLAR"
(FIRST NATIONAL)

PIERRE FRESNAY, ORANE DEMAZIS IN
"MARIUS" DIRECTED BY ALEXANDER KORDA

CHARPIN AND RAIMU IN "FANNY"
DIRECTED BY MARC ALLEGRET

ANDRÉ FOUCHÉ AND RAIMU IN
"CESAR" DIRECTED BY MARCEL PAGNOL

MARCEL PAGNOL PRODUCTIONS OF FRENCH TRILOGY

WILL ROGERS IN
"TOO BUSY TO WORK"
(FOX)

ROBERT MONTGOMERY, JOAN
CRAWFORD IN "LETTY LYNTON"
(M-G-M)

DICKIE MOORE IN
"OLD MAN MINICK"
(WARNER BROS.)

TOM DOUGLAS, RICHARD ARLEN
IN "SKY BRIDE"
(PARAMOUNT)

CHARLEY CHASE
IN HAL ROACH
COMEDIES

KATHARINE HEPBURN, DOUGLAS FAIRBANKS, JR., FRED
SANTLEY, ADOLPHE MENJOU Above: ADOLPHE MENJOU,
KATHARINE HEPBURN IN "MORNING GLORY" (RKO)

JEAN PARKER, JOAN BENNETT, SPRING BYINGTON, FRANCES DEE,
KATHARINE HEPBURN IN "LITTLE WOMEN"
(RKO)

(RKO-RADIO)

LITTLE WOMEN

Executive Producer, Merian C. Cooper; Associate Producer, Kenneth MacGowan; Director, George Cukor; Screenplay by Sarah Y. Mason and Victor Heerman; Based on Novel by Louisa May Alcott; Editor, Jack Kitchin. Released Nov. 16, 1933.

CAST

Jo	Katharine Hepburn
Amy	Joan Bennett
Meg	Frances Dee
Beth	Jean Parker
Laurie	Douglass Montgomery
Fritz Bhaer	Paul Lukas
Marmee	Spring Byington
Aunt March	Edna May Oliver
Mr. Laurence	Henry Stephenson
Mr. March	Samuel Hinds
Brooke	John Davis Lodge
Hannah	Mabel Colcord
Mamie	Nydia Westman

ERIC LINDEN, FRANCES DEE, LAURA HOPE CREWS, IRENE
DUNNE, JOEL McCREA IN "THE SILVER CORD"
(RKO)

KATHARINE HEPBURN, COLIN CLIVE IN
"CHRISTOPHER STRONG" (RKO)

GEORGE WALSH   MARIE PREVOST   NEIL HAMILTON   ANNA Q. NILSSON   JACK HOLT   CORINNE GRIFFITH

SILENT SCREEN STARS IN TALKIES

DIANA WYNYARD

BILL BOYD

DOLORES DEL RIO

ROBERT MONTGOMERY

THELMA TODD

CARY GRANT

EDNA MAY OLIVER IN
"LITTLE WOMEN"
(RKO)

1933 After her film debut in "A Bill of Divorcement," Katharine Hepburn was starred in her second film, "Christopher Strong." She won an Academy Award for her performance in her third film, "Morning Glory." Other Award winners were Charles Laughton for "The Private Life of Henry VIII"; "Cavalcade" won an Award as the best picture, and Frank Lloyd, its director, was also honored; and Walt Disney won another "Oscar" for "Three Little Pigs," a short subject. Jesse Lasky, during his first year with Fox, produced two outstanding films, "Zoo in Budapest" and "Berkeley Square" with Leslie Howard re-creating his stage role. "She Done Him Wrong," the screen version of Mae West's stage hit "Diamond Lil," had great success. Other outstanding films were "Little Women," "State Fair," "Dinner at Eight" and Warner Brothers' musical "42nd Street." Paramount made "Alice in Wonderland" with an unknown, Charlotte Henry, as Alice, and surrounded her with an all-star cast. Frank Capra, former gag-man for Hal Roach, was gaining prestige as a director with "Lady for a Day" and "The Bitter Tea of General Yen." Eugene O'Neill's "The Emperor Jones" was made into an operatic film, composed by Louis Gruenberg, with Paul Robeson in the title role. Fred Astaire and Nelson Eddy both made their film debuts supporting Joan Crawford in "Dancing Lady." "Only Yesterday" brought stage actress Margaret Sullavan to screen stardom in her first picture. Mary Pickford produced and starred in "Secrets" with Leslie Howard. It was her last screen appearance. "King Kong," a thriller made by Merian C. Cooper and Ernest B. Schoedsach, heretofore known for their documentary films, was noteworthy because of its fine miniature work and its trick photography. Garbo appeared in "Queen Christina." It reunited her with John Gilbert. Laurence Olivier had been picked by M-G-M as her leading man, but she insisted on Gilbert. Kate Smith, of radio fame, made a picture, "Hello, Everybody!" for Paramount and proved she was not film material. Max Baer, of the sports world, starred with Myrna Loy in "The Prizefighter and the Lady." Jack Dempsey and Primo Carnera played supporting roles. George Arliss continued his portraits of famous historical figures in "Voltaire."

LESLIE HOWARD IN
"BERKELEY SQUARE"
(FOX)

GRANT MITCHELL, LOUISE CLOSSER HALE, JEAN HARLOW,
WALLACE BEERY, EDMUND LOWE, KAREN MORLEY, BILLIE BURKE

JEAN HARLOW

(M-G-M) **DINNER AT EIGHT**

BILLIE DOVE

ESTELLE TAYLOR

TOM MOORE

OWEN MOORE

MATT MOORE

MARY MacLAREN

EVELYN BRENT

SILENT SCREEN STARS IN TALKIES 1933

JOAN CRAWFORD
IN "DANCING LADY"
(M-G-M)

ALINE MacMAHON, GINGER ROGERS, GUY KIBBEE,
JOAN BLONDELL, WARREN WILLIAM AND ABOVE SCENE
FROM "GOLD DIGGERS OF 1933"

GEORGE ARLISS
IN "VOLTAIRE"

MARGARET LINDSAY, GEORGE ARLISS, DORIS KENYON,
DAVID TORRENCE, MURRAY KINNELL IN "VOLTAIRE"

WARNER BROS. PRODUCTIONS

PHILIP REED, RUTH CHATTERTON
IN "FEMALE"

LBERT ROLAND

ENID BENNETT

JOHN BOLES

GERTRUDE ASTOR

GEORGE LEWIS

MAY ROBSON

ROBERT YOUNG

| MARY BRIAN | BESSIE LOVE | MONTE BLUE | FLORENCE LAWRENCE | BERT LYTELL | FLORENCE TURNER | KING BAGGOT |

SILENT SCREEN STARS IN TALKIES

RUBY KEELER

RUBY KEELER, DICK POWELL Above: UNA MERKEL, RUBY KEELER, GEORGE E. STONE, WARNER BAXTER, GINGER ROGERS IN "42nd ST." DIRECTED BY LLOYD BACON (WARNER BROS.)

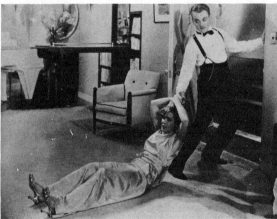

ANNA NEAGLE, FERDINAND GRAVET IN "BITTER SWEET" (UNITED ARTISTS)

MAE CLARKE, JAMES CAGNEY IN "LADY KILLER" (WARNER BROS.)

CLARA BOW IN "HOOPLA" (FOX)

 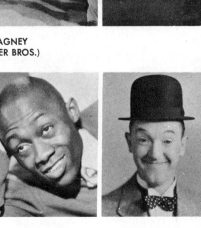 

| LLOYD HAMILTON | BERT WHEELER | ROBERT WOOLSEY | STEPIN FETCHIT | STAN LAUREL | OLIVER HARDY | AL ST. JOHN |

1933

51

MARY NOLAN

GLORIA SWANSON, LAURENCE OLIVIER
IN "PERFECT UNDERSTANDING"
(UNITED ARTISTS)

WILLIAM HAINES

CHARLES LAUGHTON, CAROLE LOMBARD,
KENT TAYLOR IN "WHITE WOMAN"
(PARAMOUNT)

MARY ASTOR

GLORIA SWANSON

GINGER ROGERS IN
"GOLD DIGGERS OF 1933"
(WARNER BROS.)

DAVID MANNERS IN
"ROMAN SCANDALS"
(UNITED ARTISTS)

KAY FRANCIS

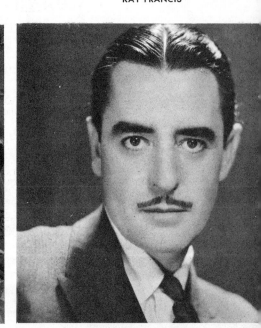

POLA NEGRI

GLORIA STUART, EDDIE CANTOR IN "ROMAN SCANDALS"
PRODUCED BY SAMUEL GOLDWYN, DIRECTED
BY FRANK TUTTLE (UNITED ARTISTS)

JOHN GILBERT

HELEN BRODERICK

FRANK MORGAN, ALICE BRADY, RUSSELL HARDIE,
MADGE EVANS IN "BROADWAY TO HOLLYWOOD"
(M-G-M)

HENRY GARAT

HUGH SINCLAIR, CONSTANCE BENNETT,
MINOR WATSON IN "OUR BETTERS"
(RKO)

LIL DAGOVER

1933

(UNITED ARTISTS)

THE PRIVATE LIFE OF HENRY VIII

Produced by London Films Productions Ltd.; Director, Alexander Korda; Story and Dialogue by Lajos Biro and Arthur Wimperis; Scenario by Arthur Wimperis; Sets Designed by Vincent Korda; Costumes by John Armstrong; Photographed by Georges Perinal. Released Nov. 3, 1933.

CAST

Henry VIII	Charles Laughton
Thomas Culpepper	Robert Donat
Henry's Old Nurse	Lady Tree
Katheryn Howard	Binnie Barnes
Ann of Cleves	Elsa Lanchester
Anne Boleyn	Merle Oberon
Cromwell	Franklin Dyall
Wriothesley	Miles Mander
Jane Seymour	Wendy Barrie
Thomas Peynell	John Loder
Katherine Parr	Everly Gregg
Cranmer	Laurence Hanray
Duke of Cleves	William Austin
Holbein	John Turnbull
Duke of Norfolk	Frederick Cully
French Executioner	Gibb McCaughlin
English Executioner	Sam Livesey
Cernell	Claude Allister

CHARLES LAUGHTON
Top: BINNIE BARNES, ELSA LANCHESTER,
CHARLES LAUGHTON, MERLE OBERON, EVERLY GREGG

CHARLES LAUGHTON, ELSA LANCHESTER Above:
CHARLES LAUGHTON, WENDY BARRIE Top:
JOHN LODER, CHARLES LAUGHTON, ROBERT DONAT

EDGAR CONNOR, HARRY LANGDON, AL JOLSON,
MADGE EVANS IN "HALLELUJAH, I'M A BUM"

WALLACE BEERY, JACKIE COOPER,
IN "THE BOWERY"

RONALD COLMAN, HALLIWELL HOBBES, RONALD COLMAN
IN "THE MASQUERADER"

UNITED ARTISTS RELEASES 1933

NED SPARKS, LUCIEN LITTLEFIELD, HARVEY CLARK, CHARLOTTE HENRY IN "ALICE IN WONDERLAND"

CHARLOTTE HENRY IN "ALICE IN WONDERLAND"

LOUISE FAZENDA, CHARLOTTE HENRY, EDNA MAY OLIVER IN "ALICE IN WONDERLAND"

(FOX)

CAVALCADE

Adapted from the play by Noel Coward; Director, Frank Lloyd; Screenplay by Reginald Berkeley; Continuity, Sonya Levien; Editor, Margaret Clancey. Released Jan. 4, 1933.

CAST

Jane Marryot	Diana Wynyard
Robert Marryot	Clive Brook
Fanny Bridges	Ursula Jeans
Alfred Bridges	Herbert Mundin
Ellen Bridges	Una O'Connor
Annie	Merle Tottenham
Margaret Harris	Irene Browne
Cook	Beryl Mercer
Edward Marryot	John Warburton
Joe Marryot	Frank Lawton
Edith Harris	Margaret Lindsay
Mr. Snapper	Tempe Pigott
George Granger	Billy Bevan
Ronnie James	Desmond Roberts
Uncle Dick	Frank Atkinson
Mirabelle	Ann Shaw
Tommy Jolly	William Stanton
Lieutenant Edgar	Stuart Hall
Duchess of Churt	Mary Forbes
Edward (aged 12)	Dick Henderson, Jr.
Joey (aged 8)	Douglas Scott

NILS ASTHER IN "STRANGE RHAPSODY" (M-G-M)

FRANK LAWTON, URSULA JEANS IN "CAVALCADE"

BERYL MERCER IN "CAVALCADE"

COLLEEN MOORE IN "THE POWER AND THE GLORY" (FOX)

ELISSA LANDI, DAVID MANNERS IN "THE WARRIOR'S HUSBAND" (FOX)

MARION DAVIES IN "PEG O' MY HEART" (M-G-M)

JOAN CRAWFORD, FRED ASTAIRE IN "DANCING LADY" (M-G-M)

GILBERT ROLAND, MAE WEST, NOAH BEERY Center: CARY GRANT, MAE WEST Top: OWEN MOORE, MAE WEST IN "SHE DONE HIM WRONG" FROM MAE WEST'S FAMOUS STAGE SUCCESS, "DIAMOND LIL" DIRECTED BY LOWELL SHERMAN

EDWARD ARNOLD, MAE WEST IN "I'M NO ANGEL"

MAE WEST IN "SHE DONE HIM WRONG"

PARAMOUNT FEATURES 1933

"POPEYE," THE SAILOR MAN, ONE OF
THE MOST POPULAR SCREEN CARTOONS
(PARAMOUNT)

"THE THREE LITTLE PIGS"
WALT DISNEY'S ACADEMY AWARD-
WINNING CARTOON

"THE NIGHT BEFORE CHRISTMAS"
A SILLY SYMPHONY
WALT DISNEY PRODUCTION

TALLULAH BANKHEAD

JANET GAYNOR, HENRY
GARAT IN "ADORABLE"
(FOX)

WEBER AND FIELDS
IN "BROADWAY TO
HOLLYWOOD" (M-G-M)

BEN ALEXANDER

BARBARA BONDERESS, GRETA GARBO, JOHN GILBERT
Above: JOHN GILBERT, GRETA GARBO
IN "QUEEN CHRISTINA" (M-G-M)

GREAT GARBO IN
"QUEEN CHRISTINA" DIRECTED
BY ROUBEN MAMOULIAN (M-G-M)

PAUL ROBESON Above: DUDLEY DIGGES,
PAUL ROBESON IN "THE EMPEROR JONES"
DIRECTED BY DUDLEY MURPHY (UNITED ARTISTS)

BARBARA STANWYCK, NILS ASTHER, WALTER
CONNOLLY IN "THE BITTER TEA OF GENERAL YEN"
DIRECTED BY FRANK CAPRA (COLUMBIA)

EDWARD G. ROBINSON, KAY FRANCIS,
GEORGE BLACKWOOD IN "I LOVED A WOMAN"
(FIRST NATIONAL)

KATHLEEN BURKE, RICHARD ARLEN IN
"THE ISLAND OF LOST SOULS"
(PARAMOUNT)

FAY WRAY, BRUCE CABOT
IN "KING KONG"
(RKO)

"KING KONG" (RKO)
PRODUCED BY MERIAN C. COOPER, ERNEST B. SCHOEDSACH

JUDITH ANDERSON, GEORGE BANCROFT
IN "BLOOD MONEY"
(PARAMOUNT)

GINGER ROGERS, FRED ASTAIRE IN
"FLYING DOWN TO RIO"
(RKO)

MARY PICKFORD, LESLIE HOWARD IN "SECRETS"
DIRECTED BY FRANK BORZAGE
(UNITED ARTISTS)

MARGARET SULLAVAN, JOHN BOLES IN
"ONLY YESTERDAY" DIRECTED BY
JOHN M. STAHL (UNIVERSAL)

THELMA TODD, BEBE DANIELS, JOHN BARRYMORE
IN "COUNSELLOR AT LAW"
(UNIVERSAL)

MYRNA LOY, JOHN BARRYMORE
IN "TOPAZE" DIRECTED BY
HARRY D'ARRAST (RKO)

LIONEL BARRYMORE, MARIE DRESSLER BEULAH BONDI,
HELEN SHIPMAN, RUSSELL HARDIE, HELEN MACK IN
"CHRISTOPHER BEAN" (M-G-M)

CLIVE BROOK   FRANCES DEE   HERBERT MARSHALL   MERLE OBERON   JOAN BENNETT   WARREN WILLIAM

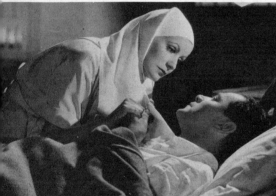

GRETA GARBO, HERBERT MARSHALL Above: GRETA GARBO, GEORGE BRENT IN "THE PAINTED VEIL" (M-G-M)

GRETA GARBO IN "THE PAINTED VEIL" (M-G-M)

KATHARINE HEPBURN IN "THE LITTLE MINISTER" (RKO)

JOHN BEAL, KATHARINE HEPBURN IN "THE LITTLE MINISTER" Above: KATHARINE HEPBURN IN "SPITFIRE" (RKO)

HAROLD LLOYD, ALAN DINEHART IN "THE CAT'S PAW" (PARAMOUNT)

WALLACE BEERY IN "VIVA VILLA!" (M-G-M)

WALLACE BEERY, STUART ERWIN, LEO CARRILLO IN "VIVA VILLA!" DIRECTED BY JOHN CONWAY. (M-G-M)

WELDON HEYBURN   UNA MERKEL   RUSSELL HARDIE   MADGE EVANS   PRESTON FOSTER   LEILA HYAMS

JOAN BLONDELL   CHESTER MORRIS   MARGARET SULLAVAN   DAVID MANNERS   DOROTHY MACKAILL   PAT O'BRIEN

1934 "It Happened One Night" won five Academy Awards. These were for the best picture; for the direction of Frank Capra; for the best screenplay by Robert Riskin; and for the performances of Clark Gable and Claudette Colbert, its stars. Outstanding films included "One Night of Love," "The House of Rothschild," "The Barretts of Wimpole Street," "Broadway Bill," "The Lost Patrol," "Twentieth Century," "Viva Villa!" and Fannie Hurst's "Imitation of Life." Some of the classics reaching the screen were Dumas' "The Count of Monte Cristo," Stevenson's "Treasure Island," Dickens' "Great Expectations" and Hawthorne's "The Scarlet Letter." Samuel Goldwyn imported a Russian actress, Anna Sten, and spent a small fortune on publicity trying to make a great star of her, but her first film, "Nana," was a great disappointment. Her accent was thick, her acting inferior, and she never reached the heights. W. Somerset Maugham's "Of Human Bondage," filmed with Leslie Howard and Bette Davis, put the latter in the star class. Dashiell Hammett's detective story "The Thin Man" starred William Powell and Myrna Loy and was the first of several successful Thin Man pictures. Ernst Lubitsch made the first talkie version of "The Merry Widow" with Jeanette MacDonald and Maurice Chevalier. Donald Duck made his film debut in a small role in Walt Disney's short, "The Orphan's Benefit." Shirley Temple became established as box-office after "Stand Up and Cheer" and "Little Miss Marker" were released. Pauline Lord, famous stage star, made her film debut in "Mrs. Wiggs of the Cabbage Patch." Cecil B. De Mille produced and directed an elaborate film, "Cleopatra," with Claudette Colbert in the title role. Douglas Fairbanks appeared in his last picture, "The Private Life of Don Juan," filmed in London with Alexander Korda. Hal Roach was making successful short comedies; some with comics Laurel and Hardy. George Sidney and Charlie Murray duplicated in the talkies the success they had in the silents with their comedy series, "The Cohens and the Kellys." Alice Fay, a New York chorus girl, made her film debut in a leading role opposite Rudy Vallee in "George White's Scandals of 1934."

BORIS KARLOFF IN "THE LOST PATROL" DIRECTED BY JOHN FORD (RKO)

ROGER IMHOF, AL SHEAN, JUNE LANG, JOHN BOLES, JOSEPH CAWTHORN, GLORIA SWANSON, DOUGLASS MONTGOMERY IN "MUSIC IN THE AIR" (FOX)

W. C. FIELDS IN "IT'S A GIFT" (PARAMOUNT)

REGINALD DENNY, BORIS KARLOFF, BILLY BEVAN, SAMMY STEIN, ALAN HALE, PAUL HANSON, WALLACE FORD, VICTOR McLAGLEN, J. M. KERRIGAN IN "THE LOST PATROL" (RKO)

MELVYN DOUGLAS   ALISON SKIPWORTH   RALPH FORBES   ELEANOR BOARDMAN   CONRAD NAGEL   RALPH BYRD

ROBERT YOUNG, LORETTA YOUNG, GEORGE ARLISS (also above) IN "HOUSE OF ROTHSCHILD" (UNITED ARTISTS)

LESLIE HOWARD, BETTE DAVIS IN "OF HUMAN BONDAGE" DIRECTED BY JOHN CROMWELL (RKO)

WARNER BAXTER

GRACE MOORE, TULLIO CARMINATI IN "ONE NIGHT OF LOVE" DIRECTED BY VICTOR SCHERTZINGER (COLUMBIA)

SHIRLEY TEMPLE, ADOLPHE MENJOU IN "LITTLE MISS MARKER" DIRECTED BY ALEXANDER HALL (PARAMOUNT)

WARNER BAXTER, MYRNA LOY IN "BROADWAY BILL" (COLUMBIA) A FRANK CAPRA PRODUCTION

PAULINE LORD (also above), VIRGINIA WEIDLER, ZASU PITTS IN "MRS. WIGGS OF THE CABBAGE PATCH" (PARAMOUNT)

CLARK GABLE, CLAUDETTE COLBERT IN "IT HAPPENED ONE NIGHT" (COLUMBIA)

CLAUDETTE COLBERT

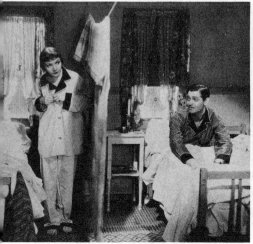

CLAUDETTE COLBERT, CLARK GABLE IN "IT HAPPENED ONE NIGHT" (COLUMBIA) A FRANK CAPRA PRODUCTION

JAMES DUNN, SHIRLEY TEMPLE IN "STAND UP AND CHEER" (FOX)

JOHNNY MACK BROWN, MAE WEST IN "IT AIN'T NO SIN" (PARAMOUNT)

JACKIE COOPER, WALLACE BEERY, NIGEL BRUCE IN "TREASURE ISLAND" DIRECTED BY VICTOR FLEMING (M-G-M)

JACK LA RUE   LUPE VELEZ   WALTER PIDGEON   MARY NASH, GENEVIEVE TOBIN IN "UNCERTAIN LADY" (UNIVERSAL)   JOSEPH SCHILDKRAUT   MARIAN MARSH   WALTER HUSTON

CAROLE LOMBARD, JOHN BARRYMORE IN
"20th CENTURY" DIRECTED BY
HOWARD HAWKS (COLUMBIA)

KING BAGGOT, FLORA FINCH, JACK GRAY, FLORENCE LAWRENCE, ROBERT WAYNE,
HELENE CHADWICK, MAHLON HAMILTON, NAOMI CHILDERS, JULES COWLES, PIONEER
FILM PLAYERS AWARDED M-G-M CONTRACTS BY LOUIS B. MAYER

JEANETTE MacDONALD, MAURICE CHEVALIER
IN "THE MERRY WIDOW" DIRECTED
BY ERNST LUBITSCH (M-G-M)

STERLING HOLLOWAY, MARY BOLAND
IN "DOWN TO THEIR LAST YACHT"
(RKO)

JOHN LODGE, MARLENE DIETRICH, C. AUBREY SMITH
IN "THE SCARLET EMPRESS" DIRECTED BY
JOSEF VON STERNBERG (PARAMOUNT)

ERIC LINDEN   JETTA GOUDAL   WILLIAM GARGAN   GARY COOPER, MARION DAVIES, WALTER LONG IN "OPERATOR 13" (M-G-M)   WALTER MILLER   JOAN MARSH   JACK OAKIE

RANDOLPH SCOTT

HELEN CHANDLER

DICK POWELL

FRANCES DRAKE, CHARLES RAY
IN "LADIES SHOULD LISTEN"
(PARAMOUNT)

LAURENCE OLIVIER

FAY WRAY

GEORGE BRENT

CLAUDETTE COLBERT, MARY BOLAND,
HERBERT MARSHALL, WILLIAM GARGAN
IN "FOUR FRIGHTENED PEOPLE"
DIRECTED BY CECIL B. DE MILLE (PARAMOUNT)

HENRY HULL, GEORGE BREAKSTON,
ALAN HALE Above: PHILLIPS HOLMES,
FLORENCE REED, JANE WYATT, ALAN HALE
IN "GREAT EXPECTATIONS" (UNIVERSAL)

PAUL LUKAS, JOHN DARROW, WYNNE
GIBSON IN "I GIVE MY LOVE"
(UNIVERSAL)

KENT TAYLOR, WILL ROGERS, EVELYN VENABLE IN "DAVID
HARUM" DIRECTED BY JAMES CRUZE (FOX)
Above: WILL ROGERS

DOLORES DEL RIO
IN "MADAME DU BARRY"
(WARNER BROS.)

FRANKIE DARROW

RALPH BELLAMY

KAREN MORLEY

JANE BAXTER, RICHARD TAUBER
IN "BLOSSOM TIME"
(B.I.P.)

BUSTER CRABBE

ANN DVORAK

PHILLIPS HOLMES

1934

JOHN LODER   FRANCIS LEDERER   JEANETTE MacDONALD   DOUGLAS FAIRBANKS, JR.   JOHN WAYNE

SIDNEY BLACKMER, ELISSA LANDI, ROBERT DONAT
IN "THE COUNT OF MONTE CRISTO" DIRECTED
BY ROWLAND V. LEE (UNITED ARTISTS)

CLARA KIMBALL YOUNG, KING BAGGOT
IN "ROMANCE IN THE RAIN"
(UNIVERSAL)

CHARLES BOYER, JEAN PARKER, LORETTA YOUNG
IN "CARAVAN" (FOX)

JOHN LODER, CHARLES BOYER IN
"THUNDER IN THE EAST"
(UNITED ARTISTS)

CLAUDE RAINS, MARGO IN
"CRIME WITHOUT PASSION"
(PARAMOUNT)

JIMMY DURANTE, STUART ERWIN,
ROBERT ARMSTRONG IN "PALOOKA"
(UNITED ARTISTS)

HUGH WILLIAMS, H. B. WARNER
IN "SORRELL AND SON"
(UNITED ARTISTS)

CARL BRISSON, JESSIE RALPH, JACK OAKIE,
GERTRUDE MICHAEL, VICTOR McLAGLEN IN
"MURDER AT THE VANITIES"
(PARAMOUNT)

NORMA SHEARER, MRS. PATRICK
CAMPBELL IN "RIPTIDE" (M-G-M)

JANE WYATT, KATHLEEN HOWARD, C. AUBREY
SMITH, MRS. PATRICK CAMPBELL, DIANA
WYNYARD, REGINALD DENNY IN "ONE
MORE RIVER" (UNIVERSAL)

TOM BROWN   CAROLE LOMBARD   DOUGLASS MONTGOMERY, MARGARET SULLAVAN IN "LITTLE MAN WHAT NOW?" (UNIVERSAL)   DAVID MANNERS   ANN SHERIDAN

HOBART CAVANAUGH, HAL LeROY, PATRICIA ELLIS IN "HAROLD TEEN" (WARNER BROS.)   MAGGIE DIRRANE, TIGER KING, MICHAEL DILLANE IN "MAN OF ARAN" DIRECTED BY ROBERT FLAHERTY (GAUMONT)   CAROLE LOMBARD, RAY MILLAND, BING CROSBY, LEON ERROL IN "WE'RE NOT DRESSING" (PARAMOUNT)

FISKE O'HARA, JANET GAYNOR, JAMES DUNN IN "CHANGE OF HEART"   THOMAS MEIGHAN, JACKIE COOPER IN "PECK'S BAD BOY"   WILL ROGERS, PEGGY WOOD IN "HANDY ANDY"   LILIAN HARVEY, GENE RAYMOND IN "I AM SUZANNE"

FOX PRODUCTIONS

DAVID TORRENCE, DONALD CRISP, HELEN HAYES, DUDLEY DIGGES IN "WHAT EVERY WOMAN KNOWS" (M-G-M)   TED HEALY AND THE THREE STOOGES IN "MEET THE BARON" (M-G-M)   MINOR WATSON, JOAN BENNETT, CHARLES RUGGLES, FRANCIS LEDERER IN "THE PURSUIT OF HAPPINESS" (PARAMOUNT)

1934

ELIZABETH BERGNER
IN "CATHERINE THE GREAT"
(UNITED ARTISTS)

DOUGLAS FAIRBANKS, JR.
IN "CATHERINE THE GREAT"
(UNITED ARTISTS)

JEAN PARKER, RUSSELL HARDIE
IN "SEQUOIA"
(M-G-M)

FREDRIC MARCH IN
"THE AFFAIRS OF CELLINI"
(UNITED ARTISTS)

ALICE FAYE IN
"GEORGE WHITE'S SCANDALS
OF 1934" (FOX)

DOUGLAS FAIRBANKS, JR., FLORA ROBSON, ELIZABETH
BERGNER Above: DOUGLAS FAIRBANKS, JR., ELIZABETH
BERGNER IN "CATHERINE THE GREAT"

DOUGLAS FAIRBANKS IN "THE PRIVATE
LIFE OF DON JUAN"
UNITED ARTISTS PRODUCTIONS

JESSIE RALPH, FAY WRAY, FRANK MORGAN, FREDRIC
MARCH Above: FREDRIC MARCH, CONSTANCE
BENNETT IN "THE AFFAIRS OF CELLINI"

GEORGE M. COHAN, WALTER GILBERT, DOROTHY
BURGESS, WYNNE GIBSON IN "GAMBLING"
(FOX)

BENITA HUME, MERLE OBERON, DOUGLAS
FAIRBANKS, JOAN GARDNER IN "THE PRIVATE
LIFE OF DON JUAN" (UNITED ARTISTS)

RUDY VALLEE, ALICE FAYE IN "GEORGE
WHITE'S SCANDALS OF 1934"
(FOX)

GEORGE M. COHAN
IN "GAMBLING"
(FOX)

HENRY WILCOXON IN
"CLEOPATRA"
(PARAMOUNT)

NORMA SHEARER IN "THE BARRETTS
OF WIMPOLE STREET" DIRECTED
BY SIDNEY FRANKLIN (M-G-M)

DOUGLASS MONTGOMERY
IN "MUSIC IN THE AIR"
(FOX)

PAT PATERSON IN
"LOTTERY LOVER"
(FOX)

JOHNNY WEISSMULLER, MAUREEN O'SULLIVAN, PAUL CAVANAGH,
NEIL HAMILTON Above: JOHNNY WEISSMULLER, MAUREEN
O'SULLIVAN IN "TARZAN AND HIS MATE" (M-G-M)

ASTA, WILLIAM POWELL, MYRNA LOY
IN "THE THIN MAN" DIRECTED BY
W. S. VAN DYKE (M-G-M)

MAUREEN O'SULLIVAN, NORMA SHEARER, CHARLES
LAUGHTON, WITH THE BROTHERS Above: FREDRIC MARCH,
CHARLES LAUGHTON, NORMA SHEARER IN "THE
BARRETTS OF WIMPOLE STREET" (M-G-M)

CLAUDETTE COLBERT IN "CLEOPATRA"
(PARAMOUNT)

HENRY WILCOXON,
CLAUDETTE COLBERT
IN "CLEOPATRA"

WARREN WILLIAM,
GERTRUDE MICHAEL
IN "CLEOPATRA"

WARREN WILLIAM, CLAUDETTE COLBERT
IN "CLEOPATRA"
(PARAMOUNT)

A CECIL B. DE MILLE PRODUCTION 1934

BETTE DAVIS, WHO WON ACADEMY AWARD FOR HER
PERFORMANCE, WITH FRANCHOT TONE IN "DANGEROUS"

EUGENE PALLETTE, BETTE DAVIS, PAUL
MUNI IN "BORDERTOWN"

WARNER BROS. PRODUCTIONS

WILLIAM GARGAN, PAUL MUNI, KAREN
MORLEY IN "BLACK FURY"

BILL ROBINSON IN "THE
BIG BROADCAST OF 1935"
(PARAMOUNT)

G. P. HUNTLEY, JR., MIRIAM HOPKINS, FRANCES DEE IN "BECKY SHARP,"
FIRST AMERICAN ALL-TECHNICOLOR TALKING FILM MADE BY PIONEER
PICTURES, DIRECTED BY ROUBEN MAMOULIAN, RELEASED BY R.K.O.

IRENE DUNNE
IN "SWEET ADELINE"
(WARNER BROS.)

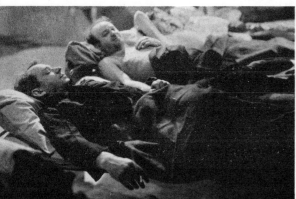

JULIE HAYDON, HOPE WILLIAMS, NOEL COWARD
Above: CHARLES MacARTHUR, BEN HECHT,
WRITER-PRODUCERS AS ACTORS IN
"THE SCOUNDREL" (PARAMOUNT)

GEORGE ARLISS IN "CARDINAL RICHELIEU"
A DARRYL ZANUCK PRODUCTION
(UNITED ARTISTS)

HALLIWELL HOBBES, GEORGE ARLISS, MAUREEN
O'SULLIVAN, EDWARD ARNOLD Above: HALLIWELL
HOBBES, MAUREEN O'SULLIVAN, CESAR ROMERO, GEORGE
ARLISS IN "CARDINAL RICHELIEU" (UNITED ARTISTS)

FREDRIC MARCH, MERLE OBERON, HERBERT MARSHALL IN "THE DARK ANGEL" DIRECTED BY SIDNEY FRANKLIN (SAMUEL GOLDWYN PRODUCTION)

BRIAN DONLEVY, JOEL McCREA, EDWARD G. ROBINSON, WALTER BRENNAN IN "BARBARY COAST" (SAMUEL GOLDWYN PRODUCTION)

LESLIE BANKS, PAUL ROBESON, ROBERT COCHRANE IN "SAUNDERS OF THE RIVER" (ALEXANDER KORDA PRODUCTION)

UNITED ARTISTS RELEASES

1935 An Academy Award went to "Mutiny on the Bounty" as the best picture of the year. Three Awards went to "The Informer": John Ford for his direction, Victor McLaglen for his acting, and Dudley Nichols for his screenplay. Bette Davis won her first Award for her performance in "Dangerous." Walt Disney won another Award for his short "Three Orphan Kittens." Winfield R. Sheehan resigned as vice-president and production chief when Fox merged with Twentieth Century. Joseph M. Schenck became chairman of the newly formed 20th Century-Fox, and Darryl F. Zanuck was appointed production head. Jesse L. Lasky left Fox and formed the Pickford-Lasky Productions for United Artists release. Warner Brothers imported Max Reinhardt, famous European impresario, to direct an elaborate production of "A Midsummer Night's Dream." It was the first Shakespearean film shown in legitimate theatres. Nearly half the theatres in the United States were now using a double-feature policy. "Becky Sharp" was the first American all-talkie to be filmed in Technicolor. Bill Boyd made the first of the "Hopalong Cassidy" films, a series that later brought him greater fame when shown on television. Noel Coward made his American talkie debut in "The Scoundrel." In "Captain Blood," Errol Flynn appeared in his first starring role. Fred MacMurray, Charles Boyer and Ann Sheridan were three newcomers signed by Paramount. Luise Rainer, a Viennese actress, appeared in her first American film, "Escapade." The best films of the year, besides the Award winners, included "David Copperfield," "Lives of a Bengal Lancer," "Ruggles of Red Gap," "Naughty Marietta," "Top Hat," "Roberta," "Anna Karenina" and a French import, "La Maternelle" ("Children of Montmartre"). Will Rogers was killed with flyer Wiley Post in an airplane crash in Alaska. Thelma Todd was found dead under mysterious circumstances. Comedian Lloyd Hamilton also died.

MAY ROBSON IN "GRAND OLD GIRL" (RKO)

ERROL FLYNN IN HIS FIRST STARRING FILM "CAPTAIN BLOOD" (WARNER BROS.)

PAUL MUNI, AKIM TAMIROFF, HENRY O'NEILL, DONALD WOODS Above: PAUL MUNI, JOSEPHINE HUTCHINSON, ANITA LOUISE, NILES WELCH IN "THE STORY OF LOUIS PASTEUR" DIRECTED BY WILLIAM DIETERLE

PAUL MUNI IN "THE STORY OF LOUIS PASTEUR"

WARNER BROS. PRODUCTIONS

HENRY STEPHENSON, OLIVIA DE HAVILLAND, ERROL FLYNN Above: ERROL FLYNN IN "CAPTAIN BLOOD" DIRECTED BY MICHAEL CURTIZ

MAMO, MOVITA, CLARK GABLE, FRANCHOT TONE
Above: (left) CLARK GABLE (center) FRANCHOT TONE, CLARK GABLE, CHARLES LAUGHTON (right)
CHARLES LAUGHTON IN "MUTINY ON THE BOUNTY" DIRECTED BY FRANK LLOYD (M-G-M)

LORETTA YOUNG   CHARLES FARRELL   JANET GAYNOR   RICHARD BARTHELMESS

MARGOT GRAHAME, VICTOR McLAGLEN

PRESTON FOSTER, JOE SAWYER, VICTOR McLAGLEN
Above: VICTOR McLAGLEN

IN "THE INFORMER" DIRECTED BY JOHN FORD (RKO)

ANN HARDING, JOHN HALLIDAY, GARY COOPER
IN "PETER IBBETSON"
(PARAMOUNT)

1935

GARY COOPER
IN "LIVES OF A BENGAL
LANCER" (PARAMOUNT)

GARY COOPER, RICHARD CROMWELL, FRANCHOT TONE, C. AUBREY
SMITH IN "LIVES OF A BENGAL LANCER"
DIRECTED BY HENRY HATHAWAY (PARAMOUNT)

(M-G-M)

DAVID COPPERFIELD

Producer, David O. Selznick; Director, George Cukor; Based on Novel by Charles Dickens; Adapted by Hugh Walpole; Screenplay by Howard Estabrook; Photographed by Oliver T. Marsh; Score by Herbert Stothart; Art Director, Cedric Gibbons; Wardrobe by Dolly Tree; Film Editor, Robert J. Kern. Released January 18, 1935.

CAST

Micawber	W. C. Fields
Dan Peggotty	Lionel Barrymore
Dora	Maureen O'Sullivan
Agnes	Madge Evans
Aunt Betsey	Edna May Oliver
Mr. Wickfield	Lewis Stone
David, The Man	Frank Lawton
David, The Child	Freddie Bartholomew
Mrs. Copperfield	Elizabeth Allan
Uriah Heep	Roland Young
Mr. Murdstone	Basil Rathbone
Clickett	Elsa Lanchester
Mrs. Micawber	Jean Cadell
Nurse Peggotty	Jessie Ralph
Mr. Dick	Lennox Pawle
Jane Murdstone	Violet Kemble-Cooper
Mrs. Gummidge	Una O'Connor
Ham	John Buckler
Steerforth	Hugh Williams
Limmiter	Ivan Sampson
Barkis	Herbert Mundin
Little Em'ly, The Child	Fay Chaldecott
Agnes, The Child	Marilyn Knowlden
Little Em'ly, The Woman	Florine McKinney
Dr. Chillip	Harry Beresford
The Vicar	Hugh Walpole

UNA O'CONNOR, JESSIE RALPH, JOHN BUCKLER, FLORINE McKINNEY, HUGH WILLIAMS, LIONEL BARRYMORE, FRANK LAWTON
Top: W. C. FIELDS, FREDDIE BARTHOLOMEW

W. C. FIELDS, JEAN CADELL, FREDDIE BARTHOLOMEW, ELSA LANCHESTER Top: BASIL RATHBONE, JESSIE RALPH, FREDDIE BARTHOLOMEW, ELIZABETH ALLAN Center: EDNA MAY OLIVER

FRANK LAWTON
Center: ELIZABETH ALLAN, FREDDIE BARTHOLOMEW

WALLACE FORD MARTHA SLEEPER EDWARD WOODS ADRIENNE AMES FRANCIS LEDERER RUBY KEELER BRIAN AHERNE

FRITZ LEIBER, BLANCHE YURKA, LUCILLE LAVERNE, MITCHELL LEWIS
Above: (left) DONALD WOODS, RONALD COLMAN, (right) ELIZABETH ALLAN, RONALD COLMAN,
EDNA MAY OLIVER IN SCENES FROM "A TALE OF TWO CITIES" (M-G-M)

CONSTANCE BENNETT

BUDDY EBSEN, ELEANOR POWELL, ROBERT
TAYLOR IN "BROADWAY MELODY OF 1936"
(M-G-M)

JANE WYATT

BING CROSBY, MARY BOLAND,
JOAN BENNETT IN "TWO FOR
TONIGHT" (PARAMOUNT)

WILLIAM COLLIER, JR.

CLARK GABLE, JEAN HARLOW, ROSALIND
RUSSELL, C. AUBREY SMITH IN
"CHINA SEAS" (M-G-M)

1935

LORETTA YOUNG, HENRY WILCOXON Above: IAN KEITH, HENRY WILCOXON, LORETTA YOUNG

C. AUBREY SMITH, HENRY WILCOXON, LUMSDEN HARE, MONTAGU LOVE

ALAN HALE, HENRY WILCOXON, MONTAGU LOVE Above: HENRY WILCOXON

"THE CRUSADES" A CECIL B. DeMILLE PRODUCTION (PARAMOUNT)

CHARLES LAUGHTON IN "LES MISERABLES" (20th CENTURY-FOX)

RITA HAYWORTH IN "PADDY O'DAY" (20th CENTURY-FOX)

WILLIAM POWELL WITH LUISE RAINER IN HER FIRST AMERICAN FILM "ESCAPADE" DIRECTED BY ROBERT Z. LEONARD (M-G-M)

CHARLES (BUDDY) ROGERS IN "OLD MAN RHYTHM" (RKO)

MARGARET SULLAVAN IN "THE GOOD FAIRY" (UNIVERSAL)

PETER LORRE, MARIAN MARSH, MRS. PATRICK CAMPBELL IN "CRIME AND PUNISHMENT" (COLUMBIA)

1935

DOUGLASS MONTGOMERY, HEATHER ANGEL, VALERIE HOBSON IN "THE MYSTERY OF EDWIN DROOD" (UNIVERSAL)

ELSA LANCHESTER, BORIS KARLOFF IN "BRIDE OF FRANKENSTEIN" (UNIVERSAL)

FREDRIC MARCH, CHARLES LAUGHTON Above:
CEDRIC HARDWICKE, FREDRIC MARCH IN "LES MISERABLES"
DIRECTED BY RICHARD BOLESLAWSKI (20th CENTURY-FOX)

ALLAN JONES, WALTER WOOLF KING, KITTY
CARLISLE Above: GROUCHO, HARPO, CHICO MARX,
ALLAN JONES IN "A NIGHT AT THE OPERA" (M-G-M)

LESLIE HOWARD Above: MERLE OBERON, LESLIE
HOWARD IN "THE SCARLET PIMPERNEL" DIRECTED BY
HAROLD YOUNG (UNITED ARTISTS)

FRED ASTAIRE IN
"TOP HAT"
(RKO)

CLARK GABLE, LORETTA
YOUNG IN "CALL OF THE
WILD" (20th CENTURY-FOX)

JOHN LODER, ANNA MAY
WONG IN "JAVA HEAD"
A BASIL DEAN PRODUCTION

ANN SHERIDAN, RANDOLPH SCOTT, MRS. LESLIE
CARTER IN "ROCKY MOUNTAIN MYSTERY"
(PARAMOUNT)

CONRAD VEIDT, PEGGY
ASHCROFT IN "THE WANDERING
JEW" (OLYMPIC)

CHARLES BOYER, CLAUDETTE
COLBERT IN "PRIVATE
WORLDS" (PARAMOUNT)

1935

BASIL RATHBONE, GRETA GARBO, FREDDIE BARTHOLOMEW
"ANNA KARENINA" DIRECTED BY CLARENCE BROWN (M-G-M)

GRETA GARBO, FREDRIC MARCH

HELEN GAHAGAN
IN "SHE" (RKO)

ROSCO ATES

DOROTHY JORDAN

GLADYS SWARTHOUT
IN "ROSE OF THE RANCHO"
(PARAMOUNT)

HERMAN BRIX (ATHLETE) WHO LATER BECAME
BRUCE BENNETT IN "NEW ADVENTURES
OF TARZAN" (BTZ)

MARLENE DIETRICH
IN "THE DEVIL IS A WOMAN" DIRECTED
BY JOSEF VON STERNBERG (PARAMOUNT)

RANDOLPH SCOTT, VICTOR VARCONI, IRENE
DUNNE IN "ROBERTA" DIRECTED
BY WILLIAM A. SEITER (RKO)

(WARNER BROTHERS)

A MIDSUMMER NIGHT'S DREAM

Directed by Max Reinhardt and William Dieterle; Adapted from William Shakespeare's classic and arranged for the screen by Charles Kenyon and Mary C. McCall, Jr., Musical arrangement by Erich Wolfgang Korngold, with Mendelssohn's "A Midsummer Night's Dream" music; Dances directed by Nijinska; Costumes by Max Ree; Photography by Hal Mohr. Released October 16, 1935.

CAST

Bottom	James Cagney
Flute	Joe E. Brown
Snout	Hugh Herbert
Quince	Frank McHugh
Oberon	Victor Jory
Hermia	Olivia De Havilland
Demetrius	Ross Alexander
Egeus	Grant Mitchell
First Fairy	Nini Theilade
Hippolyta	Verree Teasdale
Lysander	Dick Powell
Helena	Jean Muir
Theseus	Ian Hunter
Titania	Anita Louise
Puck	Mickey Rooney
Snug	Dewey Robinson
Philostrate	Hobart Cavanaugh
Starveling	Otis Harlan
Ninny's Tomb	Arthur Treacher
Mustard Seed	Billy Barty

VICTOR JORY, JAMES CAGNEY, ANITA LOUISE
Above: HUGH HERBERT, FRANK McHUGH, ARTHUR TREACHER,
OTIS HARLAN, DEWEY ROBINSON, JAMES CAGNEY, JOE E. BROWN

DICK POWELL, JEAN MUIR Above: VERREE TEASDALE,
IAN HUNTER, OLIVIA DE HAVILLAND, GRANT MITCHELL,
DICK POWELL, ROSS ALEXANDER

| FRANK McHUGH | VICTOR JORY | JOE E. BROWN | ANITA LOUISE | VERREE TEASDALE | DICK POWELL | IAN HUNTER | HOBART CAVANAUGH |

OLIVIA DE HAVILLAND   MICKEY ROONEY   **1935**   ROSS ALEXANDER   JAMES CAGNEY

KATHARINE HEPBURN, FRED MacMURRAY

ANN SHOEMAKER, FRED MacMURRAY, HATTIE McDANIEL, KATHARINE HEPBURN, FRED STONE
IN "ALICE ADAMS" DIRECTED BY GEORGE STEVENS (RKO)

BRIAN DONLEVY, SYLVIA SIDNEY   PAUL LUKAS
IN "MARY BURNS, FUGITIVE" (PARAMOUNT)

CONSTANCE   FRED MacMURRAY, CLAUDETTE COLBERT
CUMMINGS   IN "THE GILDED LILY" (PARAMOUNT)

MARY BOLAND, CHARLES RUGGLES, MAUDE EBURNE
Above: CHARLES LAUGHTON IN "RUGGLES OF RED GAP"
DIRECTED BY LEO McCAREY (PARAMOUNT)

BASIL RATHBONE, LOUIS CALHERN, PRESTON FOSTER
Center: GLORIA SHEA, PRESTON FOSTER Top:
SCENE FROM "LAST DAYS OF POMPEII" (RKO)

JOHN BEAL, CHARLES BOYER, KATHARINE HEPBURN,
IN "BREAK OF HEARTS" (RKO) Above: KATHARINE HEPBURN,
BRIAN AHERNE IN "SYLVIA SCARLETT" (RKO)

LIONEL BELMORE, LORETTA YOUNG, RONALD COLMAN
IN "CLIVE OF INDIA"
(UNITED ARTISTS)

PAULETTE ELAMBERT, MADELEINE RENAUD IN
"LA MATERNELLE" DIRECTED BY
JEAN BENOIT-LEVY AND MARIE EPSTEIN

GRIFFITH JONES, ELISABETH BERGNER, HUGH
SINCLAIR IN "ESCAPE ME NEVER"
(UNITED ARTISTS)

LEWIS STONE

JOHN BEAL

BONITA GRANVILLE, SPRING BYINGTON,
MICKEY ROONEY IN "AH, WILDERNESS"
DIRECTED BY CLARENCE BROWN (M-G-M)

LAWRENCE GRAY

LEE TRACY

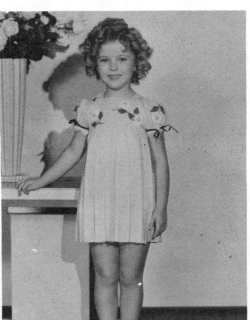

JESSIE MATTHEWS, BARRY MacKAY
IN "EVERGREEN"
(GAUMONT BRITISH)

ARLINE JUDGE

DICKIE MOORE

IRVIN S. COBB
IN "STEAMBOAT 'ROUND THE BEND"
(FOX)

SLIM SUMMERVILLE, SHIRLEY TEMPLE, GUY KIBBEE, SARA
HADEN IN "CAPTAIN JANUARY" Above: POODLES
HANNEFORD, SHIRLEY TEMPLE IN "OUR LITTLE GIRL"

BILL ROBINSON, SHIRLEY TEMPLE, JACK HOLT IN
"THE LITTLEST REBEL" Above: IN "CURLY TOP"

SHIRLEY TEMPLE, LIONEL BARRYMORE, EVELYN VENABLE,
JOHN LODGE IN "THE LITTLE COLONEL" Above: SHIRLEY
TEMPLE, JANE WITHERS IN "BRIGHT EYES"

SHIRLEY TEMPLE PICTURES **1935** PRODUCED BY 20th CENTURY-FOX

MARLENE DIETRICH IN "THE GARDEN OF ALLAH" (SELZNICK INTERNATIONAL)

RAY MILLAND, DOROTHY LAMOUR IN "THE JUNGLE PRINCESS" (PARAMOUNT)

LORETTA YOUNG, DON AMECHE IN "RAMONA" (FOX)

KAY FRANCIS IN "WHITE ANGEL" (WARNER BROS.)

JIMMY SAVO IN "ONCE IN A BLUE MOON" (A HECHT-MacARTHUR PRODUCTION)

CHARLES BOYER, MARLENE DIETRICH IN "THE GARDEN OF ALLAH" DIRECTED BY RICHARD BOLESLAWSKI (SELZNICK INTERNATIONAL)

FRANCHOT TONE, GRACE MOORE IN "THE KING STEPS OUT" (COLUMBIA)

GLADYS GEORGE IN "VALIANT IS THE WORD FOR CARRIE" (PARAMOUNT)

RUTH CHATTERTON, WALTER HUSTON Above: RUTH CHATTERTON, MARIA OUSPENSKAYA IN "DODSWORTH" DIRECTED BY WILLIAM WYLER (A SAMUEL GOLDWYN PRODUCTION)

CLARK GABLE IN "CAIN AND MABEL" (WARNER BROS.)

CLARK GABLE, JACK HOLT, SPENCER TRACY, JEANETTE MacDONALD Above: CLARK GABLE IN "SAN FRANCISCO" DIRECTED BY W. S. VAN DYKE (M-G-M)

ROBERT CUMMINGS

IDA LUPINO

DAVID NIVEN

LIONEL BARRYMORE IN
"THE DEVIL-DOLL" (M-G-M)

1936 Eighty-five per cent of the U. S. film theatres were operating with a double-feature policy. Managements were resorting to give-away gimmicks to attract customers. Academy Awards went to "The Great Ziegfeld" for the best picture, Luise Rainer for her performance in that picture, and Paul Muni for his portrayal in "The Story of Louis Pasteur." For the first time, the Academy gave awards for the best supporting players, and the best musical composition. These went to Gale Sondergaard for her performance in "Anthony Adverse" and Walter Brennan for his performance in "Come and Get It." "The Way You Look Tonight" (by Jerome Kern and Dorothy Fields) from "Swing Time" won the best song award. Frank Capra won as the best director for "Mr. Deeds Goes to Town," which, incidentally, broke some sort of record by running six months at the Blue Mouse Theatre in Portland, Oregon. Animated cartoons were becoming more popular. The industry was becoming more color-conscious, and both "Ramona" and "The Garden of Allah" were filmed in color. Carl Laemmle sold his Universal Company to Charles R. Rogers. Irving Thalberg, John Gilbert and Henry B. Walthall died. Charlie Chaplin released "Modern Times," his last film without dialogue. Several outstanding French films, artistic in character, were playing in small "art" theatres in the larger cities throughout the U.S.A. Universal filmed another version of "Show Boat." The outstanding films included M-G-M's star-studded "Romeo and Juliet," "San Francisco," "Dodsworth," "The Green Pastures," "Mr. Deeds Goes to Town," "Anthony Adverse," "My Man Godfrey," "The Voice of Bugle Ann," and Garbo's version of "Camille." Robert Taylor, Carole Lombard, Cary Grant, Alice Faye and Errol Flynn were among the younger stars with box-office draw.

FRED MacMURRAY IN
"THE TEXAS RANGERS"
(PARAMOUNT)

JEANETTE MacDONALD, NELSON EDDY
IN "ROSE MARIE" (M-G-M)

SIMONE SIMON IN
"GIRLS' DORMITORY"
(20th CENTURY-FOX)

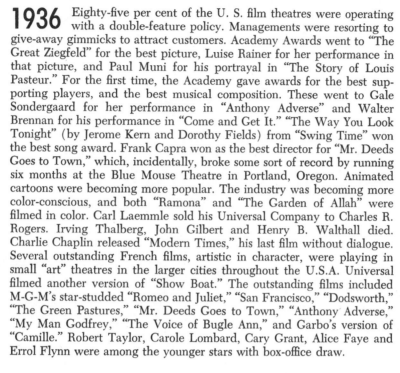

FREDRIC MARCH, KATHARINE HEPBURN Above: ALAN
MOWBRAY, FLORENCE ELDRIDGE, RALPH FORBES
IN "MARY OF SCOTLAND" DIRECTED BY JOHN FORD (RKO)

KATHARINE HEPBURN IN
"MARY OF SCOTLAND"
(RKO)

RANDOLPH SCOTT, PHILLIP REED, HENRY WILCOXON, BINNIE
BARNES, HEATHER ANGEL Above: HEATHER ANGEL, PHILLIP
REED, BRUCE CABOT IN "THE LAST OF THE MOHICANS"
(UNITED ARTISTS)

GRETA GARBO AS MARGUERITE GAUTIER
IN "CAMILLE"
DIRECTED BY GEORGE CUKOR (M-G-M)

GRETA GARBO, ROBERT TAYLOR Above: (left) GRETA GARBO, ROBERT TAYLOR (right)
GRETA GARBO, ROBERT TAYLOR, JESSIE RALPH Top: LAURA HOPE CREWS, LENORE ULRIC,
REX O'MALLEY, GRETA GARBO Below: GRETA GARBO, HENRY DANIELL, LENORE ULRIC, ROBERT TAYLOR

FREDRIC MARCH, DONALD WOODS, EDMUND GWENN
Above: FREDRIC MARCH IN "ANTHONY ADVERSE"
DIRECTED BY MERVYN LeROY (WARNER BROS.)

UNA O'CONNOR, DENIS O'DEA Above: BARRY
FITZGERALD IN "THE PLOW AND THE STARS"
DIRECTED BY JOHN FORD (RKO)

LAURENCE OLIVIER, ELISABETH BERGNER Top: LAURENCE
OLIVIER IN WILLIAM SHAKESPEARE'S "AS YOU LIKE IT"
DIRECTED BY PAUL CZINNER (20th CENTURY-FOX)

ELISSA LANDI, DOUGLAS FAIRBANKS, JR.
IN "THE AMATEUR GENTLEMAN"
(UNITED ARTISTS)

JAN KIEPURA
IN "GIVE US THIS NIGHT"
(PARAMOUNT)

1936

JEAN ARTHUR, GARY COOPER, JAMES ELLISON
IN CECIL B. De MILLE'S "THE PLAINSMAN"
(PARAMOUNT)

LESLIE HOWARD, NORMA SHEARER Above: JOHN
BARRYMORE, REGINALD DENNY, LESLIE HOWARD,
JOHN BARRYMORE, MAURICE MURPHY.

(M-G-M)

ROMEO AND JULIET

Adapted from Shakespeare's play by Talbot Jennings; Directed by George Cukor; Musical Score by Herbert Stothart; Settings by Cedric Gibbons and Oliver Messel; Costumes by Oliver Messel and Adrian; Dance Director, Agnes DeMille; Photographed by William Daniels; Film Editor, Margaret Booth. Released September 3, 1936.

CAST

Juliet	Norma Shearer
Romeo	Leslie Howard
Mercutio	John Barrymore
Nurse	Edna May Oliver
Tybalt	Basil Rathbone
Lord Capulet	C. Aubrey Smith
Peter	Andy Devine
Paris	Ralph Forbes
Benvolio	Reginald Denny
Balthasar	Maurice Murphy
Prince of Verona	Conway Tearle
Friar Laurence	Henry Kolker
Lord Montague	Robert Warwick
Lady Montague	Virginia Hammond
Lady Capulet	Violet Kemble-Cooper

VIOLET KEMBLE-COOPER, NORMA SHEARER, EDNA
MAY OLIVER, C. AUBREY SMITH Above: LESLIE HOWARD,
NORMA SHEARER

RALPH FORBES   LESLIE HOWARD   ANDY DEVINE   REGINALD DENNY   NORMA SHEARER   EDNA MAY OLIVER

(M-G-M)

THE GREAT ZIEGFELD

Producer, Hunt Stromberg; Director, Robert Z. Leonard; Screenplay by William Anthony McGuire; Music and Lyrics by Walter Donaldson, Harold Adamson, Con Conrad, Herb Magidson; Dances and Ensembles staged by Seymour Felix; Film Editor, William S. Gray; Music Director, Arthur Lange. Released April 19, 1936.

CAST

Florenz Ziegfeld, Jr.	William Powell
Billie Burke	Myrna Loy
Anna Held	Luise Rainer
Billings	Frank Morgan
Fannie Brice	Fannie Brice
Audrey Dane	Virginia Bruce
Sampston	Reginald Owen
Ray Bolger	Ray Bolger
Sidney	Ernest Cossart
Dr. Ziegfeld	Joseph Cawthorne
Sandow	Nat Pendleton
Harriet Hoctor	Harriet Hoctor
Mary Lou	Jean Chatburn
Erlanger	Paul Irving
Costumer	Herman Bing
Pianist	Charles Judels
Marie	Marcelle Corday
Sage	Raymond Walburn
Will Rogers	A. A. Trimble
Eddie Cantor	Buddy Doyle

NAT PENDLETON   FANNIE BRICE   WILLIAM POWELL, FRANK MORGAN, MYRNA LOY
Above: LUISE RAINER, WILLIAM POWELL   "THE GREAT ZIEGFELD"

LUISE RAINER, WHO WON ACADEMY AWARD FOR HER PERFORMANCE AS ANNA HELD

PAUL ROBESON, IRENE DUNNE
"SHOW BOAT"

(UNIVERSAL)

SHOW BOAT

Producer, Carl Laemmle, Jr.; Director, James Whale; Screenplay and Lyrics by Oscar Hammerstein II; Based on Novel by Edna Ferber and Musical Play by Oscar Hammerstein II and Jerome Kern; Musical Director, Victor Baravelle; Film Editor, Milton Carruth. Released May 13, 1936.

CAST

Magnolia Hawks	Irene Dunne
Gaylord Ravenal	Allan Jones
Cap'n Andy Hawks	Charles Winninger
Joe	Paul Robeson
Julie	Helen Morgan
Parthy	Helen Westley
Steve (Julie's Husband)	Donald Cook
Ellie (Frank's wife)	Queenie Smith
Frank Schultz	Sammy White
Queenie (Joe's wife)	Hattie McDaniel
Rubberface	Francis X. Mahoney
Sheriff Vallon	Charles Middleton
Pete	Arthur Hohl
Windy	J. Farrell MacDonald
Green	Charles Wilson
Kim (as a baby)	Patricia Barry
Kim (as a child)	Marilyn Knowlden
Kim	Sunny O'Dea
Guest	Flora Finch
Landlady	Mae Beatty
Sam (the janitor)	Clarence Muse
Hillbilly Patron	Stanley Fields

HELEN MORGAN   ALLAN JONES
Above: PAUL ROBESON, IRENE DUNNE, HATTIE McDANIEL, HELEN MORGAN

IRENE DUNNE   QUEENIE SMITH
Above: PAUL ROBESON, HATTIE McDANIEL, IRENE DUNNE, CHARLES WINNINGER

ROBERT TAYLOR

CAROLE LOMBARD

CARY GRANT

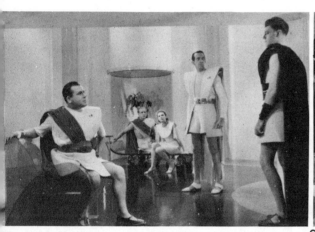

PEARL ARGYLE, RAYMOND MASSEY, ANTHONY HOLLES IN "THINGS TO COME," AN ALEXANDER KORDA PRODUCTION

GERTRUDE LAWRENCE, CHARLES LAUGHTON IN "REMBRANDT," AN ALEXANDER KORDA PRODUCTION (UNITED ARTISTS PRODUCTIONS)

JOEL McCREA, FRANCES FARMER, WALTER BRENNAN MADY CHRISTIANS IN "COME AND GET IT" DIRECTED BY HOWARD HAWKS AND WILLIAM WYLER

RAYMOND MASSEY IN "THINGS TO COME" (UNITED ARTISTS)

CAROLE LOMBARD, WILLIAM POWELL IN "MY MAN GODFREY" DIRECTED BY GREGORY LA CAVA (UNIVERSAL)

DOROTHY LAMOUR IN "THE JUNGLE PRINCESS" (PARAMOUNT)

CHARLES BOYER

JEAN MUIR

FRED MacMURRAY

ANN SOTHERN

TYRONE POWER

JOHN LODGE

SARI MARITZA

HUMPHREY BOGART, ERIN O'BRIEN-MOORE, ANN
SHERIDAN, DICK FORAN IN "BLACK LEGION"
(WARNER BROS.)

GEORGE BRENT, BETTE DAVIS IN
"THE GOLDEN ARROW"
(FIRST NATIONAL)

FRED MacMURRAY, SYLVIA SIDNEY, HENRY
FONDA IN "THE TRAIL OF THE LONESOME PINE"
DIRECTED BY HENRY HATHAWAY (PARAMOUNT)

LESLIE HOWARD, DICK FORAN, BETTE DAVIS, HUMPHREY BOGART
IN "THE PETRIFIED FOREST" DIRECTED BY ARCHIE MAYO
(WARNER BROS.)

RAYMOND WALBURN, GARY COOPER Above: JEAN
ARTHUR, GARY COOPER IN "MR. DEEDS GOES TO TOWN"
DIRECTED BY FRANK CAPRA (COLUMBIA)

LESLIE HOWARD

WYNNE GIBSON

GEORGE RAFT

LUCILLE BALL

NILS ASTHER

JEAN PARKER

TOMMY CONLON

GEORGE SANDERS

MADELEINE CARROLL, TYRONE POWER
IN "LLOYDS OF LONDON"
(20th CENTURY-FOX)

MADELEINE CARROLL

WALLACE BEERY, JOHN BOLES
IN "MESSAGE TO GARCIA"
(20th CENTURY-FOX)

SMITH BALLEW

LUCILLE BALL, GENE RAYMOND, JACK OAKIE,
FRANK JENKS, MISCHA AUER, LILY PONS
IN "THAT GIRL FROM PARIS" (RKO)

REX INGRAM IN
"THE GREEN PASTURES"
(WARNER BROS.)

MADELEINE CARROLL, GARY COOPER IN
"THE GENERAL DIED AT DAWN"
(PARAMOUNT)

ROSALIND RUSSELL IN
"CRAIG'S WIFE"
(COLUMBIA)

Top: KENNETH HOWELL, SHIRLEY DEANE Center: JUNE CARLSON,
FLORENCE ROBERTS, JED PROUTY, SPRING BYINGTON, GEORGE ERNEST
Bottom: WILLIAM MAHIN OF "THE JONES FAMILY" COMEDY SERIES (20th CENTURY-FOX)

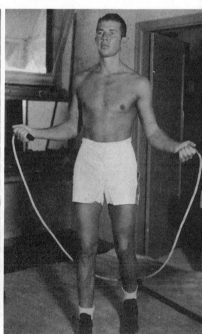

BRUCE CABOT
(RKO)

JOHNNY DOWNS, STUART ERWIN, BETTY GRABLE, JUDY
GARLAND, PATSY KELLY IN "PIGSKIN PARADE"
(20th CENTURY-FOX)

IRVING CUMMINGS (center), FAMOUS DIRECTOR
AND FORMER SILENT SCREEN STAR, WITH JUDY
STOREY, DIXIE DUNBAR, SIMONE SIMON AND
SHIRLEY DEANE IN "GIRLS' DORMITORY" (20th CENTURY-FOX)

NIGEL BRUCE, VICTOR McLAGLEN, CLAUDETTE COLBERT,
RONALD COLMAN IN "UNDER TWO FLAGS" DIRECTED
BY FRANK LLOYD (20th CENTURY-FOX)

MARLENE DIETRICH, GARY COOPER IN "DESIRE" DIRECTED BY FRANK BORZAGE (PARAMOUNT)

UNA O'CONNOR IN "LITTLE LORD FAUNTLEROY" (UNITED ARTISTS)

ERROL FLYNN IN "THE CHARGE OF THE LIGHT BRIGADE" (WARNER BROS.)

ADOLPHE MENJOU, HAROLD LLOYD, LIONEL STANDER IN "THE MILKY WAY" (PARAMOUNT)

JESSIE MATTHEWS IN "FIRST A GIRL" (GAUMONT BRITISH)

NAT PENDLETON, PATRICIA ELLIS, JAMES MELTON IN "SING ME A LOVE SONG" (WARNER BROS.)

JUDY GARLAND IN "PIGSKIN PARADE" (20th CENTURY-FOX)

1936

JEAN HARLOW

ROCHELLE HUDSON

DANIELLE DARRIEUX, CHARLES BOYER IN "MAYERLING"
DIRECTED BY ANATOLE LITVAK

ERROL FLYNN

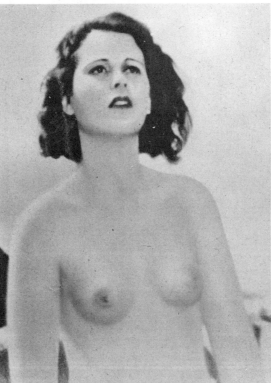

CLAUDE RAINS, DONALD BRIGGS, EDWARD NORRIS
Above: LANA TURNER, LINDA PERRY
IN "THEY WON'T FORGET" (WARNER BROS.)

HEDY KEISLER (HEDY LAMARR)
IN "EXTASE" ("ECSTASY")
CZECHOSLOVAKIAN FILM

FAY HOLDEN, ROBERT CUMMINGS, LUANA WALTERS
Above: FRANCES DEE GARY COOPER IN "SOULS AT
SEA" DIRECTED BY HENRY HATHAWAY (PARAMOUNT)

ROBERT YOUNG, TOM BROWN, JAMES STEWART,
LIONEL BARRYMORE IN "NAVY BLUE AND GOLD"
(M-G-M)

JACK OAKIE, MILTON BERLE, ANN MILLER, BOB
BURNS, KENNY BAKER IN "RADIO CITY REVELS"
(RKO)

RICHARD CROMWELL, GENE GARRICK, ANDY DEVINE,
JOHN KING IN "THE ROAD BACK"
(UNIVERSAL)

BING CROSBY

DEANNA DURBIN

FRED ASTAIRE

1937 Seventy per cent of the world's movie fare emanated from Hollywood at this time. Better pictures were being made. Stage successes, best-selling novels, and literary classics were brought to the screen by the so-called genius of the film capital. Five hundred eighty-eight pictures were made and the investment in this West Coast product was one hundred eight million dollars. Among the many distinguished films released were "The Life of Emile Zola" which won the Academy Award as the best picture of the year, "The Good Earth," "Lost Horizon," "Captains Courageous," "Make Way for Tomorrow," "Dead End," "Night Must Fall," "The Hurricane," a new version of "The Prisoner of Zenda," "Stage Door," and two captivating comedies, "The Awful Truth" and "Nothing Sacred." In the foreign field, "Mayerling" was outstanding. Walt Disney created one of his all-time great films, "Snow White and the Seven Dwarfs." It had grossed over eight million before its 1958 re-release. Luise Rainer won her second Academy Award for her portrayal in "The Good Earth," and Spencer Tracy won his first for "Captains Courageous." "A Family Affair" was an unpretentious little film released by M-G-M. It was the first of the famous Andy Hardy series which starred Mickey Rooney in the title role. From Czechoslovakia came "Ecstasy" which created a stir because of a nude swimming sequence by its star Hedy Keisler. M-G-M grabbed her and changed her name to Hedy LaMarr. Other new faces on the Hollywood scene were Lana Turner, who made her film debut in "They Won't Forget," Wayne Morris in "Kid Galahad," and Jon Hall in "The Hurricane." Jean Harlow died at the height of her career. Deanna Durbin, a youngster with a lovely voice, came into her own in "One Hundred Men and A Girl." Leopold Stokowski, famous conductor, was one of the men. Clark Gable made what was considered his worst film, "Parnell." Joe Louis, heavyweight boxing champion, made a film, "Spirit of Youth."

CHESTER MORRIS, HELEN MACK
IN "I PROMISE TO PAY"
(COLUMBIA)

BETTY GRABLE, BUSTER CRABBE
IN "THRILL OF A LIFETIME"
(PARAMOUNT)

ROLAND YOUNG, CARY GRANT, CONSTANCE
BENNETT IN "TOPPER"
(M-G-M)

BARBARA STANWYCK IN "STELLA
DALLAS" DIRECTED BY KING VIDOR
A SAMUEL GOLDWYN PRODUCTION

LYNN CARVER, JOHN BEAL, EMMA DUNN, GLADYS GEORGE,
REGINALD OWEN, WARREN WILLIAM IN "MADAME X"
DIRECTED BY SAM WOOD (M-G-M)

CONSTANCE COLLIER   RICHARD CARLE   FAY BAINTER   FRED STONE   BILLIE BURKE   HENRY HULL   HENRIETTA CROSMAN

STAGE STARS IN TALKIES

CLARENCE MUSE, JOE LOUIS IN "SPIRIT OF YOUTH" (GRAND NATIONAL)   SYLVIA SIDNEY, HENRY FONDA IN "YOU ONLY LIVE ONCE" DIRECTED BY FRITZ LANG (UNITED ARTISTS)   RUSSELL HICKS, WARD BOND, JAMES ELLISON IN "23½ HOURS" (GRAND NATIONAL)

LUISE RAINER (in bed)   LUISE RAINER, PAUL MUNI

SCENES FROM "THE GOOD EARTH" DIRECTED BY SIDNEY FRANKLIN (M-G-M)

WARNER OLAND   ESTHER RALSTON   TOM KEENE (FORMERLY GEORGE DURYEA)   GEORGE MURPHY   RALPH GRAVES   BETTY FURNESS   PERCY MARMONT

JOHNNY MACK BROWN   JANE BRYAN   LEIF ERICKSON   FRANCES FARMER   JAMES STEWART   ZASU PITTS   MICHAEL WHALEN

ROLAND YOUNG, CEDRIC HARDWICKE, PAUL ROBESON, ANNA LEE, JOHN LODER IN "KING SOLOMON'S MINES" (GAUMONT BRITISH)

MARLENE DIETRICH, ROBERT DONAT IN "KNIGHT WITHOUT ARMOR" (UNITED ARTISTS)

SABU IN "ELEPHANT BOY" DIRECTED BY ROBERT FLAHERTY (UNITED ARTISTS)

JOHN HOWARD, RONALD COLMAN, EDWARD EVERETT HORTON   H. B. WARNER, ISABEL JEWELL, EDWARD EVERETT HORTON, RONALD COLMAN, THOMAS MITCHELL

SCENES FROM "LOST HORIZON" DIRECTED BY FRANK CAPRA (COLUMBIA)

MAE CLARKE   HENRY FONDA   VIRGINIA FIELD   FRANCHOT TONE   JOAN FONTAINE   JOHN PAYNE   ANNE SHIRLEY

ROBERT WARRICK, JOSEPH SCHILDKRAUT Top: JOSEPH
SCHILDKRAUT, WHO WON AN ACADEMY AWARD
FOR HIS PORTRAYAL OF CAPT. DREYFUS

PAUL MUNI IN
"THE LIFE OF EMILE ZOLA"
DIRECTED BY WILLIAM DIETERLE (WARNER BROS.)

DOPEY, GRUMPY, SLEEPY, SNEEZY, DOC, HAPPY, SNOW WHITE, BASHFUL
WALT DISNEY'S FIRST FULL-LENGTH FEATURE PRODUCTION "SNOW WHITE AND THE SEVEN DWARFS" (RKO)

KATHARINE HEPBURN, GINGER ROGERS, EVE ARDEN IN "STAGE DOOR"
DIRECTED BY GREGORY LA CAVA (RKO)

IRENE DUNNE, CARY GRANT IN
"THE AWFUL TRUTH"
DIRECTED BY LEO McCAREY (COLUMBIA)

CARY GRANT, GRACE MOORE
IN "WHEN YOU'RE IN LOVE"
(COLUMBIA)

BETTE DAVIS, MAYO METHOT, HUMPHREY BOGART
IN "MARKED WOMAN"
(WARNER BROS.)

BRIAN AHERNE, OLIVIA DE HAVILLAND
IN "THE GREAT GARRICK"
(WARNER BROS.)

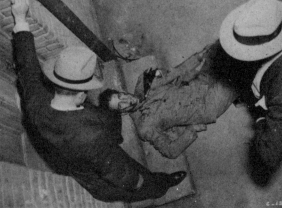

FLORA ROBSON, LAURENCE OLIVIER, VIVIEN LEIGH IN
"FIRE OVER ENGLAND" (UNITED ARTISTS)

HUMPHREY BOGART, also above WITH
MARJORIE MAIN IN SCENES FROM
"DEAD END" (UNITED ARTISTS)

CAROLE LOMBARD, WALTER CONNOLLY, FREDRIC MARCH
IN "NOTHING SACRED"
DIRECTED BY WILLIAM WELLMAN (UNITED ARTISTS)

BOBBY BREEN
IN "HAWAII CALLS"
(RKO)

JEANETTE MacDONALD, ALLAN JONES
IN "THE FIREFLY"
(M-G-M)

JON HALL, DOROTHY LAMOUR (also above)
IN "THE HURRICANE"
DIRECTED BY JOHN FORD (UNITED ARTISTS)

NELSON EDDY, JEANETTE MacDONALD
IN "MAYTIME" (M-G-M)

CHARLES WINNINGER, MAE WEST, CHARLES
BUTTERWORTH IN "EVERY DAY'S A HOLIDAY"
(PARAMOUNT)

ROLAND VARNO, WILLIAM BAKEWELL, FRANCHOT TONE, KATHARINE HEPBURN
IN SIR JAMES M. BARRIE'S "QUALITY STREET"
DIRECTED BY GEORGE STEVENS (RKO)

FRED MacMURRAY, GLADYS SWARTHOUT
IN "CHAMPAGNE WALTZ"
(PARAMOUNT)

FLORA ROBSON IN
"FIRE OVER ENGLAND"
(UNITED ARTISTS)

MICKEY ROONEY, FREDDIE BARTHOLOMEW Top: SPENCER TRACY,
FREDDIE BARTHOLOMEW, CHARLEY GRAPEWIN, LIONEL BARRYMORE
IN "CAPTAINS COURAGEOUS" DIRECTED BY VICTOR FLEMING (M-G-M)

JOHN LODER
IN "DR. SYN"
(GAUMONT BRITISH)

C. AUBREY SMITH, DAVID NIVEN, RONALD COLMAN, MADELEINE CARROLL
IN "THE PRISONER OF ZENDA"
DIRECTED BY JOHN CROMWELL (UNITED ARTISTS)

NINO MARTINI IN
"MUSIC FOR MADAME"
(RKO)

CHARLES BOYER, MARIA OUSPENSKAYA, GRETA GARBO
Top: GRETA GARBO, CHARLES BOYER, GEORGE HOUSTON,
ALAN MARSHALL IN "CONQUEST" (M-G-M)

GRETA GARBO, CHARLES BOYER
IN "CONQUEST" DIRECTED
BY CLARENCE BROWN (M-G-M)

JANET GAYNOR, FREDRIC MARCH, ADOLPHE MENJOU,
LIONEL STANDER, VINCE BARNETT Top: MARCH,
JOSEPH SCHILDKRAUT, GAYNOR IN "A STAR IS BORN"
DIRECTOR: WILIAM WELLMAN (UNITED ARTISTS)

MARY BOLAND

BRUCE CABOT

JEAN HARLOW
BORN MARCH 3, 1911
DIED JUNE 8, 1937

CESAR ROMERO

ELISSA LANDI

LANA TURNER IN
"THEY WON'T FORGET"
(WARNER BROS.)

DEANNA DURBIN, LEOPOLD STOKOWSKI
IN "ONE HUNDRED MEN AND A GIRL"
DIRECTED BY HENRY KOSTER (UNIVERSAL)

FERNAND GRAVET
IN "THE KING AND THE CHORUS
GIRL" (WARNER BROS.)

GARY COOPER

WILLIAM HOLDEN IN
"GOLDEN BOY" (COLUMBIA)

JEAN ARTHUR, HALLIWELL HOBBES, DUB TAYLOR, SPRING BYINGTON, ANN MILLER, MISCHA AUER
IN FRANK CAPRA'S PRODUCTION OF "YOU CAN'T TAKE IT WITH YOU" (COLUMBIA)

LEE J. COBB, JOSEPH CALLEIA, WILLIAM HOLDEN
IN "GOLDEN BOY" DIRECTED BY
ROUBEN MAMOULIAN (COLUMBIA)

JEAN DIXON, KATHARINE HEPBURN, EDWARD EVERETT HORTON,
LEW AYRES, CARY GRANT IN "HOLIDAY"
DIRECTED BY GEORGE CUKOR (COLUMBIA)

MAXIE ROSENBLOOM, JOE CREHAN, WAYNE MORRIS,
DICKIE JONES IN "THE KID COMES BACK"
(WARNER BROS.)

"FERDINAND THE BULL" A WALT DISNEY
SILLY SYMPHONY
(RKO)

EDDIE ALBERT, WAYNE MORRIS, RONALD REAGAN,
JOHNNIE DAVIS IN "BROTHER RAT"
(WARNER BROS.)

MICKEY ROONEY, FRANKIE THOMAS, SPENCER TRACY
IN "BOYS' TOWN"
DIRECTED BY NORMAN TAUROG (M-G-M)

BETTE DAVIS
IN "JEZEBEL" DIRECTED
BY WILLIAM WYLER (WARNER BROS.)

KIRSTEN FLAGSTAD IN
"THE BIG BROADCAST OF 1938"
(PARAMOUNT)

1938 "You Can't Take It With You," taken from a Pulitzer Prize-winning play, won an Academy Award as the best picture of the year, and Frank Capra, its director, also received an "Oscar." Bette Davis and Fay Bainter each took home an "Oscar" for their performances in "Jezebel," and Walter Brennan was voted one for his supporting role in "Kentucky." Color in motion pictures advanced scientifically as well as in popularity. Television, now in the experimental stage, was slowly drawing closer to practical reality. "Ferdinand the Bull," a Walt Disney short cartoon, won an Academy Award and was popular. Among the better films were "Boys Town," "The Citadel," "Of Human Hearts," "Marie Antoinette," "Three Comrades," "Pygmalion," "Alexander's Ragtime Band," "Algiers," "Holiday," "Test Pilot," "Sing You Sinners," and "The Adventures of Robin Hood." Among the classics filmed were Dickens' "A Christmas Carol," Kipling's "Kidnapped," and Mark Twain's "The Adventures of Tom Sawyer." "Grand Illusion" and "The Lady Vanishes" were the outstanding imports. Judy Garland was beginning to be noticed in several M-G-M productions. Other new faces gracing the screen were William Holden, Paulette Goddard, John Garfield, Betty Grable, Roy Rogers, John Payne, and David Niven. "Blondie," starring Arthur Lake and Penny Singleton, was another popular series to make its initial appearance. Two new Tarzans arrived in the persons of athletes Glenn Morris and Bruce Bennett (formerly Herman Brix). Deaths of the year included Max Factor, Hollywood's famous make-up artist, Warner Oland, famous for his Charlie Chan character, and Pearl White, famous serial queen of the silent screen. Mme. Kirsten Flagstad, famous opera diva, made her film debut singing several Wagnerian arias in "The Big Broadcast of 1938." Paderewski, internationally famous pianist, made his initial film, "Moonlight Sonata," with Marie Tempest, noted English actress, as his leading lady.

CHARLES LAUGHTON IN
"THE BEACHCOMBER"
(PARAMOUNT)

CARY GRANT, KATHARINE HEPBURN
IN "BRINGING UP BABY"
(RKO)

SIGRID GURIE, GARY COOPER IN "THE ADVENTURES
OF MARCO POLO" A SAMUEL GOLDWYN
PRODUCTION (UNITED ARTISTS)

GORDON OLIVER, GEORGE BRENT, FAY BAINTER, RICHARD
CROMWELL, HENRY O'NEILL, MARGARET LINDSAY, BETTE
DAVIS IN "JEZEBEL" (WARNER BROS.)

ROBERT PRESTON   GRACIE FIELDS   REGINALD DENNY   JOAN DAVIS   DONALD O'CONNOR   SYBIL JASON   DON AMECHE

JUNE STOREY, ALICE BRADY, ANDY DEVINE, DON AMECHE, TYRONE POWER IN "IN OLD CHICAGO" DIRECTED BY HENRY KING (20th CENTURY-FOX) MISS BRADY WON AN ACADEMY AWARD FOR HER PERFORMANCE

TOM BROWN, LOUIS HAYWARD, JOAN FONTAINE IN "THE DUKE OF WEST POINT" (UNITED ARTISTS)

HAROLD LLOYD, WILLIAM FRAWLEY IN "PROFESSOR, BEWARE!" (PARAMOUNT)

WAYNE MORRIS IN "THE KID COMES BACK" (WARNER BROS.)

ALICE FAYE IN "IN OLD CHICAGO" (20th CENTURY-FOX)

PRISCILLA LANE, JOHN GARFIELD, MAY ROBSON
Above: GAIL PAGE, LOLA, ROSEMARY AND PRISCILLA LANE IN "FOUR DAUGHTERS" (WARNER BROS.)

DICK FORAN   IRENE HERVEY   PHILLIP REED   ELSA LANCHESTER IN "THE BEACHCOMBER" (PARAMOUNT)

CHARLES BUTTERWORTH

OLIVIA DE HAVILLAND

ROBERT DONAT

LILIAN HARVEY

ALAN BAXTER

GLADYS GEORGE

CHARLES BICKFORD

NELSON EDDY, JEANETTE MacDONALD
IN "SWEETHEARTS"
(M-G-M)

NELSON EDDY, JEANETTE MacDONALD,
WALTER PIDGEON IN "THE GIRL OF THE
GOLDEN WEST" (M-G-M)

NELSON EDDY IN
"SWEETHEARTS" (M-G-M)

JOAN BENNETT IN "VOGUES OF 1938"
A WALTER WANGER PRODUCTION
(UNITED ARTISTS)

ROBERT TAYLOR IN
"THE CROWD ROARS"
(M-G-M)

ANNABELLA IN "SUEZ"
(20th CENTURY-FOX)

DONALD WOODS

GERALDINE
FITZGERALD

LYLE TALBOT

1938

BING CROSBY, ELIZABETH PATTERSON, FRED MacMURRAY,
DONALD O'CONNOR IN "SING YOU SINNERS"
(PARAMOUNT)

JAMES CAGNEY, PAT O'BRIEN WITH "DEAD END KIDS" BOBBY
JORDAN, BILLY HALOP, HUNTZ HALL, GABRIEL DELL, BERNARD
PUNSLEY, LEO GORCEY IN "ANGELS WITH DIRTY FACES"
(WARNER BROS.)

VERA ZORINA
IN "THE GOLDWYN FOLLIES"
(UNITED ARTISTS)

FRANCHOT TONE, MARGARET SULLAVAN, ROBERT
TAYLOR, ROBERT YOUNG, LIONEL ATWILL IN
"THREE COMRADES" (M-G-M)

TYRONE POWER, NORMA SHEARER

JOSEPH SCHILDKRAUT, TYRONE POWER, ANITA LOUISE,
NORMA SHEARER, REGINALD GARDINER

ROBERT MORLEY, JOHN BARRYMORE,
NORMA SHEARER

SCENES FROM "MARIE ANTOINETTE," DIRECTED BY W. S. VANDYKE (M-G-M)

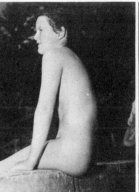

WILLIAM BOYD, RUSSELL HAYDEN IN
"HEART OF ARIZONA"
(PARAMOUNT)

CLARA KIMBALL YOUNG
IN "THE FRONTIERSMAN"
(PARAMOUNT)

TOMMY KELLY

TOMMY KELLY, MAY ROBSON, DAVID HOLT
"THE ADVENTURES OF TOM SAWYER," DAVID SELZNICK
PRODUCTION, DIRECTED BY NORMAN TAUROG (UNITED ARTISTS)

ROBERT DONAT, RALPH RICHARDSON IN
"THE CITADEL" DIRECTED BY
KING VIDOR (M-G-M)

ANN RUTHERFORD, MICKEY ROONEY, CECILIA
PARKER, LANA TURNER, JUDY GARLAND IN
"LOVE FINDS ANDY HARDY" (M-G-M)

MILIZA KORJUS, FERNAND GRAVET, LIONEL
ATWILL IN "THE GREAT WALTZ" DIRECTED BY
JULIEN DUVIVIER (M-G-M)

JACK HALEY, ALICE FAYE, DON AMECHE, TYRONE POWER IN "ALEXANDER'S RAGTIME BAND" (20th CENTURY-FOX)

C. HENRY GORDON, ELEANOR HOLM, GLENN MORRIS IN "TARZAN'S REVENGE" (20th CENTURY-FOX)

LESTER MATTHEWS, WILLIAM FARNUM, MONTAGU LOVE, RONALD COLMAN, WALTER KINGSFORD, BASIL RATHBONE IN "IF I WERE KING" (PARAMOUNT)

BEULAH BONDI, JAMES STEWART IN "OF HUMAN HEARTS" (M-G-M)

IGNACE JAN PADEREWSKI, MARIE TEMPEST IN "MOONLIGHT SONATA" DIRECTED BY LOTHAR MENDES (MALMAR PICTURES)

CLARK GABLE, SPENCER TRACY IN "TEST PILOT" (M-G-M)

GUINN WILLIAMS, JOHN BARRYMORE, GEORGE MURPHY, JOAN DAVIS IN "HOLD THAT CO-ED" (20th CENTURY-FOX)

EDNA MAY OLIVER, DONALD MEEK, SHIRLEY TEMPLE, GEORGE MURPHY IN "LITTLE MISS BROADWAY" (20th CENTURY-FOX)

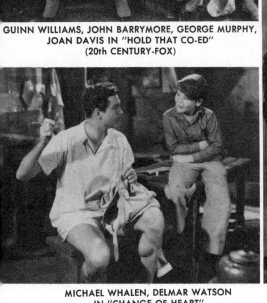

MICHAEL WHALEN, DELMAR WATSON IN "CHANGE OF HEART" (20th CENTURY-FOX)

TERRY KILBURN, REGINALD OWEN IN CHARLES DICKENS' "A CHRISTMAS CAROL" (M-G-M)

GLORIA STUART, SHIRLEY TEMPLE, HELEN WESTLEY IN "REBECCA OF SUNNYBROOK FARM" (20th CENTURY-FOX)

IGOR GORIN, SOPHIE TUCKER, GEORGE MURPHY, ELEANOR POWELL, ROBERT TAYLOR, JUDY GARLAND, BUDDY EBSEN
IN "BROADWAY MELODY OF 1938"
(M-G-M)

ESME PERCY, LESLIE HOWARD, SCOTT SUNDERLAND,
WENDY HILLER, IRENE BROWN

(M-G-M)

PYGMALION

Producer, Gabriel Pascal; Directors, Anthony Asquith and Leslie Howard; Based on Play by Bernard Shaw; Screenplay and Dialogue by Bernard Shaw; Adaptation by W. P. Lipscombe, Cecil Lewis, and Ian Dalrymple; Film Editor, David Lean; Music Director, William Axt; Musical Score by Arthur Honegger. Released November 25, 1938.

CAST

Henry Higgins	Leslie Howard
Eliza Doolittle	Wendy Hiller
Alfred Doolittle	Wilfrid Lawson
Mrs. Higgins	Marie Lohr
Colonel Pickering	Scott Sunderland
Mrs. Pearce	Jean Cadell
Freddy	David Tree
Mrs. Eynsford Hill	Everley Gregg
Clara Hill	Leueen MacGrath
Count Aristid Karpathy	Esme Percy
Ambassadress	Violet Vanbrugh
Vicar	O. B. Clarence
Duchess	Irene Brown
Grand Old Lady	Kate Cutler

"PYGMALION"

SCOTT SUNDERLAND, WENDY HILLER

MICHAEL REDGRAVE, MARGARET LOCKWOOD, DAME
MAY WHITTY IN "THE LADY VANISHES" DIRECTED
BY ALFRED HITCHCOCK (GAUMONT BRITISH)

MICHAEL REDGRAVE IN
"THE LADY VANISHES"
(GAUMONT BRITISH)

JEAN HERSHOLT WITH THE DIONNE QUINTUPLETS IN
"FIVE OF A KIND"
(20th CENTURY-FOX)

IAN HUNTER, ALAN HALE, OLIVIA DE HAVILLAND, ERROL FLYNN, HERBERT MUNDIN, PATRIC KNOWLES, EUGENE PALLETTE
Top: BASIL RATHBONE, ERROL FLYNN IN
"THE ADVENTURES OF ROBIN HOOD" (FIRST NATIONAL)

JACK CARSON, RALPH BELLAMY, LUELLA GEAR, FRED ASTAIRE, GINGER ROGERS IN "CAREFREE" (RKO)

AKIM TAMIROFF, FRANCISKA GAAL, FREDRIC MARCH
IN "THE BUCCANEER" DIRECTED BY
CECIL B. DeMILLE (PARAMOUNT)

ERROL FLYNN AS
ROBIN HOOD

ALAN HALE, JOSEPH CALLEIA, CHARLES BOYER, GENE LOCKHART IN "ALGIERS" A WALTER WANGER PRODUCTION (UNITED ARTISTS)

SABU, VALERIE HOBSON, ROGER LIVESEY IN "DRUMS" AN ALEXANDER KORDA PRODUCTION (UNITED ARTISTS)

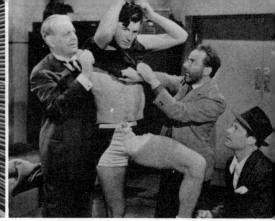

THURSTON HALL, HANK LUISETTI, FRITZ FELD, MATTY KEMP IN "CAMPUS CONFESSIONS" (PARAMOUNT)

RALPH BELLAMY, JAMES CAGNEY, PAT O'BRIEN, DICK FORAN IN "BOY MEETS GIRL" (WARNER BROS.)

FREDDIE BARTHOLOMEW, WARNER BAXTER IN "KIDNAPPED" (20th CENTURY-FOX)

BETTY GRABLE, JOHN PAYNE, CECILE CUNNINGHAM IN "COLLEGE SWING" (PARAMOUNT)

BING CROSBY, BEATRICE LILLIE IN "DR. RHYTHM" (PARAMOUNT)

DAVID SHARPE IN "DICK TRACY RETURNS" (A REPUBLIC SERIAL)

JUDY GARLAND, ALLAN JONES IN "EVERYBODY SING" (M-G-M)

JOEL McCREA IN "YOUTH TAKES A FLING" (UNIVERSAL)

OLIVER HARDY, STAN LAUREL IN "SWISS MISS" (HAL ROACH)

JACKIE COOPER, BONITA GRANVILLE, FAY BAINTER IN "WHITE BANNERS" (WARNER BROS.)

AKIM TAMIROFF, LEIF ERICKSON IN "RIDE A CROOKED MILE" (PARAMOUNT)

MORGAN WALLACE, ROY ROGERS IN "BILLY THE KID RETURNS" (REPUBLIC)

SACHA GUITRY IN "THE STORY OF A CHEAT"
("LE ROMAN D'UN TRICHEUR")
(GALLIC FILMS)

JEAN GABIN, MICHÈLE MORGAN IN
"PORT OF SHADOWS" ("QUAI DES BRUMES")
DIRECTED BY MARCEL CARNÉ

DONALD McBRIDE, GROUCHO, HARPO AND CHICO
MARX IN "ROOM SERVICE"
(RKO)

ERIC VON STROHEIM Top: JEAN GABIN, PIERRE
FRESNAY IN "GRAND ILLUSION" ("LA GRANDE
ILLUSION") DIRECTED BY JEAN RENOIR.

LARRY SIMMS, PENNY SINGLETON, ARTHUR
LAKE IN "BLONDIE"
(COLUMBIA)

SOPHIE STEWART, BARRY K.
BARNES IN "THE RETURN OF
THE SCARLET PIMPERNEL" (UNITED ARTISTS)

GLENN MORRIS IN
"TARZAN'S REVENGE"
(20th CENTURY-FOX)

MINNE DUPREE IN
"THE YOUNG IN HEART"
(UNITED ARTISTS)

BRUCE BENNETT (HERMAN BRIX)
IN "TARZAN AND THE GREEN
GODDESS" (PRI)

DEANNA DURBIN, MELVYN
DOUGLAS IN "THAT CERTAIN
AGE" (UNIVERSAL)

DAVID NIVEN, CLAUDETTE COLBERT
IN "BLUEBEARD'S EIGHTH WIFE"
(PARAMOUNT)

ROLAND YOUNG, JANET GAYNOR, BILLIE BURKE,
DOUGLAS FAIRBANKS, JR., MINNIE DUPREE IN
"THE YOUNG IN HEART" (UNITED ARTISTS)

CAROLE LOMBARD, RALPH BELLAMY,
FERNAND GRAVET IN "FOOLS FOR
SCANDAL" (WARNER BROS.)

HEDDA HOPPER
IN "LAUGH IT OFF"
(UNIVERSAL)

MARLENE DIETRICH
IN "DESTRY RIDES AGAIN"
(UNIVERSAL)

BASIL RATHBONE
AS SHERLOCK HOLMES
(20th CENTURY-FOX)

JAMES STEWART, MARLENE DIETRICH
IN "DESTRY RIDES AGAIN" DIRECTED
BY GEORGE MARSHALL (UNIVERSAL)

JOHN WAYNE
IN "STAGECOACH" DIRECTED BY
JOHN FORD (UNITED ARTISTS)

JOHN CARRADINE, ANDY DEVINE, GEORGE BANCROFT, LOUISE PLATT, DONALD MEEK,
CLAIRE TREVOR, JOHN WAYNE, BERTON CHURCHILL IN
WALTER WANGER'S PRODUCTION OF "STAGECOACH" (UNITED ARTISTS)

JOHN GARFIELD
IN "JUAREZ"

DONALD CRISP, BRIAN AHERNE, BETTE DAVIS, MICKEY KUHN, HARRY DAVENPORT,
GILBERT ROLAND IN "JUAREZ" DIRECTED BY
WILLIAM DIETERLE (WARNER BROS.)

PAUL MUNI
IN "JUAREZ"

LESLIE HOWARD, INGRID BERGMAN
IN "INTERMEZZO" DIRECTED BY
GREGORY RATOFF (UNITED ARTISTS)

WARNER BAXTER IN
"THE RETURN OF THE CISCO
KID" (20th CENTURY-FOX)

MARY MARTIN IN
"THE GREAT VICTOR
HERBERT" (PARAMOUNT)

BERT LAHR, CLAUDETTE COLBERT, HELEN WESTLEY,
CONSTANCE COLLIER IN "ZAZA" DIRECTED BY
GEORGE CUKOR (PARAMOUNT)

DON AMECHE IN
"THE THREE MUSKETEERS"
(20th CENTURY-FOX)

1939 On December 15, one of the great films of all time, "Gone With The Wind," had its world premiere in Atlanta, Georgia. It was three years in the making and cost four and one half million dollars. It won many Academy Awards: as the best picture, for art direction, film editing, color cinematography, and Vivien Leigh and Hattie McDaniel for their performances, also Victor Fleming for his direction. Other Academy "Oscars" went to Robert Donat for "Goodbye, Mr. Chips," and Thomas Mitchell for "Stage Coach." Hollywood producers kept to their large production schedules despite the war abroad and the curtailing of foreign revenues. Television was still no real threat even though N.B.C. inaugurated public service programs. Among the outstanding films were "Wuthering Heights," "Stage Coach," "Goodbye, Mr. Chips," "Mr. Smith Goes to Washington," "Ninotchka," "The Wizard of Oz," "Young Mr. Lincoln," "Juarez," "Love Affair," "The Women," and a French film, "Harvest." The "series" films were becoming very popular on family programs. Among the many series films released at this period were "Andy Hardy," "Tarzan," "Charlie Chan," "Blondie," "The Thin Man," "Hopalong Cassidy," "Dr. Kildare," "The Cisco Kid," "Maisie," "The Jones Family," "Mr. Moto," "Torchy," "Sherlock Holmes" and "Topper." Douglas Fairbanks, Sr., Carl Laemmle and Alice Brady were among death's toll. Ingrid Bergman, a Swedish actress, appeared in "Intermezzo," and Greer Garson from England played in "Goodbye, Mr. Chips." It was the American film debut of both these distinguished stars.

CLAUDETTE COLBERT
IN "ZAZA"
(PARAMOUNT)

111

BASIL RATHBONE, FRANCIS POWERS, IAN HUNTER, GEORGIA
CAINE, JOHN SUTTON IN "TOWER OF LONDON"
(UNIVERSAL)

JOSEPH SCHILDKRAUT, NIGEL BRUCE, H. B. WARNER, MARIA OUSPENSKAYA,
WILLIAM ROYLE, MYRNA LOY, GEORGE BRENT IN "THE RAINS CAME"
DIRECTED BY CLARENCE BROWN (20th CENTURY-FOX)

SONJA HENIE   WAYNE MORRIS   BETTY GRABLE   RICHARD GREENE   DOROTHY LAMOUR

GERALDINE FITZGERALD, LAURENCE OLIVIER, LEO G. CARROLL,
FLORA ROBSON Above: MERLE OBERON, LAURENCE OLIVIER IN
"WUTHERING HEIGHTS" DIRECTED BY WILLIAM WYLER
(UNITED ARTISTS)

LAURENCE OLIVIER
IN "WUTHERING HEIGHTS"
PRODUCED BY
SAMUEL GOLDWYN

ROMAN BOHNEN, BURGESS MEREDITH, BETTY FIELD, LEIGH WHIPPER
Above: LON CHANEY, JR., BURGESS MEREDITH IN
"OF MICE AND MEN" DIRECTED BY LEWIS MILESTONE
(UNITED ARTISTS)

CLARK GABLE

GRETA GARBO, ALEXANDER GRANACH, SIG RUMAN, FELIX BRESSART   GRETA GARBO   GRETA GARBO, MELVYN DOUGLAS, INA CLAIRE

SCENES FROM "NINOTCHKA" PRODUCED AND DIRECTED BY ERNST LUBITSCH (M-G-M)

ANN EVERS, CARY GRANT, JOAN FONTAINE, DOUGLAS FAIRBANKS, JR. Above: CARY GRANT, VICTOR McLAGLEN, DOUGLAS FAIRBANKS, JR. IN "GUNGA DIN" (RKO)   JAMES STEWART IN "MR. SMITH GOES TO WASHINGTON" PRODUCER-DIRECTOR, FRANK CAPRA   BEULAH BONDI, JAMES STEWART, GUY KIBBEE, RUTH DONNELLY Above: JEAN ARTHUR, JAMES STEWART, THOMAS MITCHELL IN "MR. SMITH GOES TO WASHINGTON" (COLUMBIA)

JOEL McCREA, BARBARA STANWYCK, ROBERT PRESTON IN "UNION PACIFIC" PRODUCER-DIRECTOR, CECIL B. DE MILLE (PARAMOUNT)   HEATHER ANGEL, JOHN HOWARD IN "BULLDOG DRUMMOND IN AFRICA" (PARAMOUNT)   ROBERT NEWTON, EMLYN WILLIAMS, CHARLES LAUGHTON IN "JAMAICA INN" DIRECTED BY ALFRED HITCHCOCK (PARAMOUNT)

PAUL MUNI

MADELEINE CARROLL

ROBERT MONTGOMERY

LANA TURNER

BETTY GRABLE, PHIL HARRIS, BINNIE BARNES, JACK BENNY, DOROTHY LAMOUR, EDWARD ARNOLD IN "MAN ABOUT TOWN" (PARAMOUNT)

BORIS KARLOFF
IN "SON OF FRANKENSTEIN"
(UNIVERSAL)

SUSAN HAYWARD, BOB BURNS
IN "OUR LEADING CITIZEN"
(PARAMOUNT)

RONALD COLMAN, IDA LUPINO
IN "THE LIGHT THAT FAILED"
(PARAMOUNT)

ROBERT DONAT WON AN ACADEMY
AWARD FOR HIS PERFORMANCE IN
"GOODBYE, MR. CHIPS" (M-G-M)

FRED MacMURRAY

HENRY FONDA, NANCY KELLY, HENRY HULL, TYRONE POWER
IN "JESSE JAMES" DIRECTED BY HENRY KING
(20th CENTURY-FOX)

1939

JOHN GARFIELD

JACK HALEY, RAY BOLGER, FRANK MORGAN, JUDY
GARLAND, BERT LAHR
Above: RAY BOLGER, JUDY GARLAND

(M-G-M)
THE WIZARD OF OZ

Mervyn Le Roy Production : Director Victor Fleming ; Screenplay by Noel Langley, Florence Ryerson, and Edgar Allen Woolf ; Adapted by Noel Langley from book by Frank L. Baum ; Musical adaptation Herbert Stothart ; Songs E. Y. Harburg, Harold Arlen ; Musical numbers staged by Bobby Connelly.

CAST

Dorothy	Judy Garland
Professor Marvel	Frank Morgan
Hunk	Ray Bolger
Zeke	Bert Lahr
Hickory	Jack Haley
Glenda	Billie Burke
Mrs. Gulch	Margaret Hamilton
Uncle Henry	Charley Grapewin
Nikko	Pat Walshe
Auntie Em	Clara Blandick
Toto	Toto
Munchkins	The Singer Midgets

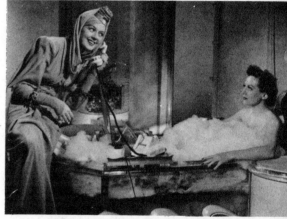

RAY BOLGER, JUDY GARLAND, JACK HALEY

SCENES FROM "THE WIZARD OF OZ"

ROSALIND RUSSELL, JOAN CRAWFORD Above: PAULETTE GODDARD, MARY BOLAND, NORMA SHEARER IN
"THE WOMEN" DIRECTED BY GEORGE CUKOR (M-G-M)

BETTE DAVIS

BETTE DAVIS, ERROL FLYNN IN
"THE PRIVATE LIVES OF ELIZABETH AND ESSEX"
DIRECTED BY MICHAEL CURTIZ (WARNER BROS.)

OLIVIA DE HAVILLAND, ERROL FLYNN

OLIVIA DE HAVILLAND, LESLIE HOWARD

OLIVIA DE HAVILLAND, WARD BOND, CLARK GABLE, LESLIE HOWARD

VIVIEN LEIGH, OLIVIA DE HAVILLAND, CLARK GABLE

LESLIE HOWARD
AS ASHLEY WILKES

VIVIEN LEIGH
AS SCARLETT O'HARA

(M-G-M)

GONE WITH THE WIND

Selznick International Production, M-G-M Release; Producer, David O. Selznick; Director, Victor Fleming; Screenplay by Sidney Howard; From the Novel by Margaret Mitchell; Production designed by William Cameron Menzies; Score by Max Steiner; Dances by Frank Floyd.

CAST

Brent Tarleton	George Reeves
Stuart Tarleton	Fred Crane
Scarlett O'Hara	Vivien Leigh
Mammy	Hattie McDaniel
Big Sam	Everett Brown
Elijah	Zack Williams
Gerald O'Hara	Thomas Mitchell
Jonas Wilkerson	Victor Jory
Ellen O'Hara	Barbara O'Neil
Suellen O'Hara	Evelyn Keyes
Carreen O'Hara	Ann Rutherford
Prissy	Butterfly McQueen
John Wilkes	Howard Hickman
India Wilkes	Alicia Rhett
Ashley Wilkes	Leslie Howard
Melanie Hamilton	Olivia de Havilland
Charles Hamilton	Rand Brooks
Frank Kennedy	Carroll Nye
Cathleen Calvert	Marcella Martin
Rhett Butler	Clark Gable
Aunt Pitty-Pat	Laura Hope Crews
Doctor Meade	Harry Davenport
Mrs. Meade	Leona Roberts
Mrs. Merriweather	Jane Darwell
Rene Picard	Albert Morin
Maybelle Merriweather	Mary Anderson
Fanny Elsing	Terry Shero
Old Levi	William McClain
Uncle Peter	Eddie Anderson
Phil Meade	Jackie Moran
Reminiscent Soldier	Cliff Edwards
Belle Watling	Ona Munson
The Sergeant	Ed Chandler
A Wounded Soldier	George Hackathorne
A Convalescent Soldier	Roscoe Ates
A Dying Soldier	John Arledge
Amputation Case	Eric Linden
A Commanding Officer	Tom Tyler
A Mounted Officer	William Bakewell
A Hungry Soldier	Louis Jean Heydt
Emmy Slattery	Isabel Jewell
Yankee Major	Robert Elliott
Johnny Gallagher	J. M. Kerrigan
Yankee Business Man	Olin Howland
Tom, Yankee Captain	Ward Bond
Nurse	Lillian Kemble Cooper

CLARK GABLE
AS RHETT BUTLER

OLIVIA DE HAVILLAND
AS MELANIE HAMILTON

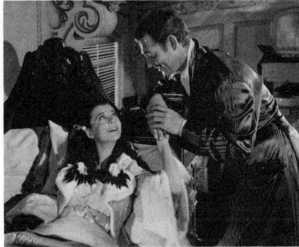

Above: OSCAR POLK, VIVIEN LEIGH,
HATTIE McDANIEL

VIVIEN LEIGH, OLIVIA DE HAVILLAND

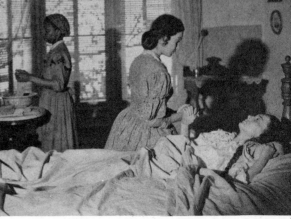

BUTTERFLY McQUEEN, VIVIEN LEIGH, OLIVIA DE HAVILLAND
Above: VIVIEN LEIGH, CLARK GABLE

"GONE WITH THE WIND"

WARD BOND, FRANCIS FORD, HENRY FONDA, CLAUDETTE
COLBERT IN "DRUMS ALONG THE MOHAWK"
DIRECTED BY JOHN FORD (20th CENTURY-FOX)

HENRY FONDA IN
"YOUNG MR. LINCOLN"
(20th CENTURY-FOX)

BETTE DAVIS, GEORGE BRENT
IN "DARK VICTORY"
DIRECTED BY EDMUND GOULDING (WARNER BROS.)

GLENDA FARRELL, BARTON MacLANE
IN "TORCHY RUNS FOR MAYOR" (WARNER BROS.)

AL JOLSON

JOHN CLEMENTS, RALPH RICHARDSON
IN "FOUR FEATHERS" (UNITED ARTISTS)

PEGGY WOOD, JOHN HYAMS, JOHN HUBBARD, JOAN
BENNETT, ADOLPHE MENJOU, WILLIAM GARGAN, LEILA
McINTYRE IN "THE HOUSEKEEPER'S DAUGHTER"
(UNITED ARTISTS)

MARY NASH, ARTHUR TREACHER, SHIRLEY TEMPLE,
IAN HUNTER IN "THE LITTLE PRINCESS"
(20th CENTURY-FOX)

ORANE DEMAZIS, FERNANDEL IN "HARVEST"
WRITTEN, DIRECTED AND PRODUCED BY MARCEL PAGNOL
(FRENCH CINEMA CENTER)

JOHNNY SHEFFIELD, MAUREEN O'SULLIVAN, JOHNNY
WEISSMULLER IN "TARZAN IN EXILE"
(M-G-M)

JOHNNY SHEFFIELD IN
"TARZAN FINDS A SON"
(M-G-M)

LOUISE FAZENDA, MIRIAM HOPKINS, BETTE DAVIS IN
"THE OLD MAID"
(WARNER BROS.)

1939

MARLENE DIETRICH

RAY MILLAND, GARY COOPER, BRIAN DONLEVY Top:
RAY MILLAND, GARY COOPER, ROBERT PRESTON IN
"BEAU GESTE" DIRECTED BY WILLIAM WELLMAN

CHARLES LAUGHTON IN
"THE HUNCHBACK OF NOTRE DAME"
DIRECTED BY WILLIAM DIETERLE (RKO)

MAUREEN O'HARA, EDMOND O'BRIEN Top:
CEDRIC HARDWICKE, RICHARD CLAYTON, CHARLES
LAUGHTON IN "THE HUNCHBACK OF NOTRE DAME"

BRIAN DONLEVY IN
"BEAU GESTE"
(PARAMOUNT)

BUSTER KEATON IN
"HOLLYWOOD CAVALCADE"
(20th CENTURY-FOX)

BILLY AND BOBBY MAUCH

ROD LaROCQUE
IN "THE HUNCHBACK OF NOTRE DAME"
(RKO)

WALTER HAMPDEN

JOHN SUTTON IN
"TOWER OF LONDON"
(UNIVERSAL)

VERA ZORINA IN
"ON YOUR TOES"
(WARNER BROS.)

GREER GARSON, ROBERT DONAT
IN "GOODBYE, MR. CHIPS"
DIRECTED BY SAM WOOD (M-G-M)

TOM BROWN
IN "EX-CHAMP"
(UNIVERSAL)

CARY GRANT
IN "GUNGA DIN"
(RKO)

EDNA MAY OLIVER, GINGER ROGERS, FRED ASTAIRE
Top: FRED ASTAIRE, LEW FIELDS IN
"THE STORY OF VERNON AND IRENE CASTLE"

GINGER ROGERS, FRED ASTAIRE IN
"THE STORY OF VERNON AND IRENE CASTLE"
DIRECTED BY H. C. POTTER (RKO)

DON AMECHE IN TITLE ROLE IN "THE STORY OF
ALEXANDER GRAHAM BELL" AND ABOVE AS STEPHEN
FOSTER IN "SWANEE RIVER" (20th CENTURY-FOX)

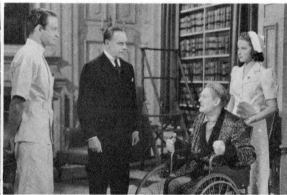

SYLVIA SIDNEY, SIDNEY LUMAT, MYRON McCORMICK
IN ". . . ONE THIRD OF A NATION . . ."
(PARAMOUNT)

BUSTER KEATON, STUART ERWIN, DON AMECHE
IN "HOLLYWOOD CAVALCADE"
(20th CENTURY-FOX)

LEW AYRES, WALTER KINGSFORD, LIONEL BARRYMORE,
LARAINE DAY IN "SECRET OF DR. KILDARE"
(M-G-M)

JACKIE COOPER IN
"EAGLE SCOUT"
(UNIVERSAL)

NORMA SHEARER IN
"IDIOT'S DELIGHT"
(M-G-M)

CHESTER CONKLIN IN
"HOLLYWOOD CAVALCADE"
(20th CENTURY-FOX)

JOAN BENNETT IN "THE
MAN IN THE IRON MASK"
(UNITED ARTISTS)

ROBERT WARWICK IN
"THE PRIVATE LIVES OF
ELIZABETH AND ESSEX"
(WARNER BROS.)

1939

CHARLES LAUGHTON, CAROLE LOMBARD
IN "THEY KNEW WHAT THEY WANTED"
DIRECTED BY GARSON KANIN (RKO)

GARY COOPER, MADELEINE CARROLL, PAULETTE GODDARD,
PRESTON FOSTER, ROBERT PRESTON Top: CECIL B. DeMILLE
DIRECTING DICK KLEIN, ROBERT PRESTON, PAULETTE
GODDARD IN "NORTHWEST MOUNTED POLICE" (PARAMOUNT)

TERRY KILBURN, THOMAS MITCHELL, EDNA BEST,
BOBBY QUILLAN, FREDDIE BARTHOLOMEW, TIM HOLT
IN "SWISS FAMILY ROBINSON" (RKO)

BETTE DAVIS IN
"THE LETTER"
(WARNER BROS.)

JANE DARWELL, SHIRLEY MILLS, DARRYL HICKMAN, FRANK SULLY, EDDIE QUILLAN, DORIS BOWDON,
RUSSELL SIMPSON, FRANK DARIEN, HENRY FONDA, O. Z. WHITEHEAD, JOHN CARRADINE IN JOHN
STEINBECK'S "THE GRAPES OF WRATH" DIRECTED BY JOHN FORD (20th CENTURY-FOX)

PAT O'BRIEN IN
"KNUTE ROCKNE—ALL AMERICAN"
(WARNER BROS.)

GRADY SUTTON, W. C. FIELDS
IN "THE BANK DICK"

DONALD WOODS, EL BRENDEL, GLORIA JEAN,
BING CROSBY IN "IF I HAD MY WAY"

MAE WEST, HARLAN BRIGGS, W. C. FIELDS
IN "MY LITTLE CHICKADEE"

1940 UNIVERSAL PRODUCTIONS

"PINOCCHIO"
A WALT DISNEY PRODUCTION
(RKO)

SNOWFLAKE, PROMISE (THE DOG), BILLY LEE
IN "THE BISCUIT EATER"
(PARAMOUNT)

"FANTASIA"
A WALT DISNEY PRODUCTION
(RKO)

1940 The war overseas, with spreading hostilities, continued to shrink the industry's foreign revenues and eleven countries were closed to American films. The one bright spot was Latin America where importation of American films continued to increase. Though America was a neutral power at this time, anti-Nazi films poured out of Hollywood. These included "The Mortal Storm," "Escape," "Four Sons," and "The Great Dictator" which was noteworthy as Charlie Chaplin's first talking picture. Walt Disney cartoons continued to delight the public with two features, "Pinocchio" and "Fantasia" which introduced "Fantasound," a method with three sound tracks on the film. It utilized the cartoon to interpret musical classics played by the Philadelphia Orchestra with Leopold Stokowski conducting. "Gone With The Wind" was rolling up unprecedented domestic grosses of over twenty-three million dollars during its first release period. Improvement in color continued with favorable effects, and Technicolor was used in eighteen feature films. Bing Crosby, whose records were topping all sales, was becoming big box office, and "Road to Singapore" in which he co-starred with Bob Hope was so popular it started a series of equally popular "road" sequels. Hedda Hopper was being advertised as an actress, radio commentator and columnist, and her column "Hedda Hopper's Hollywood" was appearing in newspapers from coast to coast. Death took Marguerite Clark, silent screen favorite, Tom Mix and Ben Turpin. John Ford directed two fine films: Eugene O'Neill's "The Long Voyage Home," and John Steinbeck's "The Grapes of Wrath" which the New York Film Critics dubbed the best picture of the year. The Academy gave the same honor to "Rebecca," directed by Alfred Hitchcock who came up with a second excellent film, "Foreign Correspondent." Other praiseworthy films were "The Biscuit Eater," "Northwest Passage," "Our Town," "Abe Lincoln in Illinois," "Boom Town," "The Philadelphia Story," "All This and Heaven Too" and the French import, "The Baker's Wife."

GINGER ROGERS IN "KITTY FOYLE"
FOR WHICH SHE WON AN
ACADEMY AWARD (RKO)

JOHN BARRYMORE
IN "THE GREAT PROFILE"
(20th CENTURY-FOX)

GLADYS COOPER, GINGER ROGERS, DENNIS MORGAN
IN "KITTY FOYLE"
DIRECTED BY SAM WOOD (RKO)

CARY GRANT, ROSALIND RUSSELL
IN "HIS GIRL FRIDAY"
DIRECTED BY HOWARD HAWKS (COLUMBIA)

MARGARET SULLAVAN, WILLIAM ORR, ROBERT STACK,
JAMES STEWART IN "THE MORTAL STORM"
DIRECTED BY FRANK BORZAGE (M-G-M)

JEANETTE MacDONALD, NELSON EDDY IN "NEW MOON"
DIRECTED BY ROBERT Z. LEONARD (M-G-M)
Top: JEANETTE MacDONALD, NELSON EDDY

JUDITH ANDERSON AS MRS. DANVERS
IN "REBECCA"

JOAN FONTAINE, LAURENCE OLIVIER, GLADYS COOPER, REGINALD DENNY IN "REBECCA"
A DAVID O. SELZNICK PRODUCTION DIRECTED BY ALFRED HITCHCOCK (UNITED ARTISTS)

ROBERT PRESTON
IN "TYPHOON"
(PARAMOUNT)

MARTHA SCOTT, WILLIAM HOLDEN
IN "OUR TOWN"
DIRECTED BY SAM WOOD (UNITED ARTISTS) **1940**

THOMAS MITCHELL, WILLIAM HOLDEN, MARTHA
SCOTT, GUY KIBBEE, STUART ERWIN, FRANK CRAVEN
Above: FRANK CRAVEN IN "OUR TOWN"

CHARLES LANG   EVE ARDEN   JOHN HOWARD   PRISCILLA LANE   CARL BRISSON   BINNIE BARNES   VICTOR MOORE

FERNANDEL AND RAIMU IN "THE WELL-DIGGER'S DAUGHTER" PRODUCED, DIRECTED AND WRITTEN BY MARCEL PAGNOL (SIRITZKY)

ROBERT MONTGOMERY IN "THE EARL OF CHICAGO" (M-G-M)

RAIMU (center) IN "THE BAKER'S WIFE" DIRECTED BY MARCEL PAGNOL

JOHN HUBBARD IN "TURNABOUT" (UNITED ARTISTS)

JOHN WAYNE, JOHN QUALEN, THOMAS MITCHELL IN "THE LONG VOYAGE HOME" DIRECTED BY JOHN FORD (UNITED ARTISTS)

RANDOLPH SCOTT, MIRIAM HOPKINS, ERROL FLYNN IN "VIRGINIA CITY" (WARNER BROS.)

NEELY EDWARDS   SPRING BYINGTON   PHILIP HUSTON   MARTHA RAYE   TERRY KILBURN   JUDY CANOVA   GEORGE BANCROFT

RICARDO CORTEZ   FLORA ROBSON   JON HALL   ILONA MASSEY   WILLIAM HENRY   BARBARA BRITTON   JOHNNY DOWNS

EDWARD G. ROBINSON, RUTH GORDON, OTTO KRUGER
IN "THE STORY OF DR. EHRLICH'S MAGIC BULLET"
(WARNER BROS.)

HARRY LAUDER IN
"SONG OF THE ROAD"
(SELECT)

ROBERT BENCHLEY, GEORGE SANDERS, JOEL McCREA
IN "FOREIGN CORRESPONDENT"
(UNITED ARTISTS)

RANDOLPH SCOTT, CARY GRANT, IRENE
DUNNE IN "MY FAVORITE WIFE"
DIRECTED BY GARSON KANIN (RKO)

ROBERT YOUNG, SPENCER TRACY, TRUMAN BRADLEY
IN "NORTHWEST PASSAGE"
DIRECTED BY KING VIDOR (M-G-M)

RICHARD ARLEN IN
"THE LEATHER PUSHERS"
(UNIVERSAL)

ALAN HALE   PATSY KELLY   ERIK RHODES   JACKIE COOGAN   DEAN JAGGER   ANDREA LEEDS

RICHARD CROMWELL

1940

CAROLE LOMBARD

JACK BENNY, FRED ALLEN IN
"LOVE THY NEIGHBOR" (PARAMOUNT)

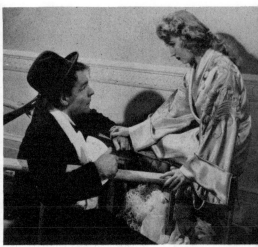

JOHN JUSTIN, JUNE DUPREZ, SABU IN
"THE THIEF OF BAGDAD" (UNITED ARTISTS)

BRIAN DONLEVY, MURIEL ANGELUS IN
"THE GREAT McGINTY" (PARAMOUNT)

RAYMOND MASSEY, RUTH GORDON
IN "ABE LINCOLN IN ILLINOIS"
DIRECTED BY JOHN CROMWELL (RKO)

BETTY FIELD, JACKIE COOPER IN
"SEVENTEEN"
(PARAMOUNT)

DENNIS O'KEEFE, RAY MILLAND, DICK PURCELL
IN "ARISE, MY LOVE"
(PARAMOUNT)

Above and Top: HENRY DANIELL, CHARLES CHAPLIN, JACK
OAKIE Center: CHARLES CHAPLIN, PAULETTE GODDARD
IN "THE GREAT DICTATOR"

CHARLES CHAPLIN IN "THE GREAT DICTATOR"
WRITTEN AND DIRECTED BY CHARLES CHAPLIN
(UNITED ARTISTS)

DUDLEY DIGGES, PETER GODFREY, DAVID NIVEN, OLIVIA
DE HAVILLAND, LIONEL PAPE IN "RAFFLES"
DIRECTED BY SAM WOOD (UNITED ARTISTS)

DESI ARNAZ IN
"TOO MANY GIRLS" (RKO)

1940

MARGARET SULLAVAN, FRANK MORGAN, JAMES STEWART
IN "THE SHOP AROUND THE CORNER"
DIRECTED BY ERNST LUBITSCH (M-G-M)

JESSIE RALPH, SHIRLEY TEMPLE, JOHNNY RUSSELL, EDDIE
COLLINS, GALE SONDERGAARD IN "THE BLUE BIRD"
DIRECTED BY WALTER LANG (20th CENTURY-FOX)

WALTER BRENNAN IN "THE
WESTERNER" (UNITED ARTISTS) FOR
WHICH HE WON AN ACADEMY AWARD

RICHARD GREENE, ALICE FAYE, FRED MacMURRAY, WARD
BOND IN "LITTLE OLD NEW YORK"
DIRECTED BY HENRY KING (20th CENTURY-FOX)

GUY KIBBEE, LINDA DARNELL, TED NORTH IN "CHAD HANNA"
DIRECTED BY HENRY KING (20th CENTURY-FOX)

DOROTHY LAMOUR, BING CROSBY, BOB HOPE IN "ROAD TO SINGAPORE"
DIRECTED BY VICTOR SCHERTZINGER
(PARAMOUNT)

HUMPHREY BOGART, ANN SHERIDAN, GEORGE RAFT
IN "THEY DRIVE BY NIGHT"
DIRECTED BY RAOUL WALSH (WARNER BROS.)

CHARLES BOYER, WALTER HAMPDEN, BETTE DAVIS
IN "ALL THIS AND HEAVEN TOO"
DIRECTED BY ANATOLE LITVAK (WARNER BROS.)

CARY GRANT IN
"THE HOWARDS OF VIRGINIA"
(COLUMBIA)

CARY GRANT, RICHARD CARLSON, CEDRIC HARDWICKE,
MARTHA SCOTT IN "THE HOWARDS OF VIRGINIA"
DIRECTED BY FRANK LLOYD (COLUMBIA)

SPENCER TRACY IN THE TITLE ROLE
IN "EDISON, THE MAN"
DIRECTED BY CLARENCE BROWN

VIVIEN LEIGH, ROBERT TAYLOR
IN "WATERLOO BRIDGE"
DIRECTED BY MERVYN LeROY

VIRGINIA WEIDLER, MICKEY ROONEY, BOBBY JORDAN
IN "YOUNG TOM EDISON"
DIRECTED BY NORMAN TAUROG

SPENCER TRACY, CLARK GABLE
IN "BOOM TOWN"
DIRECTED BY JACK CONWAY

JOHN HOWARD, CARY GRANT, KATHARINE HEPBURN, JAMES STEWART
IN "THE PHILADELPHIA STORY"
DIRECTED BY GEORGE CUKOR

EDWARD ASHLEY, ANN RUTHERFORD, MARY BOLAND, GREER
GARSON, HEATHER ANGEL, MAUREEN O'SULLIVAN, MARSHA
HUNT IN "PRIDE AND PREJUDICE"
DIRECTED BY ROBERT Z. LEONARD

LAURENCE OLIVIER, GREER GARSON
IN "PRIDE AND PREJUDICE"

NAZIMOVA, FELIX BRESSART, ROBERT TAYLOR, NORMA SHEARER
IN "ESCAPE" DIRECTED BY MERVYN LeROY

JOHN LODER, EVAN EVANS, DONALD CRISP, SARA ALLGOOD, RICHARD FRASER, JAMES MONKS,
RODDY McDOWALL, MAUREEN O'HARA, PATRIC KNOWLES IN "HOW GREEN WAS MY VALLEY"
DIRECTED BY JOHN FORD (20th CENTURY-FOX)

RODDY McDOWALL, WALTER PIDGEON
IN "HOW GREEN WAS MY VALLEY"
PRODUCED BY DARRYL ZANUCK

ROBERT MONTGOMERY
IN "HERE COMES MR. JORDAN"
(COLUMBIA)

CHARLES DINGLE, PATRICIA COLLINGE, BETTE DAVIS, TERESA WRIGHT, DAN DURYEA,
JESSIE GRAYSON, CARL BENTON REID IN "THE LITTLE FOXES"
A SAMUEL GOLDWYN PRODUCTION DIRECTED BY WILLIAM WYLER (RKO)

BETTE DAVIS
IN "THE LITTLE FOXES"
(RKO)

CLAUDE RAINS, ROBERT MONTGOMERY, JAMES GLEASON
IN "HERE COMES MR. JORDAN"
132 DIRECTED BY ALEXANDER HALL (COLUMBIA)

SPENCER TRACY, MICKEY ROONEY
IN "MEN OF BOYS TOWN"
DIRECTED BY NORMAN TAUROG (M-G-M)

MARY ASTOR, HUMPHREY BOGART, PETER LORRE
IN "THE MALTESE FALCON"
DIRECTED BY JOHN HUSTON (WARNER BROS.)

GARY COOPER AS SERGEANT YORK
FOR WHICH HE WON AN ACADEMY AWARD

JUNE LOCKHART, DICKIE MOORE, MARGARET WYCHERLY, GARY COOPER
IN "SERGEANT YORK" DIRECTED BY HOWARD HAWKS (WARNER BROS.)

1941 As the year ended and with the United States plunged into war, the full force of the film industry rallied in the nation's all-out war effort. Perhaps the most discussed and engrossing picture of the year was "Citizen Kane." The New York Film Critics voted it the best. Orson Welles, who gained fame with his Mercury Theatre, was given complete authority by RKO, and he not only authored, directed and produced the picture, but he was also its star. No one but Charlie Chaplin had ever combined so many talents to create one film. Supposedly based on the life of William Randolph Hearst and showing him in an unfavorable light, the Hearst newspapers refused to advertise, review or mention the film or Welles. The Academy chose John Ford's direction and film "How Green Was My Valley" as the best. Gary Cooper made two good films, "Sergeant York" which won him an "Oscar" and "Meet John Doe." Joan Fontaine's performance in "Suspicion" won her an Academy Award. Included in the year's best were "Here Comes Mr. Jordan," "High Sierra," "Kings Row," "One Foot in Heaven," "The Maltese Falcon," and from France "Pepe Le Moko." Stage successes to reach the screen were "The Little Foxes," "The Man Who Came to Dinner" and "Tobacco Road." Abbott and Costello were a comic team gaining public favor, and new discoveries included Gene Tierney, Joseph Cotten, Robert Stack, Veronica Lake and Sterling Hayden. Greta Garbo made what was possibly her last film, "Two-Faced Woman." In "You'll Never Get Rich" Fred Astaire danced with a new partner, Rita Hayworth. Walt Disney's famous creations, Mickey Mouse, Donald Duck and Pluto, continued to delight the world. "Major Barbara" was G. B. Shaw's second work to successfully reach the screen. Such old standbys as "Charley's Aunt," "Dr. Jekyll and Mr. Hyde," "The Sea Wolf," "Smilin' Through" and "Blood and Sand" were remade.

MARTHA SCOTT, FREDRIC MARCH
IN "ONE FOOT IN HEAVEN"
(WARNER BROS.)

CHARLES BOYER, MARGARET SULLAVAN
IN "BACK STREET"
DIRECTOR, ROBERT STEVENSON (UNIVERSAL)

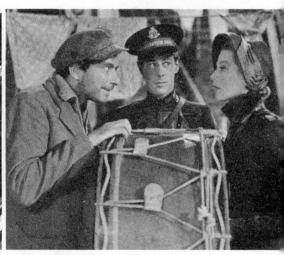

MARTHA SCOTT, WILLIAM GARGAN
IN "CHEERS FOR MISS BISHOP"
DIRECTOR, TAY GARNETT (UNITED ARTISTS)

VIVIEN LEIGH, LAURENCE OLIVIER IN "THAT HAMILTON
WOMAN" PRODUCER-DIRECTOR, ALEXANDER KORDA
(UNITED ARTISTS)

ROBERT NEWTON, REX HARRISON, WENDY HILLER
IN SHAW'S "MAJOR BARBARA"
PRODUCER-DIRECTOR, GABRIEL PASCAL (UNITED ARTISTS)

HUMPHREY BOGART
IN "HIGH SIERRA"
(WARNER BROS.)

RUSSELL SIMPSON, WALTER BRENNAN, WALTER HUSTON,
DANA ANDREWS, FLEETER (DOG) IN "SWAMP WATER"
DIRECTOR, JEAN RENOIR (20th CENTURY-FOX)

JUDY GARLAND, MICKEY ROONEY
IN "BABES ON BROADWAY"
DIRECTOR, BUSBY BERKELEY (M-G-M)

ROBERT TAYLOR, LANA TURNER
IN "JOHNNY EAGER"
DIRECTOR, MERVYN LeROY (M-G-M)

WALT DISNEY'S "DUMBO"

JEAN GABIN, MIREILLE BALIN
IN "PEPE LE MOKO"
DIRECTOR, JULIEN DUVIVIER

ANN SHERIDAN, RICHARD TRAVIS, BETTE DAVIS, MONTY WOOLLEY
IN "THE MAN WHO CAME TO DINNER"
DIRECTED BY WILLIAM KEIGHLEY (WARNER BROS.)

JOHN CARRADINE, TYRONE POWER, J. CARROL NAISH, LAIRD CREGAR
IN "BLOOD AND SAND"
DIRECTED BY ROUBEN MAMOULIAN (20th CENTURY-FOX)

EDWARD G. ROBINSON, JOHN GARFIELD, IDA LUPINO
IN "THE SEA WOLF"
DIRECTED BY MICHAEL CURTIZ (WARNER BROS.)

GEORGE MURPHY, BURGESS MEREDITH, ALAN MARSHALL
IN "TOM, DICK AND HARRY"
DIRECTED BY GARSON KANIN (RKO)

EDWARD ARNOLD, BARBARA STANWYCK, GARY COOPER,
WALTER BRENNAN IN "MEET JOHN DOE"
PRODUCER-DIRECTOR, FRANK CAPRA (WARNER BROS.)

DOROTHY COMINGORE, ORSON WELLES
Above: ORSON WELLES, RUTH WARRICK
IN "CITIZEN KANE" (RKO)

ORSON WELLES IN THE TITLE ROLE OF
"CITIZEN KANE" WHICH HE PRODUCED,
DIRECTED AND CO-AUTHORED FOR RKO

DOROTHY COMINGORE, ORSON WELLES
Above: EVERETT SLOANE, ORSON WELLES, JOSEPH
COTTEN IN "CITIZEN KANE" (RKO)

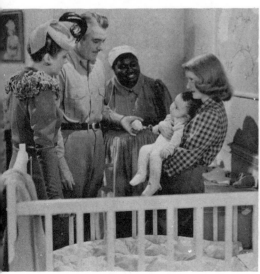

MARY ASTOR, GEORGE BRENT, HATTIE McDANIEL,
BETTE DAVIS IN "THE GREAT LIE"
(WARNER BROS.)

IRENE DUNNE, CARY GRANT
IN "PENNY SERENADE"
DIRECTED BY GEORGE STEVENS (COLUMBIA)

IAN HUNTER, DONALD CRISP, LANA TURNER,
SPENCER TRACY IN "DR. JEKYLL AND MR. HYDE"
DIRECTED BY VICTOR FLEMING (M-G-M)

1941

BING CROSBY, BOB HOPE IN "ROAD TO ZANZIBAR"
DIRECTED BY VICTOR SCHERTZINGER (PARAMOUNT)

JAMES STEWART

WALLACE BEERY IN "BARNACLE BILL"
DIRECTED BY RICHARD THORPE (M-G-M)

TYRONE POWER IN
"BLOOD AND SAND"
(20th CENTURY-FOX)

BETTY FIELD IN "THE
SHEPHERD OF THE HILLS"
(PARAMOUNT)

JON HALL, DOROTHY LAMOUR
IN "ALOMA OF THE SOUTH
SEAS" (PARAMOUNT)

MARLENE DIETRICH IN
"MANPOWER"
(WARNER BROS.)

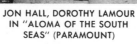

STERLING HAYDEN IN
"BAHAMA PASSAGE"
(PARAMOUNT)

CONSTANCE BENNETT, MELVYN DOUGLAS, GRETA GARBO,
ROBERT STERLING IN "TWO-FACED WOMAN"
DIRECTED BY GEORGE CUKOR (M-G-M)

GRETA GARBO
IN "TWO-FACED WOMAN" (M-G-M)

HEDY LAMARR

JOAN FONTAINE, CARY GRANT IN "SUSPICION"
DIRECTED BY ALFRED HITCHCOCK (RKO)

1941

GENE TIERNEY, WARD BOND, ZEFFIE TILBURY, ELIZABETH PATTERSON, CHARLIE
GRAPEWIN, SLIM SUMMERVILLE, WILLIAM TRACY, MARJORIE RAMBEAU IN
"TOBACCO ROAD" DIRECTOR, JOHN FORD (20th CENTURY-FOX)

JACK BENNY
IN "CHARLEY'S AUNT"
(20th CENTURY-FOX)

DON TERRY IN
"DON WINSLOW OF THE NAVY"
A UNIVERSAL SERIAL

VIVIEN LEIGH
IN "THAT HAMILTON WOMAN"
(UNITED ARTISTS)

PATRICIA COLLINGE
IN "THE LITTLE FOXES"
(RKO)

ANNE BAXTER, ARLEEN WHELAN, JIMMY ELLISON,
RICHARD HAYDEN, JACK BENNY IN
"CHARLEY'S AUNT" (20th CENTURY-FOX)

MICHAEL REDGRAVE
IN "THE STARS LOOK DOWN"
(M-G-M)

IAN HUNTER, BRIAN AHERNE, JEANETTE MacDONALD
GENE RAYMOND IN "SMILIN' THROUGH"
DIRECTOR, FRANK BORZAGE (M-G-M)

BARBARA STANWYCK, HENRY FONDA
IN "THE LADY EVE" DIRECTOR,
PRESTON STURGES (PARAMOUNT)

BILLY CONN, JEAN PARKER, JOHN
KELLY IN "THE PITTSBURGH KID"
(REPUBLIC)

TOM HARMON, ANITA LOUISE, LARRY
PARKS IN "HARMON OF MICHIGAN"
(COLUMBIA)

BUD ABBOTT, LOU COSTELLO
IN "HOLD THAT GHOST"
(UNIVERSAL)

MELVYN DOUGLAS, JOAN CRAWFORD IN
"A WOMAN'S FACE" DIRECTOR, GEORGE CUKOR
(M-G-M)

GENE RAYMOND
IN "SMILIN' THROUGH"
(M-G-M)

DOUGLAS FAIRBANKS, JR. IN
"THE CORSICAN BROTHERS"
(UNITED ARTISTS)

LANA TURNER, CLARK GABLE, CLAIRE TREVOR
IN "HONKY TONK"
DIRECTOR, JACK CONWAY (M-G-M)

EVA GABOR, RICHARD ARLEN
IN "FORCED LANDING"
(PARAMOUNT)

NAZIMOVA
IN "BLOOD AND SAND"
(20th CENTURY-FOX)

WALTER HUSTON IN
"ALL THAT MONEY CAN BUY"
(RKO)

ROBERT CUMMINGS
IN "MOON OVER MIAMI"
(20th CENTURY-FOX)

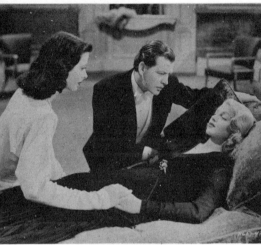

HEDY LAMARR, PHILIP DORN, LANA TURNER
IN "ZIEGFELD GIRL" DIRECTED BY ROBERT Z. LEONARD
(M-G-M)

LEIF ERIKSON, BOB HOPE, CLARENCE KOLB, EDWARD
ARNOLD, MARY FORBES, CATHERINE DOUCET, GLENN
ANDERS, ROSE HOBART, PAULETTE GODDARD IN
"NOTHING BUT THE TRUTH" (PARAMOUNT)

INGRID BERGMAN, GEORGE SANDERS,
ROBERT MONTGOMERY IN "RAGE IN HEAVEN"
(M-G-M)

RISE STEVENS, NELSON EDDY IN
"THE CHOCOLATE SOLDIER"
(M-G-M)

DANA ANDREWS, GENE TIERNEY
RANDOLPH SCOTT IN "BELLE STARR"
(20th CENTURY-FOX)

OSCAR LEVANT, MARY MARTIN,
DON AMECHE IN "KISS THE BOYS
GOODBYE" (PARAMOUNT)

VAN HEFLIN, ROBERT YOUNG,
RUTH HUSSEY IN "H. M. PULHAM, ESQ."
(M-G-M)

CHARLES COBURN, SPRING BYINGTON, JEAN ARTHUR,
ROBERT CUMMINGS IN "THE DEVIL AND MISS JONES"
DIRECTOR, SAM WOOD (RKO)

VICTOR MOORE, BOB HOPE, VERA
ZORINA IN "LOUISIANA PURCHASE"
DIRECTOR, IRVING CUMMINGS (PARAMOUNT)

IDA LUPINO, ELSA LANCHESTER, LOUIS HAYWARD,
EDITH BARRETT IN "LADIES IN RETIREMENT"
DIRECTOR, CHARLES VIDOR (COLUMBIA)

1941

BILL GOODWIN, ROBERT PRESTON, WILLIAM BENDIX
IN "WAKE ISLAND" DIRECTED BY JOHN FARROW
(PARAMOUNT)

NOEL COWARD (center) IN "IN WHICH WE SERVE" WHICH HE
WROTE, PRODUCED, DIRECTED AND SCORED
(UNITED ARTISTS)

GEORGE SANDERS IN "THE MOON
AND SIXPENCE" DIRECTOR, ALBERT LEWIN
(UNITED ARTISTS)

ALLYN JOSLYN, JUNE HAVOC, ROSALIND RUSSELL, BRIAN AHERNE, JANET BLAIR,
RICHARD QUINE, GORDON JONES IN "MY SISTER EILEEN"
DIRECTED BY ALEXANDER HALL (COLUMBIA)

NOEL COWARD
IN "IN WHICH WE SERVE"
(UNITED ARTISTS)

RICHARD BENNETT, JOSEPH COTTEN, DOLORES COSTELLO,
DONALD DILLAWAY, AGNES MOOREHEAD, RAY COLLINS IN
"THE MAGNIFICENT AMBERSONS" WRITTEN, PRODUCED AND
DIRECTED BY ORSON WELLES (RKO)

JINX FALKENBERG
IN "LAUGH YOUR BLUES
AWAY" (COLUMBIA)

PAUL HENREID, FRANKLIN PANGBORN, BETTE DAVIS
IN "NOW, VOYAGER" DIRECTED BY IRVING RAPPER
(WARNER BROS.)

RAY MILLAND
Top: PAULETTE GODDARD
IN "REAP THE WILD WIND"

RAY MILLAND, LYNNE OVERMAN, PAULETTE GODDARD, JOHN WAYNE
IN "REAP THE WILD WIND"
PRODUCED AND DIRECTED BY CECIL B. DeMILLE (PARAMOUNT)

HEDDA HOPPER
Top: SUSAN HAYWARD
IN "REAP THE WILD WIND"

1942 Hollywood's all-out effort for war aid included stars making personal appearances, and benefit premières of important pictures for selling war bonds. Demands and exigencies of the war curtailed television. A new high in the production of color features was reached when 25 pictures were made in Technicolor. Among the war stories filmed were "Mrs. Miniver" which won an Academy Award, Noel Coward's "In Which We Serve" which the New York Film Critics picked as the best film, "Wake Island" and "The Commandos Strike at Dawn." Walt Disney's feature contribution was "Bambi." Orson Welles followed his "Citizen Kane" with Booth Tarkington's "The Magnificent Ambersons." As light and amusing escapist films list "My Sister Eileen," "The Talk of the Town," "Holiday Inn," "The Pied Piper," "Yankee Doodle Dandy" and "The Major and the Minor." Other films entertaining the public were "The Pride of the Yankees," "The Woman of the Year," "Random Harvest" and "This Above All." Cecil B. DeMille's contribution was "Reap the Wild Wind." Academy Awards were given to Greer Garson and Teresa Wright for their performances in "Mrs. Miniver." James Cagney won an "Oscar" for his "Yankee Doodle Dandy" portrayal, and newcomer Van Heflin won his for "Johnny Eager." "White Christmas," a song from "Holiday Inn," also received an Academy citation. New and promising players were Van Johnson, Alan Ladd, Kathryn Grayson, Maria Montez, George Montgomery and Susan Hayward. Jean Gabin, French favorite, made his American film debut in "Moontide." Famous stories remade were "The Spoilers" and "Mrs. Wiggs of the Cabbage Patch." The death toll included John Barrymore, Carole Lombard, James Cruze, George M. Cohan, May Robson, Buck Jones and Edna May Oliver.

ANN SOTHERN AND SEABISCUIT
IN "PANAMA HATTIE" DIRECTED BY
NORMAN McLEOD (M-G-M)

TYRONE POWER, NIGEL BRUCE,
JOAN FONTAINE IN "THIS ABOVE ALL"
(20th CENTURY-FOX)

SPENCER TRACY, HEDY LAMARR, JOHN GARFIELD
IN "TORTILLA FLAT" DIRECTED BY VICTOR FLEMING
(M-G-M)

MARIE WILSON
IN "BROADWAY"
(UNIVERSAL)

BOB HOPE, DOROTHY LAMOUR, BING CROSBY
IN "ROAD TO MOROCCO" DIRECTED BY DAVID BUTLER
(PARAMOUNT)

DICK POWELL   OLIVIA DE HAVILLAND   ALLAN JONES   GENE TIERNEY   WARREN HULL

WALTER HUSTON, ROSEMARY DeCAMP, JEANNE CAGNEY,
JAMES CAGNEY, RICHARD WHORF, JOAN LESLIE
Above: IRENE MANNING IN "YANKEE DOODLE DANDY"

JEANNE AND JAMES CAGNEY, JOAN LESLIE
IN "YANKEE DOODLE DANDY" DIRECTED BY
MICHAEL CURTIZ (WARNER BROS.)

TERESA WRIGHT, GARY COOPER
Above: GARY COOPER, BILL DICKEY IN "THE PRIDE
OF THE YANKEES" DIRECTOR, SAM WOOD (RKO)

TIM HOLT IN
"THE MAGNIFICENT
AMBERSONS" (RKO)

BETTY FIELD IN
"GREAT WITHOUT GLORY"
(PARAMOUNT)

JOHN LODER, DIANA BARRYMORE, JON HALL,
ROBERT STACK IN "EAGLE SQUADRON"
(UNIVERSAL)

HELMUT DANTINE
IN "MRS. MINIVER"
(M-G-M)

AGNES MOOREHEAD
IN "THE MAGNIFICENT
AMBERSONS" (RKO)

142

CAROLE LANDIS   CARY GRANT   ARLEEN WHELAN   RANDOLPH SCOTT   JEAN PARKER

RANDOLPH SCOTT, MARLENE DIETRICH, JOHN WAYNE
Above: HARRY CAREY, JOHN WAYNE, RANDOLPH SCOTT
IN "THE SPOILERS" DIRECTOR, RAY ENRIGHT (UNIVERSAL)

FRED ASTAIRE, RITA HAYWORTH
IN "YOU WERE NEVER LOVELIER"
DIRECTOR, WILLIAM SEITER (COLUMBIA)

EDDIE ANDERSON, ETHEL WATERS, PAUL ROBESON
Above: CHARLES BOYER, RITA HAYWORTH
IN "TALES OF MANHATTAN" (20th CENTURY-FOX)

ROBERT STACK   **VERONICA LAKE**   **VAN JOHNSON**   **SUSAN HAYWARD**   **GEORGE MONTGOMERY**

1942

BING CROSBY, MARJORIE REYNOLDS, FRED ASTAIRE, VIRGINIA DALE
IN "HOLIDAY INN" MUSIC AND LYRICS BY IRVING BERLIN
PRODUCER-DIRECTOR, MARK SANDRICH (PARAMOUNT)

RAY MILLAND, GINGER ROGERS
IN "THE MAJOR AND THE MINOR"
DIRECTED BY BILLY WILDER (PARAMOUNT)

RONALD COLMAN, GREER GARSON
IN "RANDOM HARVEST"
DIRECTED BY MERVYN LeROY (M-G-M)

GEORGE MURPHY, JUDY GARLAND, GENE KELLY
IN "FOR ME AND MY GAL" DIRECTED BY
BUSBY BERKELEY (M-G-M)

JACK CARSON, ERROL FLYNN, WILLIAM FRAWLEY,
ALAN HALE, ARTHUR SHIELDS IN "GENTLEMAN JIM"
DIRECTOR, RAOUL WALSH (WARNER BROS.)

HEDY LAMARR
IN "WHITE CARGO"
(M-G-M)

RICHARD DENNING
IN "BEYOND THE BLUE
HORIZON" (PARAMOUNT)

GREER GARSON
IN "RANDOM HARVEST"
(M-G-M)

ROBERT DONAT
IN "THE YOUNG MR. PITT"
(20th CENTURY-FOX)

MARIA MONTEZ
IN "ARABIAN NIGHTS"
(RKO)

ERROL FLYNN
IN "GENTLEMAN JIM"
(WARNER BROS.)

ROSEMARY DeCAMP, SABU
IN "THE JUNGLE BOOK"
(UNITED ARTISTS)

GREER GARSON, CHRISTOPHER SEVERN, WALTER PIDGEON,
CLARE SANDARS IN "MRS. MINIVER"
DIRECTED BY WILLIAM WYLER (M-G-M)

DOROTHY LAMOUR, RICHARD DENNING
IN "BEYOND THE BLUE HORIZON"
(PARAMOUNT)

ROBERT BENCHLEY, VERONICA LAKE, FREDRIC MARCH,
SUSAN HAYWARD, ROBERT WARWICK
IN "I MARRIED A WITCH" (UNITED ARTISTS)

SPENCER TRACY, KATHARINE HEPBURN
IN "WOMAN OF THE YEAR"
DIRECTED BY GEORGE STEVENS (M-G-M)

GEORGE SANDERS, ANTHONY QUINN, TYRONE
POWER IN "THE BLACK SWAN"
(20th CENTURY FOX)

MARY THOMAS, CAROLYN LEE, FAY BAINTER
BILLY LEE, BETTY BREWER IN "MRS.
WIGGS OF THE CABBAGE PATCH" (PARAMOUNT)

WALT DISNEY'S "BAMBI"
FULL-LENGTH, TECHNICOLOR FEATURE (RKO)

1942

VERONICA LAKE, ALAN LADD
IN "THIS GUN FOR HIRE"
(PARAMOUNT)

KATINA PAXINOU
Top: AKIM TAMIROFF

ERIC FELDARY, MIKHAIL RASUMNY, VLADIMIR SOKOLOFF, ARTURO DE CORDOVA, KATINA
PAXINOU, AKIM TAMIROFF, INGRID BERGMAN, GARY COOPER
"FOR WHOM THE BELL TOLLS" PRODUCER-DIRECTOR, SAM WOOD (PARAMOUNT)

INGRID BERGMAN
Top: GARY COOPER

JOAN FONTAINE
IN "THE CONSTANT
NYMPH" (WARNER BROS.)

WILLARD PARKER
IN "WHAT A WOMAN!"
(COLUMBIA)

LENA HORNE
IN "THOUSANDS CHEER"
(M-G-M)

TIM HOLT
IN "HITLER'S CHILDREN"
(RKO)

BARBARA STANWYCK
IN "LADY OF BURLESQUE"
(UNITED ARTISTS)

IRVING BERLIN
IN "THIS IS THE ARMY"
(WARNER BROS.)

MICHAEL O'SHEA, PINKY LEE, BARBARA STANWYCK
IN "LADY OF BURLESQUE"
DIRECTOR, WILLIAM WELLMAN (UNITED ARTISTS)

"THIS IS THE ARMY" DIRECTED BY
MICHAEL CURTIZ MUSIC AND LYRICS
BY IRVING BERLIN (WARNER BROS.)

BONITA GRANVILLE, TIM HOLT, KENT SMITH
IN "HITLER'S CHILDREN"
DIRECTOR, EDWARD DMYTRYK (RKO)

HUMPHREY BOGART
IN "SAHARA" DIRECTOR,
ZOLTAN KORDA (COLUMBIA)

KATHARINE CORNELL, ALINE MacMAHON, LON McALLISTER, MICHAEL HARRISON
IN "STAGE DOOR CANTEEN"
DIRECTED BY FRANK BORZAGE (UNITED ARTISTS)

JENNIFER JONES IN
"THE SONG OF BERNADETTE"
(20th CENTURY-FOX)

JOSEPH COTTEN, TERESA WRIGHT
IN "SHADOW OF A DOUBT"
DIRECTOR, ALFRED HITCHCOCK (UNIVERSAL)

1943

The year saw a decisive shift in the course of the war with the scales tipped in the favor of the United Nations. Dominant among the most important pictures were those dealing with the war or aspects of it. Among them: "Guadalcanal Diary," "Bataan," "Destination Tokyo," "This Is the Army," "A Guy Named Joe," "Cry Havoc," "Air Force," "The Immortal Sergeant," "So Proudly We Hail," "Stage Door Canteen," "Hitler's Children" and "The Cross of Lorraine." "Casablanca," which won an Academy Award, was released when public interest in the historic meeting of Roosevelt, Churchill and Stalin at the Casablanca Conference was highest. The film version of the stage success, "Watch On the Rhine," was picked as the year's best picture by the New York Film Critics. Color was used more widely than ever. Escapist entertainment included "The More the Merrier," "Holy Matrimony," "Lassie Come Home," "Claudia," "Hello, Frisco, Hello," "Princess O'Rourke," "My Friend Flicka" and the English importation "Jeannie." Other outstanding films were "For Whom the Bell Tolls," "Madame Curie," "Heaven Can Wait" and "Shadow of a Doubt." Claude Rains appeared in a remake of "The Phantom of the Opera." Frank Sinatra, a singer of popular tunes, made an inauspicious film debut in "Higher and Higher." The Academy gave an award to William Saroyan's "The Human Comedy" as the best original story. Death toll: veterans Hobart Bosworth, Kate Price, Charles Ray, Conrad Veidt and Leslie Howard, a war victim.

LASSIE, RODDY McDOWALL
IN "LASSIE COME HOME"
DIRECTOR, FRED WILCOX (M-G-M)

EDGAR BARRIER, BETTY FIELD
IN "FLESH AND FANTASY"
DIRECTOR, JULIEN DUVIVIER (UNIVERSAL)

JAMES
STEPHENSON

ANN
RUTHERFORD

TONIO
SELWART

DOROTHY McGUIRE, INA CLAIRE, ROBERT YOUNG
IN "CLAUDIA" DIRECTOR, EDMUND GOULDING
(20th CENTURY-FOX)

RICHARD TRAVIS

SUSAN PETERS

RODDY McDOWALL

SUSANNA FOSTER

JAMES CRAIG

RUTH HUSSEY

DESI ARNAZ

PAUL LUKAS, BETTE DAVIS, BEULAH BONDI, DONALD BUKA, ERIC ROBERTS,
JANIS WILSON IN "WATCH ON THE RHINE"
DIRECTED BY HERMAN SHUMLIN (WARNER BROS.)

CARMEN MIRANDA
IN "DOWN ARGENTINE WAY"
(20th CENTURY-FOX)

DENNIS MORGAN
IN "THE DESERT SONG"
DIRECTED BY ROBERT FLOREY (WARNER BROS.)

NAZIMOVA

OLIVIA DE HAVILLAND
IN "PRINCESS O'ROURKE" DIRECTED BY
NORMAN KRASNA (WARNER BROS.)

JAMES ELLISON

MARIA MONTEZ

ALAN CURTIS

GRACIE ALLEN

BRODERICK CRAWFORD

LARAINE DAY

CHARLES DRAKE

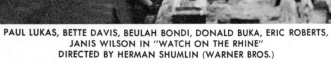

ADOLPH MENJOU   KATHRYN GRAYSON   JOHN LODER   DIANA BARRYMORE   DENNIS MORGAN   ANNE BAXTER   GLENN FORD

ALAN LADD
IN "CHINA"
(PARAMOUNT)

HUMPHREY BOGART, CLAUDE RAINS, PAUL HENREID, INGRID BERGMAN
IN "CASABLANCA" DIRECTED BY MICHAEL CURTIZ
(WARNER BROS.)

RODDY McDOWALL
IN "MY FRIEND FLICKA"
(20th CENTURY-FOX)

GRACE GEORGE
IN "JOHNNY COME LATELY"
(UNITED ARTISTS)

MARJORIE LORD, MARGARET HAMILTON, GEORGE CLEVELAND,
GRACE GEORGE, JAMES CAGNEY IN "JOHNNY COME LATELY"
DIRECTED BY WILLIAM K. HOWARD (UNITED ARTISTS)

DAN DAILEY   MARGARET O'BRIEN   JOSEPH COTTEN   MAUREEN O'HARA   WILLIAM HOLDEN   MARGARET LOCKWOOD   RICHARD NEY

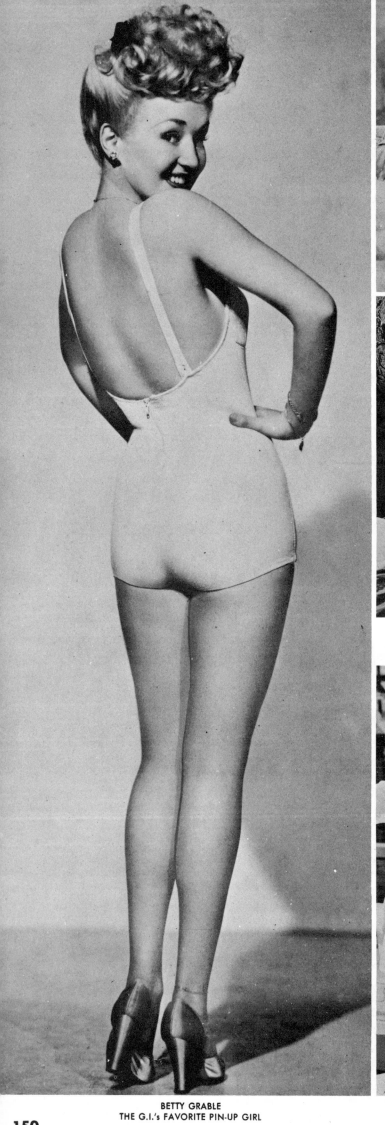

BETTY GRABLE
THE G.I.'s FAVORITE PIN-UP GIRL

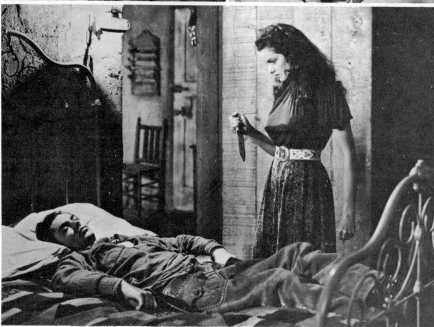

Above and Top: JACK BUETEL, JANE RUSSELL
IN "THE OUTLAW"
PRODUCED AND DIRECTED BY HOWARD HUGHES

FRANK SINATRA, MICHELE
MORGAN IN "HIGHER AND
HIGHER" (RKO)

JOEL McCREA, JEAN ARTHUR
IN "THE MORE THE MERRIER"
DIRECTED BY GEORGE STEVENS (COLUMBIA)

JANE WYATT, RICHARD DIX
IN "THE KANSAN"
(UNITED ARTISTS)

SONJA HENIE, GEARY STEFAN
IN "WINTERTIME"
(20th CENTURY-FOX)

GENE KELLY, JEAN PIERRE AUMONT
IN "THE CROSS OF LORRAINE"
(M-G-M)

ANN SOTHERN, FAY BAINTER, JOAN
BLONDELL, MARSHA HUNT, MARGARET
SULLAVAN IN "CRY HAVOC" (M-G-M)

RICHARD CRANE, ANN RUTHERFORD
IN "HAPPY LAND"
(20th CENTURY-FOX)

EUGENE PALLETTE, MARJORIE MAIN, ALLYN JOSLYN, GENE
TIERNEY, CHARLES COBURN, DON AMECHE, SPRING BYINGTON,
LOUIS CALHERN IN "HEAVEN CAN WAIT" (20th CENTURY-FOX)

ERICH VON STROHEIM
IN "FIVE GRAVES TO
CAIRO" (PARAMOUNT)

DANA ANDREWS, ANTHONY QUINN, FRANCIS FORD, LEIGH WHIPPER,
JANE DARWELL, FRANK CONROY IN "THE OX-BOW INCIDENT"
DIRECTED BY WILLIAM A. WELLMAN (20th CENTURY-FOX)

KENNY BOWERS, JACK JORDAN, LUCILLE BALL,
TOMMY DIX, WILLIAM GAXTON IN "BEST FOOT
FORWARD" DIRECTOR, EDWARD BUZZELL (M-G-M)

PHILIP REED, BETTE DAVIS, DOLORES MORAN
IN "OLD ACQUAINTANCE" DIRECTED BY
VINCENT SHERMAN (WARNER BROS.)

MARTHA SCOTT, JUNE HAVOC, ADOLPHE MENJOU,
POLA NEGRI IN "HI DIDDLE DIDDLE"
DIRECTOR, ANDREW STONE (UNITED ARTISTS)

CLAUDE RAINS IN "THE PHANTOM OF THE OPERA"
DIRECTOR, ARTHUR LUBIN
(UNIVERSAL)

BARBARA MULLEN, MICHAEL REDGRAVE
IN "JEANNIE" (ENGLISH FILMS)

BETTY BLYTHE, WILLIAM BOYD, ANDY CLYDE,
ROBERT MITCHUM IN "BAR 20"
(UNITED ARTISTS)

1943

MORTON LOWRY, MELVILLE COOPER, HENRY FONDA, THOMAS MITCHELL,
BRAMWELL FLETCHER, ALLYN JOSLYN IN "THE IMMORTAL SERGEANT"
DIRECTED BY JOHN M. STAHL (20th CENTURY-FOX)

RALPH BYRD, ROBERT ROSE, LIONEL STANDER, WILLIAM BENDIX, PRESTON FOSTER,
LLOYD NOLAN, RICHARD JAECKEL, ANTHONY QUINN AND U.S. MARINES
IN "GUADALCANAL DIARY" DIRECTOR, LEWIS SEILER (20th CENTURY-FOX)

SONNY TUFTS IN
"SO PROUDLY WE HAIL"
(PARAMOUNT)

BING CROSBY IN
"DIXIE" (PARAMOUNT)

FARLEY GRANGER

BARRY NELSON, ROBERT WALKER, DESI ARNAZ, ROBERT TAYLOR
IN "BATAAN"
DIRECTED BY TAY GARNETT (M-G-M)

GILBERT ROLAND

DANA ANDREWS, JANE WITHERS, ERIC ROBERTS,
ANNE BAXTER, FARLEY GRANGER IN "THE NORTH
STAR" DIRECTOR, LEWIS MILESTONE (RKO)

WALTER HUSTON, ANN SHERIDAN, ERROL FLYNN,
JUDITH ANDERSON IN "EDGE OF DARKNESS"
DIRECTOR, LEWIS MILESTONE (WARNER BROS.)

BARRY NELSON, SPENCER TRACY, VAN JOHNSON,
IRENE DUNNE, WARD BOND IN "A GUY NAMED JOE"
DIRECTOR, VICTOR FLEMING (M-G-M)

JUNE HAVOC, JACK OAKIE, ALICE FAYE, JOHN PAYNE
IN "HELLO, FRISCO, HELLO"
DIRECTED BY BRUCE HUMBERSTONE (20th CENTURY-FOX)

GREER GARSON, WALTER PIDGEON
IN "MADAME CURIE"
DIRECTED BY MERVYN LeROY (M-G-M)

CONRAD VEIDT

CHARLES "BUDDY" ROGERS

CORNEL WILDE

RONALD REAGAN

BUTCH JENKINS, DARRYL HICKMAN, MICKEY ROONEY, FAY BAINTER
IN "THE HUMAN COMEDY"
DIRECTED BY CLARENCE BROWN (M-G-M)

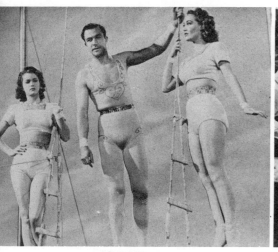

GENE KELLY
IN "THOUSANDS CHEER"
DIRECTED BY GEORGE SIDNEY (M-G-M)

MONTY WOOLLEY, LAIRD CREGAR, GRACIE FIELDS
IN "HOLY MATRIMONY" (20th CENTURY-FOX)

GEORGE MURPHY, CONSTANCE MOORE, EDDIE
CANTOR, JOAN DAVIS IN "SHOW
BUSINESS" (RKO)

1943

ROBERT WALKER, VAN JOHNSON, SPENCER TRACY
IN "THIRTY SECONDS OVER TOKYO"
DIRECTED BY MERVYN LeROY (M-G-M)

KURT KREUGER
IN "MLLE. FIFI"
(RKO)

RAYMOND MASSEY, CARY GRANT, JEAN ADAIR, JOSEPHINE HULL
IN "ARSENIC AND OLD LACE"
DIRECTED BY FRANK CAPRA (WARNER BROS.)

FARLEY GRANGER
IN "THE PURPLE HEART"
(20th CENTURY-FOX)

RICHARD CRANE
IN "NONE SHALL ESCAPE"
(COLUMBIA)

LON McCALLISTER
IN "WINGED VICTORY"
(20th CENTURY-FOX)

JOSEPH COTTEN
IN "SINCE YOU WENT AWAY"
(UNITED ARTISTS)

LON McCALLISTER, BARRY NELSON, RUNE HULTMAN, MARK
DANIELS, DON TAYLOR Above: MARK DANIELS, DON TAYLOR,
EDMOND O'BRIEN, KEVIN McCARTHY IN "WINGED
VICTORY" DIRECTED BY GEORGE CUKOR

GUY MADISON IN
"SINCE YOU WENT AWAY"
DIRECTED BY JOHN CROMWELL
(UNITED ARTISTS)

ROBERT WALKER, JENNIFER JONES, GUY MADISON
Above: JOSEPH COTTEN, JENNIFER JONES, SHIRLEY
TEMPLE, CLAUDETTE COLBERT IN "SINCE YOU WENT AWAY"

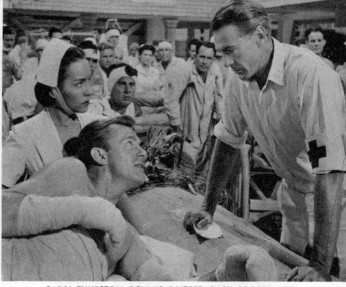

GEORGE OFFERMAN, JR., ROBERT WALKER, KEENAN WYNN
IN "SEE HERE, PRIVATE HARGROVE"
DIRECTED BY WESLEY RUGGLES (M-G-M)

MARLENE DIETRICH
ENTERTAINED TROOPS
OVERSEAS

CAROL THURSTON, DENNIS O'KEEFE, GARY COOPER AND
WOUNDED SAILORS IN "THE STORY OF DR. WASSELL"
PRODUCER-DIRECTOR, CECIL B. DeMILLE (PARAMOUNT)

ROBERT STACK
U.S. NAVY

1944 The war years were drawing to a close. Among the many Hollywood personalities actively engaged in the war effort were Capt. Clark Gable, A.A.F., Maj. James Stewart, A.A.F.; Lt. Douglas Fairbanks, Jr., Lt. Cmdr. Robert Montgomery, Lt. Richard Barthelmess, Lt. Robert Taylor, Lt. Wayne Morris, Lt. Robert Stack, Lt. George O'Brien and Lt. Charles "Buddy" Rogers, all of the U.S. Navy; Lt. Richard Greene of the British Army, and many other patriotic actors. Of the women, Marlene Dietrich was outstanding in her tireless efforts to entertain overseas troops. Among the war films which continued to reach the public were "The Story of Dr. Wassell," "The Purple Heart," "Winged Victory," "30 Seconds Over Tokyo" and "See Here, Private Hargrove." Notable film fare included "Going My Way," "Wilson," "Double Indemnity," "Meet Me in St. Louis," "Gaslight," "Laura," "National Velvet," "None But The Lonely Heart," "The Keys to the Kingdom," "Since You Went Away," and a French import, "Un Carnet de Bal." "Going My Way" won Academy Awards for the best picture, best direction by Leo McCarey, and best performances by Bing Crosby and Barry Fitzgerald. Also, it was voted best picture by the New York Film Critics. Academy Awards also went to Ingrid Bergman for "Gaslight" and Ethel Barrymore for "None But The Lonely Heart." Gregory Peck, Lauren Bacall, Cornel Wilde, Bill Williams, Faye Emerson, and Charles Korvin were some of the new faces gracing the screen.

CLARK GABLE
U.S. ARMY

MICKEY ROONEY
U.S. ARMY

RICHARD CONTE, FARLEY GRANGER, DANA ANDREWS, CHARLES RUSSELL, DONALD BARRY,
KEVIN O'SHEA, SAM LEVENE, JOHN CRAVEN IN "THE PURPLE HEART"
DIRECTED BY LEWIS MILESTONE (20th CENTURY-FOX)

DOUGLAS FAIRBANKS, JR.
U.S. NAVY

BARRY FITZGERALD

BARRY FITZGERALD, RISE STEVENS, BING CROSBY
IN "GOING MY WAY" PRODUCED AND DIRECTED BY LEO McCAREY
(PARAMOUNT)

BING CROSBY

ORSON WELLES, MARGARET O'BRIEN, JOAN FONTAINE
IN "JANE EYRE" DIRECTOR, ROBERT STEVENSON
(20th CENTURY-FOX)

BOB CROSBY, GRACE
McDONALD IN "MY GAL
LOVES MUSIC" (UNIVERSAL)

LOU COSTELLO, BUD ABBOTT
IN "IN SOCIETY"
(UNIVERSAL)

ROSE STRADNER, THOMAS MITCHELL, GREGORY PEC
IN "THE KEYS OF THE KINGDOM"
DIRECTED BY JOHN M. STAHL (20th CENTURY-FOX)

BILL EDWARDS, GAIL RUSSELL, JAMES BROWN,
DIANA LYNN IN "OUR HEARTS WERE YOUNG
AND GAY" (PARAMOUNT)

BEATRICE LILLIE, ROLAND CULVER, GOOGIE WITHERS,
CLIVE BROOK IN "ON APPROVAL"
(ENGLISH FILMS)

DEREK HARRIS (later JOHN DEREK), SHIRLEY TEMPLE,
SPRING BYINGTON IN "I'LL BE SEEING YOU"
DIRECTOR, WILLIAM DIETERLE (UNITED ARTISTS)

MICHAEL REDGRAVE, JAMES MASON
IN "THUNDER ROCK"
(ENGLISH FILMS)

DOROTHY GISH IN
"OUR HEARTS WERE YOUNG
AND GAY" (PARAMOUNT)

FREDRIC MARCH IN
"THE ADVENTURES OF MARK
TWAIN" (WARNER BROS.)

RICHARD WARING, BETTE DAVIS
IN "MR. SKEFFINGTON"
DIRECTED BY VINCENT SHERMAN (WARNER BROS.)

FRANCIS LEDERER, LYNN BARI, BLANCHE YURKA, DONALD WOODS, JOAN LORRING, AKIM TAMIROFF, NAZIMOVA IN "THE BRIDGE OF SAN LUIS REY" DIRECTED BY ROWLAND V. LEE (UNITED ARTISTS)

ROBERT PAIGE, DEANNA DURBIN IN "CAN'T HELP SINGING" (UNIVERSAL)

RAY MILLAND, GINGER ROGERS, WARNER BAXTER, JON HALL IN "LADY IN THE DARK" DIRECTED BY MITCHELL LEISEN (PARAMOUNT)

MARGARET O'BRIEN, JUDY GARLAND, HENRY DANIELS, JR. IN "MEET ME IN ST. LOUIS" DIRECTED BY VINCENTE MINNELLI (M-G-M)

RUTH FORD, ALEXANDER KNOX, RUTH NELSON, MARY ANDERSON, MADELEINE FORBES IN "WILSON" DIRECTOR, HENRY KING (20th CENTURY-FOX)

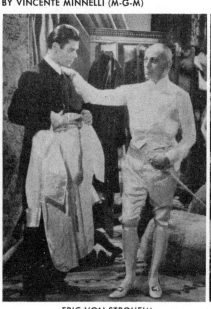

FIBBER McGEE AND MOLLY IN "HEAVENLY DAYS" (RKO)

ERIC VON STROHEIM IN "L'ALIBI" (COLUMBIA)

JOEL McCREA, ANTHONY QUINN IN "BUFFALO BILL" (20th CENTURY-FOX)

HOAGY CARMICHAEL, HUMPHREY BOGART, LAUREN BACALL IN "TO HAVE AND HAVE NOT" (WARNER BROS.)

CLIFTON WEBB, GENE TIERNEY, VINCENT PRICE, JUDITH ANDERSON Top: CLIFTON WEBB, DANA ANDREWS IN "LAURA" PRODUCER-DIRECTOR, OTTO PREMINGER (20th CENTURY-FOX)

TURHAN BEY, KATHARINE HEPBURN IN "DRAGON SEED" DIRECTED BY JACK CONWAY (M-G-M)

LUCILLE MARSH, EVE ARDEN, OTTO KRUGER, GENE KELLY, RITA HAYWORTH, LEE BOWMAN   Top: GENE KELLY, RITA HAYWORTH, PHIL SILVERS, ED BROPHY IN "COVER GIRL" DIRECTED BY CHARLES VIDOR (COLUMBIA)

FRANK SINATRA   MARILYN MAXWELL   JEFFREY LYNN   LAIRD CREGAR   RICHARD ARLEN   CLAIRE TREVOR   DICK HAYMES

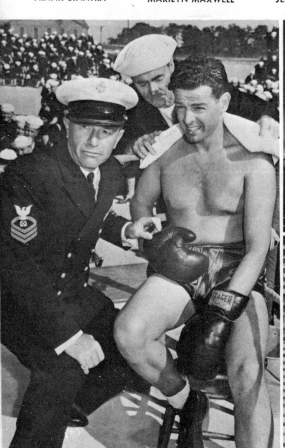

1944

ROBERT ARMSTRONG, ROBERT LOWERY IN "THE NAVY WAY" (PARAMOUNT)

MICKEY ROONEY, BUTCH JENKINS, ELIZABETH TAYLOR, KING CHARLES Above: MICKEY ROONEY, ELIZABETH TAYLOR IN "NATIONAL VELVET" (M-G-M)

IRENE DUNNE, ALAN MARSHALL IN "THE WHITE CLIFFS OF DOVER" DIRECTED BY CLARENCE BROWN (M-G-M)

HENRY HULL, JOHN HODIAK, HUME CRONYN, TALLULAH BANKHEAD, MARY ANDERSON
IN "LIFEBOAT" DIRECTED BY ALFRED HITCHCOCK
(20th CENTURY-FOX)

BARBARA STANWYCK, FRED MacMURRAY
IN "DOUBLE INDEMNITY"
DIRECTED BY BILLY WILDER (PARAMOUNT)

ALBERT DEKKER   ROD CAMERON   DON CASTLE   SIGNE HASSO   BILL WILLIAMS   FAYE EMERSON   ROBERT PAIGE

ROBERT LEWIS
IN "DRAGON SEED"
(M-G-M)

JULIA DEAN IN
"THE CURSE OF THE
CAT PEOPLE" (RKO)

CHARLES KORVIN
IN "ENTER ARSENE LUPIN"
(UNIVERSAL)

INGRID BERGMAN, CHARLES BOYER, BARBARA EVEREST
IN "GASLIGHT" DIRECTED BY GEORGE CUKOR (M-G-M)

1944

ETHEL BARRYMORE
IN "NONE BUT THE LONELY
HEART" (RKO)

159

TURHAN BEY IN
"NIGHT IN PARADISE"
(UNIVERSAL)

LLOYD NOLAN, JOAN BLONDELL, TED DONALDSON, DOROTHY McGUIRE, JAMES
DUNN, PEGGY ANN GARNER IN "A TREE GROWS IN BROOKLYN"
DIRECTED BY ELIA KAZAN (20th CENTURY-FOX)

LAWRENCE TIERNEY
IN "DILLINGER"
(MONOGRAM)

PATRIC KNOWLES, RAY MILLAND, CECIL KELLAWAY, PAULETTE
GODDARD IN "KITTY"
DIRECTED BY MITCHELL LEISEN (PARAMOUNT)

BURGESS MEREDITH
IN "THE STORY OF
G.I. JOE"

ROBERT MITCHUM, BURGESS MEREDITH
IN "THE STORY OF G.I. JOE"
DIRECTED BY WILLIAM A. WELLMAN (UNITED ARTISTS)

SHARON McMANUS, GENE KELLY
IN "ANCHORS AWEIGH"
(M-G-M)

KATHRYN GRAYSON
IN "ANCHORS AWEIGH"
(M-G-M)

BORIS KARLOFF
IN "THE BODY SNATCHER"
(RKO)

ROBERT WALKER, JUDY GARLAND
IN "THE CLOCK"
DIRECTOR, VINCENTE MINNELLI (M-G-M)

FRED MacMURRAY
IN "CAPTAIN EDDIE"
(20th CENTURY-FOX)

RAY MILLAND, HOWARD DA SILVA
IN "THE LOST WEEKEND"
DIRECTED BY BILLY WILDER (PARAMOUNT)

BETTE DAVIS IN
"THE CORN IS GREEN"
(WARNER BROS.)

CORNEL WILDE, MERLE OBERON, PAUL MUNI
IN "A SONG TO REMEMBER"
DIRECTED BY CHARLES VIDOR (COLUMBIA)

MERLE OBERON IN
"A SONG TO REMEMBER"
(COLUMBIA)

BETTE DAVIS, JOHN DALL
IN "THE CORN IS GREEN"
DIRECTED BY IRVING RAPPER (WARNER BROS.)

ROBERT MONTGOMERY, JOHN WAYNE
IN "THEY WERE EXPENDABLE"
DIRECTOR, JOHN FORD (M-G-M)

1945 With the war in Europe over in May and the surrender of Japan in August, the film industry turned its attention to peacetime operation. Will H. Hays, who had been president of Motion Picture Producers and Distributors of America since its inception in 1922, resigned and was succeeded by Eric Johnston, an industrialist. "The Lost Weekend" received both an Academy Award and a citation from the New York Film Critics as the best picture of the year. Both organizations also cited Ray Milland as the best male star performer, and Billy Wilder received an Academy Award for his direction. An Academy Award went to Joan Crawford for her brilliant portrayal in "Mildred Pierce." The New York Critics picked Ingrid Bergman as the best female star performer of the year for "Spellbound." Among the outstanding films were "A Tree Grows in Brooklyn," "A Song to Remember," "The Story of G. I. Joe," "The Corn Is Green," "Anchors Aweigh," "A Walk in the Sun," "Our Vines Have Tender Grapes," "The Fighting Lady," "The House on 92nd Street," "A Bell for Adano" and a re-make of "State Fair." Among new faces were Rory Calhoun, Lawrence Tierney and Hurd Hatfield. Death claimed Alla Nazimova, famed stage and silent screen star. Roy Rogers, with George "Gabby" Hayes as his side-kick and Dale Evans his love interest, was the top cowboy star at the box office.

SPENCER TRACY, KATHARINE HEPBURN
IN "WITHOUT LOVE" DIRECTOR,
HAROLD S. BUCQUET (M-G-M)

HENRY MORGAN, MARCEL DALIO, JOHN HODIAK, WILLIAM BENDIX, JOHN RUSSELL Top: GLENN LANGAN IN "A BELL FOR ADANO" DIRECTOR, HENRY KING (20th CENTURY-FOX)

DICK HAYMES, FAY BAINTER, JEANNE CRAIN, CHARLES WINNINGER Top: DICK HAYMES, JEANNE CRAIN, DANA ANDREWS IN "STATE FAIR" DIRECTOR, WALTER LANG (20th CENTURY-FOX)

JOHN WARBURTON, JERRY AUSTIN, GARY COOPER, INGRID BERGMAN IN "SARATOGA TRUNK" DIRECTED BY SAM WOOD (WARNER BROS.)

SONNY TUFTS, LILLIAN GISH (also above), LLOYD BRIDGES, BILLY DeWOLFE, BILL EDWARDS IN "MISS SUSIE SLAGLE" (PARAMOUNT)

HURD HATFIELD, ANGELA LANSBURY IN "THE PICTURE OF DORIAN GRAY" DIRECTED BY ALBERT LEWIN (M-G-M)

GREGORY PECK, INGRID BERGMAN IN "SPELLBOUND" DIRECTOR, ALFRED HITCHCOCK (UNITED ARTISTS)

INGRID BERGMAN IN "SARATOGA TRUNK" (WARNER BROS.)

HURD HATFIELD IN "THE PICTURE OF DORIAN GRAY" (M-G-M)

ANN HARDING, BILL WILLIAMS, ROBERT YOUNG IN "THOSE ENDEARING YOUNG CHARMS" DIRECTOR, LEWIS ALLEN (RKO

KATHARINE HEPBURN
1945

BOB HOPE, BING CROSBY
IN "THE ROAD TO UTOPIA"
(PARAMOUNT)

JACK CARSON, JOAN CRAWFORD, ANN BLYTH
IN "MILDRED PIERCE" DIRECTED BY
MICHAEL CURTIZ (WARNER BROS.)

MARGARET O'BRIEN, EDWARD G. ROBINSON
BUTCH JENKINS IN "OUR VINES HAVE
TENDER GRAPES" (M-G-M)

TOM DRAKE

MARSHALL THOMPSON

PHYLLIS THAXTER

LAWRENCE TIERNEY

ANN TODD

ZACHARY SCOTT

ERICH VON STROHEIM

GEORGE "GABBY" HAYES, ROY ROGERS,
DALE EVANS IN "BELLS OF ROSARITA"
(REPUBLIC)

GRACIE FIELDS, KURT KREUGER, CONSTANCE BENNETT
IN "PARIS UNDERGROUND" DIRECTED BY
GREGORY RATOFF (UNITED ARTISTS)

ROGER LIVESEY, DEBORAH KERR, ANTON WALBROOK
IN "COLONEL BLIMP" PRODUCED AND DIRECTED BY
POWELL AND PRESSBURGER (UNITED ARTISTS)

LEO G. CARROLL, WILLIAM EYTHE, SIGNE HASSO
IN "THE HOUSE ON 92nd STREET"
(20th CENTURY-FOX)

DANA ANDREWS
IN "A WALK IN THE SUN"
DIRECTOR, LEWIS MILESTONE (20th CENTURY-FOX)

VIVIAN BLAINE, PERRY COMO, DENNIS O'KEEFE,
CARMEN MIRANDA IN "DOLL FACE"
(20th CENTURY-FOX)

RUTH DONNELLY, INGRID BERGMAN, BING CROSBY
IN "THE BELLS OF ST. MARY'S"
AUTHOR-PRODUCER-DIRECTOR, LEO McCAREY (RKO)

GREER GARSON, DAN DURYEA, GLADYS COOPER, MARSHALL THOMPSON,
MARSHA HUNT, GREGORY PECK IN "THE VALLEY OF DECISION"
DIRECTED BY TAY GARNETT (M-G-M)

WILLIAM MARSHALL   FORREST TUCKER   ELLA RAINS   SIDNEY TOLER   ALEXIS SMITH   JOHN SUTTON   ROBERT STERLING

DONALD WOODS, DANNY KAYE, VERA-ELLEN
IN "WONDER MAN" DIRECTED BY
BRUCE HUMBERSTONE (RKO)

ALAN REED, PEGGY ANN GARNER, RORY CALHOUN,
GEORGE RAFT IN "NOB HILL" DIRECTED BY
HENRY HATHAWAY (20th CENTURY-FOX)

FRED ALLEN, RUDY VALLEE, VICTOR MOORE,
DON AMECHE IN "IT'S IN THE BAG"
(UNITED ARTISTS)

ROBERT ALDA IN
"RHAPSODY IN BLUE" DIRECTED BY
IRVING RAPPER (WARNER BROS.)

DEANNA DURBIN IN
"LADY ON A TRAIN" (UNIVERSAL)

GEORGE ROUQUIER'S "FARREBIQUE"
(SIRITSKY INTERNATIONAL)

CHARLES BOYER

ANN TODD, JAMES MASON
IN "THE SEVENTH VEIL" DIRECTED
BY COMPTON BENNETT (UNIVERSAL)

BILL BOYD AS HOPALONG CASSIDY, A ROLE HE
PORTRAYED IN DOZENS OF FILMS

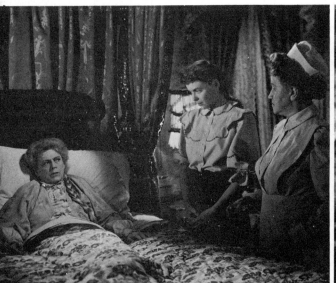

ETHEL BARRYMORE, DOROTHY McGUIRE, SARA ALLGOOD
IN "THE SPIRAL STAIRCASE" DIRECTED
BY ROBERT SIODMAK (RKO)

CLAUDE JARMAN, JR.
IN "THE YEARLING"
(M-G-M)

JANE WYMAN, CLAUDE JARMAN, JR., GREGORY
PECK IN "THE YEARLING" DIRECTED
BY CLARENCE BROWN (M-G-M)

HENRY FONDA, CATHY DOWNS
IN "MY DARLING CLEMENTINE"
(20th CENTURY-FOX)

1946 Laurence Olivier produced, directed and acted in the year's most distinguished film, Shakespeare's "Henry V." Other films of quality from abroad were Shaw's "Caesar and Cleopatra" starring Vivien Leigh and Claude Rains, "Open City" which introduced Anna Magnani to American audiences, and "Children of Paradise" with France's distinguished troupers Jean-Louis Barrault and Arletty. "The Best Years of Our Lives," a Samuel Goldwyn production, was chosen by the Academy and the New York Film Critics as the best film. William Wyler for his direction and Fredric March and Harold Russell for their acting in this picture, all received Academy Awards. An "Oscar" was also won by Olivia De Havilland for "To Each His Own" and by Anne Baxter for "The Razor's Edge." James Mason made a fine impression with his performance in the English importation "The Seventh Veil" and was promptly grabbed by Hollywood. Other new faces gracing the screen were John Lund, Douglas Dick and Larry Parks who scored with his impersonation in "The Jolson Story." Walt Disney made "Song of the South," a full-length feature with live actors. Bill Boyd was in his twelfth year with his popular "Hopalong Cassidy" series. Death took William S. Hart, George Arliss, W. C. Fields, Laurette Taylor and Florence Turner, the original "Vitagraph Girl." Among the classics to reach the screen were "Two Years Before the Mast," "Black Beauty," and re-makes of "The Virginian" with Joel McCrea and "Monsieur Beaucaire" with Bob Hope.

JEAN ARTHUR

DEAN JAGGER, ROSALIND RUSSELL
IN "SISTER KENNY" DIRECTED
BY DUDLEY NICHOLS (RKO)

IDA LUPINO, OLIVIA DE HAVILLAND,
NANCY COLEMAN, ARTHUR KENNEDY
IN "DEVOTION" (WARNER BROS.)

MONTY WOOLLEY, DONALD WOODS, DOROTHY MALONE, CARY
GRANT, ALEXIS SMITH IN "NIGHT AND DAY" DIRECTED
BY MICHAEL CURTIZ (WARNER BROS.)

CAESAR AND CLEOPATRA

Producer-Director, Gabriel Pascal; Author, George Bernard Shaw. Produced in England by J. Arthur Rank and released by United Artists.

CAST

Caesar......................................Claude Rains
Cleopatra...................................Vivien Leigh
Apollodorus...........................Stewart Granger
Ftatateeta..................................Flora Robson
Pothinus........................Francis L. Sullivan
Rufio..Basil Sydney
Britannus..................................Cecil Parker
Lucius Septimius...................Raymond Lovell
Achillas..............................Antony Eustrel
Theodotus.............................Ernest Thesiger
Ptolemy ....Anthony Harvey
Nubian Slave............................Robert Adams
Cleopatra's Attendants........ Olga Edwardes,
                                                Harda Swanhilde
Centurions.............................Michael Rennie,
                                                James McKechnie
Major Domo................................Esme Percy
Belzanor ....Stanley Holloway
Bel Aftris.......................................Leo Genn
1st Nobleman...............................Felix Aylmer

VIVIEN LEIGH
Top: STEWART GRANGER, BASIL SYDNEY,
VIVIEN LEIGH, CLAUDE RAINS

VIVIEN LEIGH, CLAUDE RAINS
Top: VIVIEN LEIGH, FLORA ROBSON, CLAUDE RAINS

CLAUDE RAINS

SCENES FROM "CAESAR AND CLEOPATRA" (UNITED ARTISTS)

**FLORA ROBSON IN
"CAESAR AND CLEOPATRA"
(UNITED ARTISTS)**

**LARRY PARKS IN
"THE JOLSON STORY"
(COLUMBIA)**

**GENE TIERNEY IN
"THE RAZOR'S EDGE"
(20th CENTURY-FOX)**

**BILL WILLIAMS IN
"TILL THE END OF TIME"
(RKO)**

**MYRNA LOY IN
"THE BEST YEARS OF
OUR LIVES" (RKO)**

HENRY V

Producer-Director, Laurence Olivier; Associate Producer, Dallas Bower; Author, William Shakespeare; Score, William Walton; Cameramen, Robert Krasker, Jack Hildyard; Costumes by Roger Furse. Produced in England by Two Cities, Ltd. and released by United Artists.

CAST

King Henry V	Laurence Olivier
Ancient Pistol	Robert Newton
Chorus	Leslie Banks
Princess Katherine	Renee Asherson
Fluellen	Esmond Knight
Constable of France	Leo Genn
Archbishop of Canterbury	Felix Aylmer
Mountjoy	Ralph Truman
Duke of Exeter	Nicholas Hannen
Charles VI of France	Harcourt Williams
Bishop of Ely	Robert Helpmann
Alice	Ivy St. Helier
Mistress Quickly	Freda Jackson
Duke of Berri	Ernest Thesiger
Williams	Jimmy Hanley
The Dauphin	Max Adrian
Jamy	John Laurie
Duke of Orleans	Francis Lister
MacMorris	Niall MacGinnis
Duke of Burgundy	Valentine Dyall
Sir John Falstaff	George Robey
Duke of Bourbon	Russell Thorndike
Duke of Gloucester	Michael Warre
Queen Isabel of France	Janet Burnell

LAURENCE OLIVIER, RENEE ASHERSON

LAURENCE OLIVIER

SCENES FROM "HENRY V" (UNITED ARTISTS)

DANNY KAYE IN "THE KID FROM BROOKLYN" (RKO)

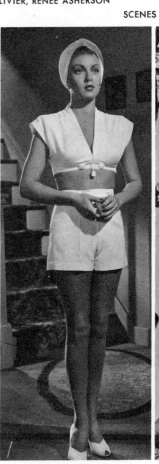

LANA TURNER IN "THE POSTMAN ALWAYS RINGS TWICE" (M-G-M)

CORNEL WILDE IN "THE BANDIT OF SHERWOOD FOREST" (COLUMBIA)

RITA HAYWORTH IN "GILDA" (COLUMBIA)

BURT LANCASTER IN "THE KILLERS" (UNIVERSAL)

1946

169

JOAN FONTAINE, MARK STEVENS
IN "FROM THIS DAY FORWARD"
(RKO)

INGRID BERGMAN, CARY GRANT
IN "NOTORIOUS" PRODUCED AND
DIRECTED BY ALFRED HITCHCOCK (RKO)

SONNY TUFTS, RUTH WARRICK
IN "SWELL GUY"
(UNIVERSAL)

JEANNE CRAIN, ALAN YOUNG, GLENN LANGAN,
VANESSA BROWN Above: JEANNE CRAIN
IN "MARGIE" (20th CENTURY-FOX)

TOM DRAKE, CHARLES COBURN, BEVERLY
TYLER IN "THE GREEN YEARS"
DIRECTED BY VICTOR SAVILLE (M-G-M)

FREDA FLIER, CONSTANTINE, MIRIAM SHILLER, MICHAEL
CHEKHOV, JUDITH ANDERSON Above: CHARLES MARSHALL
LIONEL STANDER, JUDITH ANDERSON, VIOLA ESSEN,
IVAN KIROV IN "SPECTER OF THE ROSE" (REPUBLIC)

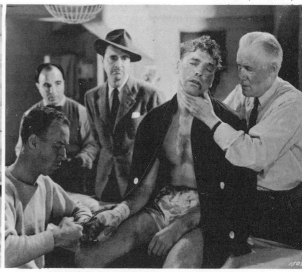

CORNEL WILDE, CONSTANCE BENNETT, WALTER
BRENNAN, DOROTHY GISH IN "CENTENNIAL
SUMMER" (20th CENTURY-FOX)

JAMES BASKETT, BOBBY DRISCOLL
IN WALT DISNEY'S "SONG OF
THE SOUTH" (RKO)

SAM LEVENE, BURT LANCASTER (his first picture),
CHARLES D. BROWN IN "THE KILLERS"
(UNIVERSAL)

MARILYN MAXWELL, RED SKELTON
IN "THE SHOW-OFF"
(M-G-M)

HAROLD RUSSELL, DANA ANDREWS, FREDRIC MARCH
IN "THE BEST YEARS OF OUR LIVES"
DIRECTED BY WILLIAM WYLER (RKO)

DAVID NIVEN, ROGER LIVESEY, KIM
HUNTER IN "STAIRWAY TO HEAVEN"
(UNIVERSAL)

FRANK LATIMORE, ANNE BAXTER, HERBERT
MARSHALL, JOHN PAYNE, GENE TIERNEY, CLIFTON
WEBB Above: TYRONE POWER, ANNE BAXTER, GENE
TIERNEY IN "THE RAZOR'S EDGE" (20th CENTURY-FOX)

OLIVIA DeHAVILLAND, JOHN LUND
IN "TO EACH HIS OWN" DIRECTED
BY MITCHELL LEISEN (PARAMOUNT)

JEAN-LOUIS BARRAULT, ARLETTY
Above: JEAN-LOUIS BARRAULT
IN "CHILDREN OF PARADISE" (PATHÉ)

DOUGLAS DICK, ROBERT YOUNG, ANN RICHARDS
IN "THE SEARCHING WIND" DIRECTED BY
WILLIAM DIETERLE (PARAMOUNT)

VIVIANE ROMANCE
IN "CARMEN"
1946

ANNA MAGNANI
IN "OPEN CITY"
DIRECTED BY ROBERTO ROSSELLINI

JEAN PIERRE AUMONT

DIANA LYNN

ROBERT WALKER

"BUTCH" JENKINS

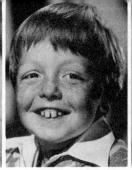
RICHARD CRANE

JANE WYMAN

ARTHUR KENNEDY

CONSTANCE COLLIER, CECIL KELLAWAY, BOB HOPE, JOSEPH SCHILDKRAUT, REGINALD OWEN IN "MONSIEUR BEAUCAIRE" (PARAMOUNT)

ROBERT MITCHUM, KATHARINE HEPBURN IN "UNDERCURRENT" (M-G-M)

JAMES STEWART, H. B. WARNER IN "IT'S A WONDERFUL LIFE" (RKO)

ALAN LADD, BRIAN DONLEVY, BARRY FITZGERALD IN "TWO YEARS BEFORE THE MAST" (PARAMOUNT)

CHARLES RUGGLES, PETER LAWFORD, "BUTCH" JENKINS IN "MY BROTHER TALKS TO HORSES" (M-G-M)

ANITA LOUISE, CORNEL WILDE IN "THE BANDIT OF SHERWOOD FOREST" (COLUMBIA)

EDWARD G. ROBINSON, LORETTA YOUNG, ORSON WELLES IN "THE STRANGER" (RKO)

HAL HACKETT, DOROTHY FORD, MICKEY ROONEY IN "LOVE LAUGHS AT ANDY HARDY" (M-G-M)

FORREST TUCKER, ERROL FLYNN IN "NEVER SAY GOODBYE" (WARNER BROS.)

BARBARA BRITTON, JOEL McCREA IN "THE VIRGINIAN" (PARAMOUNT)

JOHNNY WEISSMULLER, BRENDA JOYCE, JOHNNY SHEFFIELD IN "TARZAN AND THE LEOPARD WOMAN" (RKO)

DANE CLARK

BRIAN DONLEVY

VERA-ELLEN

EDMUND LOWE

MARIE WILSON

RICHARD CARLSON

EDWARD ARNOLD

172

PERRY COMO   VIRGINIA GILMORE   RICHARD DENNING   JUNE HAVER   ALLAN JONES   ESTHER WILLIAMS   GIG YOUNG

TOM DRAKE, LASSIE, ELIZABETH TAYLOR IN "COURAGE OF LASSIE" (M-G-M)

JUNE HAVER, GEORGE MONTGOMERY, VIVIAN BLAINE, FRANK LATIMORE, CHARLES SMITH, VERA-ELLEN, CELESTE HOLM IN "THREE LITTLE GIRLS IN BLUE" (20th CENTURY-FOX)

LEW AYRES, OLIVIA DE HAVILLAND (in dual role) IN "DARK MIRROR" (UNIVERSAL)

  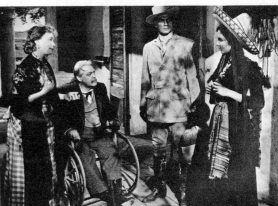

EVELYN ANKERS, RICHARD DENNING, TERRY KILBURN, MONA FREEMAN IN "BLACK BEAUTY" (20th CENTURY-FOX)

IRENE DUNNE, REX HARRISON IN "ANNA AND THE KING OF SIAM" DIRECTOR, JOHN CROMWELL (20th CENTURY-FOX)

LILLIAN GISH, LIONEL BARRYMORE, JOSEPH COTTEN, JENNIFER JONES IN "DUEL IN THE SUN" DIRECTOR, KING VIDOR (SELZNICK)

JOAN CAULFIELD, FRED ASTAIRE, BING CROSBY IN "BLUE SKIES" (PARAMOUNT)

LUCILLE BALL IN "LOVER COME BACK" (UNIVERSAL)

PETER GLENVILLE IN "MADONNA OF THE SEVEN MOONS" (UNIVERSAL)

GENE TIERNEY, VINCENT PRICE, GLENN LANGAN IN "DRAGONWYCK" (20th CENTURY-FOX)

CHARLES COBURN   DEAN STOCKWELL   DAME MAY WHITTY   RAIMU   CHARLOTTE GREENWOOD   CLIFTON WEBB   HENRY WILCOXON

JEANNE CRAIN   RORY CALHOUN   BARBARA STANWYCK   LOUIS JOURDAN   PAULETTE GODDARD   LIONEL BARRYMORE

TYRONE POWER, COLEEN GRAY, MIKE MAZURKI
IN "NIGHTMARE ALLEY"
(20th CENTURY-FOX)

KEN MURRAY'S "BILL AND COO"
WHICH RECEIVED A SPECIAL
ACADEMY AWARD (REPUBLIC)

RICHARD LONG, FRED MacMURRAY, CLAUDETTE
COLBERT IN "THE EGG AND I"
(UNIVERSAL)

BRUCE BENNETT

JIMMY LYDON, MARTIN MILNER, ELIZABETH TAYLOR, ZASU PITTS,
JOHNNY CALKINS, IRENE DUNNE, WILLIAM POWELL, DEREK SCOTT
IN "LIFE WITH FATHER" (WARNER BROS.)

BEULAH BONDI

NYDIA WESTMAN, RONALD COLMAN, RICHARD HAYDN, VANESSA BROWN,
PEGGY CUMMINS, RICHARD NEY, PERCY WARAM, EDNA BEST,
MILDRED NATWICK IN "THE LATE GEORGE APLEY" (20th CENTURY-FOX)

RAYMOND MASSEY, JOAN CRAWFORD, VAN HEFLIN
IN "POSSESSED" (WARNER BROS.)

DOLORES DEL RIO, HENRY FONDA
IN "THE FUGITIVE" (RKO)

ROBERT MONTGOMERY, WANDA HENDRIX, FRED CLARK
IN "RIDE THE PINK HORSE" (UNIVERSAL)

174

OLIVIA DE HAVILLAND

WALLACE BEERY

AVA GARDNER

JEAN MARAIS

LAUREN BACALL

STERLING HAYDEN

LINDA DARNELL, CORNEL WILDE

GLENN LANGAN

LINDA DARNELL

GLENN LANGAN, RICHARD GREENE, LINDA DARNELL, JESSICA TANDY

SCENES FROM "FOREVER AMBER" DIRECTED BY OTTO PREMINGER (20th CENTURY-FOX)

JOHN LUND, BETTY HUTTON IN "THE PERILS OF PAULINE" (PARAMOUNT)

1947 J. Arthur Rank, British film tycoon, was a name to reckon with in the film industry. He was a factor in telescoping Universal, International and United World Pictures into Universal-International Productions Company. English films were receiving fine reception with American audiences. Among the year's popular British releases were "Odd Man Out," "Black Narcissus," Noel Coward's "This Happy Breed," and Dickens' "Nicholas Nickleby" and "Great Expectations." The New York Film Critics and the Academy picked "Gentleman's Agreement" as the best film. An "Oscar" went to Elia Kazan for directing it. Other Academy Award winners were Loretta Young for "The Farmer's Daughter," Ronald Colman for "A Double Life" and Edmund Gwenn for "Miracle on 34th Street." Three best selling books made into films were "Forever Amber," "The Late George Apley" and "The Egg and I." Vittorio de Sica's "Shoe Shine" and "To Live in Peace," two outstanding Italian films, received critical acclaim. Broadway successes to reach the screen were "Life with Father," "The Voice of the Turtle" and "Dear Ruth." Eugene O'Neill's "Mourning Becomes Electra" was filmed but was a box-office failure. Charlie Chaplin, who had become a controversial figure because of his political views, met his first financial failure with "Monsieur Verdoux." Death took Ernst Lubitsch, Grace Moore, Harry Carey and J. Warren Kerrigan, matinee idol of the silent screen.

CARY GRANT, SHIRLEY TEMPLE IN "THE BACHELOR AND THE BOBBY-SOXER" (RKO)

ROBERT RYAN, ROBERT MITCHUM, ROBERT YOUNG IN "CROSSFIRE" (RKO)

MARLENE DIETRICH, RAY MILLAND IN "GOLDEN EARRINGS" DIRECTED BY MITCHELL LEISEN (PARAMOUNT)

BRIAN DONLEVY, RICHARD WIDMARK, VICTOR MATURE IN "KISS OF DEATH" (20th CENTURY-FOX)

175

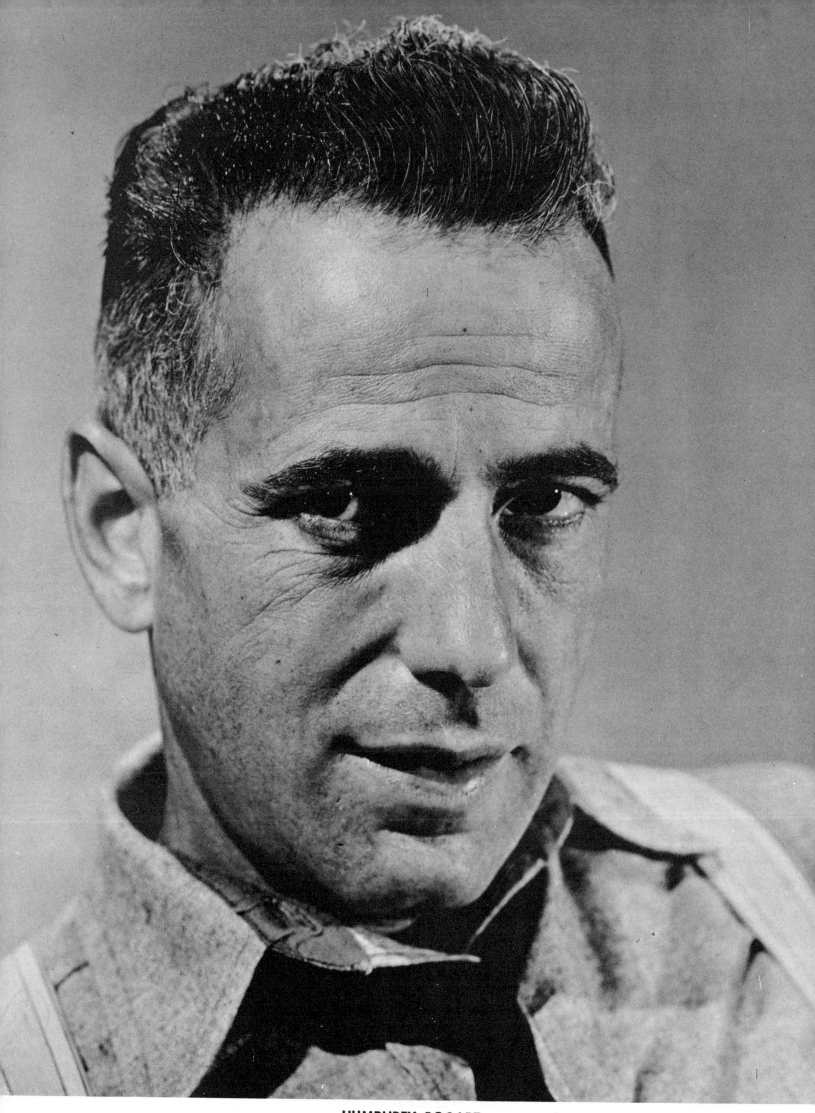

HUMPHREY BOGART

JOAN TETZEL, GREGORY PECK, ETHEL BARRYMORE, CHARLES COBURN, ANN TODD IN ALFRED HITCHCOCK'S "THE PARADINE CASE" (SELZNICK)

HOWARD DUFF, JEFF COREY, JACK OVERMAN, BURT LANCASTER, JOHN HOYT IN "BRUTE FORCE" (UNIVERSAL)

CLARK GABLE, AVA GARDNER, DEBORAH KERR, GLORIA HOLDEN, ADOLPHE MENJOU IN "THE HUCKSTERS" (M-G-M)

CARMEN MIRANDA, GROUCHO MARX, GLORIA JEAN, STEVE COCHRAN IN "COPACABANA" (UNITED ARTISTS)

"SALT WATER TABBY" ONE OF THE POPULAR TOM AND JERRY CARTOONS (M-G-M)

KIRK DOUGLAS, WENDELL COREY, BURT LANCASTER IN "I WALK ALONE" (PARAMOUNT)

CHARLES CHAPLIN IN "MONSIEUR VERDOUX" (UNITED ARTISTS)

CHARLES CHAPLIN, MARTHA RAYE IN "MONSIEUR VERDOUX" WRITTEN, PRODUCED AND DIRECTED BY CHARLES CHAPLIN (UNITED ARTISTS)

KATHARINE HEPBURN, PAUL HENREID IN "SONG OF LOVE" (M-G-M)

BING CROSBY AND THE ANDREWS SISTERS (PATTY, LAVERNE AND MAXINE) IN "ROAD TO RIO" (PARAMOUNT)

BARBARA HALE, BILL WILLIAMS IN "A LIKELY STORY" (RKO)

GORDON JONES, DANNY KAYE, ANN RUTHERFORD, THURSTON HALL, FAY BAINTER, FLORENCE BATES IN "THE SECRET LIFE OF WALTER MITTY" (RKO)

1947

JEAN SIMMONS, DEBORAH KERR, DAVID FARRAR
IN "BLACK NARCISSUS" WRITTEN, PRODUCED AND DIRECTED
BY MICHAEL POWELL AND EMERIC PRESSBURGER (RANK-UNIVERSAL)

EDMUND GWENN, NATALIE WOOD, JOHN PAYNE
IN "MIRACLE ON 34th STREET" DIRECTED BY
GEORGE SEATON (20th CENTURY-FOX)

ALF KJELLIN
IN "TORMENT"
(OXFORD)

ALEC GUINNESS IN
'GREAT EXPECTATIONS'
(UNIVERSAL)

DEREK BOND, AUBREY WOODS
IN "NICHOLAS NICKLEBY"
(J. ARTHUR RANK)

EDWARD ARNOLD, MARY PHILIPS, WILLIAM HOLDEN,
JOAN CAULFIELD, BILLY DE WOLFE IN
"DEAR RUTH" (PARAMOUNT)

JOHN MILLS, FINLAY CURRIE Above: JEAN
SIMMONS, MARTITA HUNT, ANTHONY WAGER
IN "GREAT EXPECTATIONS" (UNIVERSAL)

DOUGLAS FAIRBANKS, JR.
IN "SINBAD THE SAILOR"
(RKO)

VITTORIO DE SICA'S "SHOE SHINE"
Above: GAR MOORE, ALDO FABRIZI IN
"TO LIVE IN PEACE" (ITALIAN FILMS)

SPENCER TRACY, KATHARINE HEPBURN
IN "THE SEA OF GRASS"
(M-G-M)

ROBERT NEWTON, JAMES MASON, ELWYN BROOK-JONES, F. J. McCORMICK
IN "ODD MAN OUT" (UNIVERSAL)

PAULETTE GODDARD, GARY COOPER
IN "UNCONQUERED" PRODUCER-DIRECTOR,
CECIL B. DeMILLE (PARAMOUNT)

DENNIS MORGAN, KRISTEN MORGAN
IN "MY WILD IRISH ROSE"
(WARNER BROS.)

ROSALIND RUSSELL, MICHAEL REDGRAVE, KATINA
PAXINOU IN "MOURNING BECOMES ELECTRA"
DIRECTED BY DUDLEY NICHOLS (RKO)

LEE J. COBB, JEAN PETERS, CESAR ROMERO,
TYRONE POWER IN "CAPTAIN FROM CASTILE"
(20th CENTURY-FOX)

ROBERT NEWTON, CELIA JOHNSON
IN "THIS HAPPY BREED" (UNIVERSAL)

SAM LEVENE, JAMES DOBSON
IN "BOOMERANG" (20th CENTURY-FOX)

GENE TIERNEY, WHITFORD KANE
IN "THE GHOST AND MRS. MUIR"
(20th CENTURY-FOX)

KEITH ANDES, LEX BARKER, JAMES ARNESS, JOSEPH
COTTEN, LORETTA YOUNG Above: ETHEL BARRYMORE,
JOSEPH COTTEN, LORETTA YOUNG IN "THE FARMER'S
DAUGHTER" (RKO)

LANA TURNER, RICHARD HART, VAN HEFLIN, GIGI
PERREAU IN "GREEN DOLPHIN STREET"
(M-G-M)

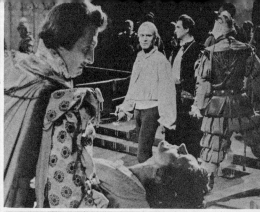

HAMLET

By William Shakespeare; Producer-Director, Laurence Olivier; Music by William Walton; A. J. Arthur Rank Production released by Universal-International.

CAST

Hamlet	Laurence Olivier
The Queen	Eileen Herlie
The King	Basil Sydney
Ophelia	Jean Simmons
Polonius	Felix Aylmer
Horatio	Norman Wooland
Laertes	Terence Morgan
Gravedigger	Stanley Holloway
Osric	Peter Cushing
Bernardo	Esmond Knight
Marcellus	Anthony Quayle
First Player	Harcourt Williams
Francisco	John Laurie

LAURENCE OLIVIER, BASIL SYDNEY, EILEEN HERLIE, JEAN SIMMONS
Top: LAURENCE OLIVIER, JEAN SIMMONS Top center: LAURENCE OLIVIER
Center: EILEEN HERLIE, LAURENCE OLIVIER

SCENES FROM "HAMLET" (UNIVERSAL)

JEAN SIMMONS   EILEEN HERLIE

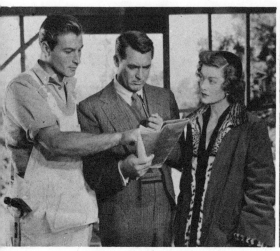

LEX BARKER, CARY GRANT, MYRNA LOY
IN "MR. BLANDINGS BUILDS HIS DREAM HOUSE"
(SELZNICK)

"LOUISIANA STORY"
PRODUCED AND DIRECTED BY
ROBERT FLAHERTY

MARIA MICHI, GAR MOORE
IN ROBERTO ROSSELLINI'S
"PAISAN"

CHARLES BOYER, INGRID BERGMAN
IN "ARCH OF TRIUMPH"
(UNITED ARTISTS)

WALTER HUSTON, HUMPHREY BOGART, TIM HOLT
IN "THE TREASURE OF THE SIERRA MADRE"
DIRECTED BY JOHN HUSTON (WARNER BROS.)

ESTHER WILLIAMS, PETER LAWFORD
IN "ON AN ISLAND WITH YOU"
(M-G-M)

1948 Fresh from his success with "Henry V," Laurence Olivier again produced, directed and acted in a Shakespearean film. This time he chose "Hamlet," and it was voted the best film of the year by the Academy. The New York Film Critics chose "The Treasure of the Sierra Madre" for their citation. Both, however, acclaimed Olivier's performance as the best among the males. Academy "Oscars" also went to Jane Wyman for "Johnny Belinda," Claire Trevor for "Key Largo" and Walter Huston for "The Treasure of the Sierra Madre." Other exceptional films were "The Snake Pit," "The Search," "Easter Parade," "The Naked City" and "Sitting Pretty." David W. Griffith, who perhaps contributed more than any one man to the development and improvement of motion pictures, died in Hollywood, July 27, 1948, a forgotten man. Other deaths were Warren William, Dame May Whitty, Carole Landis and King Baggot. Important imports included "Red Shoes" from England, Roberto Rossellini's "Paisan" from Italy, and from France, Jean Cocteau's "The Eternal Return" and "Beauty and the Beast." Jean Marais, Paris film idol, starred in the latter two. Broadway successes to reach the screen included William Saroyan's prize play, "The Time of Your Life," "I Remember Mama," "All My Sons," "Command Decision," "State of the Union," and a re-make of "One Sunday Afternoon." New faces were Montgomery Clift, Beatrice Pearson and Barbara Bel Geddes.

JUNE HAVER, LON McCALLISTER
IN "SUMMER LIGHTNING"
(20th CENTURY-FOX)

JANE WYMAN, CHARLES BICKFORD, LEW
AYRES IN "JOHNNY BELINDA"
(WARNER BROS.)

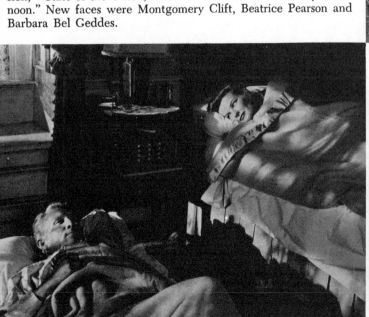

DEANNA DURBIN, DICK HAYMES
IN "UP IN CENTRAL PARK"
(UNIVERSAL)

SPENCER TRACY, KATHARINE HEPBURN
IN "STATE OF THE UNION" PRODUCED
AND DIRECTED BY FRANK CAPRA (M-G-M)

LOUIS JOURDAN, JOAN FONTAINE
IN "LETTER FROM AN UNKNOWN WOMAN"
(UNIVERSAL)

WALTER REED

GAIL PAGE

MICHAEL REDGRAVE

MICHELE MORGAN

GEORGE SANDERS

JANE POWELL

VINCENT PRICE

RITA HAYWORTH, GLENN FORD
IN "THE LOVES OF CARMEN"
(COLUMBIA)

MONTGOMERY CLIFT, IVAN JANDL, WENDELL COREY
IN "THE SEARCH" DIRECTED BY
FRED ZINNEMANN (M-G-M)

INGRID BERGMAN
IN "JOAN OF ARC"
(RKO)

ROCK HUDSON, ROBERT STACK, EDMOND O'BRIEN
IN "FIGHTER SQUADRON"
(WARNER BROS.)

CLIFTON WEBB
IN "SITTING PRETTY"
(20th CENTURY-FOX)

RICHARD DERR, INGRID BERGMAN, RAY TEAL
IN "JOAN OF ARC" DIRECTED BY
VICTOR FLEMING (RKO)

GAR MOORE

ANN MILLER

LARRY PARKS

ANTHONY QUINN

TURHAN BEY

GAIL PATRICK

HAL HACKETT

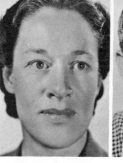

| DENNIS O'KEEFE | ANNE REVERE | GEORGE MURPHY | JUNE ALLYSON | WALTER PIDGEON | JANET BLAIR | ROBERT RYAN |

MADELEINE SOLOGNE, JEAN MARAIS
IN "THE ETERNAL RETURN"
(DISCINA)

JEAN ARTHUR, JOHN LUND, MARLENE DIETRICH
IN "A FOREIGN AFFAIR" DIRECTED BY
BILLY WILDER (PARAMOUNT)

JEAN MARAIS IN JEAN COCTEAU'S
"BEAUTY AND THE BEAST"
(LOPERT)

JAMES CAGNEY, JEANNE CAGNEY, WAYNE MORRIS
IN "THE TIME OF YOUR LIFE"
DIRECTED BY H. C. POTTER (UNITED ARTISTS)

DOROTHY MALONE, DENNIS MORGAN
IN "ONE SUNDAY AFTERNOON"
(WARNER BROS.)

PHILIP DORN, BARBARA BEL GEDDES, STEVEN BROWN,
IRENE DUNNE, PEGGY McINTIRE, JUNE HEDIN IN
"I REMEMBER MAMA" (RKO)

| JACK OAKIE | MARY ASTOR | RICHARD DERR | ENID MARKEY | LOUIS HAYWARD | ELIZABETH PATTERSON | LLOYD NOLAN |

JOAN FONTAINE, BING CROSBY, BUTTONS
IN "THE EMPEROR WALTZ"
(PARAMOUNT)

FRED ASTAIRE, JUDY GARLAND
IN "EASTER PARADE" DIRECTED
BY CHARLES WALTERS (M-G-M)

LORETTA YOUNG, DOUGLAS DICK
IN "THE ACCUSED"
(PARAMOUNT)

TONY MARTIN, YVONNE DE CARLO, HUGO
HAAS, DOUGLAS DICK IN "CASBAH"
(UNIVERSAL)

BARBARA STANWYCK IN
"SORRY WRONG NUMBER"
(PARAMOUNT)

MADY CHRISTIANS, HOWARD DUFF, BURT LANCASTER,
LOUISA HORTON, EDWARD G. ROBINSON
IN "ALL MY SONS" (UNIVERSAL)

JOHN GARFIELD, BEATRICE PEARSON
IN "FORCE OF EVIL"
(M-G-M)

JOHN IRELAND, MONTGOMERY CLIFT,
JOANNE DRU IN "RED RIVER"
(UNITED ARTISTS)

DAVID NIVEN, FARLEY GRANGER
IN "ENCHANTMENT"
(RKO)

CLAIRE TREVOR
IN "KEY LARGO"
(WARNER BROS.)

ROBERT STACK
IN "FIGHTER SQUADRON"
(WARNER BROS.)

ROBERT STACK, ILKA CHASE, JOHN LUND
IN "MISS TATLOCK'S MILLIONS"
(PARAMOUNT)

RONALD COLMAN AS OTHELLO IN "A DOUBLE LIFE" (UNIVERSAL)

JENNIFER JONES IN "PORTRAIT OF JENNIE" (SELZNICK)

BING CROSBY IN "THE EMPEROR WALTZ" (PARAMOUNT)

BARBARA BEL GEDDES IN "I REMEMBER MAMA" (RKO)

DOUGLAS DICK IN "THE ACCUSED" (PARAMOUNT)

JANE RUSSELL IN "PALE FACE" (PARAMOUNT)

JOHN HODIAK, BRIAN DONLEVY, WALTER PIDGEON, CLARK GABLE, VAN JOHNSON IN "COMMAND DECISION" (M-G-M)

ROBERT HELPMANN, MOIRA SHEARER, LEONIDE MASSINE IN "RED SHOES" (J. ARTHUR RANK)

GLENN LANGAN, LEO GENN, FRANK CONROY, HOWARD FREEMAN, OLIVIA DE HAVILLAND IN "THE SNAKE PIT" (20th CENTURY-FOX)

OLIVIA DE HAVILLAND IN "THE SNAKE PIT" DIRECTED BY ANATOLE LITVAK (20th CENTURY-FOX)

CONSTANCE COLLIER, JOAN CHANDLER, DOUGLAS DICK, CEDRIC HARDWICKE, JOHN DALL, FARLEY GRANGER, JAMES STEWART IN "ROPE" (WARNER BROS.)

PAULETTE GODDARD, DIANA WYNYARD, HUGH WILLIAMS IN "AN IDEAL HUSBAND" (20th CENTURY-FOX)

WILLIAM BENDIX, DICK FOOTE IN "STREETS OF LAREDO" (PARAMOUNT)

1948

RAY MILLAND, CHARLES LAUGHTON IN "THE BIG CLOCK" (PARAMOUNT)

DOUGLAS FAIRBANKS, JR., BETTY GRABLE IN "THAT LADY IN ERMINE" (20th CENTURY-FOX)

BARRY FITZGERALD, DON TAYLOR, HOWARD DUFF,
DOROTHY HART IN "THE NAKED CITY"
(UNIVERSAL)

RONALD COLMAN, SHELLEY WINTERS
IN "A DOUBLE LIFE" DIRECTED BY GEORGE CUKOR
(UNIVERSAL)

GREG McCLURE, GEORGE MONTGOMERY,
DOROTHY LAMOUR IN "LULU BELLE"
(COLUMBIA)

LANA TURNER

BURT LANCASTER

HELEN HAYES , KIERON MOORE, VIVIEN LEIGH
IN "ANNA KARENINA"
(20th CENTURY-FOX)

RODDY McDOWALL, SUE
ENGLAND IN "KIDNAPPED"
(MONOGRAM)

NATALIE WOOD

LOTTE LEHMANN, KARIN BOOTH, MARGARET O'BRIEN
GEORGE MURPHY, DANNY THOMAS,
ROBERT PRESTON IN "BIG CITY" (M-G-M)

H. B. WARNER, PATRICIA MORISON, JON HALL
IN "THE PRINCE OF THIEVES"
(COLUMBIA)

EDMUND GWENN, WILLIAM HOLDEN, JEANNE CRAIN
IN "APARTMENT FOR PEGGY"
(20th CENTURY-FOX)

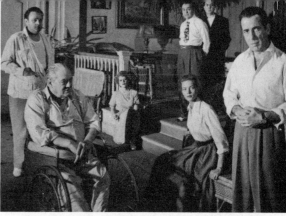

DAN SEYMOUR, LIONEL BARRYMORE, CLAIRE TREVOR,
EDWARD G. ROBINSON, THOMAS GOMEZ, LAUREN BACALL,
HUMPHREY BOGART IN "KEY LARGO" (WARNER BROS.)

LORETTA YOUNG

BOB HOPE

WALTER SLEZAK, GENE KELLY, GLADYS COOPER,
JUDY GARLAND IN "THE PIRATE"
(M-G-M)

GREER GARSON IN
"JULIA MISBEHAVES" (M-G-M)

1948

ANN BLYTH, EDMOND O'BRIEN, FREDRIC MARCH,
FLORENCE ELDRIDGE IN "ANOTHER PART
OF THE FOREST" (UNIVERSAL)

ETHEL WATERS, JEANNE CRAIN, WILLIAM LUNDIGAN
IN "PINKY"
DIRECTED BY ELIA KAZAN (20th CENTURY-FOX)

BEATRICE PEARSON, RICHARD HYLTON, MEL FERRER
IN "LOST BOUNDARIES"
DIRECTED BY ALFRED L. WERKER (FILM CLASSICS)

DONALD HOUSTON, JEAN SIMMONS
IN "BLUE LAGOON"
(J. ARTHUR RANK—UNIVERSAL)

JEFF COREY, JAMES EDWARDS, STEVE BRODIE, DOUGLAS DICK
IN "HOME OF THE BRAVE" A STANLEY KRAMER
PRODUCTION DIRECTED BY MARK ROBSON (UNITED ARTISTS)

KEEFE BRASSELLE, SALLY FORREST
IN "NOT WANTED" DIRECTED
BY ELMER CLIFTON (FILM CLASSICS)

ANN RUTHERFORD, ERROL FLYNN IN
"ADVENTURES OF DON JUAN" DIRECTED BY
VINCENT SHERMAN (WARNER BROS.)

DONALD THOMPSON
IN "THE QUIET ONE"
(FILM DOCUMENTS)

MICKEY KNOX, JOSHUA SHELLEY, TONY CURTIS, RICHARD JAECKEL,
PETER FERNANDEZ, AL RAMSEN IN "CITY ACROSS THE RIVER"
PRODUCED AND DIRECTED BY MAXWELL SHANE (UNIVERSAL)

ARTHUR KENNEDY, KIRK DOUGLAS
IN "CHAMPION" DIRECTED
BY MARK ROBSON (UNITED ARTISTS)

ANNE SEYMOUR, JOHN DEREK, BRODERICK CRAWFORD, JOHN IRELAND
IN "ALL THE KING'S MEN" WRITTEN
AND DIRECTED BY ROBERT ROSSEN (COLUMBIA)

BRODERICK CRAWFORD, WALTER BURKE, RALPH
DUMKE, WILL WRIGHT, JOHN IRELAND, MERCEDES
McCAMBRIDGE IN "ALL THE KING'S MEN"

JUNE HAVER, RAY BOLGER IN
"LOOK FOR THE SILVER LINING"
(WARNER BROS.)

1949 The year was not a banner one with regard to the quality of the pictures turned out in Hollywood, nor was it good from a box-office viewpoint. Among the pictures worth mentioning, four of them, "Pinky," "Lost Boundaries," "Home of the Brave" and "Intruder in the Dust," dealt with the controversial race question; and two of them, "Champion" and "The Set-up," started a cycle of prize-fight pictures. Other stand-out pictures were "The Heiress," "The Window," "The Quiet One" and "Adam's Rib." Both the New York Film Critics and the Motion Picture Academy voted "All the King's Men" the best picture of 1949. Both also picked Broderick Crawford as the best actor for his performance in that film, and Olivia de Havilland as the best actress for hers in "The Heiress." The New York Film Critics also chose Carol Reed as the best director for "The Fallen Idol," and the Italian film "The Bicycle Thief" as the best foreign language picture. The year also saw the reunion of Fred Astaire and Ginger Rogers as a dancing team in "The Barkleys of Broadway"; the debut of a new comic team, Dean Martin and Jerry Lewis, in "My Friend Irma"; other new faces to attract attention were Mario Lanza, Tony Curtis, Jeff Chandler, Sally Forrest and Keefe Brasselle; and the retirement of Johnny Weissmuller in the role of Tarzan and his replacement by Lex Barker. Walt Disney contributed animated cartoon features of "Cinderella" and "Ichabod and Mr. Toad." Re-makes were made of "A Connecticut Yankee in King Arthur's Court" and "Little Women." Among the veterans who were still starring in films were Clark Gable, Joan Crawford, Claudette Colbert, Barbara Stanwyck, Spencer Tracy, James Cagney and Robert Montgomery. Death took its toll of four outstanding figures of filmdom: actors Richard Dix and Wallace Beery, and directors Sam Wood and Victor Fleming.

KATHRYN GRAYSON, MARIO LANZA
IN "THAT MIDNIGHT KISS"
(M-G-M)

PAUL STEWART, BOBBY DRISCOLL
IN "THE WINDOW"
DIRECTED BY TED TETZLAFF (RKO)

BOBBY DRISCOLL
IN "THE WINDOW"
(RKO)

JEFF CHANDLER, DANA ANDREWS, STEPHEN McNALLY, MARTA
TOREN IN "SWORD IN THE DESERT"
DIRECTED BY GEORGE SHERMAN (UNIVERSAL)

DANNY KAYE

MARSHA HUNT

TONY CURTIS

JOAN CAULFIELD

SONNY TUFTS

MARJORIE MAIN

VAN HEFLIN

PAUL DOUGLAS IN
"EVERYBODY DOES IT"
(20th CENTURY-FOX)

JOAN CRAWFORD
IN "FLAMINGO ROAD"
(WARNER BROS.)

RED SKELTON
IN "NEPTUNE'S
DAUGHTER" (M-G-M)

MARCIA VAN DYKE
IN "IN THE GOOD OLD
SUMMERTIME" (M-G-M)

GINGER ROGERS AND FRED ASTAIRE REUNITED AS A
DANCE TEAM IN "THE BARKLEYS OF BROADWAY"
DIRECTED BY CHARLES WALTERS (M-G-M)

MARGARET O'BRIEN (BETH), ELIZABETH TAYLOR (AMY), JUNE ALLYSON (JO), JANET LEIGH (MEG),
ELIZABETH PATTERSON (HANNAH) IN "LITTLE WOMEN"
PRODUCED AND DIRECTED BY MERVYN LeROY (M-G-M)

RICHARD HART

BEATRICE PEARSON

ROSS HUNTER

ANGELA LANSBURY

RICHARD HYLTON

MARY YOUNG

PAUL KELLY

| RAY MILLAND | BETTY FIELD | GUY MADISON | ANN SHERIDAN | KIRK DOUGLAS | BETTY HUTTON | JAMES MASON |

GREGORY PECK IN
"THE GREAT SINNER"
(M-G-M)

MILTON BERLE IN
"ALWAYS LEAVE THEM LAUGHING"
(WARNER BROS.)

MONTGOMERY CLIFT
IN "THE HEIRESS"
(PARAMOUNT)

LEON ERROL, JOE KIRKWOOD, JR. IN
"JOE PALOOKA IN THE BIG FIGHT" (MONOGRAM)

OLIVIA DE HAVILLAND, MONTGOMERY CLIFT, RALPH RICHARDSON
IN "THE HEIRESS" PRODUCED AND
DIRECTED BY WILLIAM WYLER (PARAMOUNT)

| LOU COSTELLO | BUD ABBOTT | GLENN LANGAN | BRENDA JOYCE | SYDNEY GREENSTREET | JOAN LESLIE | JOHN ARCHER |

1949

BETTE DAVIS

ALICE PEARCE, FRANK SINATRA, BETTY GARRETT, GENE KELLY, ANN MILLER, JULES MUNSHIN IN "ON THE TOWN" (M-G-M)

JOAN CRAWFORD, DAVID BRIAN, SYDNEY GREENSTREET IN "FLAMINGO ROAD" (WARNER BROS.)

DON ALVARADO, RAMON NOVARRO, JANE GREER, ROBERT MITCHUM IN "THE BIG STEAL" (RKO)

MEG RANDALL, RICHARD LONG, ROSEMARY DeCAMP, WILLIAM BENDIX, LANNY RESS IN "THE LIFE OF RILEY" (UNIVERSAL)

RUSS TAMBLYN IN "THE KID FROM CLEVELAND" (REPUBLIC)

SPENCER TRACY, JUDY HOLLIDAY, KATHARINE HEPBURN IN "ADAM'S RIB" DIRECTED BY GEORGE CUKOR (M-G-M)

JOHN LUND IN "RIDE OF VENGEANCE" (PARAMOUNT)

JAMES STEWART IN "THE STRATTON STORY" (M-G-M)

VAN JOHNSON IN "BATTLEGROUND" (M-G-M)

FRANK SINATRA IN "THE KISSING BANDIT" (M-G-M)

ROBERT RYAN IN "THE SET-UP" (RKO)

RICHARD TODD IN "THE HASTY HEART" (WARNER BROS.)

HUGH DEMPSTER, RICHARD GREENE, JOHN SUTTON, GEORGE SANDERS, MADELEINE CARROLL IN "THE FAN" (20th CENTURY-FOX)

MARIE WILSON, DIANA LYNN, DEAN MARTIN, JERRY LEWIS IN "MY FRIEND IRMA" (PARAMOUNT)

1949

RICHARD JAECKEL, JOHN WAYNE, FORREST TUCKER, JOHN AGAR, ARTHUR FRANZ IN "SANDS OF IWO JIMA" (REPUBLIC)

MICHELE MORGAN, RALPH RICHARDSON, DENIS O'DEA
BOBBY HENREY, JACK HAWKINS, BERNARD LEE
IN "THE FALLEN IDOL" (SELZNICK)

MASSIMO GIROTTI
IN "THE IRON CROWN"
(MINERVA)

LINDA DARNELL, ANN SOTHERN, JEANNE CRAIN
IN "A LETTER TO THREE WIVES" WRITTEN AND
DIRECTED BY JOSEPH L. MANKIEWICZ (20th CENTURY-FOX)

HUGH MARLOWE, CELESTE HOLM, LORETTA YOUNG
IN "COME TO THE STABLE"
(20th CENTURY-FOX)

ENZO STAIOLA, LAMBERTO MAGGIORANI
IN "THE BICYCLE THIEF"
(MAYER-BURSTYN)

HUMPHREY BOGART, JOHN DEREK, ALLENE ROBERTS
IN "KNOCK ON ANY DOOR"
(COLUMBIA)

AUDIE MURPHY IN HIS
FIRST STARRING ROLE IN
"BAD BOY" (ALLIED ARTISTS)

FARLEY GRANGER
IN "ROSEANNA McCOY"
(RKO)

GEORGE "GABBY" HAYES
IN "EL PASO"
(PARAMOUNT)

SMILEY BURNETT IN
"BANDITS OF EL DORADO"
(COLUMBIA)

GARY MERRILL, GREGORY PECK, DEAN JAGGER
IN "TWELVE O'CLOCK HIGH"
(20th CENTURY-FOX)

DISNEY'S "ICHABOD AND MR. TOAD" AND
Above: "CINDERELLA" (RKO)

JENNIFER JONES, LOUIS JOURDAN, VAN HEFLIN
IN "MADAME BOVARY"
(M-G-M)

194   1949

CHARLTON HESTON AS MARK ANTONY IN "JULIUS CAESAR" (AVON)

TYRONE POWER IN "PRINCE OF FOXES" (20th CENTURY-FOX)

VICTOR MATURE

DOUGLAS FAIRBANKS, JR. IN "THE FIGHTING O'FLYNN" (UNIVERSAL)

WILLIAM BENDIX, BING CROSBY, HENRY WILCOXON IN "A CONNECTICUT YANKEE" (PARAMOUNT)

ELIZABETH PATTERSON, ELZIE EMMANUEL, CLAUDE JARMAN, JR., IN "INTRUDER IN THE DUST" (M-G-M)

BURT LANCASTER, CORINNE CALVET, CLAUDE RAINS, PAUL HENREID IN "ROPE OF SAND" (PARAMOUNT)

ERROL FLYNN, GREER GARSON, WALTER PIDGEON IN "THAT FORSYTHE WOMAN" (M-G-M)

LEX BARKER AS TARZAN (RKO)

1949

EDITH EVANS IN "THE WOMAN OF DOLWYN" (LOPERT)

ROBERT MONTGOMERY, JANE COWL IN "ONCE MORE, MY DARLING" (UNIVERSAL)

JOSE FERRER
AS "CYRANO DE BERGERAC"
(UNITED ARTISTS)

WILLIAM PRINCE, MALA POWERS, JOSE FERRER
IN "CYRANO DE BERGERAC" DIRECTED
BY MICHAEL GORDON (UNITED ARTISTS)

ORSON WELLES
AS "MACBETH"
(REPUBLIC)

JOHN DEREK IN
"ROGUES OF SHERWOOD FOREST"
(COLUMBIA)

ORSON WELLES AS MACBETH, ERSKINE SANFORD AS DUNCAN,
RODDY McDOWALL AS MALCOLM IN "MACBETH"
PRODUCED AND DIRECTED BY ORSON WELLES (REPUBLIC)

SILVANA MANGANO
IN "BITTER RICE"
(I.F.E.)

ALAN HALE, JOHN DEREK, BILLY BEVAN, BILLY HOUSE
IN "ROGUES OF SHERWOOD FOREST"
(COLUMBIA)

DEAN STOCKWELL, ERROL FLYNN
IN "KIM" DIRECTED BY
VICTOR SAVILLE (M-G-M)

GREER GARSON, WILLIAM FOX, WALTER PIDGEON
IN "THE MINIVER STORY"
DIRECTED BY H. C. POTTER (M-G-M)

SPENCER TRACY, ELIZABETH TAYLOR
IN "FATHER OF THE BRIDE" DIRECTED
BY VINCENTE MINNELLI (M-G-M)

BETTE DAVIS, GARY MERRILL, ANNE BAXTER, GEORGE SANDERS
IN "ALL ABOUT EVE" WRITTEN AND DIRECTED BY
JOSEPH L. MANKIEWICZ (20th CENTURY-FOX)

JAMES STEWART, CHARLES DRAKE, PEGGY
DOW, JOSEPHINE HULL, WILLIAM LYNN
IN "HARVEY" (UNIVERSAL)

FARLEY GRANGER, ANN BLYTH
IN "OUR VERY OWN" DIRECTED
BY DAVID MILLER (RKO)

1950 From a box-office standpoint, the year was a bad one, and exhibitors all over the country were blaming it on television. No longer could a popular star attract customers unless the picture was a good one. The day of name "draws" was past. People were shopping around and only good pictures were making money. Among the pictures with popular appeal as well as box-office power were Cecil B. DeMille's spectacle "Samson and Delilah," "The Third Man," "Sunset Boulevard" which brought Gloria Swanson into the limelight again, "All About Eve," "King Solomon's Mines" and "The Asphalt Jungle" in which Marilyn Monroe received notice in a small role. Stanley Kramer, rising young independent producer, was responsible for two outstanding films, the classic "Cyrano de Bergerac" with Jose Ferrer, and "The Men" which brought Marlon Brando, a rising young stage actor, to the attention of motion picture audiences. Mr. Ferrer won an Academy Award for his performance. Judy Holliday also won an "Oscar" for repeating her stage performance of Billie Dawn in the film "Born Yesterday." Both the Academy and the New York Film Critics voted "All About Eve," written and directed by Joseph L. Mankiewicz, the best picture of the year. The best foreign films were "Bitter Rice," "Devil in the Flesh" and "Kind Hearts and Coronets." Death took its toll of Al Jolson, Maurice Costello, matinee idol of the early pioneer days, Sid Grauman, Hollywood showman, director Rex Ingram, and character players Walter Huston, Alan Hale, Sara Allgood and Emil Jannings.

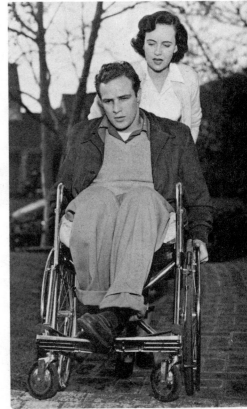

MARLON BRANDO, TERESA WRIGHT
IN "THE MEN" DIRECTED BY
FRED ZINNEMANN (UNITED ARTISTS)

SAM JAFFEE, JEAN HAGEN, STERLING HAYDEN
IN "THE ASPHALT JUNGLE" DIRECTED
BY JOHN HUSTON (M-G-M)

FRANCIS, DONALD O'CONNOR
IN "FRANCIS" DIRECTED
BY ARTHUR LUBIN (UNIVERSAL)

KIRK DOUGLAS, GERTRUDE LAWRENCE, JANE WYMAN,
ARTHUR KENNEDY IN "THE GLASS MENAGERIE"
DIRECTED BY IRVING RAPPER (WARNER BROS.)

ROBERT CUMMINGS   MONTGOMERY CLIFT   JUDITH ANDERSON   SCOTT BRADY   YVONNE DE CARLO   JOHN AGAR   WILLIAM BENDI

HEDY LAMARR, VICTOR MATURE   HENRY WILCOXON, ANGELA LANSBURY, VICTOR MATURE   VICTOR MATURE
Above: (L) HENRY WILCOXON, (C) VICTOR MATURE
SCENES FROM "SAMSON AND DELILAH" PRODUCED AND DIRECTED BY CECIL B. DeMILLE (PARAMOUNT)

FARLEY GRANGER, ADELE JERGENS, DANA ANDREWS
IN "EDGE OF DOOM"
DIRECTED BY MARK ROBSON (RKO)

RICHARD CARLSON, DEBORAH KERR, STEWART GRANGER
IN "KING SOLOMON'S MINES" DIRECTED BY
COMPTON BENNETT AND ANDREW MARTON (M-G-M)

VALLI, JOSEPH COTTEN, TREVOR HOWARD
IN "THE THIRD MAN"
PRODUCER-DIRECTOR, CAROL REED (SELZNICK)

JACK CARSON   CARLETON CARPENTER   HELMUT DANTINE   KEEFE BRASSELLE   DAN DURYEA   ROBERT LOWERY   EDDIE ALBERT

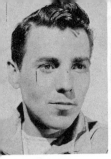
WILLIAM EYTHE

HELEN HAYES

DANA ANDREWS

JOAN BENNETT

LEX BARKER

PIER ANGELI

CHARLES LAUGHTON

GLORIA SWANSON, WILLIAM HOLDEN

ERICH VON STROHEIM, GLORIA SWANSON
Above: ANNA Q. NILSSON, H. B. WARNER, GLORIA SWANSON
SCENES FROM "SUNSET BOULEVARD" DIRECTED BY BILLY WILDER (PARAMOUNT)

DEBRA PAGET, JEFF CHANDLER, JAMES STEWART
IN "BROKEN ARROW" DIRECTED BY
DELMER DAVES (20th CENTURY-FOX)

CECILE AUBRY, TYRONE POWER, JACK HAWKINS
IN "THE BLACK ROSE" DIRECTED BY
HENRY HATHAWAY (20th CENTURY-FOX)

GLORIA SWANSON
IN "SUNSET BOULEVARD"
(PARAMOUNT)

MACDONALD CAREY

ANN BLYTH

GOWER CHAMPION

MARGE CHAMPION

RICHARD CONTE

JOHN CARROLL

RAYMOND BURR

RICARDO MONTALBAN
IN "RIGHT CROSS"
(M-G-M)

JOAN CAULFIELD
IN "THE PETTY GIRL"
(COLUMBIA)

DENISE DARCEL, LEX BARKER IN
"TARZAN AND THE SLAVE GIRL"
(RKO)

GERTRUDE LAWRENCE
IN "THE GLASS MENAGERIE"
(WARNER BROS.)

MARIO VITALE
IN "STROMBOLI"
(RKO)

JIMMY CONLIN, HAROLD LLOYD
IN "MAD WEDNESDAY" WRITTEN AND
DIRECTED BY PRESTON STURGES (RKO)

HAROLD LLOYD
IN "MAD WEDNESDAY"
(RKO)

WALTER HUSTON, BARBARA STANWYCK, WENDELL COREY
IN "THE FURIES" DIRECTED BY ANTHONY MANN
(PARAMOUNT)

ROBERT NEWTON, BOBBY DRISCOLL
IN "TREASURE ISLAND"
(RKO)

JON HALL
IN "HURRICANE ISLAND"
(COLUMBIA)

SALLY FORREST IN
"THE YOUNG LOVERS"
(EAGLE LION)

JEAN MARAIS
IN "ORPHEUS"
(PAULVE)

MARJORIE MAIN, PERCY KILBRIDE
IN "MA AND PA KETTLE GO TO TOWN"
(UNIVERSAL)

SPENCER TRACY
1950

DORIS DAY, LAUREN BACALL, KIRK DOUGLAS
IN "YOUNG MAN WITH A HORN"
DIRECTED BY MICHAEL CURTIZ (WARNER BROS.)

JOHN BARRYMORE, JR., JOHN ARCHER
IN "HIGH LONESOME"
(EAGLE LION)

MYRNA LOY, CLIFTON WEBB, JEANNE CRAIN, BENNIE
BARTLETT IN "CHEAPER BY THE DOZEN" DIRECTED
BY WALTER LANG (20th CENTURY-FOX)

BARRY JONES
IN "SEVEN DAYS TO NOON"
(MAYLUX)

INGRID BERGMAN, MARIO VITALE
IN "STROMBOLI" WRITTEN, PRODUCED AND
DIRECTED BY ROBERTO ROSSELLINI (RKO)

JOHN AGAR, SUZANNE DALBERT, FRANK LOVEJOY
IN "BREAKTHROUGH"
(WARNER BROS.)

HOWARD KEEL, BETTY HUTTON IN
"ANNIE GET YOUR GUN"
DIRECTED BY GEORGE SIDNEY (M-G-M)

JUDY HOLLIDAY, BRODERICK CRAWFORD, WILLIAM HOLDEN
IN "BORN YESTERDAY"
DIRECTED BY GEORGE CUKOR (COLUMBIA)

ANN HARDING, LOUIS CALHERN
IN "THE MAGNIFICENT YANKEE"
DIRECTED BY JOHN STURGES (M-G-M)

NICK CRAVAT, VIRGINIA MAYO, ROBERT DOUGLAS
BURT LANCASTER IN "THE FLAME AND THE
ARROW" (WARNER BROS.)

VICTOR MATURE, BETTY GRABLE, PHIL HARRIS
IN "WABASH AVENUE" DIRECTED BY
HENRY KOSTER (20th CENTURY-FOX)

VERA-ELLEN, RED SKELTON, FRED ASTAIRE
IN "THREE LITTLE WORDS"
DIRECTED BY RICHARD THORPE (M-G-M)

WENDELL COREY, JOAN CRAWFORD
IN "HARRIET CRAIG"
DIRECTED BY VINCENT SHERMAN (COLUMBIA)

DENNIS PRICE, ALEC GUINNESS
IN "KIND HEARTS AND CORONETS"
(J. ARTHUR RANK)

QUEENIE SMITH, JIMMY DURANTE
IN "THE GREAT RUPERT"
(EAGLE LION)

SESSUE HAYAKAWA, CLAUDETTE COLBERT
IN "THREE CAME HOME" DIRECTED BY
JEAN NEGULESCO (20th CENTURY-FOX)

TONY CURTIS, RICHARD LONG, SCOTT BRADY, DEWEY
MARTIN IN "KANSAS RAIDERS"
(UNIVERSAL)

WENDELL COREY, MARGARET SULLAVAN, NATALIE
WOOD IN "NO SAD SONGS FOR ME" DIRECTED
BY RUDOLPH MATÉ (COLUMBIA)

GENE NELSON, DORIS DAY, JAMES CAGNEY, VIRGINIA
MAYO, GORDON MacRAE IN "THE WEST POINT STORY"
DIRECTED BY ROY DEL RUTH (WARNER BROS.)

MARGARET LEIGHTON, NOEL COWARD
IN "THE ASTONISHED HEART"
(J. ARTHUR RANK—UNIVERSAL)

ALLAN NIXON IN
"PREHISTORIC WOMEN"
(EAGLE LION)

MARILYN MONROE IN
"THE ASPHALT JUNGLE"
DIRECTOR, JOHN HUSTON (M-G-M)

WILLARD PARKER
IN "BODYHOLD"
(COLUMBIA)

GREG SHERWOOD, DEWEY MARTIN
IN "THE GOLDEN GLOVES STORY"
(EAGLE LION)

CELESTE HOLM, RONALD COLMAN
IN "CHAMPAGNE FOR CAESAR" DIRECTED
BY RICHARD WHORF (UNITED ARTISTS)

ZERO MOSTEL, JACK PALANCE, RICHARD WIDMARK
IN "PANIC IN THE STREETS" DIRECTED BY
ELIA KAZAN (20th CENTURY-FOX)

GERARD PHILIPE, MICHELINE PRESLE
IN "DEVIL IN THE FLESH"
(A.F.E.)

MARLON BRANDO, KIM HUNTER

MARLON BRANDO, VIVIEN LEIGH
SCENES FROM "A STREETCAR NAMED DESIRE" DIRECTED BY ELIA KAZAN (WARNER BROS.)

VIVIEN LEIGH

ELIZABETH TAYLOR, MONTGOMERY CLIFT Above:
MONTGOMERY CLIFT, RAYMOND BURR IN "A PLACE IN THE
SUN" PRODUCER-DIRECTOR GEORGE STEVENS (PARAMOUNT)

LEO GENN, MARINA BERTI, ROBERT TAYLOR
SCENES FROM "QUO VADIS"
DIRECTED BY MERVYN LeROY (M-G-M)

PETER USTINOV, PATRICIA LAFFAN, ROBERT TAYLOR

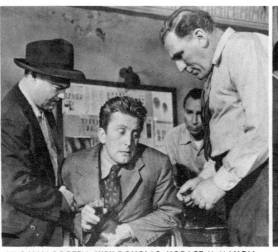

DENIS O'DEA, VIRGINIA MAYO, GREGORY PECK
IN "CAPTAIN HORATIO HORNBLOWER"
DIRECTED BY RAOUL WALSH (WARNER BROS.)

LUIS VAN ROOTEN, KIRK DOUGLAS, HORACE McMAHON,
WILLIAM BENDIX IN "DETECTIVE STORY"
PRODUCER-DIRECTOR, WILLIAM WYLER (PARAMOUNT)

MAURICE EVANS, KEENAN WYNN, ETHEL
BARRYMORE, ANGELA LANSBURY IN "KIND LADY"
DIRECTED BY JOHN STURGES (M-G-M)

JOHNNY SHEFFIELD, ANN TODD
IN "BOMBA AND THE ELEPHANT
STAMPEDE" (MONOGRAM)

KATHARINE HEPBURN, HUMPHREY BOGART
IN "THE AFRICAN QUEEN"
DIRECTED BY JOHN HUSTON (UNITED ARTISTS)

DEBRA PAGET, LOUIS JOURDAN
IN "BIRD OF PARADISE"
(20th CENTURY-FOX)

1951 Television brought chaos and fear into the heart of Hollywood, and at this time the leading motion picture companies forbade any of their contract players to appear in this new intruding medium. Exhibitors were alarmed at the noticeable drop in box-office receipts. Academy Awards went to "An American in Paris," an M-G-M original musical directed by Vincente Minnelli, as the best picture; to George Stevens as best director for "A Place in the Sun," and to Vivien Leigh for her performance in "A Streetcar Named Desire" and Humphrey Bogart for his in "The African Queen." The New York Film Critics voted "A Streetcar Named Desire," directed by Elia Kazan, the best film, Miss Leigh best actress for her performance in same, and Arthur Kennedy the best actor for his in "Bright Victory." Among the other films to receive critical acclaim were "Detective Story," "The African Queen," "A Place in the Sun," "The Great Caruso" and an elaborate re-make of "Quo Vadis." Other stories re-filmed were Edna Ferber's "Show Boat" and Dickens' "Oliver Twist." Walt Disney contributed his version of "Alice in Wonderland." Anthony Dexter, an unknown, starred in the life of Valentino. "The Red Badge of Courage" was a controversial film. Ezio Pinza, of opera fame, made his film debut in "Mr. Imperium," a mediocre film. Rock Hudson, in minor roles, was attracting attention and fans. Death took veterans Warner Baxter, Jack Holt, and Ralph Forbes, also youngsters Robert Walker and Maria Montez, and Robert F. Flaherty, famous director-producer.

ALEC GUINNESS AS FAGIN, JOHN HOWARD
DAVIES AS OLIVER IN "OLIVER TWIST"
(J. ARTHUR RANK—EAGLE LION)

GENE KELLY
IN "AN AMERICAN IN PARIS"
DIRECTED BY VINCENTE MINNELLI (M-G-M)

FARLEY GRANGER, ROBERT WALKER
IN "STRANGERS ON A TRAIN"
DIRECTED BY ALFRED HITCHCOCK (WARNER BROS.)

AUDIE MURPHY
IN "THE RED BADGE OF COURAGE"
DIRECTED BY JOHN HUSTON (M-G-M)

RICHARD BASEHART, PAUL DOUGLAS, BARBARA BEL
GEDDES IN "FOURTEEN HOURS" DIRECTED BY
HENRY HATHAWAY (20th CENTURY-FOX)

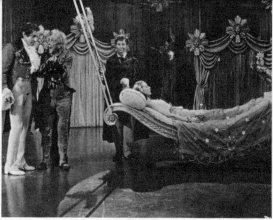

MICHELE MORGAN, HENRI VIDAL
IN "FABIOLA"
(UNITED ARTISTS)

ROBERT ROUNSEVILLE, ROBERT HELPMANN, PAMELA
BROWN, MOIRA SHEARER IN "TALES OF HOFFMAN"
(UNITED ARTISTS)

ALEC GUINNESS, IRENE DUNNE
IN "THE MUDLARK" DIRECTED BY JEAN
NEGULESCO (20th CENTURY-FOX)

MASSIMO GIROTTI
IN "FABIOLA"
(UNITED ARTISTS)

RHONDA FLEMING
IN "LITTLE EGYPT"
(UNIVERSAL)

ROBERT STACK IN
"THE BULLFIGHTER AND
THE LADY" (REPUBLIC)

JEROME COURTLAND
IN "THE BAREFOOT
MAILMAN" (COLUMBIA)

MOIRA SHEARER IN
"TALES OF HOFFMAN"
(UNITED ARTISTS)

ANDREW RAY
IN "THE MUDLARK"
(20th CENTURY-FOX)

CORINNE CALVET, DANNY KAYE
IN "ON THE RIVIERA"
(20th CENTURY-FOX)

LANA TURNER, EZIO PINZA
IN "MR. IMPERIUM"
(M-G-M)

JOHN ERICSON, PIER ANGELI
IN "TERESA"
(M-G-M)

MARILYN MONROE, ALBERT DEKKER
IN "AS YOUNG AS YOU FEEL"
(20th CENTURY-FOX)

ROBERT STACK, GILBERT ROLAND
IN "THE BULLFIGHTER AND THE LADY"
(REPUBLIC)

RADHA, THOMAS BREEN, ADRIENNE CORRI
IN "THE RIVER"
(UNITED ARTISTS)

BOURVIL, JOAN GREENWOOD
IN "MR. PEEK-A-BOO"
(UNITED ARTISTS)

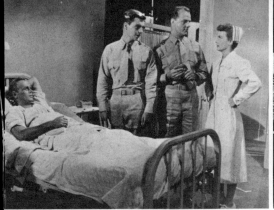

RICHARD WIDMARK, ROBERT WAGNER, KARL
MALDEN, MARION MARSHALL IN "HALLS OF
MONTEZUMA" (20th CENTURY-FOX)

ANTHONY DEXTER AS VALENTINO
IN "VALENTINO" DIRECTED BY
LEWIS ALLEN (COLUMBIA)

SHEPARD MENKEN, PAUL JAVOR, IAN WOLFE, CARL
MILLETAIRE, LUDWIG DONATH, MARIO LANZA IN
"THE GREAT CARUSO" DIRECTED BY RICHARD THORPE (M-G-M)

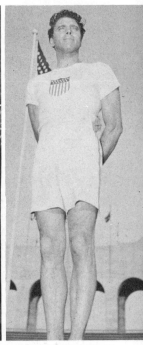

JAMES MASON
IN "THE DESERT FOX"
(20th CENTURY-FOX)

JUDY CANOVA
IN "HONEYCHILE"
(REPUBLIC)

JOHN DEREK
IN "SATURDAY'S HERO"
(COLUMBIA)

CARLETON CARPENTER
IN "THE WHISTLE AT EATON
FALLS" (COLUMBIA)

JOAN BLONDELL
IN "THE BLUE VEIL"
(RKO)

BURT LANCASTER IN
"JIM THORPE—ALL AMERICAN"
(WARNER BROS.)

ROBERT MITCHUM

IDA LUPINO

JOHN LUND

ARLENE DAHL

DOUGLAS DICK

GLORIA DE HAVEN

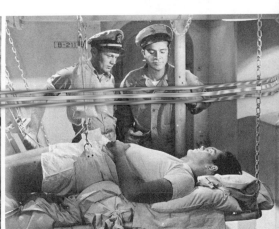

DALE ROBERTSON, BETTY GRABLE, DAN DAILEY
IN "CALL ME MISTER"
(20th CENTURY-FOX)

ALLAN NIXON, BEVERLY MICHAELS
IN "PICK UP" (COLUMBIA)

RICHARD WIDMARK, DANA ANDREWS, JEFFREY HUNTER
IN "THE FROGMEN"
(20th CENTURY-FOX)

1951

BARBARA STANWYCK

JAMES CAGNEY

SHIRLEY TEMPLE

DANA ANDREWS, DOROTHY McGUIRE, PEGGY DOW, FARLEY GRANGER, MILDRED DUNNOCK, ROBERT KEITH IN "I WANT YOU" DIRECTED BY MARK ROBSON (RKO)

"ALICE IN WONDERLAND" (WALT DISNEY)

BERT LAHR, MAXIE ROSENBLOOM, VINCENT EDWARDS, JACK CARSON IN "MR. UNIVERSE" (EAGLE LION)

GUY MADISON

RITA HAYWORTH

FARLEY GRANGER

VIRGINIA MAYO

RALPH MEEKER

GENE KELLY

JOAN CRAWFORD

ROBERT STACK

JEFF CHANDLER, ROCK HUDSON
IN "IRON MAN" DIRECTED BY
JOSEPH PEVNEY (UNIVERSAL)

KATHRYN GRAYSON, AGNES MOOREHEAD, GOWER AND
MARGE CHAMPION, JOE E. BROWN, HOWARD KEEL IN
"SHOW BOAT" DIRECTED BY GEORGE SIDNEY (M-G-M)

FRANK LOVEJOY, ROBERT YOUNG, JOAN CRAWFORD
IN "GOODBYE, MY FANCY" DIRECTED BY
VINCENT SHERMAN (WARNER BROS.)

ETHEL BARRYMORE   JULIA DEAN

MARJORIE RAMBEAU   JANE COWL

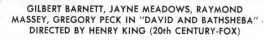

GILBERT BARNETT, JAYNE MEADOWS, RAYMOND
MASSEY, GREGORY PECK IN "DAVID AND BATHSHEBA"
DIRECTED BY HENRY KING (20th CENTURY-FOX)

LEO COLEMAN, ANNA MARIA ALBERGHETTI
IN "THE MEDIUM" DIRECTED BY
GIAN-CARLO MENOTTI (TRANSFILM)

1951

PHILIP LOEB, GERTRUDE BERG, LARRY ROBINSON,
ELI MINTZ, ARLENE McQUADE IN "MOLLY"
(PARAMOUNT)

TYRONE POWER
IN "THE MISSISSIPPI GAMBLER"
(UNIVERSAL)

RITA HAYWORTH IN
"AFFAIR IN TRINIDAD"
(COLUMBIA)

SHIRLEY BOOTH
IN "COME BACK, LITTLE SHEBA"
(PARAMOUNT)

ROY ROGERS AND TRIGGER

FREDRIC MARCH
IN "DEATH OF A SALESMAN"
(COLUMBIA)

BURT LANCASTER, SHIRLEY BOOTH, RICHARD JAECKEL, TERRY MOORE
IN "COME BACK, LITTLE SHEBA"
DIRECTED BY DANIEL MANN (PARAMOUNT)

JOHN DEREK IN
"PRINCE OF PIRATES"
(COLUMBIA)

ROYAL BEAL, MILDRED DUNNOCK, FREDRIC MARCH, KEVIN McCARTHY,
CAMERON MITCHELL IN "DEATH OF A SALESMAN"
DIRECTED BY LASLO BENEDEK (COLUMBIA)

BING CROSBY, DOROTHY LAMOUR, BOB HOPE
IN "ROAD TO BALI" DIRECTED BY HAL WALKER
(PARAMOUNT)

GRACE KELLY, GARY COOPER
IN "HIGH NOON"
DIRECTED BY FRED ZINNEMANN (UNITED ARTISTS)

CHARLES CHAPLIN
IN "LIMELIGHT"
(UNITED ARTISTS)

1952 Another big money-maker from Cecil B. DeMille's hand, "The Greatest Show on Earth," was chosen the best picture of the year by the Motion Picture Academy. They also voted Shirley Booth's performance in "Come Back, Little Sheba" the best; Gary Cooper received an "Oscar" for his in "High Noon." The New York Film Critics picked Stanley Kramer's production "High Noon," directed by Fred Zinnemann, as the best picture. Other films that were among the "best" lists were John Ford's "The Quiet Man," "Ivanhoe," "Come Back, Little Sheba," "Singing in the Rain," "Five Fingers," "The Snows of Kilimanjaro," "Viva Zapata!" and "With a Song in My Heart." Alec Guinness was popular with American audiences and both his "The Lavender Hill Mob" and "The Man in the White Suit" were hits. Other foreign successes include "Breaking Through the Sound Barrier," "Rasho-Mon," "Ways of Love" and "Forbidden Games." Joan Crawford, whose career outlasted all feminine stars in the history of motion pictures, had another popular film in "Sudden Fear." Cinerama made its first appearance. Re-makes were made of "The Merry Widow," "The Prisoner of Zenda" and "Scaramouche." Ray Bolger filmed his stage success, "Where's Charley?". Chaplin appeared in "Limelight" which was the last he filmed in this country. New faces to attract attention were Grace Kelly and Tab Hunter. Dean Martin and Jerry Lewis were riding high as a comedy team. Mario Lanza, with his glorious voice, was proving a big box-office draw. Ever-popular Bing Crosby and Bob Hope continued to make their "road" series — this year's was "Road to Bali." Will Rogers, Jr., enacted the role of his father in "The Story of Will Rogers." George Bernard Shaw's play "Androcles and the Lion," filmed by RKO, was poorly received by the press and public.

GARY COOPER
IN "HIGH NOON"
(UNITED ARTISTS)

WILL ROGERS, JR.
IN "THE STORY OF WILL ROGERS"
(WARNER BROS.)

CHARLES CHAPLIN, JR., CHARLES CHAPLIN, WHEELER DRYDEN, ANDRE EGLEVSKY, CLAIRE BLOOM IN "LIMELIGHT" PRODUCED, DIRECTED, WRITTEN AND SCORED BY CHARLES CHAPLIN (UNITED ARTISTS)

JAMES MASON
IN "FIVE FINGERS"
(20th CENTURY-FOX)

LAURENCE OLIVIER, JENNIFER JONES, EDDIE ALBERT IN "CARRIE" PRODUCED AND DIRECTED BY WILLIAM WYLER (PARAMOUNT)

ROBERT WALKER, HELEN HAYES, DEAN JAGGER IN "MY SON JOHN" PRODUCED AND DIRECTED BY LEO McCAREY (PARAMOUNT)

CLIFTON WEBB, ROBERT WAGNER, RUTH HUSSEY IN "STARS AND STRIPES FOREVER" DIRECTED BY HENRY KOSTER (20th CENTURY-FOX)

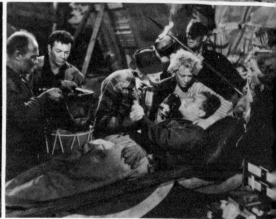

LYLE BETTGER, GLORIA GRAHAME

CORNEL WILDE, BETTY HUTTON, CHARLTON HESTON
Above: GLORIA GRAHAME, EMMETT KELLY, BETTY HUTTON, CORNEL WILDE, DOROTHY LAMOUR, LYLE BETTGER

FRANK WILCOX, CORNEL WILDE, JAMES STEWART, BETTY HUTTON, CHARLTON HESTON, GLORIA GRAHAME

SCENES FROM "THE GREATEST SHOW ON EARTH" PRODUCED AND DIRECTED BY CECIL B. DeMILLE (PARAMOUNT)

RICHARD CONTE IN "THE FIGHTER" (UNITED ARTISTS)

LANA TURNER IN "THE MERRY WIDOW" (M-G-M)

JAMES STEWART IN "THE GREATEST SHOW ON EARTH" (PARAMOUNT)

TAB HUNTER IN "ISLAND OF DESIRE" (UNITED ARTISTS)

VIRGINIA MAYO IN "SHE'S WORKING HER WAY THROUGH COLLEGE" (WARNER BROS.)

JOHN BOLES IN "BABES IN BAGDAD" (UNITED ARTISTS)

JAMES ROBERTSON JUSTICE, ANTHONY FORWOOD,
RICHARD TODD IN "STORY OF ROBIN HOOD"
(WALT DISNEY—RKO)

KIRK DOUGLAS, DEWEY MARTIN
IN "THE BIG SKY"
(RKO)

DONALD O'CONNOR, DEBBIE REYNOLDS, GENE KELLY,
JEAN HAGEN, MILLARD MITCHELL IN "SINGING
IN THE RAIN" (M-G-M)

ZION NATIONAL PARK
Above: VENICE

THIS IS CINERAMA

Cinerama is a new multi-dimensional motion picture medium which employs a three-lensed camera, a giant curved screen approximately six times the size of the normal movie screen and requires three projectors to fill this vast space. It provides an amazing wide-angle panorama of 146 degrees which approximates the complete vision range of the human eye. It achieves the unique effect of three dimensions and "puts the audience in the picture." Fred Waller was the inventor of Cinerama. Hazard Reeves developed the "stereophonic" Cinerama — sound process used, and Lowell Thomas was instrumental in its presentation. Merian C. Cooper and Robert L. Bendick were the producers. "This Is Cinerama" was the first of this new medium presented to the public. It had a variety of subjects, among them a ride on a roller coaster, an actual La Scala audience witnessing the Triumphal March and the Temple Dance of the opera "Aida," the Regatta in Venice, the Rally of the Clans in Edinburgh, water skiing in Cypress Gardens, Florida, an airplane voyage across America from New York Harbor to San Francisco's Golden Gate, and other events. "This Is Cinerama" opened September 30, 1952, on Broadway and played 122 weeks. It has since been shown in all the larger cities in the United States, and most of the world's capitals.

SCENES FROM "THIS IS CINERAMA"

NIAGARA FALLS
Above: ROLLER COASTER

URSULA THEISS
IN "MONSOON"
(UNITED ARTISTS)

MAURICE EVANS
IN "ANDROCLES AND THE
LION" (RKO)

GYPSY ROSE LEE
IN "BABES IN BAGDAD"
(UNITED ARTISTS)

RICHARD TODD IN
"STORY OF ROBIN HOOD"
(RKO)

MARILYN MONROE
IN "CLASH BY NIGHT"
(RKO)

ANTHONY DEXTER
IN "THE BRIGAND"
(COLUMBIA)

1952

LON McCALLISTER   DOROTHY McGUIRE   GENE NELSON   DONNA REED   BARRY SULLIVAN   GINGER ROGERS   HURD HATFIELD

EDITH EVANS, DOROTHY TUTIN, JOAN GREENWOOD, MICHAEL REDGRAVE, MICHAEL DENISON, MARGARET RUTHERFORD, MILES MALLESON IN "THE IMPORTANCE OF BEING EARNEST" (J. ARTHUR RANK—UNIVERSAL)

ALEC GUINNESS IN "THE LAVENDER HILL MOB" (UNIVERSAL)

DENHOLM ELLIOTT, ANN TODD, NIGEL PATRICK IN "BREAKING THROUGH THE SOUND BARRIER" (UNITED ARTISTS)

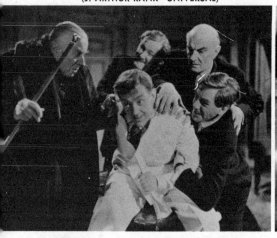

ERNEST THESIGER, ALEC GUINNESS, HOWARD MARION-CRAWFORD, DESMOND ROBERTS, MICHAEL GOUGH IN "THE MAN IN THE WHITE SUIT" (UNIVERSAL)

TOSHIRO MIFUNE, MACHIKO KYO IN "RASHO-MON" (DAIEI)

ROBERT DONAT, FRANCIS L. SULLIVAN IN "THE WINSLOW BOY" (EAGLE LION)

LUCIEN HUBERT, GEORGES POUJOULY, BRIGITTE FOSSEY IN "FORBIDDEN GAMES" (TIMES)

ANNA MAGNANI IN "THE MIRACLE" FROM "WAYS OF LOVE" (BURSTYN)

MARJORIE STEELE, ROBERT PRESTON IN "FACE TO FACE" (RKO)

FRANK LATIMORE   SHELLEY WINTERS   KEENAN WYNN   MARTHA SCOTT   JOHNNY SANDS   ALIDA VALLI   RON RANDELL

214

TONY MARTIN

VIRGINIA MAYO

DAVID NIVEN

ELEANOR PARKER

RED SKELTON

JANE WYMAN

DALE ROBERTSON

JACK PALANCE, JOAN CRAWFORD
IN "SUDDEN FEAR"
DIRECTED BY DAVID MILLER (RKO)

ALLYN McLERIE, RAY BOLGER, MARY GERMAINE
IN "WHERE'S CHARLEY?"
DIRECTED BY DAVID BUTLER (WARNER BROS.)

ANNE FRANCIS, DALE ROBERTSON, CHARLES KORVIN,
ADELINE DE WALT REYNOLDS IN "LYDIA BAILEY"
DIRECTED BY JEAN NEGULESCO (20th CENTURY-FOX)

CANADA LEE, ALBERTINA TEMBA
IN "CRY, THE BELOVED COUNTRY"
(UNITED ARTISTS)

KURT KASZNAR, CHARLES BOYER, BOBBY DRISCOLL,
MARSHA HUNT, LOUIS JOURDAN IN "THE HAPPY TIME"
DIRECTED BY RICHARD FLEISCHER (COLUMBIA)

UNA MERKEL, DAVID WAYNE, THELMA RITTER, SUSAN
HAYWARD IN "WITH A SONG IN MY HEART"
DIRECTED BY WALTER LANG (20th CENTURY-FOX)

AVA GARDNER, GREGORY PECK IN
"THE SNOWS OF KILIMANJARO"
DIRECTED BY HENRY KING (20th CENTURY-FOX)

BARRY SULLIVAN, LANA TURNER, DICK POWELL, WALTER
PIDGEON IN "THE BAD AND THE BEAUTIFUL"
DIRECTED BY VINCENTE MINNELLI (M-G-M)

BETTE DAVIS, GARY MERRILL
IN "PHONE CALL FROM A STRANGER"
DIRECTED BY JEAN NEGULESCO (20th CENTURY-FOX)

RICHARD TODD

GAIL RUSSELL

EDMOND O'BRIEN

DEBRA PAGET

WILLARD PARKER

PATRICIA NEAL

ALDO RAY

1952

215

ALDO RAY, SPENCER TRACY, KATHARINE HEPBURN
IN "PAT AND MIKE"
DIRECTED BY GEORGE CUKOR (M-G-M)

JERRY LEWIS, DEAN MARTIN
IN "SAILOR BEWARE"
(PARAMOUNT)

JUDY HOLLIDAY, MADGE KENNEDY, ALDO RAY
IN "THE MARRYING KIND"
DIRECTED BY GEORGE CUKOR (COLUMBIA)

ELIZABETH TAYLOR, ROBERT TAYLOR
IN "IVANHOE"
DIRECTED BY RICHARD THORPE (M-G-M)

FERNANDO LAMAS, LANA TURNER
IN "THE MERRY WIDOW"
DIRECTED BY CURTIS BERNHARDT (M-G-M)

VICTOR MATURE, JEAN SIMMONS, ALAN YOUNG
IN "ANDROCLES AND THE LION"
DIRECTED BY CHESTER ERSKINE (RKO)

BURT LANCASTER
IN "THE CRIMSON PIRATE"
DIRECTED BY ROBERT SIODMAK (WARNER BROS.)

TAB HUNTER, DONALD GRAY, LINDA DARNELL
IN "ISLAND OF DESIRE" DIRECTED
BY STUART HEISLER (UNITED ARTISTS)

DANNY KAYE IN
"HANS CHRISTIAN ANDERSON"
DIRECTED BY CHARLES VIDOR (RKO)

ROBERT COOTE, STEWART GRANGER, LOUIS CALHERN,
DEBORAH KERR IN "THE PRISONER OF ZENDA"
DIRECTED BY RICHARD THORPE (M-G-M)

SPENCER TRACY, GENE TIERNEY
IN "PLYMOUTH ADVENTURE" DIRECTED
BY CLARENCE BROWN (M-G-M)

STEWART GRANGER, HENRY WILCOXON, PATRICK CONWAY, REX
REASON, ELEANOR PARKER IN "SCARAMOUCHE"
DIRECTED BY GEORGE SIDNEY (M-G-M)

MARIO LANZA IN
"BECAUSE YOU'RE MINE"
(M-G-M)

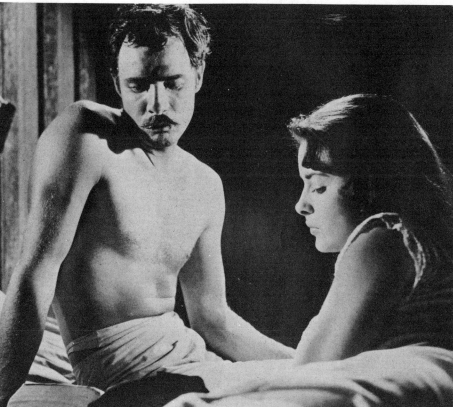

MARLON BRANDO, JEAN PETERS
IN "VIVA ZAPATA!"
DIRECTED BY ELIA KAZAN (20th CENTURY-FOX)

STEWART GRANGER
IN "SCARAMOUCHE"
(M-G-M)

LEX BARKER, JOYCE MacKENZIE
IN "TARZAN AND THE SHE-DEVIL"
(RKO)

BARRY FITZGERALD, JOHN WAYNE, MAUREEN O'HARA
IN "THE QUIET MAN" DIRECTED BY JOHN FORD (REPUBLIC)

KEITH ANDES, MARILYN MONROE
IN "CLASH BY NIGHT"
DIRECTED BY FRITZ LANG (RKO)

1952

KATHRYN GRAYSON, JAMES WHITMORE, KEENAN WYNN, HOWARD KEEL, WILLARD PARKER
Top: (L) TOMMY RALL, ANN MILLER, BOB FOSSE, BOBBY VAN, (R) KATHRYN GRAYSON, HOWARD KEEL
SCENES FROM "KISS ME, KATE" DIRECTED BY GEORGE SIDNEY (M-G-M)

HOWARD KEEL

LESLIE CARON, MEL FERRER
IN "LILI"
DIRECTED BY CHARLES WALTERS (M-G-M)

FRED ASTAIRE, NANETTE FABRAY, JACK BUCHANAN
OSCAR LEVANT IN "THE BAND WAGON"
DIRECTED BY VINCENTE MINNELLI (M-G-M)

MICHAEL WILDING, JOAN CRAWFORD
IN "TORCH SONG"
DIRECTED BY CHARLES WALTERS (M-G-M)

ALDO RAY, RITA HAYWORTH
IN "MISS SADIE THOMPSON"
DIRECTED BY CURTIS BERNHARDT (COLUMBIA)

DONALD O'CONNOR, ETHEL MERMAN, GEORGE SANDERS
VERA-ELLEN IN "CALL ME MADAM"
DIRECTED BY WALTER LANG (20th CENTURY-FOX)

BURT LANCASTER, DEBORAH KERR

MONTGOMERY CLIFT, FRANK SINATRA, BURT LANCASTER Top: (L) FRANK SINATRA, (C) DONNA REED, MONTGOMERY CLIFT, FRANK SINATRA, (R) MONTGOMERY CLIFT
SCENES FROM "FROM HERE TO ETERNITY" DIRECTED BY FRED ZINNEMANN (COLUMBIA)

RICHARD BURTON, OLIVIA DE HAVILLAND, RONALD SQUIRE IN "MY COUSIN RACHEL" DIRECTED BY HENRY KOSTER (20th CENTURY-FOX)

1953 Both the film industry and the exhibitors were determined to curb the current menace and combat the steadily increasing inroads television was making on the box office. Drive-in theatres sprang up throughout the country and were popular; 3-D, or three-dimensional films, were introduced with the use of polaroid glasses which were furnished by theatre managements. "Bwana Devil" was the first of many 3-D films which paying customers flocked to see. However, this proved to be a novelty the public soon tired of, and within a year 3-D was on its way out. 20th Century-Fox came up with Cinema-Scope, a wide-screen process that became popular and is still in use. Paramount produced films in VistaVision, while Todd-AO and Cinemiracle were other processes used to lure people from their home TV screens back to the theatre screen. Stereophonic Sound entered the picture. While the novelty lasted, people were interested. "The Robe," the first film released in CinemaScope, established one of the all-time-high movie grosses in the history of the film industry. To help matters, too, there were a large number of high-quality films released. These included "Shane," "Roman Holiday," "Lili," "Moulin Rouge," "Stalag 17," "The Cruel Sea," "Julius Caesar" and "From Here to Eternity" which was chosen the best film of the year by both the Academy and the New York Film Critics. Julie Harris made her film debut in her stage success, "The Member of the Wedding," and Anthony Perkins made his first film appearance in "The Actress." Walt Disney released his version of "Peter Pan." Death took veterans William Farnum, Lewis Stone and Herbert Rawlinson.

ALAN LADD, VAN HEFLIN, JEAN ARTHUR, BRANDON DE WILDE IN "SHANE" DIRECTED BY GEORGE STEVENS (PARAMOUNT)

JANET LEIGH, TONY CURTIS IN "HOUDINI" DIRECTED BY GEORGE MARSHALL (PARAMOUNT)

DORIS DAY, ALLYN McLERIE, HOWARD KEEL IN "CALAMITY JANE" DIRECTED BY DAVID BUTLER (WARNER BROS.)

RICHARD JAECKEL	BARBARA HALE	PETER LAWFORD	WANDA HENDRIX	HOWARD DUFF	MONA FREEMAN	ROBERT HORTON

PETER GRAVES, KEITH LARSEN, EMORY PARNELL, ROBERT STACK, CHARLES NOLTE, ROBERT WILKE, JOHN DOUCETTE IN "WAR PAINT" (UNITED ARTISTS)

NIGEL BRUCE, ROBERT STACK IN "BWANA DEVIL" (UNITED ARTISTS) FIRST 3-D FILM TO BE RELEASED

WILLIAM HOLDEN, MAGGIE McNAMARA, DAVID NIVEN IN "THE MOON IS BLUE" PRODUCED AND DIRECTED BY OTTO PREMINGER (UNITED ARTISTS)

LYLE BETTGER, ANNE BAXTER, JAY C. FLIPPEN IN "THE CARNIVAL STORY" DIRECTED BY KURT NEUMANN (RKO)

WALT DISNEY'S FULL-LENGTH ALL-CARTOON FEATURE "PETER PAN" (RKO)

JANE WYMAN, TOMMY RETTIG IN "SO BIG" DIRECTED BY ROBERT WISE (WARNER BROS.)

NORMA NIELSON, JEAN SIMMONS, DAWN BENDER, SPENCER TRACY, TERESA WRIGHT, ANTHONY PERKINS IN "THE ACTRESS" DIRECTOR, GEORGE CUKOR (M-G-M)

JOHN WAYNE, GERALDINE PAGE, TOM IRISH, WARD BOND IN "HONDO" DIRECTED BY JOHN FARROW (WARNER BROS.)

ANGELA CLARK, ROBERT WAGNER, GILBERT ROLAND, GLORIA GORDON IN "BENEATH THE 12-MILE REEF" DIRECTED BY ROBERT D. WEBB (20th CENTURY-FOX)

ROBERT ARTHUR	JANET LEIGH	KEITH ANDES	KATY JURADO	KURT KREUGER	ADELE JERGENS	JAMES DOBSON

JOHN HODIAK   LINDA DARNELL   CHARLTON HESTON   GLORIA GRAHAME   JEFFREY HUNTER   DORIS DAY   JOHN DEREK

CLAUDE DAUPHIN, BING CROSBY, CHRISTIAN FOURCADE
IN "LITTLE BOY LOST"
DIRECTED BY GEORGE SEATON (PARAMOUNT)

RORY CALHOUN, LAUREN BACALL, CAMERON MITCHELL,
MARILYN MONROE IN "HOW TO MARRY A MILLIONAIRE"
DIRECTED BY JEAN NEGULESCO (20th CENTURY-FOX)

ANNA MARIA ALBERGHETTI, LAURITZ MELCHIOR,
ROSEMARY CLOONEY IN "THE STARS ARE SINGING"
DIRECTED BY NORMAN TAUROG (PARAMOUNT)

MARILYN MONROE, JANE RUSSELL
IN "GENTLEMEN PREFER BLONDES"
DIRECTED BY HOWARD HAWKS (20th CENTURY-FOX)

PETER GRAVES, WILLIAM HOLDEN, NEVILLE BRAND,
RICHARD ERDMAN IN "STALAG 17" PRODUCED AND
DIRECTED BY BILLY WILDER (PARAMOUNT)

SARA HADEN, BARBARA HALE, ANNE FRANCIS, JAMES
CAGNEY, JOHN McINTIRE IN "A LION IS IN THE STREETS"
DIRECTED BY RAOUL WALSH (WARNER BROS.)

JULIE HARRIS, ETHEL WATERS, BRANDON DE WILDE
IN "THE MEMBER OF THE WEDDING"
DIRECTED BY FRED ZINNEMANN (COLUMBIA)

HARPER CARTER, BARBARA STANWYCK, AUDREY DALTON,
CLIFTON WEBB IN "TITANIC"
DIRECTED BY JEAN NEGULESCO (20th CENTURY-FOX)

PAUL DOUGLAS   BILL ELLIOTT   ANN HARDING   SESSUE HAYAKAWA   JOSEPHINE HULL   TAYLOR HOLMES   EDWARD G. ROBINSON

1953

221

VICTOR MATURE, JAY NOVELLO, RICHARD BURTON, DAWN ADDAMS   JEAN SIMMONS, RICHARD BURTON
SCENES FROM "THE ROBE" DIRECTED BY HENRY KOSTER (20th CENTURY-FOX)   JEFF MORROW, VICTOR MATURE, RICHARD BURTON

SUZANNE FLON, ZSA ZSA GABOR, JOSÉ FERRER
IN "MOULIN ROUGE"
DIRECTED BY JOHN HUSTON (UNITED ARTISTS)

GREGORY PECK, AUDREY HEPBURN, EDDIE ALBERT
IN "ROMAN HOLIDAY"
PRODUCED AND DIRECTED BY WILLIAM WYLER (PARAMOUNT)

LAURENCE OLIVIER IN
"THE BEGGAR'S OPERA"
(WARNER BROS.)

ZSA ZSA GABOR
IN "LILI"
(M-G-M)

ELROY "CRAZYLEGS" HIRSCH IN
"CRAZYLEGS, ALL-AMERICAN"
(REPUBLIC)

JANE RUSSELL
IN "THE FRENCH LINE"
(RKO)

JEFF CHANDLER
IN "THE IRON MAN"
(UNIVERSAL)

JACK RAINE, EDMOND O'BRIEN, WILLIAM COTTRELL, TOM POWERS, JOHN HOYT, JOHN GIELGUD, JAMES MASON, MARLON BRANDO

(M-G-M)

JULIUS CAESAR

By William Shakespeare; Director, Joseph L. ankiewicz; Producer, John Houseman; Mucal Score by Miklos Rozsa.

CAST

arpenter	John Doucette
arullus	George Macready
avius	Michael Pate
lius Caesar	Louis Calhern
asca	Edmond O'Brien
lpurnia	Greer Garson
ortia	Deborah Kerr
ark Antony	Marlon Brando
rutus	James Mason
assius	John Gielgud
oothsayer	Richard Hale
cero	Alan Napier
nna	William Cottrell
ucius	John Hardy
ecius Brutus	John Hoyt
etellus Cimber	Tom Powers
ebonius	Jack Raine
garius	Ian Wolfe
rvant to Caesar	Chester Stratton
ablius	Lumsden Hare
rtemidorus	Morgan Farley
opilius Lena	Victor Perry
rvant to Antony	Bill Phipps
ctavius Caesar	Douglas Watson
ficer to Octavius	Michael Tolan
arro	John Lupton
audius	Preston Hanson
tinius	John Parrish
tus	Joe Waring
ardanius	Stephen Roberts
olumnius	Thomas Browne Henry
rato	Edmund Purdom

tizens of Rome: Paul Guilfoyle, Lawrence bkin, David Bond, Jo Gilbert, Ann Tyrrell, hn O'Malley, Oliver Blake, Alvin Hurwitz, nald Elson.

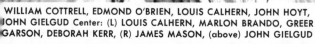

WILLIAM COTTRELL, EDMOND O'BRIEN, LOUIS CALHERN, JOHN HOYT, JOHN GIELGUD Center: (L) LOUIS CALHERN, MARLON BRANDO, GREER GARSON, DEBORAH KERR, (R) JAMES MASON, (above) JOHN GIELGUD

MARLON BRANDO AS MARK ANTONY
SCENES FROM "JULIUS CAESAR" (M-G-M)

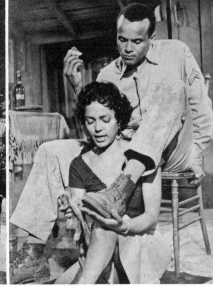

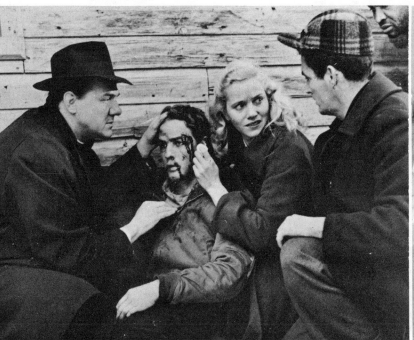

STEWART GRANGER, PETER USTINOV, ROSEMARY HARRIS
IN "BEAU BRUMMELL"
DIRECTED BY CURTIS BERNHARDT (M-G-M)

DANNY KAYE, VERA-ELLEN, BING CROSBY
IN IRVING BERLIN'S "WHITE CHRISTMAS"
DIRECTED BY MICHAEL CURTIZ (PARAMOUNT)

DINAH SHERIDAN, JOHN GREGSON, KAY KENDALL,
KENNETH MORE IN "GENEVIEVE"
(J. ARTHUR RANK-UNIVERSAL)

EDMUND PURDOM, BELLA DARVI
IN "THE EGYPTIAN" DIRECTED BY
MICHAEL CURTIZ (20th CENTURY-FOX)

JEAN PETERS, LOUIS JOURDAN, MAGGIE McNAMARA, DOROTHY McGUIRE
IN "THREE COINS IN THE FOUNTAIN"
DIRECTED BY JEAN NEGULESCO (20th CENTURY-FOX)

DOROTHY DANDRIDGE, HARRY BELAFONTE
IN "CARMEN JONES" PRODUCED AND DIRECTED
BY OTTO PREMINGER (20th CENTURY-FOX)

MARLON BRANDO IN
"THE WILD ONE" DIRECTED BY
LASLO BENEDEK (COLUMBIA)

KARL MALDEN, MARLON BRANDO, EVA MARIE SAINT
IN "ON THE WATERFRONT"
DIRECTED BY ELIA KAZAN (COLUMBIA)

MARLON BRANDO
IN "DESIREE" DIRECTED BY
HENRY KOSTER (20th CENTURY-FOX)

ROBERT FRANCIS IN
"THEY RODE WEST"
(COLUMBIA)

Front: VIRGINIA GIBSON, RUTA KILMONIS, NANCY KILGAS, HOWARD KEEL, JANE POWELL, NORMA DOGGETT, JULIE NEWMEYER, BETTY CARR Back row: TOMMY RALL, MATT MATTOX, RUSS TAMBLYN, MARC PLATT, JEFF RICHARDS, JACQUES D'AMBOISE IN "SEVEN BRIDES FOR SEVEN BROTHERS" DIRECTED BY STANLEY DONEN (M-G-M)

DANNY KAYE IN
"KNOCK ON WOOD"
(PARAMOUNT)

DAN O'HERLIHY
IN "ADVENTURES OF ROBINSON CRUSOE"
(UNITED ARTISTS)

1954 The showing of films in CinemaScope was gaining in popularity and exhibitors were put to the added expense of installing wide screens in their theatres to accommodate it. This was Marlon Brando's year. Besides winning an "Oscar" and being picked by the New York Film Critics as the best male actor for his performance in "On the Waterfront," he also appeared in "The Wild One" and "Desiree." Grace Kelly received an "Oscar" for "The Country Girl" and Eva Marie Saint, a newcomer, was also cited for her performance in "On the Waterfront." The best foreign film was the Japanese "Gate of Hell." Two English films, "Genevieve" and "Mr. Hulot's Holiday," found great favor. Among other popular films were "Three Coins in the Fountain," "Rear Window," "The Caine Mutiny," "The Country Girl," "The High and the Mighty," and a delightful original musical "Seven Brides for Seven Brothers." Re-makes were made of "A Star Is Born" with Judy Garland and James Mason in the Janet Gaynor and Fredric March roles, "The Magnificent Obsession," "Beau Brummell," "Rose-Marie" and "Romeo and Juliet." Bob Mathias, famous athlete, apparently was the right type. He starred in a film based on his own life. Death claimed Lionel Barrymore, Bert Lytell and Sydney Greenstreet.

GRACE KELLY
IN "THE COUNTRY GIRL"
DIRECTED BY GEORGE SEATON (PARAMOUNT)

PHIL GARRIS, JUNE ALLYSON, JAMES STEWART
IN "THE GLENN MILLER STORY"
DIRECTED BY ANTHONY MANN (UNIVERSAL)

KEEFE BRASSELLE
IN "THE EDDIE CANTOR
STORY" (WARNER BROS.)

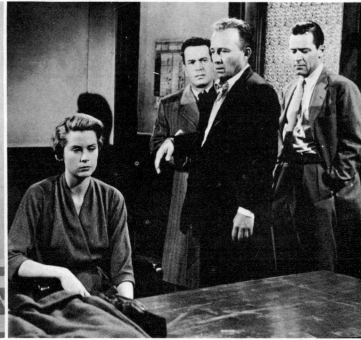

GRACE KELLY, GENE REYNOLDS, BING CROSBY, WILLIAM HOLDEN
IN "THE COUNTRY GIRL"
(PARAMOUNT)

225

DONALD O'CONNOR   WENDELL COREY   RHONDA FLEMING   ROBERT FRANCIS   BARBARA BEL GEDDES   STEVE FORREST   VINCENT EDWARD

MEL FERRER, AVA GARDNER, STANLEY BAKER, ANNE
CRAWFORD, FELIX AYLMER, ROBERT TAYLOR, MAUREEN
SWANSON IN "KNIGHTS OF THE ROUND TABLE" (M-G-M)

KAZUO HASEGAWA, ISAO YAMAGATO, MACHIKO KY
IN "GATE OF HELL"
(DAIEI)

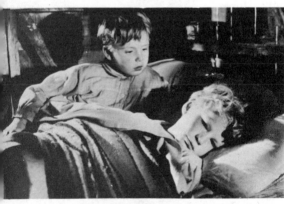

JACQUES TATI, NICHELLE ROLLA
IN "MR. HULOT'S HOLIDAY"
(ORAIN)

TONY CURTIS IN
"THE BLACK SHIELD OF FALWORTH"
(UNIVERSAL)

WILLIAM HOLDEN, AUDREY HEPBURN, HUMPHREY BOGA
IN "SABRINA" PRODUCED AND DIRECTED
BY BILLY WILDER (PARAMOUNT)

VINCENT WINTER, JON WHITELEY
IN "THE LITTLE KIDNAPPERS"
(UNITED ARTISTS)

JOHNNY RAY, MITZI GAYNOR, DAN DAILEY, ETHEL MERMAN,
DONALD O'CONNOR, MARILYN MONROE IN "THERE'S NO
BUSINESS LIKE SHOW BUSINESS" (20th CENTURY-FOX)

ROCK HUDSON, JANE WYMAN, BARBARA RUSH
IN "MAGNIFICENT OBSESSION" DIRECTED BY
DOUGLAS SIRK (UNIVERSAL)

SYDNEY CHAPLIN   DAVID BRIAN   CORINNE CALVET   REX ALLEN   FAITH DOMERGUE   CAMERON MITCHELL   ROGER MOORE

WILLIAM LUNDIGAN

JENNIFER JONES

JEFF CHANDLER

DEBORAH KERR

AUDIE MURPHY

JUDY HOLLIDAY

STEWART GRANGER

ROSSANO BRAZZI, AVA GARDNER, VALENTINA CORTESA
"THE BAREFOOT CONTESSA" WRITTEN AND DIRECTED
BY JOSEPH L. MANKIEWICZ (UNITED ARTISTS)

FREDRIC MARCH, BARBARA STANWYCK, WALTER PIDGEON,
WILLIAM HOLDEN IN "EXECUTIVE SUITE"
DIRECTED BY ROBERT WISE (M-G-M)

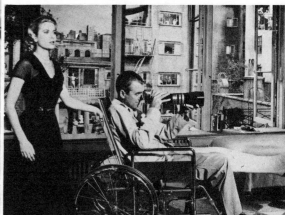

RICHARD CARLSON, JULIA ADAMS, RICHARD DENNING
IN "CREATURE FROM THE BLACK LAGOON"
(UNIVERSAL)

GREER GARSON
IN "HER TWELVE MEN"
(M-G-M)

GRACE KELLY, JAMES STEWART
IN "REAR WINDOW"
DIRECTED BY ALFRED HITCHCOCK (PARAMOUNT)

MARJORIE MAIN, HOWARD KEEL, BERT LAHR,
ANN BLYTH IN "ROSE MARIE" PRODUCED AND
DIRECTED BY MERVYN LeROY (M-G-M)

LAUREN BACALL, CORNEL WILDE, JUNE ALLYSON, FRED
MacMURRAY, CLIFTON WEBB, ARLENE DAHL, ELLIOTT REID,
VAN HEFLIN IN "WOMAN'S WORLD" DIRECTED BY
JEAN NEGULESCO (20th CENTURY-FOX)

HENRY BRANDON, GARY COOPER, BURT LANCASTER
IN "VERA CRUZ" DIRECTED BY
ROBERT ALDRICH (UNITED ARTISTS)

JOHN BARRYMORE, JR.

RICHARD BASEHART

MARIE WINDSOR

JACQUES SERNAS

TERESA WRIGHT

RICHARD WIDMARK

RICARDO MONTALBAN

1954

227

BOB MATHIAS IN "THE BOB MATHIAS STORY" (ALLIED ARTISTS)

ROBERT WAGNER IN "PRINCE VALIANT" (20th CENTURY-FOX)

JANE POWELL IN "THREE SAILORS AND A GIRL" (WARNER BROS.)

MARILYN MONROE IN "THERE'S NO BUSINESS LIKE SHOW BUSINESS" (20th CENTURY-FOX)

GENE NELSON IN "THREE SAILORS AND A GIRL" (WARNER BROS.)

ROBERT TAYLOR IN "KNIGHTS OF THE ROUND TABLE" (M-G-M)

WARD BOND, BOB MATHIAS IN "THE BOB MATHIAS STORY" (ALLIED ARTISTS)

CHARLES BICKFORD, JUDY GARLAND, JAMES MASON, JACK CARSON IN "A STAR IS BORN" DIRECTED BY GEORGE CUKOR (WARNER BROS.)

JOSÉ FERRER, VAN JOHNSON, HUMPHREY BOGART
Above: HUMPHREY BOGART, CLAUDE AKINS, ROBERT FRANCIS, FRED MacMURRAY IN "THE CAINE MUTINY" DIRECTED BY EDWARD DMYTRYK (COLUMBIA)

SUSAN SHENTALL, LAURENCE HARVEY IN "ROMEO AND JULIET" (J. ARTHUR RANK-UNITED ARTISTS)

WILLIAM CAMPBELL, WALLY BROWN, ROBERT STACK, JOHN WAYNE IN "THE HIGH AND THE MIGHTY" DIRECTED BY WILLIAM A. WELLMAN (WARNER BROS.)

EDMUND PURDOM, JANE POWELL, STEVE REEVES, DEBBIE REYNOLDS, VIC DAMONE IN "ATHENA" DIRECTED BY RICHARD THORPE (M-G-M)

JUDY GARLAND
1954

MARILYN MONROE

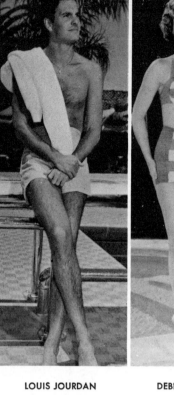

LOUIS JOURDAN

DEBBIE REYNOLDS

ROBERT FRANCIS

LANA TURNER
IN 'THE PRODIGAL''
DIRECTED BY RICHARD THORPE (M-G-M)

JEFFREY HUNTER

RUTH ROMAN

RICHARD CRANE

230

RICHARD TODD, JEAN PETERS, LES TREMAYNE
IN "A MAN CALLED PETER"
DIRECTED BY HENRY KOSTER (20th CENTURY-FOX)

DEWEY MARTIN, MARY MURPHY, FREDRIC MARCH, RICHARD
EYER, MARTHA SCOTT, HUMPHREY BOGART IN "THE
DESPERATE HOURS" PRODUCED AND DIRECTED BY
WILLIAM WYLER (PARAMOUNT)

JAMES CAGNEY, DORIS DAY
IN "LOVE ME OR LEAVE ME"
DIRECTED BY CHARLES VIDOR (M-G-M)

KAY KENDALL, ROBERT TAYLOR
IN "QUENTIN DURWARD"
DIRECTED BY RICHARD THORPE (M-G-M)

1955

The new producing firm of Harold Hecht and Burt Lancaster came up with a winner in an unpretentious film called "Marty." Written by Paddy Chayefsky, directed by Delbert Mann, with newcomers Ernest Borgnine and Betsy Blair in the leading roles, and made with normal-size film and in black and white, it was chosen the best picture of the year by both the Academy and the New York Film Critics. Anna Magnani, famous Italian actress, won an "Oscar" for her American debut performance in "The Rose Tattoo." "Oklahoma," filmed in Todd-AO, did not repeat its stage success. James Dean, a newcomer from the stage, had great success in his first two films "East of Eden" and "Rebel Without a Cause." His untimely death in an automobile accident at the age of twenty-four cut short what promised to be a brilliant career. Death in an airplane accident also claimed Robert Francis, another promising newcomer. Other deaths included those of John Hodiak, Carmen Miranda, and veterans Alice Joyce, Theda Bara, Carlyle Blackwell and Tom Moore. John Wayne was top man in the box-office polls for the tenth consecutive year. Marilyn Monroe and Rock Hudson were also top favorites. Eva Le Gallienne of stage fame made her film debut in "Prince of Players." "Umberto D" and "Diabolique" were the best foreign films released.

EVELYN ELLIS, GLENN FORD, ELEANOR
PARKER, ROGER MOORE IN
"INTERRUPTED MELODY" DIRECTED
BY CURTIS BERNHARDT (M-G-M)

CARY GRANT, GRACE KELLY
IN "TO CATCH A THIEF"
DIRECTED BY ALFRED HITCHCOCK (PARAMOUNT)

JACK LEMMON, JAMES CAGNEY, HENRY FONDA, WILLIAM
POWELL IN "MISTER ROBERTS" DIRECTED BY
JOHN FORD AND MERVYN LeROY (WARNER BROS.)

JENNIFER JONES, WILLIAM HOLDEN
IN "LOVE IS A MANY SPLENDORED THING"
DIRECTED BY HENRY KING (20th CENTURY-FOX)

MARIA PIA CASILIO, FLICK, CARLO
BATTISTI IN VITTORIO DE SICA'S
"UMBERTO D"

RICHARD BURTON, EVA LE GALLIENNE
IN "PRINCE OF PLAYERS"
(20th CENTURY-FOX)

RON RANDELL, JULIE HARRIS, LAURENCE
HARVEY IN "I AM A CAMERA"
(DCA)

JEAN CARSON, EDWARD ANDREWS
IN "PHENIX CITY STORY"
(ALLIED ARTISTS)

JAMES DEAN

DICK DAVALOS, JAMES DEAN, JULIE HARRIS
IN "EAST OF EDEN"
DIRECTED BY ELIA KAZAN (WARNER BROS.)

IDA LUPINO, JACK PALANCE
IN "THE BIG KNIFE"
(UNITED ARTISTS)

JOHNNY WEISSMULLER
AS JUNGLE JIM WITH KIMBA
(COLUMBIA)

JAMES DEAN, SAL MINEO, NATALIE WOOD
IN "REBEL WITHOUT A CAUSE"
DIRECTED BY NICHOLAS RAY (WARNER BROS.)

WALT DISNEY'S "LADY AND
THE TRAMP" FIRST ALL-CARTOON
FEATURE IN CINEMASCOPE

GENE NELSON, GORDON MacRAE, SHIRLEY JONES, CHARLOTTE
GREENWOOD, JAY C. FLIPPEN IN "OKLAHOMA!"
DIRECTED BY FRED ZINNEMANN (MTC)

TOMMY DURAN, JIMMY BAIRD, LINDA BENNETT, LYDIA REED, PAUL DeROLF, LEE ERICKSON, BILLY GRAY, BOB HOPE IN "THE SEVEN LITTLE FOYS" DIRECTED BY MELVILLE SHAVELSON (PARAMOUNT)

TAB HUNTER, ALDO RAY, WILLIAM CAMPBELL IN "BATTLE CRY" DIRECTED BY RAOUL WALSH (WARNER BROS.)

NADENE ASHDOWN, GRACE KELLY, CHERYL LYNN CALLAWAY, WILLIAM HOLDEN IN "THE BRIDGES AT TOKO-RI" (PARAMOUNT)

ESTHER MINCIOTTI, BETSY BLAIR, ERNEST BORGNINE IN "MARTY" DIRECTED BY DELBERT MANN (UNITED ARTISTS)

OLIVIA DE HAVILLAND

WILDFIRE, DEAN JAGGER, RICHARD ANDERSON, SALLY FRASER, EDMUND GWENN IN "IT'S A DOG'S LIFE" (M-G-M)

DEWEY MARTIN, JACK HAWKINS IN "LAND OF THE PHARAOHS" (WARNER BROS.)

CHARD EGAN, JANE RUSSELL, ROBERT KEITH, GILBERT ROLAND, LORI NELSON IN "UNDERWATER" (RKO)

BURT LANCASTER, ANNA MAGNANI SCENES FROM "THE ROSE TATTOO" DIRECTED BY DANIEL MANN (PARAMOUNT)

ANNA MAGNANI, BEN COOPER

1955

MARGO, SUSAN HAYWARD, DONALD BARRY, EDDIE ALBERT IN "I'LL CRY TOMORROW" DIRECTED BY DANIEL MANN (M-G-M)

233

TAB HUNTER   CARA WILLIAMS   GEORGE NADER   JUNE HAVER   ALDO RAY

EDMUND PURDOM   PAT CROWLEY   ALEX NICOL   HILDEGARDE NEFF, DONALD WOLFIT IN "SVENGALI" (M-G-M)   JACK LEMMON   VIVECA LINDFORS   RICHARD LONG

BETSY PALMER, TYRONE POWER, ROBERT FRANCIS, MAUREEN O'HARA IN "THE LONG GRAY LINE" DIRECTED BY JOHN FORD (COLUMBIA)   SIDNEY POITIER (left), GLENN FORD (center) IN "BLACKBOARD JUNGLE" DIRECTED BY RICHARD BROOKS (M-G-M)   JANE POWELL, VIC DAMONE, ANN MILLER, TONY MARTIN, DEBBIE REYNOLDS, RUSS TAMBLYN IN "HIT THE DECK" DIRECTED BY ROY ROWLAND (M-G-M)

MICHAEL WILDING, LESLIE CARON IN "THE GLASS SLIPPER" (M-G-M)   GINA LOLLOBRIGIDA, ROBERTO RISSO IN "FRISKY" (TITANUS)   FOLK SUNDQUIST, ULLA JACOBSSON IN "ONE SUMMER OF HAPPINESS" (NORISK TONEFILM)   JAMES DALY, GARY COOPER, RALPH BELLAMY IN "THE COURT MARTIAL OF BILLY MITCHELL" (WARNER BROS.)   SUSAN STRASBERG, JOHN KERR IN "THE COBWEB" (M-G-M)

234

ROBERT STACK IN
"THE IRON GLOVE"
(COLUMBIA)

BETTE DAVIS IN
"THE VIRGIN QUEEN"
(20th CENTURY-FOX)

ROCK HUDSON IN
"CAPTAIN LIGHTFOOT"
(UNIVERSAL)

MARILYN MONROE IN
"THE SEVEN YEAR ITCH"
(20th CENTURY-FOX)

JACK WEBB IN
"PETE KELLY'S BLUES"
(WARNER BROS.)

JOAN COLLINS IN "LAND
OF THE PHARAOHS"
(WARNER BROS.)

CAROLEE KELLY, LUTHER ADLER, JOAN COLLINS, FARLEY
GRANGER, CORNELIA OTIS SKINNER IN "THE GIRL IN
THE RED VELVET SWING" (20th CENTURY-FOX)

FRANK SINATRA, VIVIAN BLAINE, JEAN SIMMONS,
MARLON BRANDO, REGIS TOOMEY IN "GUYS AND
DOLLS" DIRECTED BY JOSEPH MANKIEWICZ (M-G-M)

DICK POWELL

JOAN BLONDELL

GORDON SCOTT BECOMES THE ELEVENTH TARZAN
IN "TARZAN'S HIDDEN JUNGLE"
(RKO)

LILLIAN GISH

LEW AYRES

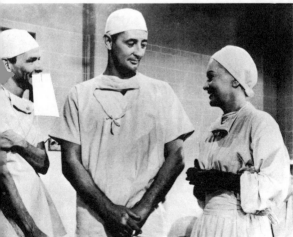

FRANK SINATRA, ROBERT MITCHUM, OLIVIA DE HAVILLAND
IN "NOT AS A STRANGER" PRODUCED AND
DIRECTED BY STANLEY KRAMER (UNITED ARTISTS)

ORSON WELLES, SUZANNE CLOUTIER IN
"OTHELLO" PRODUCED AND DIRECTED
BY ORSON WELLES (UNITED ARTISTS)

KATHARINE HEPBURN, ROSSANO BRAZZI, GAITANO AUDIERO
IN "SUMMERTIME" DIRECTED BY DAVID LEAN
(UNITED ARTISTS)

ANN MILLER, DOLORES GRAY, JUNE ALLYSON, ANN SHERIDAN, JOAN BLONDELL, JOAN COLLINS IN "THE OPPOSITE SEX" DIRECTED BY DAVID MILLER (M-G-M)

BURT LANCASTER, GINA LOLLOBRIGIDA, TONY CURTIS IN "TRAPEZE" DIRECTED BY CAROL REED (UNITED ARTISTS)

MARILYN MONROE, DON MURRAY IN "BUS STOP" DIRECTED BY JOSHUA LOGAN (20th CENTURY-FOX)

ANTHONY QUINN, JULIE ROBINSON, KIRK DOUGLAS IN "LUST FOR LIFE" DIRECTED BY VINCENTE MINNELLI (M-G-M)

BURT LANCASTER, KATY JURADO, JOHNNY PULEO, TONY CURTIS IN "TRAPEZE" (UNITED ARTISTS)

MACHIKO KYO, MARLON BRANDO, EDDIE ALBERT, GLENN FORD, JUN NEGAMI IN "THE TEAHOUSE OF THE AUGUST MOON" DIRECTED BY DANIEL MANN (M-G-M)

KIRK DOUGLAS AS VAN GOGH IN "LUST FOR LIFE" (M-G-M)

KIM NOVAK, ROSALIND RUSSELL, SUSAN STRASBERG, BETTY FIELD Above: ARTHUR O'CONNELL, ROSALIND RUSSELL, WILLIAM HOLDEN, SUSAN STRASBERG IN "PICNIC" DIRECTED BY JOSHUA LOGAN (COLUMBIA)

MARLON BRANDO IN "THE TEAHOUSE OF THE AUGUST MOON" (M-G-M)

CLAYTON MOORE, SILVER, JAY SILVERHEELS
IN "THE LONE RANGER"
DIRECTED BY STUART HEISLER (WARNER BROS.)

GIULIETTA MASINA IN "LA STRADA"
DIRECTED BY FEDERICO FELLINI
(PONTI-DE LAURENTIIS)

HELEN HAYES, INGRID BERGMAN
IN "ANASTASIA"
DIRECTED BY ANATOLE LITVAK (20th CENTURY-FOX)

GREGORY PECK AS CAPTAIN AHAB
IN "MOBY DICK" PRODUCED AND
DIRECTED BY JOHN HUSTON
(WARNER BROS.)

1956 Two films were released this year that are probably destined to break the all-time box-office record now held by "Gone With the Wind." They are Michael Todd's "Around the World in Eighty Days" and Cecil B. De Mille's re-make of "The Ten Commandments." The Todd film has already grossed thirty-three million dollars and has won many Academy awards and other honors. Mr. De Mille has gone on record with the claim that his film will gross over one hundred million dollars. Other re-makes were "The Spoilers," "Moby Dick," "The Swan," "The Opposite Sex" (formerly "The Women") and "High Society" which was originally "The Philadelphia Story." "High Society" was Grace Kelly's last film before she became Princess Grace of Monaco. Recently Hollywood was relying more and more on Broadway for film fodder. Stage successes to reach the cinema screens this year included "The King and I," "Anastasia," "The Tea-house of the August Moon," "Picnic," "Bus Stop," "Tea and Sympathy," "The Rainmaker" and "Carousel." Among the better films were "Lust For Life," "The Man with the Golden Arm," "Somebody Up There Likes Me" and "Baby Doll." Giulietta Masina, an Italian star, scored great success with "La Strada." From England came Laurence Olivier's superb production of "Richard III" and two pleasant comedies, "Wee Geordie" introducing Bill Travers to American audiences, and "The Ladykillers" with Alec Guinness and Katie Johnson. Elvis Presley, a rock 'n' roll singing idol of the teen-agers, made his film debut in "Love Me Tender."

CECIL PARKER, KATIE JOHNSON,
ALEC GUINNESS IN
"THE LADYKILLERS"
(J. ARTHUR RANK)

YUL BRYNNER IN "THE KING
AND I" DIRECTED BY WALTER
LANG (20th CENTURY-FOX)

BING CROSBY, JOHN LUND, GRACE KELLY, FRANK SINATRA
IN "HIGH SOCIETY" MUSIC BY COLE PORTER
DIRECTED BY CHARLES WALTERS (M-G-M)

ELVIS PRESLEY
IN "LOVE ME TENDER"
(20th CENTURY-FOX)

FERNANDO LAMAS

JEFF RICHARDS

JOAN COLLINS

RICHARD BURTON

MARISA PAVAN

RICHARD EGAN

STEVE COCHRAN

MAE MARSH, FAY WRAY, ALAN LADD
IN "HELL ON FRISCO BAY"
DIRECTED BY FRANK TUTTLE (WARNER BROS.)

KIM NOVAK, FRANK SINATRA IN "THE MAN
WITH THE GOLDEN ARM" PRODUCED AND
DIRECTED BY OTTO PREMINGER (UNITED ARTISTS

DOROTHY McGUIRE, ANTHONY PERKINS, GARY COOPER
IN "FRIENDLY PERSUASION" PRODUCED AND
DIRECTED BY WILLIAM WYLER (ALLIED ARTISTS)

ROCK HUDSON, ELIZABETH TAYLOR, MERCEDES McCAMBRIDGE
Above: JAMES DEAN IN "GIANT" PRODUCED AND
DIRECTED BY GEORGE STEVENS (WARNER BROS.)

DEBORAH KERR, JOHN KERR
IN "TEA AND SYMPATHY"
DIRECTED BY VINCENTE MINNELLI (M-G-M)

PAUL NEWMAN, EILEEN HECKART
IN "SOMEBODY UP THERE LIKES ME"
DIRECTED BY ROBERT WISE (M-G-M)

STEVE ALLEN IN "THE
BENNY GOODMAN STORY"
DIRECTOR, VALENTINE
DAVIES (UNIVERSAL)

BURT LANCASTER, KATHARINE
HEPBURN IN "THE RAINMAKER"
DIRECTED BY JOSEPH ANTHONY
(PARAMOUNT)

GORDON MacRAE, SHIRLEY JONES
IN "CAROUSEL" DIRECTED BY HENRY KING
(20th CENTURY-FOX)

DEWEY MARTIN

TOM TRYON

BETSY DRAKE

MICHAEL WILDING

JANE WITHERS

RUSS TAMBLYN

JAMES ARNESS

ERNEST BORGNINE   EVA MARIE SAINT   ROBERT WAGNER   MITZI GAYNOR   GORDON MacRAE   JEAN SIMMONS   HOWARD KEEL

JACK OAKIE, CANTINFLAS, DAVID NIVEN, VICTOR
McLAGLEN, EDMUND LOWE, SHIRLEY MacLAINE
Above: CANTINFLAS, DAVID NIVEN

CANTINFLAS, DAVID NIVEN

DAVID NIVEN, BASIL SYDNEY, TREVOR HOWARD, ROLAND
SQUIRE, ROBERT MORLEY, FINLAY CURRIE
Above' TOLEDO, SPAIN

SCENES FROM MICHAEL TODD'S "AROUND THE WORLD IN 80 DAYS" DIRECTED BY MICHAEL ANDERSON (UNITED ARTISTS)

CANTINFLAS IN "AROUND
THE WORLD IN 80 DAYS"
(UNITED ARTISTS)

GRACE KELLY, ALEC GUINNESS, JESSIE ROYCE LANDIS, BRIAN AHERNE, LOUIS JOURDAN
IN "THE SWAN"
DIRECTED BY CHARLES VIDOR (M-G-M)

JACQUES SERNAS, ROSSANA PODESTA
IN "HELEN OF TROY" DIRECTED BY
ROBERT WISE (WARNER BROS.)

FRANK LOVEJOY   BILLY GILBERT   JERRY LEWIS   LUCILLE BALL AND
DESI ARNAZ   DEAN MARTIN   PHYLLIS KIRK   KURT KASZNAR

239

RICHARD BURTON IN "ALEXANDER THE GREAT" (UNITED ARTISTS)

GRACE KELLY IN "HIGH SOCIETY" (M-G-M)

TONY CURTIS IN "THE SQUARE JUNGLE" (UNIVERSAL)

BILL TRAVERS IN "WEE GEORDIE" (TIMES)

EVE ARDEN IN "OUR MISS BROOKS" (WARNER BROS.)

ROGER MOORE IN "DIANE" (M-G-M)

JOHN GIELGUD, MARY KERRIDGE, PAUL HUSON, CEDRIC HARDWICKE, LAURENCE OLIVIER
Above: LAURENCE OLIVIER, CLAIRE BLOOM
SCENES FROM "RICHARD III" PRODUCED AND DIRECTED BY LAURENCE OLIVIER (LOPERT)

LAURENCE OLIVIER AS RICHARD III

HENRY FONDA, AUDREY HEPBURN Above: MEL FERRER, AUDREY HEPBURN IN "WAR AND PEACE" DIRECTED BY KING VIDOR (PONTI-DE LAURENTIIS-PARAMOUNT)

CARROL BAKER, ELI WALLACH IN "BABY DOLL" DIRECTED BY ELIA KAZAN (WARNER BROS.)

JEFF CHANDLER, RORY CALHOUN IN "THE SPOILERS" DIRECTED BY JESSE HIBBS (UNIVERSAL)

KATHARINE HEPBURN, BOB HOPE IN "THE IRON PETTICOAT" DIRECTED BY RALPH THOMAS (M-G-M)

(PARAMOUNT)

THE TEN COMMANDMENTS

Producer-Director, Cecil B. De Mille; Screenplay by Aeneas MacKenzie, Jesse L. Lasky, Jr., Jack Gariss and Frederic M. Frank; Based on The Holy Scriptures, "Prince Of Egypt" by Dorothy Clarke Wilson, "Pillar Of Fire" by Rev. J. H. Ingraham, "On Eagle's Wings" by Rev. A. E. Southon; Choreography by LeRoy Prinz and Ruth Godfrey; Costumes by Edith Head, Ralph Jester, John Jensen, Dorothy Jeakins and Arnold Friberg; Music by Elmer Bernstein; Associate Producer, Henry Wilcoxon; Assistant Directors, Francisco Day, Michael Moore, Edward Salven, Daniel McCauley, Fouad Aref; In VistaVision and Technicolor.

CAST

Moses	Charlton Heston
Nefretiri	Anne Baxter
Sephora	Yvonne De Carlo
Joshua	John Derek
Bithiah	Nina Foch
Memnet	Judith Anderson
Aaron	John Carradine
Jannes	Douglass Dumbrille
Pentaur	Henry Wilcoxon
Mered	Donald Curtis
Amminadab	H. B. Warner
Rameses	Yul Brynner
Dathan	Edward G. Robinson
Lilia	Debra Paget
Sethi	Cedric Hardwicke
Yochabel	Martha Scott
Baka	Vincent Price
Miriam	Olive Deering
Abiram	Frank DeKova
Jethro	Eduard Franz
Hur Ben Caleb	Lawrence Dobkin
Elisheba	Julia Faye
Jethro's Daughters	Lisa Mitchell, Joanna Merlin, Joyce Vanderveen, Noelle Williams, Pat Richards, Diane Hall
Rameses' Charioteer	Abbas El Boughdadly
The Infant Moses	Fraser Heston
Gershom	Tommy Duran
Rameses' Son	Eugene Mazzola
Korah	Ramsay Hill
Princess Tharbia	Esther Brown
The Blind One	John Miljan
Simon	Francis J. McDonald
Rameses I	Ian Keith
Eleazar	Paul DeRolf
Korah's Wife	Joan Woodbury
King of Ethiopia	Woodrow Strode

CHARLTON HESTON, YUL BRYNNER (also at top)
Top center: EUGENE MAZZOLA, YUL BRYNNER, ANNE BAXTER, CEDRICK HARDWICKE, CHARLTON HESTON, JOHN CARRADINE

JOHN DEREK, DEBRA PAGET, OLIVE DEERING, YVONNE DE CARLO, CHARLTON HESTON (also at top)

HENRY WILCOXON   YVONNE DE CARLO   JUDITH ANDERSON   JOHN DEREK   VINCENT PRICE   ANNE BAXTER   EDWARD G. ROBINSON

1956

ALAN LADD

PAT HINGLE, ARTHUR STORCH, BEN GAZZARA IN "THE STRANGE ONE" DIRECTED BY JACK GARFEIN (COLUMBIA)

PATRICIA NEAL, PERCY WARAM, ANDY GRIFFITH IN "A FACE IN THE CROWD" DIRECTED BY ELIA KAZAN (WARNER BROS.)

GREER GARSON

AVA GARDNER, MEL FERRER, TYRONE POWER, ROBERT EVANS, EDDIE ALBERT, ERROL FLYNN IN "THE SUN ALSO RISES" DIRECTED BY HENRY KING (20th CENTURY-FOX)

JOAN BLONDELL, SAMMY OGG, KATHARINE HEPBURN, SPENCER TRACY, SUE RANDALL, DINA MERRILL IN "THE DESK SET" DIRECTED BY WALTER KING (20th CENTURY-FOX)

EARL HOLLIMAN, JEFF RICHARDS, ANNE FRANCIS IN "DON'T GO NEAR THE WATER" DIRECTED BY CHARLES WALTERS (M-G-M)

DOROTHY MALONE, JAMES CAGNEY IN "MAN OF A THOUSAND FACES" DIRECTED BY JOSEPH PEVNEY (UNIVERSAL)

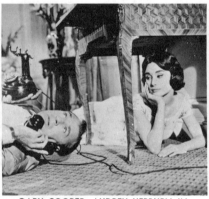

GARY COOPER, AUDREY HEPBURN IN "LOVE IN THE AFTERNOON" PRODUCED AND DIRECTED BY BILLY WILDER (ALLIED ARTISTS)

TONY RANDALL, JAYNE MANSFIELD IN "WILL SUCCESS SPOIL ROCK HUNTER?" PRODUCED AND DIRECTED BY FRANK TASHLIN (20th CENTURY-FOX)

BILL TRAVERS, JENNIFER JONES IN "TH BARRETTS OF "WIMPOLE STREET" DIRECTE BY SIDNEY FRANKLIN (M-G-M)

ELIZABETH TAYLOR

MARIO LANZA

AUDREY HEPBURN

GREGORY PECK

GEOFFREY HORNE, SESSUE HAYAKAWA, ALEC GUINNESS   ALEC GUINNESS   WILLIAM HOLDEN, JACK HAWKINS, GEOFFREY HORNE

SCENES FROM "THE BRIDGE ON THE RIVER KWAI" DIRECTED BY DAVID LEAN (COLUMBIA)

1957 With the exception of Paramount, all the major film companies, who had been blaming their troubles on television, had sold all their output prior to 1948 to their arch-enemy, and by 1958 Paramount had joined the parade. Television indeed had taken its toll on Hollywood. Most of the major studios were making fewer films, and some of them were shut down entirely for long periods. More American films were being shot in foreign lands than ever before in the history of motion pictures. It was cheaper. One encouraging note: while the quantity was less, the quality, on the whole, was better. The year's output included such fine films as "The Bridge on the River Kwai," "Sayonara," "Peyton Place," "Heaven Knows, Mr. Allison," "Twelve Angry Men," "The Young Strangers," "Edge of the City" and "A Hatful of Rain." In the foreign field, two newcomers were good box-office bets. French actress Brigitte Bardot was a sensation in "And God Created Woman," and Maria Schell, a Swiss actress, was equally effective in "Gervaise." Other new faces included Joanne Woodward, Robert Evans, James MacArthur, Jean Seberg and Diane Varsi. Death took Humphrey Bogart, Norma Talmadge, Oliver Hardy, Erich Von Stroheim and Louis B. Mayer.

JOANNE WOODWARD, LEE J. COBB IN "THE THREE FACES OF EVE" PRODUCED, DIRECTED AND WRITTEN BY NUNNALLY JOHNSON (20th CENTURY-FOX)

ROBERT MITCHUM, DEBORAH KERR IN "HEAVEN KNOWS, MR. ALLISON" DIRECTED BY JOHN HUSTON (20th CENTURY-FOX)

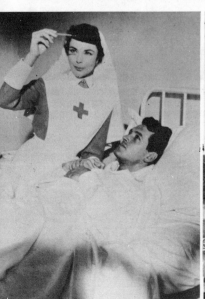

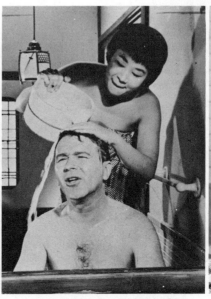

ROCK HUDSON, JENNIFER JONES IN "A FAREWELL TO ARMS" DIRECTED BY CHARLES VIDOR (20th CENTURY-FOX)   ANTHONY FRANCIOSA, ANNA MAGNANI, JOSEPH CALLEIA IN "WILD IS THE WIND" DIRECTED BY GEORGE CUKOR (PARAMOUNT)   RED BUTTONS, MIYOSHI UMEKI   MIIKO TAKA, MARLON BRANDO SCENES FROM "SAYONARA" DIRECTED BY JOSHUA LOGAN (WARNER BROS.)

DOROTHY MALONE

JOHN SAXON

LESLIE CARON

DON MURRAY

PIPER LAURIE

HUGH O'BRIAN

LORI NELSON

TAINA ELG, MITZI GAYNOR, KAY KENDALL, GENE KELLY IN "LES GIRLS" DIRECTED BY GEORGE CUKOR (M-G-M)

HOPE LANGE, RUSS TAMBLYN, DIANE VARSI, DAVID NELSON Above: LEE PHILIPS, LANA TURNER, DIANE VARSI IN "PEYTON PLACE" DIRECTED BY MARK ROBSON (20th CENTURY-FOX)

DAVID NIVEN, AVA GARDNER, STEWART GRANGER IN "THE LITTLE HUT" DIRECTED BY MARK ROBSON (M-G-M)

LISA GAYE, JOHN ARCHER, LISA MONTELL, STEVE DUNNE, ANNA MARIA ALBERGHETTI, DEWEY MARTIN, EVA BARTOK, DEAN MARTIN IN "TEN THOUSAND BEDROOMS" DIRECTED BY RICHARD THORPE (M-G-M)

PASCAL LAMORISSE IN "THE RED BALLOON" (LOPERT)

JOHN RAITT, DORIS DAY IN "THE PAJAMA GAME" (WARNER BROS.)

JOANNE GILBERT, ED WYNN, JOSÉ FERRER IN "THE GREAT MAN" DIRECTED BY JOSÉ FERRER (UNIVERSAL)

RICK JASON

ELAINE STEWART

GEORGE NADER

SHEREE NORTH

WILLIAM HOPPER

DIANA DORS

PHIL CAREY

JOHN KERR

NATALIE WOOD

BILL TRAVERS

JAYNE MANSFIELD

PAUL NEWMAN

KIM NOVAK

JACK PALANCE

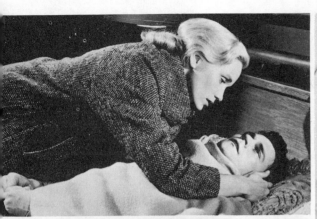

DON MURRAY, ANTHONY FRANCIOSA, EVA MARIE SAINT, LLOYD NOLAN Above: EVA MARIE SAINT, DON MURRAY IN "A HATFUL OF RAIN" DIRECTED BY FRED ZINNEMANN (20th CENTURY-FOX)

SOPHIA LO... "BOY ON A ... (20th CENTU...

...MERY CLIFT, ELIZABETH TAYLOR, TOM DRAKE ...Y CLIFT, ROD TAYLOR, EVA MARIE SAINT IN ...DIRECTED BY EDWARD DMYTRYK (M-G-M)

WHIT BISSELL, KIM HUNTER, JAMES MacARTHUR, JAMES GREGORY IN "THE YOUNG STRANGER" DIRECTED BY JOHN FRANKENHEIMER (UNIVERSAL)

HARR... IN "IS... ROB...

...TAINE ...CTED BY ...Y-FOX)

JACK WARDEN, EDWARD BINNS, E. G. MARSHALL, JOHN FIEDLER, HENRY FONDA, ED BEGLEY, ROBERT WEBBER, JACK KLUGMAN, GEORGE VOSKOVEC, MARTIN BALSAM, JOSEPH SWEENEY IN "12 ANGRY MEN" DIRECTED BY SIDNEY LUMET (UNITED ARTISTS)

MAMIE VAN DOREN

JACK LORD

SHIRLEY Mac...

...ROD STEIGER

THELMA RITTER

CLIFF ROBERTSON

DANA WYNTER

1957

245

MARLON BRANDO

ANNA MAGNANI

WILLIAM HOLDEN

ELVIS PRESLEY
IN "JAILHOUSE ROCK"
(M-G-M)

KIM NOVAK IN
"PAL JOEY" DIRECTED BY
GEORGE SIDNEY (COLUMBIA)

ANTHONY PERKINS IN
"FEAR STRIKES OUT" DIRECTED BY
ROBERT MULLIGAN (PARAMOUNT)

AUDREY HEPBURN IN
"FUNNY FACE" DIRECTED BY
STANLEY DONEN (PARAMOUNT)

PAT BOONE IN "BERNARDINE"
DIRECTED BY HENRY LEVIN
(20th CENTURY-FOX)

VAN JOHNSON

BEN GAZZARA IN
"THE STRANGE ONE"
(COLUMBIA)

GEORGE MONTGOMERY
AND DINAH SHORE

JEAN SEBERG
IN "SAINT JOAN"
(UNITED ARTISTS)

TAB HUNTER

INGRID BERGMAN
1957

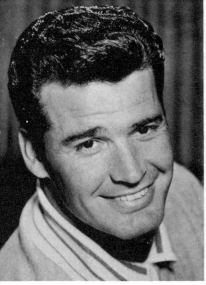

JAMES GARNER SOPHIA LOREN ANTHONY PERKINS BRIGITTE BARDOT

PETER FINCH, AUDREY HEPBURN
IN "THE NUN'S STORY"
DIRECTED BY FRED ZINNEMANN (WARNER BROS.)

SOPHIA LOREN, ANTHONY PERKINS
IN "DESIRE UNDER THE ELMS" DIRECTED
BY DELBERT MANN (PARAMOUNT)

NICK ADAMS, ANDY GRIFFITH, MYRON McCORMICK
IN "NO TIME FOR SERGEANTS"
DIRECTED BY MERVYN LeROY (WARNER BROS.)

LESLIE CARON, LOUIS JOURDAN
Above: LESLIE CARON

MAURICE CHEVALIER, LESLIE CARON, LOUIS JOURDAN
SCENES FROM "GIGI" DIRECTED BY VINCENTE MINNELLI (M-G-M)

HERMIONE GINGOLD, MAURICE
CHEVALIER Above: LOUIS JOURDAN

"WINDJAMMER"
LOUIS DE ROCHEMONT'S MODERN
ADVENTURE IN CINEMIRACLE

ROSSANO BRAZZI, MITZI GAYNOR

JUANITA HALL, JOHN KERR, RAY WALSTON
SCENES FROM "SOUTH PACIFIC"
DIRECTED BY JOSHUA LOGAN (20th CENTURY-FOX)

1958 To combat the TV menace, Hollywood produced better and more mature films. These included the excellent "Witness for the Prosecution," "Paths of Glory," "God's Little Acre," Stanley Kramer's racially-topical "The Defiant Ones," the sex-steeped "Cat on a Hot Tin Roof," and the searing attack on capital punishment, "I Want to Live," for which Susan Hayward won an Oscar. David Niven and Wendy Hiller received best actor and supporting actress Oscars for their performances in "Separate Tables." Other awards went to Burl Ives for his supporting role in the epic western, "The Big Country," and to the delightful "Gigi" which won most of the other Oscars, including best film, and best director (Vincente Minnelli). French comedian Jacques Tati's "My Uncle" won the best foreign film award. The year's big hits included "Auntie Mame," "The Brothers Karamazov," "The Young Lions," "South Pacific," "The Vikings," and "Indiscreet." Brigitte Bardot was still the most popular foreign star and Ingmar Bergman whose "Seventh Seal" and "Smiles of a Summer Night" were shown this year, the most admired foreign director. Death took Ronald Colman, Robert Donat, Edna Purviance, Estelle Taylor, silent star H. B. Warner, Hollywood pioneer producer Jesse L. Lasky and producer Mike Todd.

TYRONE POWER, MARLENE DIETRICH
IN "WITNESS FOR THE PROSECUTION"
DIRECTED BY BILLY WILDER (UNITED ARTISTS)

CAROL LYNLEY, JAMES MacARTHUR
IN "THE LIGHT IN THE FOREST" DIRECTED
BY HERSCHEL DAUGHERTY (DISNEY)

MARLON BRANDO, MAY BRITT Above: MONTGOMERY
CLIFT, DEAN MARTIN IN "THE YOUNG LIONS" DIRECTED
BY EDWARD DMYTRYK (20th CENTURY-FOX)

ERICH MARIA REMARQUE, JOHN GAVIN
IN "A TIME TO LOVE AND A TIME TO DIE"
DIRECTED BY DOUGLAS SIRK (UNIVERSAL)

YUL BRYNNER, MARIA SCHELL Above: YUL BRYNNER,
RICHARD BASEHART, WILLIAM SHATNER, HARRY TOWNES,
CLAIRE BLOOM IN "THE BROTHERS KARAMAZOV"
DIRECTED BY RICHARD BROOKS (M-G-M)

249

JAMES MacARTHUR

DIANE VARSI

STEPHEN BOYD

ANITA EKBERG

RAY STRICKLYN

CAROLYN JONES

BARRY COE

ELIZABETH TAYLOR, PAUL NEWMAN
IN "CAT ON A HOT TIN ROOF"
DIRECTED BY RICHARD BROOKS (M-G-M)

CLINT WALKER
IN "FORT DOBBS" DIRECTED
BY GORDON DOUGLAS (WARNER BROS.)

HENRY AMARGO, ROBERT GIST, GREG ROMAN, L. Q. JONE
ALDO RAY IN "THE NAKED AND THE DEAD"
DIRECTED BY RAOUL WALSH (RKO-WARNER BROS.)

MARIA SCHELL IN "THE
BROTHERS KARAMAZOV"
(M-G-M)

JOHN GAVIN IN
"A TIME TO LOVE AND A TIME
TO DIE" (UNIVERSAL)

KEVIN CORCORAN
IN "OLD YELLER"
DIRECTED BY ROBERT STEVENSON (DISNEY)

JAMES GARNER IN "DARBY'S
RANGERS" DIRECTED BY WILLIAM
WELLMAN (WARNER BROS.)

KIM STANLEY IN "TH
GODDESS" DIRECTED BY J
CROMWELL (COLUMBIA

CARY GRANT, INGRID BERGMAN IN
"INDISCREET" PRODUCED AND DIRECTED
BY STANLEY DONEN (WARNER BROS.)

SPENCER TRACY, FELIPE PAZOS
IN "THE OLD MAN AND THE
SEA" DIRECTED BY JOHN
STURGES (WARNER BROS.)

SOPHIA LOREN, WILLIAM HOLDEN
IN "THE KEY" DIRECTED BY
CAROL REED (COLUMBIA)

CHANA EDEN, CHRISTOPHER PLUMMER
IN "ACROSS THE EVERGLADES" DIRECTED
BY NICHOLAS RAY (WARNER BROS.)

ROBERT EVANS

SUZY PARKER

DAVID NELSON

JOANNE WOODWARD

SAL MINEO

MARIA SCHELL

GEOFFREY HORNE

PAUL FORD, SHIRLEY BOOTH, ANTHONY PERKINS, ROBERT MORSE IN "THE MATCHMAKER" DIRECTED BY JOSEPH ANTHONY (PARAMOUNT)

ANTHONY PERKINS IN "THIS ANGRY AGE" DIRECTED BY RENÉ CLÉMENT (COLUMBIA)

RAY STRICKLYN, GARY COOPER, DIANE VARSI, GERALDINE FITZGERALD IN "TEN NORTH FREDERICK" DIRECTED BY PHILIP DUNNE (20th CENTURY-FOX)

ED WYNN IN "MARJORIE MORNINGSTAR" DIRECTED BY IRVING RAPPER (WB)

AUDREY HEPBURN IN "THE NUN'S STORY" (WARNER BROS.)

ALAN LADD, DAVID LADD IN "THE PROUD REBEL" DIRECTED BY MICHAEL CURTIZ (BUENA VISTA)

LILI ST. CYR IN "THE NAKED AND THE DEAD" (RKO-WARNER BROS.)

JAMES MacARTHUR IN "THE LIGHT IN THE FOREST" (DISNEY)

KIRK DOUGLAS, WAYNE MORRIS IN "PATHS OF GLORY" DIRECTED BY STANLEY KUBRICK (UNITED ARTISTS)

FRANCHOT TONE, DOLORES DORN-HEFT IN "UNCLE VANYA"

BOB HOPE, FERNANDEL IN "PARIS HOLIDAY" DIRECTED BY GERD OSWALD (UNITED ARTISTS)

JACK LORD, ROBERT RYAN, TINA LOUISE IN "GOD'S LITTLE ACRE" DIRECTED BY ANTHONY MANN (UNITED ARTISTS)

HOPE LANGE   ORSON WELLES·   GLORIA GRAHAME   EFREM ZIMBALIST JR.   ANNA KASHFI   CHRISTOPHER PLUMMER

GLENN FORD, SHIRLEY MacLAINE IN "THE SHEEPMAN"
DIRECTED BY GEORGE MARSHALL (M-G-M)

JAMES STEWART, KIM NOVAK
IN "VERTIGO" DIRECTED BY
ALFRED HITCHCOCK (PARAMOUNT)

ALFONSA BEDOYA, CHARLES BICKFORD, JEAN SIMMONS, CHARLTON HESTON
CARROLL BAKER, GREGORY PECK, BURL IVES, CHUCK CONNORS IN
"THE BIG COUNTRY" DIRECTED BY WILLIAM WYLER (UNITED ARTISTS)

JEAN SIMMONS IN
"HOME BEFORE DARK"
DIRECTED BY MERVYN LE ROY (WARNER BROS.)

ROBERT TAYLOR, RICHARD WIDMARK
IN "THE LAW AND JAKE WADE"
DIRECTED BY JOHN STURGES (M-G-M)

ERNEST BORGNINE, GLENN FORD
IN "TORPEDO RUN"
DIRECTED BY JOSEPH PEVNEY (M-G-M)

CURT JURGENS, ROBERT MITCHUM
IN "THE ENEMY BELOW" DIRECTED
BY DICK POWELL (20th CENTURY-FOX)

CORAL BROWNE, ROSALIND RUSSELL
IN "AUNTIE MAME"
DIRECTOR, MORTON DA COSTA (WARNER BROS.)

GUNNAR BJORNSTRAND, EVA DAHLBECK
IN "SMILES OF A SUMMER NIGHT"
DIRECTED BY INGMAR BERGMAN (RANK)

ROMY SCHNEIDER

ROBERT STACK

PAUL NEWMAN

RICHARD BOONE

EARTHA KITT

AUDIE MURPHY

GENE KELLY, NATALIE WOOD
IN "MARJORIE MORNINGSTAR" DIRECTED
BY IRVING RAPPER (WARNER BROS.)

CHRISTOPHER LEE, MELISSA STRIBLING
IN "HORROR OF DRACULA"
DIRECTED BY TERENCE FISHER (HAMMER FILMS)

JOHN WAYNE IN "THE BARBARIAN
AND THE GEISHA" DIRECTED BY JOHN
HUSTON (20th CENTURY-FOX)

BURT LANCASTER, CLARK GABLE
IN "RUN SILENT, RUN DEEP"
DIRECTED BY ROBERT WISE (U.A.)

DAVID NIVEN, WENDY HILLER IN
"SEPARATE TABLES" DIRECTED BY
DELBERT MANN (UNITED ARTISTS)

TERRY-THOMAS, PETER SELLERS
IN "TOM THUMB"
DIRECTED BY GEORGE PAL (M-G-M)

LANA TURNER, SEAN CONNERY IN
"ANOTHER TIME, ANOTHER PLACE"
DIRECTED BY LEWIS ALLEN (PARAMOUNT)

KIRK DOUGLAS, JANET LEIGH IN
"THE VIKINGS" DIRECTED BY
RICHARD FLEISCHER (UNITED ARTISTS)

ROBERT DONAT, CURT JURGENS, INGRID BERGMAN
IN "THE INN OF THE SIXTH HAPPINESS"
DIRECTOR, MARK ROBSON (20th CENTURY-FOX)

253

ELIZABETH TAYLOR

TONY CURTIS, CARA WILLIAMS, SIDNEY POITIER
IN "THE DEFIANT ONES"
DIRECTED BY STANLEY KRAMER (UNITED ARTISTS)

KAY KENDALL, REX HARRISON IN
"THE RELUCTANT DEBUTANTE"
DIRECTED BY VINCENTE MINNELLI (M-G-M)

JULIETTE GRECO, RICHARD TODD IN
"THE NAKED EARTH" DIRECTED BY
VINCENT SHERMAN (20th CENTURY-FOX)

ALEC GUINNESS IN "THE HORSE'S MOUTH"
DIRECTED BY RONALD NEAME (U.A.)

VAN JOHNSON, SEAN CONNERY,
MARTINE CAROL IN
"ACTION OF THE TIGER" (M-G-M)

JEAN SEBERG, DEBORAH KERR
IN "BONJOUR TRISTESSE"

HOPE LANGE, BETTY FIELD,
ARTHUR KENNEDY

HOPE LANGE, LANA TURNER

"PEYTON PLACE" DIRECTED BY MARK ROBSON (20th CENTURY-FOX)

ROBERT TAYLOR, JOHN CASSAVETES IN "SADDLE THE WIND" DIRECTED BY ROBERT PARRISH (M-G-M)

JOSE FERRER, VIVECA LINDFORS
IN "I ACCUSE!"
DIRECTED BY JOSE FERRER (M-G-M)

DANNY KAYE, PIER ANGELI
IN "MERRY ANDREW"
DIRECTOR, MICHAEL KIDD (M-G-M)

JULIETTE GRECO, TREVOR HOWARD,
GREGOIRE ASLAN IN "THE ROOTS OF HEAVEN"
(20th CENTURY-FOX)

MELINA MERCOURI, PIERRE VANECK IN
"HE WHO MUST DIE" DIRECTOR,
JULES DASSIN (KASSLER FILMS)

FRANK SINATRA, TONY CURTIS
IN "KINGS GO FORTH"
DIRECTED BY DELMER DAVES (U.A.)

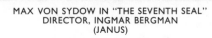

MAX VON SYDOW IN "THE SEVENTH SEAL"
DIRECTOR, INGMAR BERGMAN
(JANUS)

SUSAN HAYWARD
IN "I WANT TO LIVE"
DIRECTED BY ROBERT WISE (U.A.)

BARBARA MURRAY, DIRK BOGARDE
IN "CAMPBELL'S KINGDOM"
DIRECTOR, RALPH THOMAS (RANK)

CLAIRE MAURIER, ALBERT REMY
IN "THE 400 BLOWS"
DIRECTOR, FRANÇOIS TRUFFAUT (ZENITH INTERNATIONAL)

SIMONE SIGNORET, LAURENCE HARVEY
IN "ROOM AT THE TOP"
DIRECTOR, JACK CLAYTON (CONTINENTAL)

FRED ASTAIRE, GREGORY PECK,
AVA GARDNER IN "ON THE BEACH"
DIRECTOR, STANLEY KRAMER (U.A.)

CLAIRE BLOOM, RICHARD BURTON IN
"LOOK BACK IN ANGER" DIRECTOR,
TONY RICHARDSON (WARNER BROS.)

BRIGITTE BARDOT IN
"LOVE IS MY PROFESSION"
(KINGSLEY INTERNATIONAL)

JOHN WAYNE IN "THE HORSE SOLDIERS"
DIRECTED BY JOHN FORD (UNITED ARTISTS)

VICTOR SJÖSTRÖM IN "WILD STRAWBERRIES"
DIRECTED BY INGMAR BERGMAN (JANUS)

RITA HAYWORTH, GARY COOPER
IN "THEY CAME TO CORDURA"
DIRECTOR, ROBERT ROSSEN (COLUMBIA)

JUANITA MOORE, TERRY BURNHAM,
LANA TURNER IN "IMITATION OF LIFE"
DIRECTOR, DOUGLAS SIRK (UNIVERSAL)

DORIS DAY, ROCK HUDSON IN
"PILLOW TALK" DIRECTOR,
MICHAEL GORDON (UNIVERSAL)

ELKE SOMMER

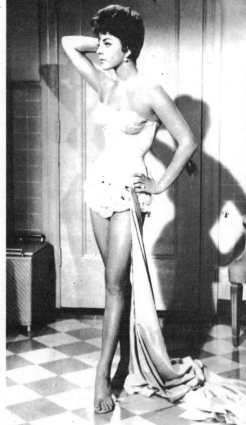

JOAN COLLINS

1959

The year of the epics. M-G-M released their mammoth re-make "Ben Hur," which raced home with most of the year's Oscars, collecting eleven including best actor, Charlton Heston ; best picture ; best director, William Wyler ; and best supporting actor, Hugh Griffith. It then went ahead to become one of the top ten money-makers of all time. The Italians, cashing in on the success of the promotion-made "Hercules," supplied a never-ending stream of mythological musclemen (mostly Steve Reeves) in the scantiest of clothes and even less plot for audiences who could not seem to get enough of these films. The other sure-fire foreign star at the box office remained Brigitte Bardot with such commercially titled films as "Love Is My Profession." Marilyn Monroe scored her biggest personal hit in one of the year's most popular comedies "Some Like It Hot," and Lana Turner came back to the screen in another re-make to do even better than the original, "Imitation of Life." The re-make of the classic German film, "The Blue Angel," which introduced the then unknown Marlene Dietrich, failed to repeat the trick for the Swedish discovery Mai Britt, who did not survive. Doris Day and Rock Hudson began their very successful partnership as a team in formula comedies, with the smash hit "Pillow Talk." Other hits were "Rio Bravo," "Porgy and Bess," "Anatomy of a Murder," "North by Northwest," "Suddenly Last Summer," and "On the Beach." From France came the "new wave" success, "400 Blows," and Jeanne Moreau made an impression in the heavily-censored "The Lovers" that established her as the new earth-mother of the boudoir. England sent Hayley Mills in her debut film "Tiger Bay," which also introduced another promising newcomer, Horst Buchholz. Simone Signoret was voted the best actress Oscar for her superbly drawn performance in the English film "Room at the Top." The Brazilian-made "Black Orpheus" won the Oscar for the best foreign feature. Another Oscar went to Shelley Winters for best supporting actress in "The Diary of Anne Frank." The exciting new faces included Troy Donahue, Lee Remick, Tuesday Weld, George Peppard, Laurence Harvey and Millie Perkins. Death took one of Hollywood's most famous directors and film pioneers, Cecil B. De Mille. Others who died in 1959 included famous fashion designer Adrian, Ethel Barrymore, Lou Costello, Paul Douglas, Errol Flynn, Kay Kendall, Mario Lanza, Victor McLaglen, Gilda Gray, Werner Krauss, Edmund Gwenn and Gerard Philipe.

FRED MacMURRAY, JAMES COBURN
IN "FACE OF A FUGITIVE"
DIRECTOR, PAUL WENDKOS (COLUMBIA)

GARY COOPER IN "THE
WRECK OF THE MARY DEARE"
DIRECTOR, MICHAEL ANDERSON (M-G-M)

RICHARD WIDMARK, TINA LOUISE, LEE
J. COBB, EARL HOLLIMAN IN "THE TRAP"
DIRECTED BY NORMAN PANAMA (PARAMOUNT)

CHARLTON HESTON AS BEN HUR
(M-G-M)

DAVID NIVEN, SHIRLEY MacLAINE
IN "ASK ANY GIRL"
DIRECTOR, CHARLES WALTER (M-G-M)

SIMONE SIGNORET

ANTHONY FRANCIOSA, AVA GARDNER
IN "THE NAKED MAJA"
DIRECTED BY HENRY KOSTER (U.A.)

JACK HAWKINS AS QUINTUS ARRIUS
Above: CHARLTON HESTON

THE CHARIOT RACE
"BEN HUR" DIRECTED BY WILLIAM WYLER (M-G-M)

HAYA HARAREET. Above:
HUGH GRIFFITH, STEPHEN BOYD

VINCENT PRICE   BETTE DAVIS   STEVE McQUEEN   JACK HAWKINS   JACK PALANCE   MARGARET LEIGHTON

ELIZABETH TAYLOR, MONTGOMERY CLIFT
"SUDDENLY LAST SUMMER" DIRECTOR, JOSEPH L. MANKIEWICZ (COLUMBIA)

ELIZABETH TAYLOR

FRANK SINATRA, ELEANOR PARKER
IN "A HOLE IN THE HEAD"
DIRECTED BY FRANK CAPRA (U.A.)

NIKOLAI CHERKASSOV IN
"IVAN THE TERRIBLE" PART II
DIRECTOR, EISENSTEIN (JANUS)

SANDRA DEE, TROY DONAHUE, RICHARD EGAN
IN "A SUMMER PLACE" DIRECTOR, DELMER DAVES
(WARNER BROS.)

MAI BRITT, CURT JURGENS
IN "THE BLUE ANGEL"
(20th CENTURY-FOX)

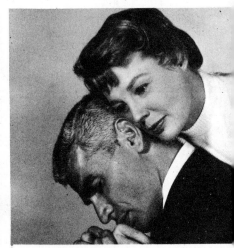

JERRY LEWIS, JULIE NEWMAR, WILLIAM
LANTEAU, STUBBY KAYE IN "LI'L ABNER"
DIRECTOR, MELVIN FRANK (PARAMOUNT)

DEAN STOCKWELL, BRADFORD DILLMAN,
ORSON WELLES IN "COMPULSION"
DIRECTOR, RICHARD FLEISCHER (20th CENTURY-FOX)

JEFF CHANDLER, JUNE ALLYSON
IN "A STRANGER IN MY ARMS"
DIRECTOR, HELMUT KAUTNER (UNIVERSAL)

YVONNE DE CARLO

ROBERT VAUGHAN

CAPUCINE

JOEL McCREA

SESSUE HAYAKAWA

CAROLYN JONES

CAT FISH ROW SCENE FROM "PORGY AND BESS"
DIRECTED BY OTTO PREMINGER (COLUMBIA)

DAVID WAYNE, PAUL MUNI IN "THE LAST ANGRY MAN"
DIRECTED BY DANIEL MANN (COLUMBIA)

GREGORY PECK, DEBORAH KERR IN
"THE BELOVED INFIDEL" DIRECTOR,
HENRY KING (20th CENTURY-FOX)

SAMMY DAVIS JR., EARTHA KITT
IN "ANNA LUCASTA" (U.A.)

ALEC GUINNESS IN
"THE SCAPEGOAT"
DIRECTOR, ROBERT HAMER (M-G-M)

SEAN CONNERY, JANET MUNRO IN
"DARBY O'GILL AND THE LITTLE PEOPLE"
DIRECTOR, ROBERT STEVENSON (BUENA VISTA)

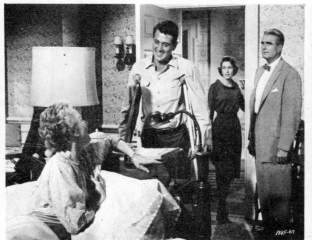
ANNA LEE, ROCK HUDSON, STACY GRAHAM,
KENT SMITH IN "THIS EARTH IS MINE"
DIRECTOR, HENRY KING (UNIVERSAL)

PAT BOONE, PETER RONSON, JAMES MASON, ARLENE
DAHL IN "A JOURNEY TO THE CENTRE OF THE EARTH"
DIRECTED BY HENRY LEVIN (20th CENTURY-FOX)

FAY SPAIN

JOHN SAXON

RHONDA FLEMING

SAL MINEO

LINDA CHRISTIAN

TREVOR HOWARD

JOSEPH SCHILDKRAUT, GUSTI HUBER, MILLIE PERKINS, LOU JACOBI,
SHELLEY WINTERS, RICHARD BEYMER, DIANE BAKER

"THE DIARY OF ANNE FRANK" DIRECTED BY GEORGE STEVENS (20th CENTURY-FOX)

SHELLEY WINTERS

JOHN WAYNE, DEAN MARTIN, RICKY
NELSON IN "RIO BRAVO"
(WARNER BROS.)

YUL BRYNNER, DEBORAH KERR
IN "THE JOURNEY"
DIRECTED BY ANATOLE LITVAK (M-G-M)

VIVECA LINDFORS IN "THE TEMPEST"
(PARAMOUNT)

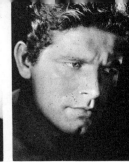

JOANNE WOODWARD   JEFF CHANDLER   JACK LEMMON   CARROLL BAKER   BOB HOPE   STEPHEN BOYD

LEE REMICK IN "ANATOMY OF A MURDER" (COLUMBIA)

KATHARINE HEPBURN IN "SUDDENLY LAST SUMMER" (COLUMBIA)

RITA HAYWORTH

JAYNE MANSFIELD, KENNETH MORE IN "THE SHERIFF OF FRACTURED JAW" (20th CENTURY-FOX)

VERA MILES, JAMES STEWART IN "THE F.B.I. STORY" DIRECTOR, MERVYN LE ROY (WARNER BROS.)

ALEXIS SMITH, PAUL NEWMAN IN "THE YOUNG PHILADELPHIANS" (WARNER BROS.)

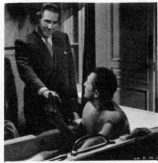

MICKEY ROONEY IN "THE LAST MILE" DIRECTED BY HOWARD W. KOCH (U.A.)

DONALD WOLFIT, ROBERT MITCHUM IN "THE ANGRY HILLS" (M-G-M)

UNA MERKEL, PAUL DOUGLAS, DEBBIE REYNOLDS, TONY RANDALL IN "THE MATING GAME" (M-G-M)

ANTHONY QUINN, HENRY FONDA IN "WARLOCK" DIRECTED BY EDWARD DMYTRYK (20th CENTURY-FOX)

JEAN-MARC BORY, JEANNE MOREAU
IN "THE LOVERS"
DIRECTOR, LOUIS MALLE (ZENITH)

CARY GRANT, EVA MARIE SAINT, JAMES MASON
IN "NORTH BY NORTHWEST" DIRECTED BY
ALFRED HITCHCOCK (M-G-M)

CARY GRANT, JOAN O'BRIEN, DINA
MERRILL, TONY CURTIS IN "OPERATION
PETTICOAT" (UNIVERSAL)

JOAN COLLINS, PAUL NEWMAN IN
"RALLY ROUND THE FLAG BOYS"
DIRECTOR, LEO McCAREY (20th CENT. FOX)

FRANK SINATRA, GINA LOLLOBRIGIDA
IN "NEVER SO FEW"
DIRECTOR, JOHN STURGES (M-G-M)

ARTHUR O'CONNELL, EVE ARDEN, JAMES STEWART IN "ANATOMY OF A MURDER"
DIRECTED BY OTTO PREMINGER (COLUMBIA)

HAYLEY MILLS, JOHN MILLS IN "TIGER BAY"
DIRECTOR, J. LEE THOMPSON (CONTINENTAL)

HOWARD KEEL IN "THE BIG FISHERMAN" (BUENA VISTA)

SOPHIA LOREN IN "THE BLACK ORCHID" DIRECTOR, MARTIN RITT (PARAMOUNT)

DOROTHY McGUIRE, RICHARD EGAN IN "A SUMMER PLACE" (WARNER BROS.)

LAURENCE OLIVIER, SHEREE WINTON IN "THE DEVIL'S DISCIPLE" (U.A.)

STEVE REEVES IN "HERCULES" (WARNER BROS.)

HARRY BELAFONTE, INGER STEVENS IN "THE WORLD, THE FLESH AND THE DEVIL" (M-G-M)

BRENO MELLO IN "BLACK ORPHEUS" DIRECTED BY MARCEL CAMUS (LOPERT)

LOUIS ARMSTRONG, DANNY KAYE IN "THE FIVE PENNIES" DIRECTED BY MELVILLE SHAVELSON (PARAMOUNT)

ARTHUR KENNEDY, FRANK SINATRA IN "SOME CAME RUNNING" (M-G-M)

TONY CURTIS, JACK LEMMON

JACK LEMMON, MARILYN MONROE

"SOME LIKE IT HOT" DIRECTED BY BILLY WILDER (UNITED ARTISTS)

CAPUCINE, JOHN WAYNE IN
"NORTH TO ALASKA" DIRECTED BY
HENRY HATHAWAY (20th CENTURY-FOX)

TATIANA SAMOILOVA, ALEXEI BATALOV
IN "THE CRANES ARE FLYING" DIRECTED
BY M. KALATOZOV (WARNER BROS.)

MARIA SCHELL, GLENN FORD,
IN "CIMARRON" DIRECTED BY
ANTHONY MANN (M-G-M)

DEAN MARTIN, JUDY HOLLIDAY IN
"BELLS ARE RINGING" DIRECTED BY
VINCENTE MINNELLI (M-G-M)

RALPH BELLAMY, GREER GARSON, IN
"SUNRISE AT CAMPOBELLO" DIRECTED BY
VINCENT J. DONAHUE (WARNER BROS.)

JAMES MASON IN
"A TOUCH OF LARCENY" DIRECTED BY
GUY HAMILTON (PARAMOUNT)

JANE FONDA, ANTHONY PERKINS,
IN "TALL STORY"
DIRECTOR, JOSHUA LOGAN (WARNER BROS.)

RICHARD ATTENBOROUGH
IN "THE ANGRY SILENCE"
DIRECTED BY BRYAN FORBES (VALIANT)

KAY KENDALL, YUL BRYNNER IN
"ONCE MORE WITH FEELING" DIRECTED
BY STANLEY DONEN (COLUMBIA)

HAYLEY MILLS, ADOLPH MENJOU, IN "POLLYANNA" DIRECTED BY DAVID SWIFT (BUENA VISTA)

AUDREY HEPBURN, BURT LANCASTER IN "THE UNFORGIVEN" DIRECTED BY JOHN HUSTON (UNITED ARTISTS)

DEBORAH KERR IN "THE SUNDOWNERS" DIRECTED BY FRED ZINNEMANN (WARNER BROS.)

MAMIE VAN DOREN

1960 The last year for some time in which most of the year's big money-makers were domestic, although the flood of cheaply fabricated Italian epics reached its height. Hollywood was still making its own all-star epics to combat the TV monster, and "Spartacus," "Exodus," and "The Alamo" did well. Among the better films were Hitchcock's frightening exercise in terror "Psycho;" another was "Elmer Gantry" which won Oscars for best actor, Burt Lancaster and best supporting actress, Shirley Jones; and "Pollyanna," whose treacle-coated plot was made palatable by the most popular child star since Shirley Temple, the English moppet, Hayley Mills. She won a special Oscar for her performance and became one of America's best-loved box office stars for several years. Billy Wilder's widely-hailed "The Apartment" won Oscars for best film, best director, and best story and screenplay. Peter Ustinov received a supporting Oscar for "Spartacus." The most discussed award was given to Elizabeth Taylor for her performance in the novelettish "Butterfield 8" not long after her dramatic fight for life in hospital. Other films of fine quality included "Heller in Pink Tights," "The Unforgiven," "The Fugitive Kind," "The Magnificent Seven" and "The Sundowners." Ingmar Bergman's excellent "The Virgin Spring" won the Oscar for best foreign feature, while the New York Film Critics awarded their prize to the French masterpiece "Hiroshima, Mon Amour." Other foreign films to gain success were the Russian-made "Ballad of a Soldier," and "The Cranes Are Flying," while the success of the Greek film "Never on a Sunday" made its star, Melina Mercouri, and its song, world famous. New faces were James Coburn, Steve McQueen, Robert Vaughan, Charles Bronson, Jane Fonda, Jim Hutton, Paula Prentiss, George Hamilton, Nancy Kwan, and Yvette Mimieux. One of the perennial symbols of Hollywood stardom, Clark Gable, "The King," died aged 59. Others to die in 1960 included Margaret Sullavan, Gregory Ratoff, Diana Barrymore, Hans Albers, and the great silent stars, Clara Kimball Young, Kathlyn Williams, Phyllis Haver and Mack Sennett.

LAURENCE HARVEY

MARILYN MONROE, YVES MONTAND, IN "LET'S MAKE LOVE" DIRECTED BY GEORGE CUKOR (20th CENTURY-FOX)

ELVIS PRESLEY, DOLORES DEL RIO, IN "FLAMING STAR" DIRECTED BY DON SIEGEL (20th CENTURY-FOX)

BRADFORD DILLMAN, JULIETTE GRECO, ORSON WELLES, IN "CRACK IN THE MIRROR" (20th CENTURY-FOX)

PETER O'TOOLE

EVA MARIE SAINT

GINA LOLLOBRIGIDA

TROY DONAHUE

MAUREEN O'HARA

DOUG McCLURE

PETER FINCH IN
"THE GREEN CARNATION"
DIRECTED BY KEN HUGHES (WARWICK)

CLARK GABLE, SOPHIA LOREN IN "IT
STARTED IN NAPLES" DIRECTED BY
MELVILLE SHAVELSON (PARAMOUNT)

LEE REMICK, MONTGOMERY CLIFT IN
"WILD RIVER" DIRECTED BY
ELIA KAZAN (20th CENTURY-FOX)

HAYLEY MILLS IN "POLLYANNA"
DIRECTED BY DAVID SWIFT
(BUENA VISTA)

DEAN STOCKWELL, WENDY HILLER
IN "SONS AND LOVERS" DIRECTED BY
JACK CARDIFF (20th CENTURY-FOX)

CAROLYN JONES, RICHARD BURTON,
SHIRLEY KNIGHT IN "ICE PALACE"
(WARNER BROS.)

SPENCER TRACY IN
"INHERIT THE WIND" DIRECTED
BY STANLEY KRAMER (UNITED ARTISTS)

268

JULIE LONDON

ALEC GUINNESS

HORST BUCHHOLZ

MARTHA HYER

SUSANNAH YORK

JANICE RULE

JOAN COLLINS

ROBERT MITCHUM, RICHARD HARRIS IN
"THE NIGHT FIGHTERS" DIRECTED BY
TAY GARNETT (UNITED ARTISTS)

DAVID NIVEN, JANIS PAIGE IN
"PLEASE DON'T EAT THE DAISIES"
DIRECTED BY CHARLES WALTERS (M-G-M)

LAURENCE OLIVIER IN
"THE ENTERTAINER" DIRECTED BY
TONY RICHARDSON (CONTINENTAL)

JIM HUTTON, PAULA PRENTISS IN
"WHERE THE BOYS ARE" DIRECTED BY
HENRY LEVIN (M-G-M)

HARDY KRUGER, MICHELINE PRESLE
IN "CHANCE MEETING" DIRECTED BY
JOSEPH LOSEY (PARAMOUNT)

AVA GARDNER, DIRK BOGARDE IN
"THE ANGEL WORE RED" DIRECTED BY
NUNNALLY JOHNSON (M-G-M)

MARILYN MONROE IN "LET'S
MAKE LOVE" DIRECTED BY GEORGE
CUKOR (20th CENTURY-FOX)

SOPHIA LOREN IN
"HELLER IN PINK TIGHTS"
(PARAMOUNT)

JACK LEMMON

JACK LEMMON, SHIRLEY MacLAINE
"THE APARTMENT" DIRECTED BY BILLY WILDER (UNITED ARTISTS)

LAURENCE OLIVIER, PETER USTINOV,
NINA FOCH, JEAN SIMMONS

PETER USTINOV

KIRK DOUGLAS, JEAN SIMMONS
"SPARTACUS" DIRECTED BY STANLEY KUBRICK (UNIVERSAL)

CHARLES LAUGHTON

PAUL NEWMAN

EVA MARIE SAINT
RALPH RICHARDSON
"EXODUS" DIRECTED BY OTTO PREMINGER (UNITED ARTISTS)

EVA MARIE SAINT, JOHN DEREK
PAUL NEWMAN,

SHIRLEY JONES, BURT LANCASTER

BURT LANCASTER
"ELMER GANTRY" DIRECTED BY RICHARD BROOKS (UNITED ARTISTS)

MELINA MERCOURI IN
"NEVER ON A SUNDAY" DIRECTED BY
JULES DASSIN (LOPERT)

SOPHIA LOREN

ELIZABETH TAYLOR

LAURENCE HARVEY, ELIZABETH TAYLOR
"BUTTERFIELD 8" DIRECTED BY DANIEL MANN (M-G-M)

SHANNA PROKHORENKO, VLADIMIR
IVASHOV IN "BALLAD OF A SOLDIER"
DIRECTED BY GRIGORI CHUKHRAI
(KINGSLEY INTERNATIONAL)

KIM NOVAK, KIRK DOUGLAS IN
"STRANGERS WHEN WE MEET"
(COLUMBIA)

BUSTER KEATON IN
"WHEN COMEDY WAS KING" DIRECTED
BY ROBERT YOUNGSON (20th CENT. FOX)

JOHN WAYNE, RICHARD WIDMARK
IN "THE ALAMO" DIRECTED BY
JOHN WAYNE (UNITED ARTISTS)

ELVIS PRESLEY IN
"G.I. BLUES" DIRECTED BY
NORMAN TAUROG (PARAMOUNT)

JOHN MILLS, ALEC GUINNESS IN
"TUNES OF GLORY" DIRECTED BY
RONALD NEAME (LOPERT)

MAX VON SYDOW, BIRGITTA PETTERSON,
BIRGITTA VALBERG IN "THE VIRGIN
SPRING" DIRECTED BY INGMAR BERGMAN (JANUS)

SHIRLEY MacLAINE, JULIETTE PROWSE
IN "CAN-CAN" DIRECTED BY
WALTER LANG (20th CENTURY-FOX)

LLOYD NOLAN, LANA TURNER IN
"PORTRAIT IN BLACK" DIRECTED BY
MICHAEL GORDON (UNIVERSAL)

YUL BRYNNER, STEVE McQUEEN, HORST BUCHHOLZ,
CHARLES BRONSON, ROBERT VAUGHAN, BRAD DEXTER,
JAMES COBURN IN "THE MAGNIFICENT SEVEN"
DIRECTED BY JOHN STURGES (UNITED ARTISTS)

ROBERT PRESTON, ROBERT EYER IN
"THE DARK AT THE TOP OF THE STAIRS"
DIRECTED BY DELBERT MANN (WARNER BROS.)

SYLVIA SYMS, WILLIAM HOLDEN, NANCY
KWAN IN "THE WORLD OF SUZY WONG"
DIRECTED BY RICHARD QUINE (PARAMOUNT)

EMMANUELLE RIVA, EIJI OKADA IN
"HIROSHIMA MON AMOUR"
DIRECTED BY ALAIN RESNAIS

MARLON BRANDO, ANNA MAGNANI,
JOANNA WOODWARD IN "THE FUGITIVE
KIND" DIRECTED BY SIDNEY LUMET
(UNITED ARTISTS)

RITA HAYWORTH, ANTHONY FRANCIOSA
IN "THE STORY ON PAGE ONE"
(20th CENTURY-FOX)

EDWARD G. ROBINSON, ROD STEIGER,
JOAN COLLINS, ELI WALLACH IN "SEVEN
THIEVES" DIRECTED BY H. HATHAWAY
(20th CENTURY-FOX)

JANET LEIGH, JOHN GAVIN

ANTHONY PERKINS

273

"PSYCHO" DIRECTED BY ALFRED HITCHCOCK (PARAMOUNT)

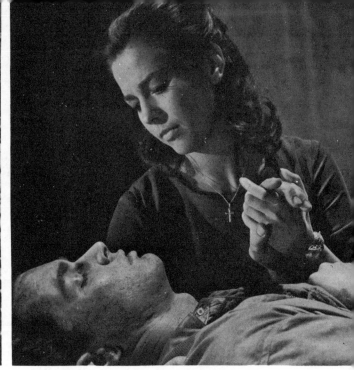

NATALIE WOOD

RICHARD BEYMER, RUSS TAMBLYN

RICHARD BEYMER, NATALIE WOOD

"WEST SIDE STORY" DIRECTED BY ROBERT WISE (UNITED ARTISTS)

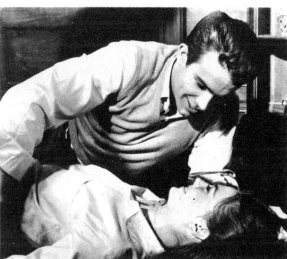

INGRID BERGMAN, YVES MONTAND IN
"GOODBYE AGAIN" DIRECTED BY
ANATOLE LITVAK (UNITED ARTISTS)

WARREN BEATTY, NATALIE WOOD IN
"SPLENDOR IN THE GRASS" DIRECTED
BY ELIA KAZAN (WARNER BROS.)

ANNE BAXTER, JOHN MILLS, ERNEST
BORGNINE IN "SEASON OF PASSION"
DIRECTED BY LESLIE NORMAN (UNITED
ARTISTS)

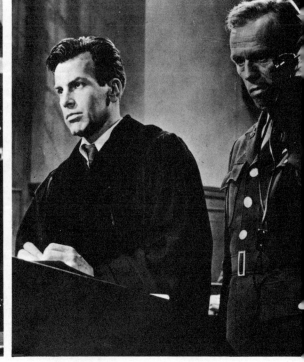

MARLENE DIETRICH, SPENCER TRACY

BURT LANCASTER

MAXIMILIAN SCHELL, RICHARD WIDMARK

274

"JUDGMENT AT NUREMBERG" DIRECTED BY STANLEY KRAMER (UNITED ARTISTS)

GUY ROLFE, VIVECA LINDFORS, HURD HATFIELD, FRANK THRING, RITA GAM IN "KING OF KINGS" DIRECTED BY N. RAY (M-G-M)

MONICA VITTI, GABRIELE FERZETTI IN "L'AVVENTURA" DIRECTED BY MICHELANGELO ANTONIONI (JANUS)

HORST BUCHHOLZ, LESLIE CARON IN "FANNY" DIRECTED BY JOSHUA LOGAN (WARNER BROS.)

1961 More and more American Companies moved to Europe to make their big films there, and more and more foreign language films found favor with American audiences. One of the best films of that or any other year was the American financed, internationally cast, Spanish made, "El Cid," starring Charlton Heston and Sophia Loren. Sophia Loren received the Oscar for her performance in the Italian film, "Two Women." It was the first time a performer nominated for a role in a foreign language film won it. An Oscar went to Maximilian Schell, for his performance in Stanley Kramer's all star courtroom drama, "Judgment at Nuremberg." A total of eleven Oscars went to one of the most widely praised musicals of all time, "West Side Story," adapted from the Broadway hit of the same name. Among its awards were ones for the best film, best director Robert Wise, best male and female co-stars George Chakiris and Rita Moreno, and the New York Film Critics choice. Outstanding successes included Disney's cartoon feature "One Hundred and One Dalmatians," "The Guns of Navarone," "Breakfast at Tiffany's," and the brilliant "The Hustler." The year's fascinating failures included the last film which Monroe and Clark Gable made, "The Misfits;" the only film Marlon Brando directed and starred in, "One Eyed Jacks," and the heavy if intriguing "King of Kings." For the second year running the Oscar for the best foreign feature went to an Ingmar Bergman film "Through a Glass Darkly," but it was the sensational Italian film, "La Dolce Vita" that broke through the American reserve to European films on a big scale, and paved the way for such successful imports as "La Notte," "Rocco and his Brothers," "L'Avventura" and others. England's excellent "Saturday Night and Sunday Morning" did well. Promising personalities for film stardom included Warren Beatty, Susan Strasberg, Keir Dullea, Pamela Tiffin, Chad Everett, Stella Stevens, Claudia Cardinale, Albert Finney, Susannah York and Connie Stevens. One of Hollywood's all-time great stars, Gary Cooper, died of cancer, aged 60. Among those who also died were Ruth Chatterton, Marion Davies, Nita Naldi, Jeff Chandler, Charles Coburn, Barry Fitzgerald, Belinda Lee, Chico Marx, Gail Russell and Anna May Wong.

GEORGE CHAKIRIS IN "WEST SIDE STORY" (U.A.)

RITA MORENO IN "WEST SIDE STORY" (U.A.)

BOB HOPE, LANA TURNER IN "BACHELOR IN PARADISE" DIRECTED BY JACK ARNOLD (M-G-M)

BETTE DAVIS, GLENN FORD IN "POCKETFUL OF MIRACLES" DIRECTED BY FRANK CAPRA (UNITED ARTISTS)

FRED ASTAIRE, DEBBIE REYNOLDS, TAB HUNTER, LILLI PALMER, GARY MERRILL, CHARLES RUGGLES IN "THE PLEASURE OF HIS COMPANY" DIRECTED BY GEORGE SEATON (PARAMOUNT)

PINA PELLICER, MARLON BRANDO IN
"ONE-EYED JACKS" DIRECTED BY
MARLON BRANDO (PARAMOUNT)

JULIE NEWMAR, JAMES MASON IN
"THE MARRIAGE-GO-ROUND" DIRECTED
BY WALTER LANG (20th CENT. FOX)

PATRICIA NEAL, AUDREY HEPBURN,
GEORGE PEPPARD IN "BREAKFAST AT
TIFFANY'S" (PARAMOUNT)

SHIRLEY MacLAINE, DEAN MARTIN IN
"ALL IN A NIGHT'S WORK" DIRECTED
BY JOSEPH ANTHONY (PARAMOUNT)

HAYLEY MILLS IN "THE PARENT TRAP"
DIRECTED BY DAVID SWIFT
(BUENA VISTA)

ROLAND WINTERS, ELVIS PRESLEY,
ANGELA LANSBURY, JOHN ARCHER IN
"BLUE HAWAII" (PARAMOUNT)

AUDREY HEPBURN IN "BREAKFAST AT TIFFANY'S"
DIRECTOR, BLAKE EDWARDS (PARAMOUNT)

SOPHIA LOREN, ELEANORA BROWN
"TWO WOMEN" DIRECTED BY VITTORIO DE SICA (EMBASSY)

SOPHIA LOREN, JEAN-PAUL BELMONDO

JANE ASHER, SUSANNAH YORK IN
"LOSS OF INNOCENCE" DIRECTED BY
LEWIS GILBERT (COLUMBIA)

AUDREY HEPBURN IN "BREAKFAST AT TIFFANY'S"
(PARAMOUNT)

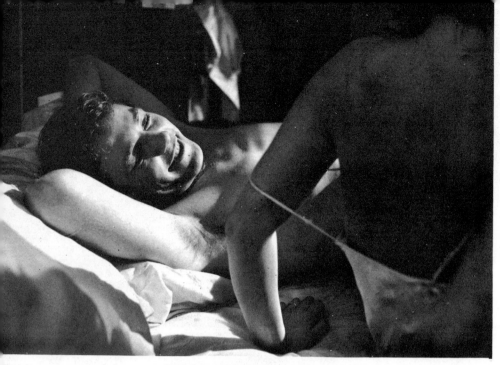

ALBERT FINNEY, RACHEL ROBERTS

ALBERT FINNEY

"SATURDAY NIGHT & SUNDAY MORNING" DIRECTED BY KAREL REISZ (CONTINENTAL)

BRIGITTE BARDOT IN "THE TRUTH" DIRECTED BY HENRI-GEORGES CLOUZOT (KINGSLEY)

JENNIFER JONES IN "TENDER IS THE NIGHT" DIRECTOR, HENRY KING (20th CENTURY-FOX)

PETER FINCH IN "NO LOVE FOR JOHNNIE" DIRECTOR, RALPH THOMAS (EMBASSY)

BURT LANCASTER, SHELLEY WINTERS IN "THE YOUNG SAVAGES" (UNITED ARTISTS)

DON AMECHE

HOPE LANGE

RENATO SALVATORI

MARTHA HYER

LOUIS JOURDAN

BRIGITTE BARDOT

PAUL NEWMAN PIPER LAURIE   PAUL NEWMAN

"THE HUSTLER" DIRECTED BY ROBERT ROSSEN (20th CENTURY-FOX)

JARL KULLE IN "THE DEVIL'S EYE" DIRECTOR, INGMAR BERGMAN (JANUS)

JEANNE MOREAU IN "LA NOTTE" DIRECTOR, ANTONIONI (LOPERT)

GERARD PHILIPE, ANNETTE VADIM IN "LES LIASONS DANGEREUSES" DIRECTED BY ROGER VADIM (ASTOR)

RENATO SALVATORI, ANNIE GIR'ARDOT IN "ROCCO AND HIS BROTHERS" DIRECTED BY LUCHINO VISCONTI (ASTOR)

JULIET PROWSE   RICHARD JOHNSON   ESTHER WILLIAMS   CONNIE STEVENS   ANNE FRANCIS   VITTORIO DE SICA

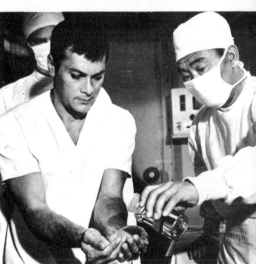

JOHN WAYNE, INA BALIN, STUART
WHITMAN IN "THE COMANCHEROS"
DIRECTED BY MICHAEL CURTIS (20th CENTURY-FOX)

GIA SCALA, ANTHONY QUINN   ANTHONY QUINN   TONY CURTIS IN "THE GREAT IMPOSTER"
DIRECTOR, ROBERT MULLIGAN (UNIVERSAL)

Above: JAMES DARREN, STANLEY BAKER, DAVID NIVEN, GREGORY PECK, ANTHONY QUINN,
ANTHONY QUAYLE IN "THE GUNS OF NAVARONE" (COLUMBIA)

CAROL LYNLEY, ROCK HUDSON IN
"THE LAST SUNSET" DIRECTED BY
ROBERT ALDRICH (UNIVERSAL)

JULIE HARRIS, LAURENCE OLIVIER IN
"THE POWER AND THE GLORY" (PARAMOUNT)

JAMES STEWART, RICHARD WIDMARK IN
"TWO RODE TOGETHER" DIRECTED BY
JOHN FORD (COLUMBIA)

SANDRA DEE, JOHN GAVIN IN
"ROMANOFF AND JULIET" DIRECTED
BY PETER USTINOV (UNIVERSAL)

GERALDINE PAGE, LAURENCE HARVEY IN
"SUMMER AND SMOKE" DIRECTED BY
PETER GLENVILLE (PARAMOUNT)

TROY DONAHUE, CLAUDETTE COLBERT IN
"PARRISH" DIRECTED BY DELMER DAVES
(WARNER BROS.)

SOPHIA LOREN AS CHIMENE

CHARLTON HESTON AS EL CID

GARY RAYMOND, JOHN FRASER

ANDREW CRUICKSHANK, SOPHIA LOREN

CHARLTON HESTON,
CHRISTOPHER RHODES

CHARLTON HESTON, MASSIMO SERRATO

GENEVIEVE PAGE, JOHN FRASER

SOPHIA LOREN, CHARLTON HESTON

SCENES FROM "EL CID" DIRECTED BY ANTHONY MANN (ALLIED ARTISTS)

Above: CLARK GABLE; ARTHUR MILLER, ELI WALLACH, MONTGOMERY CLIFT, MARILYN MONROE, JOHN HUSTON, CLARK GABLE. Below: CLARK GABLE, ELI WALLACH, MONTGOMERY CLIFT IN "THE MISFITS" DIRECTED BY JOHN HUSTON (UNITED ARTISTS)

SOPHIA LOREN, PETER SELLERS "THE MILLIONAIRESS" DIRECTED BY ANTHONY ASQUITH (20th CENT. FOX)

GARY COOPER, DEBORAH KERR, DIANE CILENTO, RAY McNALLY IN "THE NAKED EDGE" DIRECTED BY MICHAEL ANDERSON (UNITED ARTISTS)

DON AMECHE, ANGIE DICKINSON, EFREM ZIMBALIST JR. IN "A FEVER IN THE BLOOD" (WARNER BROS.)

YOKO TANI, ANTHONY QUINN, PETER O'TOOLE IN "THE SAVAGE INNOCENTS" DIRECTED BY NICHOLAS RAY (PARAMOUNT)

CARY GRANT, JEAN SIMMONS IN "THE GRASS IS GREENER" DIRECTED BY STANLEY DONEN (UNIVERSAL)

JOHN GAVIN, VERA MILES, SUSAN HAYWARD IN "BACK STREET" DIRECTED BY DAVID MILLER (UNIVERSAL)

MARY ASTOR, TUESDAY WELD, ELEANOR PARKER IN "RETURN TO PEYTON PLACE" (20th CENTURY-FOX)

BRADFORD DILLMAN   MILLIE PERKINS   SUSAN KOHNER   JENNIFER JONES

MAURICE CHEVALIER, LESLIE CARON
IN "FANNY" DIRECTED BY
JOSHUA LOGAN (WARNER BROS.)

MAX VON SYDOW, HARRIET ANDERSSON
IN "THROUGH A GLASS DARKLY" DIRECTED
BY INGMAR BERGMAN (CONTEMPORARY)

Above Left: ANITA EKBERG. Above Right: MARCELLO MASTROIANNI

"LA DOLCE VITA" DIRECTED BY FEDERICO FELLINI (ASTOR)

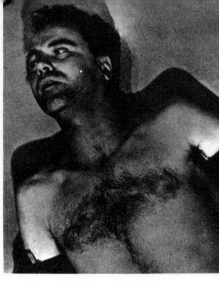

WARREN BEATTY, EVA MARIE SAINT
IN "ALL FALL DOWN" DIRECTED BY
JOHN FRANKENHEIMER (M-G-M)

LEE REMICK

JACK LEMMON

"DAYS OF WINE AND ROSES" DIRECTOR, BLAKE EDWARDS (WARNER BROS.)

LAURENCE HARVEY IN "THE
MANCHURIAN CANDIDATE" DIRECTED
BY JOHN FRANKENHEIMER (U.A.)

NATALIE WOOD AS "GYPSY"
(WARNER BROS.)

YUL BRYNNER IN "TARAS BULBA"
DIRECTOR, J. LEE THOMPSON (U.A.)

DEBORAH KERR IN "THE INNOCENTS"
DIRECTED BY JACK CLAYTON
(20th CENTURY-FOX)

KIRK DOUGLAS IN "TOWN WITHOUT
PITY" DIRECTED BY GOTTFRIED
REINHART (UNITED ARTISTS)

MAI ZETTERLING, PETER SELLERS
IN "ONLY TWO CAN PLAY" DIRECTOR,
SIDNEY GILLIATT (COLUMBIA)

SOPHIA LOREN, JULIEN BERTHEAU
IN "MADAME" DIRECTED BY
CHRISTIAN-JACQUE (EMBASSY)

GREGORY PECK, JAMES ANDERSON IN
"TO KILL A MOCKINGBIRD" DIRECTED
BY ROBERT MULLIGAN (UNIVERSAL)

MIRIAM HOPKINS, JAMES GARNER
IN "THE CHILDREN'S HOUR"
DIRECTOR, WILLIAM WYLER (U.A.)

ALEKA CATSELLI IN "ELECTRA"
DIRECTED BY MICHAEL CACOYANNIS
(LOPERT)

GREGORY PECK

1962 The first films to use Cinerama as a medium for telling a story, "The Wonderful World of the Brothers Grimm" and the epic western "How the West Was Won", were released and found public favor. "Harold Lloyd's World of Comedy" proved a surprise smash hit, and was followed by several other well-edited silent comedy compilations, including another by Harold Lloyd. Many of the year's best films were adaptations of Broadway plays; these included "Long Day's Journey into Night," "Advise and Consent," "The Music Man," "Gypsy" and "The Miracle Worker." In the latter, Anne Bancroft and Patty Duke recreated their Broadway roles to win the Oscars for best actress and best supporting actress. Gregory Peck received his Oscar for the very fine "To Kill a Mockingbird," and Ed Begley was the best supporting actor for "Sweet Bird of Youth." Undoubtedly the year's best film, and the biggest success, was "Lawrence of Arabia" which won awards for director (David Lean), composer (Maurice Jarre) and best film. Films to do well at the box-office were "The Man Who Shot Liberty Valance," "Hatari," "Lolita," "The Manchurian Candidate," "The Longest Day," "Days of Wine and Roses" and the 'sleeper' "Whatever Happened to Baby Jane?" starring Bette Davis and Joan Crawford as two old time movie queens. Made for less than a million dollars, it became one of the year's biggest money-spinners, and both ladies found new careers open to them in gothic horror stories. Other good films included "David and Lisa," "The Bird Man of Alcatraz," and "Mutiny on the Bounty" with Marlon Brando in the role originally created by Clark Gable. Other re-makes were "The Four Horsemen of the Apocalypse," "The Children's Hour," "State Fair," and "Kid Galahad." England sent the fine films "Victim" and "The Innocents." From France came "Last Year in Marienbad," "Sundays and Cybele," which won the Oscar for best foreign film, "Shoot the Piano Player," the delightful "Lola" and "Jules et Jim." Other foreign successes were "Divorce—Italian Style," "Boccaccio 70," "Barabbas," "Electra" and "Viridiana." Death robbed Hollywood and the film industry of one of its greatest stars, Marilyn Monroe, who died aged 36 from an overdose of sleeping pills. Her role in the unfinished "Something's Got to Give" was taken over by Doris Day and the film retitled "Move Over Darling." Ernie Kovacs, Charles Laughton, Frank Lovejoy, Thomas Mitchell, Hoot Gibson and Louise Beavers were some of the others who would no longer be seen. New faces soon to become stars included Peter O'Toole, Suzanne Pleshette, Robert Redford, Tom Courtenay, Terence Stamp, Sue Lyon, Shirley Knight and Janet Margolin.

DORIS DAY

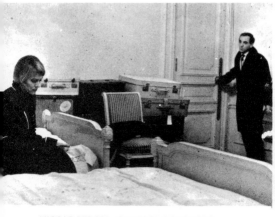

NICOLE BERGER, CHARLES AZNAVOUR
IN "SHOOT THE PIANO PLAYER"
DIRECTOR, FRANÇOIS TRUFFAUT (ASTOR)

DEAN MARTIN, LANA TURNER
IN "WHO'S GOT THE ACTION"
DIRECTOR, DANIEL MANN (PARAMOUNT)

ROBERT MITCHUM, SHIRLEY MacLAINE
IN "TWO FOR THE SEESAW"
DIRECTED BY ROBERT WISE (U.A.)

DON MURRAY

JEAN SEBERG

SHIRLEY MacLAINE

SEAN CONNERY

JANET LEIGH

MAXIMILIAN SCHE

BURT LANCASTER

BURT LANCASTER, THELMA RITTER
"THE BIRDMAN OF ALCATRAZ" DIRECTOR, JOHN FRANKENHEIMER (U.A.)

OLIVIA DE HAVILLAND, YVETTE MIMIEUX,
BARRY SULLIVAN IN "LIGHT IN THE PIAZZA"
DIRECTED BY GUY GREEN (M-G-M)

ALICE FAYE, PAT BOONE, PAMELA TIFFIN, TOM EWELL
IN "STATE FAIR" DIRECTED BY JOSE FERRER
(20th CENTURY-FOX)

CARY GRANT, DORIS DAY
IN "THAT TOUCH OF MINK"
DIRECTOR, DELBERT MANN (UNIVERSAL)

MURRAY MELVIN, RITA TUSHINGHAM
IN "A TASTE OF HONEY" DIRECTED
BY TONY RICHARDSON (CONTINENTAL)

FERNANDO REY, SILVIA PINAL IN
"VIRIDIANA" DIRECTED BY LUIS
BUÑUEL (KINGSLEY INTERNATIONAL)

DANIELLA ROCCA, MARCELLO MASTROIANNI
IN "DIVORCE-ITALIAN STYLE" DIRECTED
BY PIETRO GERMI (EMBASSY)

RICHARD TODD

JEANNE CRAIN

VITTORIO GASSMAN

DOLORES HART

TERRY-THOMAS

CONSTANCE
CUMMINGS

(Columbia)

LAWRENCE OF ARABIA

Producer, Sam Spiegel; Director, David Lean; Screenplay, Robert Bolt; Music, Maurice Jarre; Director of Photography, Fred A. Young; Costumes, Phyllis Dalton; Production Designer, John Box; Art Director, John Stoll; Produced in Super Panavision-70 and Technicolor.

CAST

Lawrence	Peter O'Toole
Prince Feisal	Alec Guinness
Audu Abu Tayi	Anthony Quinn
General Allenby	Jack Hawkins
Turkish Bey	Jose Ferrer
Colonel Brighton	Anthony Quayle
Mr. Dryden	Claude Rains
Jackson Bentley	Arthur Kennedy
General Murray	Donald Wolfit
Sherif Ali Ibn el Kharish	Omar Sharif
Gasim	I. S. Johar
Majid	Gamil Ratib
Farraj	Michel Ray
Tafas	Zia Mohyeddin
Daud	John Dimech
Medical Officer	Howard Marion Crawford
Club Secretary	Jack Gwillim
R.A.M.C. Colonel	Hugh Miller

PETER O'TOOLE, CLAUDE RAINS, JACK HAWKINS

PETER O'TOOLE, ANTHONY QUINN

Above: ALEC GUINNESS, OMAR SHARIF, PETER O'TOOLE

SCENES FROM "LAWRENCE OF ARABIA" DIRECTED BY DAVID LEAN (COLUMBIA)

RALPH RICHARDSON, KATHARINE HEPBURN
IN "LONG DAY'S JOURNEY INTO NIGHT"
DIRECTED BY SIDNEY LUMET (20th CENTURY-FOX)

HAROLD LLOYD IN "HAROLD LLOYD'S
WORLD OF COMEDY" (COLUMBIA)

ANNE BANCROFT, PATTY DUKE IN
"THE MIRACLE WORKER" DIRECTED
BY ARTHUR PENN (UNITED ARTISTS)

OSKAR WERNER, JEANNE MOREAU IN
"JULES ET JIM" DIRECTED BY
FRANÇOIS TRUFFAUT (GALA)

MELINA MERCOURI, ANTHONY PERKINS
IN "PHAEDRA" DIRECTED BY JULES
DASSIN (UNITED ARTISTS)

SYLVIA SYMS, DIRK BOGARDE IN
"VICTIM" DIRECTED BY BASIL
DEARDEN (PATHE-AMERICAN)

TERENCE STAMP

KEIR DULLEA, JANET MARGOLIN IN
"DAVID AND LISA" DIRECTED BY
FRANK PERRY (CONTINENTAL)

NATALIE WOOD

PAUL NEWMAN, GERALDINE PAGE IN
"SWEET BIRD OF YOUTH" DIRECTED
BY RICHARD BROOKS (M-G-M)

SHIRLEY JONES, ROBERT PRESTON
IN "THE MUSIC MAN" DIRECTED BY
MORTON DA COSTA (WARNER BROS.)

ROMY SCHNEIDER IN "BOCCACCIO 70"
DIRECTED BY LUCHINO VISCONTI
(EMBASSY)

ELVIS PRESLEY, LOLA ALBRIGHT, GIG YOUNG
IN "KID GALAHAD" DIRECTED BY PHIL KARLSON
(UNITED ARTISTS)

KIM NOVAK, JACK LEMMON IN
"THE NOTORIOUS LANDLADY"
DIRECTOR, RICHARD QUINE (COLUMBIA)

ANOUK AIMEE IN "LOLA"
DIRECTED BY JACQUES DEMY
(FILMS ROUND THE WORLD)

DELPHINE SEYRIG IN "LAST YEAR
IN MARIENBAD" DIRECTED BY
ALAIN RESNAIS (ASTOR)

MONICA VITTI IN "ECLIPSE"
DIRECTOR, MICHELANGELO ANTONIONI
(TIMES)

WALTER PIDGEON, CHARLES LAUGHTON

"ADVISE AND CONSENT" DIRECTED BY OTTO PREMINGER (COLUMBIA)

HENRY FONDA, GENE TIERNEY

LEE MARVIN, JAMES STEWART, JOHN WAYNE IN
"THE MAN WHO SHOT LIBERTY VALANCE"
DIRECTOR, JOHN FORD (PARAMOUNT)

VALENTIN DE VARGAS, JOHN
WAYNE IN "HATARI"
(PARAMOUNT)

JAMES MASON, SHELLEY WINTERS

"LOLITA" DIRECTED BY STANLEY KUBRICK (M-G-M)

SUE LYON AS LOLITA

TARITA, MARLON BRANDO

"MUTINY ON THE BOUNTY" DIRECTED BY LEWIS MILESTONE (M-G-M)

TREVOR HOWARD

ROBERT MITCHUM   JEFFREY HUNTER   JOHN WAYNE   CURT JURGENS   HENRY FONDA   ROBERT WAGNER

  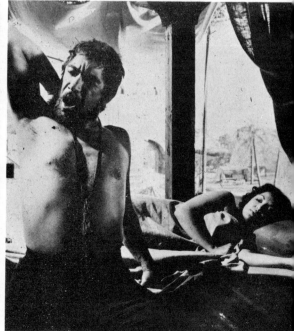

PETER LAWFORD, RICHARD TODD, FRANK HOWARD

"THE LONGEST DAY" DIRECTED BY KEN ANNAKIN, ANDREW MARTON, BERNHARD WICKI (20th CENTURY-FOX)

BARBARA STANWYCK, JANE FONDA IN "WALK ON THE WILD SIDE" DIRECTED BY EDWARD DMYTRYK (COLUMBIA)

SHIRLEY MacLAINE, YVES MONTAND IN "MY GEISHA" (PARAMOUNT)

ALAN BATES, JUNE RITCHIE IN "A KIND OF LOVING" DIRECTED BY JOHN SCHLESINGER (GOVERNOR)

  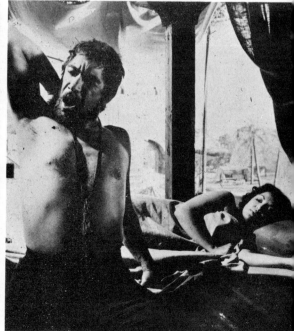

YVETTE MIMIEUX IN "THE WONDERFUL WORLD OF THE BROTHERS GRIMM" DIRECTOR, HENRY LEVIN (M-G-M)

HARDY KRUGER, PATRICIA GOZZI IN "SUNDAYS AND CYBELE" DIRECTED BY SERGE BOURGUIGNON (DAVIS-ROYAL)

ANTHONY QUINN, KATY JURADO IN "BARABBAS" DIRECTED BY RICHARD FLEISCHER (COLUMBIA)

MARILYN MONROE

KARL MALDEN, DEBBIE REYNOLDS, AGNES MOORHEAD,
BRIAN RUSSELL, CARROLL BAKER
SCENES FROM "HOW THE WEST WAS WON" DIRECTORS HENRY HATHAWAY, JOHN FORD, GEORGE MARSHALL (M-G-M)

DEBBIE REYNOLDS IN
"HOW THE WEST WAS WON"

CAROL LAWRENCE, JEAN SOREL IN
"A VIEW FROM THE BRIDGE"
DIRECTOR, SIDNEY LUMET (PARAMOUNT)

WILLIAM HOLDEN, INGRID VAN BERGEN IN
"THE COUNTERFEIT TRAITOR" DIRECTED BY
GEORGE SEATON (PARAMOUNT)

JOAN CRAWFORD, BETTE DAVIS

BETTE DAVIS

"WHATEVER HAPPENED TO BABY JANE?" DIRECTED BY ROBERT ALDRICH (WARNER BROS.)

FRANK SINATRA, DEAN MARTIN,
SAMMY DAVIS JR., PETER LAWFORD IN
"SERGEANTS THREE" (U.A.)

ANTHONY FRANCIOSA, JANE FONDA IN
"PERIOD OF ADJUSTMENT" DIRECTED
BY GEORGE ROY HILL (M-G-M)

KIRK DOUGLAS IN "LONELY
ARE THE BRAVE" DIRECTED BY
DAVID MILLER (UNIVERSAL)

TOM TRYON, JOHN HUSTON
"THE CARDINAL" DIRECTED BY OTTO PREMINGER (COLUMBIA)

TOM TRYON

THOMAS HOLTZMAN, ELSA MARTINELLI,
ANTHONY PERKINS IN "THE TRIAL"
DIRECTOR, ORSON WELLES (ASTOR)

TONY CURTIS, CLAIRE
WILCOX IN "40 POUNDS
OF TROUBLE" (UNIVERSAL)

BURT LANCASTER IN "THE LEOPARD"
DIRECTED BY LUCHINO VISCONTI
(20th CENTURY-FOX)

RACHEL ROBERTS, RICHARD HARRIS
IN "THIS SPORTING LIFE"
DIRECTOR, LINDSAY ANDERSON (RANK)

"THE BIRDS"
DIRECTED BY ALFRED HITCHCOCK
(UNIVERSAL)

SCILLA GABEL, STANLEY BAKER IN
SODOM AND GOMORRAH" DIRECTED BY
ROBERT ALDRICH (20th CENTURY-FOX)

RICHARD ATTENBOROUGH, GORDON JACKSON,
STEVE McQUEEN
"THE GREAT ESCAPE" DIRECTED BY JOHN STURGES (UNITED ARTISTS)

STEVE McQUEEN

ORSON WELLES, MARGARET
RUTHERFORD
"THE V.I.P.s" DIRECTED BY ANTHONY ASQUITH (M-G-M)

RICHARD WATTIS, ELIZABETH TAYLOR,
RICHARD BURTON

CLIFF ROBERTSON IN
"PT 109" DIRECTED BY
LESLIE H. MARTINSON (WARNER)

1963 The year's most awaited picture, "Cleopatra," starring Elizabeth Taylor, proved a first in more ways than one. At a cost of more than $30,000,000 it was certainly the most expensive film ever made, and although eventually it would recoup its costs, the casualties in its wake included two marriages, two of the film's directors, and the President of 20th Century-Fox, while it shook the foundations of the company itself. Two films, made for minute percentage of the cost of "Cleopatra" went on to break box office records all over the world. These were the English "Tom Jones" and "Dr. No." The former was an eighteenth century romp and galloped home with Oscars for best director (Tony Richardson) and best film; it also made its star, Albert Finney, an international name. "Dr. No," which introduced the fictional hero, James Bond, did the same thing for Sean Connery. Paul Newman was "Hud," one of the best American films of the year. The film won Oscars for best actress, Patricia Neal, and best supporting actor, Melvyn Douglas. Sidney Poitier was voted best actor for "Lilies of the Field." An Oscar went to Margaret Rutherford for her supporting role in "The V.I.P.s," and Federico Fellini's masterpiece "8½" was chosen best foreign film. Other films to do well were "The Leopard," "The L-Shaped Room," "This Sporting Life," "The Birds," "In The French Style" and "America, America." New screen personalities to catch the eye included Richard Chamberlain, Elke Sommer, Ursula Andress, Julie Christie, Peter Fonda, Sarah Miles, Joey Heatherton and Robert Walker Jr. Death took Jack Carson, Jean Cocteau, Dick Powell, Sabu and Monte Woolley as well as silent greats Richard Barthelmess, Adolph Menjou and Zasu Pitts.

TOM COURTENAY, JULIE CHRISTIE
IN "BILLY LIAR" DIRECTED BY
JOHN SCHLESINGER (CONTINENTAL)

MARILYN MONROE IN "MARILYN"
(SCENE FROM UNFINISHED "SOMETHING'S
GOT TO GIVE") (20th CENTURY-FOX)

SEAN CONNERY

URSULA ANDRESS

EUNICE GAYSON, SEAN CONNERY

LAURENCE OLIVIER, SIMONE SIGNORET
IN "TERM OF TRIAL" DIRECTED BY
PETER GLENVILLE (WARNER BROS.)

"DR. NO" DIRECTED BY TERENCE YOUNG (UNITED ARTISTS)

ELKE SOMMER   LILLI PALMER   BELINDA LEE   TONY RANDALL   JULIE CHRISTIE   SHIRLEY ANNE FIELD

CLIFF RICHARD, UNA STUBBS IN "SUMMER HOLIDAY" DIRECTED BY PETER YATES (AMERICAN INTERNATIONAL)

LAURENCE HARVEY, LEE REMICK IN "THE RUNNING MAN" DIRECTOR, CAROL REED (COLUMBIA)

STANLEY BAKER, JEAN SEBERG IN "IN THE FRENCH STYLE" DIRECTOR, ROBERT PARRISH (COLUMBIA)

IRENE BROWN, PETER SELLERS, ELIZA BUCKINGHAM IN "THE WRONG ARM OF THE LAW" (CONTINENTAL)

SOPHIA LOREN, MAXIMILIAN SCHELL IN "THE CONDEMNED OF ALTONA" DIRECTOR VITTORIO DE SICA (20th CENT. FOX)

LEA MASSARI IN "FOUR DAYS IN NAPLES" DIRECTED BY NANNI LOY (M-G-M)

PAUL NEWMAN, PATRICIA NEAL

PAUL NEWMAN, MELVYN DOUGLAS

MELVYN DOUGLAS

STATHIS GIALLELIS IN "AMERICA, AMERICA" (WARNER BROS.)

"HUD" DIRECTED BY MARTIN RITT (PARAMOUNT)

RICHARD BURTON, ELIZABETH TAYLOR

ELIZABETH TAYLOR

REX HARRISON

ELIZABETH TAYLOR

"CLEOPATRA" DIRECTED BY JOSEPH L. MANKIEWICZ (20th CENTURY-FOX)

PAT HINGLE, JOCELYN BRANDO,
MARLON BRANDO, SANDRA CHURCH
IN "THE UGLY AMERICAN" (U.A.)

DIRK BOGARDE IN "THE MIND
BENDERS" DIRECTED BY
BASIL DEARDEN (ALLIED ARTISTS)

BARBARA WINDSOR, JAMES BOOTH IN
"SPARROWS CAN'T SING" DIRECTED BY
JOAN LITTLEWOOD (JANUS)

GENE TIERNEY IN "TOYS IN
THE ATTIC" DIRECTED BY
GEORGE ROY HILL (UNITED ARTISTS)

GEORGE CHAKIRIS, YVETTE MIMIEUX,
CHARLTON HESTON IN "DIAMOND HEAD"
DIRECTED BY GUY GREEN (COLUMBIA)

STEVE COCHRAN, MERLE OBERON IN
"OF LOVE AND DESIRE" DIRECTOR,
RICHARD RUSH (20th CENTURY-FOX)

LESLIE CARON

JACQUES PERRIN, MARCELLO MASTROIANNI
IN "FAMILY DIARY" DIRECTED BY
VALERIO ZURLINI (M-G-M)

"HALLELUJAH, THE HILLS"
DIRECTED BY ADOLFAS MEKAS
(CONTEMPORARY FILMS)

MELINA MERCOURI, GEORGE PEPPARD
IN "THE VICTORS" DIRECTED BY
CARL FOREMAN (COLUMBIA)

YUL BRYNNER, SHIRLEY ANNE FIELD
GEORGE CHAKIRIS, BRAD DEXTER IN
"KINGS OF THE SUN" (U.A.)

JOE E. BROWN

JIMMY DURANTE

EDIE ADAMS, SID CAESAR.
Above: TERRY-THOMAS

ETHEL MERMAN

"IT'S A MAD, MAD, MAD, MAD WORLD" DIRECTED BY STANLEY KRAMER (U.A.)

CHARLTON HESTON, AVA GARDNER,
DAVID NIVEN

LEO GENN, ROBERT HELPMANN, FLORA ROBSON.
Above: DAVID NIVEN, CHARLTON HESTON

"55 DAYS AT PEKING" DIRECTED BY NICHOLAS RAY (ALLIED ARTISTS)

GIG YOUNG, KIRK DOUGLAS IN
"FOR LOVE OR MONEY" DIRECTED
BY MICHAEL GORDON (UNIVERSAL)

LEE MARVIN, DOROTHY LAMOUR IN
"DONOVAN'S REEF" DIRECTED BY
JOHN FORD (PARAMOUNT)

DORIS DAY, CHUCK CONNORS IN
"MOVE OVER DARLING" DIRECTED
BY MICHAEL GORDON (20th CENT. FOX)

CORNEL WILDE, BRIAN AHERNE, JEAN
WALLACE IN "SWORD OF LANCELOT"
DIRECTOR, CORNEL WILDE (UNIVERSAL)

URSULA ANDRESS, DEAN MARTIN IN
"4 FOR TEXAS" DIRECTED BY
ROBERT ALDRICH (WARNER BROS.)

JUDY GARLAND IN
"I COULD GO ON SINGING"
DIRECTOR, RONALD NEAME (U.A.)

299

SUSANNAH YORK

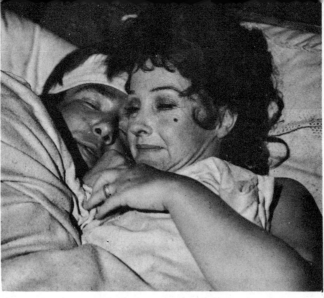

ALBERT FINNEY, JOYCE REDMAN

ALBERT FINNEY

HUGH GRIFFITH

JOYCE REDMAN, ALBERT FINNEY

HUGH GRIFFITH, EDITH EVANS

"TOM JONES" DIRECTED BY TONY RICHARDSON (UNITED ARTISTS)

ROBERT TAYLOR, LILLI PALMER IN
"THE MIRACLE OF THE WHITE STALLIONS"
DIRECTOR, ARTHUR HILLER (BUENA VISTA)

BOB HOPE, LUCILLE BALL
IN "CRITIC'S CHOICE" DIRECTED
BY DON WEIS (WARNER BROS.)

ROBERT PRESTON, JEAN SIMMONS
IN "ALL THE WAY HOME"
DIRECTED BY ALEX SEGAL (PARAMOUNT)

ROD TAYLOR, ROCK HUDSON IN
"A GATHERING OF EAGLES"
DIRECTOR, DELBERT MANN (UNIVERSAL)

KIRK DOUGLAS, GEORGE C. SCOTT IN
"THE LIST OF ADRIAN MESSENGER"
DIRECTOR, JOHN HUSTON (UNIVERSAL)

SANDRA DEE, JAMES STEWART IN "TAKE
HER, SHE'S MINE" DIRECTED BY HENRY
KOSTER (20th CENTURY-FOX)

ANOUK AIMEE   MARCELLO MASTROIANNI   CLAUDIA CARDINALE   TOM BELL, LESLIE CARON IN
"THE L-SHAPED ROOM" DIRECTED
BY BRYAN FORBES (COLUMBIA)

"8½" DIRECTED BY FEDERICO FELLINI (COLUMBIA)

SIDNEY POITIER IN
"LILIES OF THE FIELD"
(U.A.)

JOLANTA UMECKA, ZYGMUNT MALANOWICZ IN
"KNIFE IN THE WATER" DIRECTED BY
ROMAN POLANSKI (KANAWHA)

JACK LEMMON, SHIRLEY MacLAINE IN
"IRMA LA DOUCE" DIRECTED BY BILLY WILDER
(UNITED ARTISTS)

JACK LEMMON IN "UNDER THE
YUM-YUM TREE" DIRECTED BY
DAVID SWIFT (COLUMBIA)

PAUL NEWMAN, ELKE SOMMER
IN "THE PRIZE" DIRECTED
BY MARK ROBSON (M-G-M)

"THE INCREDIBLE JOURNEY"
DIRECTED BY FLETCHER MARKLE
(BUENA VISTA)

301

CLAUDIA CARDINALE, JOHN WAYNE,
RITA HAYWORTH IN "CIRCUS WORLD"
DIRECTOR, HENRY HATHAWAY (PARAMOUNT)

JEANNE MOREAU IN "BAY
OF ANGELS" DIRECTED
BY JACQUES DEMY (PATHE)

KIM STANLEY, RICHARD ATTENBOROUGH
IN "SEANCE ON A WET AFTERNOON"
DIRECTOR, BRYAN FORBES (ARTIXO)

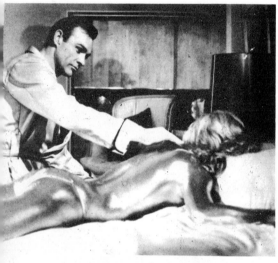

SEAN CONNERY, SHIRLEY EATON
IN "GOLDFINGER" DIRECTED BY
GUY HAMILTON (UNITED ARTISTS)

SEAN CONNERY, DANIELLE BIANCHI

LOTTE LENYA, ROBERT SHAW

"FROM RUSSIA WITH LOVE" DIRECTED BY TERENCE YOUNG (UNITED ARTISTS)

PETER SELLERS IN
"DR. STRANGELOVE" DIRECTOR,
STANLEY KUBRICK (COLUMBIA)

DOLORES DEL RIO, SAL MINEO

"CHEYENNE AUTUMN" DIRECTED BY JOHN FORD (WARNER BROS.)

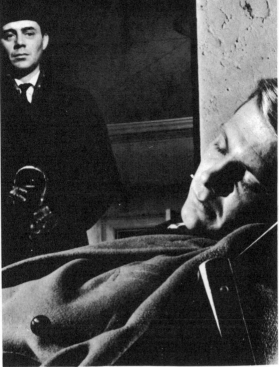

SHIRLEY MacLAINE, GENE KELLY IN "WHAT A WAY TO GO" DIRECTED BY J. LEE THOMPSON (20th CENTURY-FOX)

DIRK BOGARDE, JAMES FOX IN "THE SERVANT" DIRECTOR, JOSEPH LOSEY (LANDAU)

LILA KEDROVA, ANTHONY QUINN IN "ZORBA THE GREEK" DIRECTED BY MICHAEL CACOYANNIS (20th CENTURY-FOX)

DANIELLE BIANCHI IN "FROM RUSSIA WITH LOVE" (U.A.)

1964

1964 was again a personal triumph for the English, and for none more so than Julie Andrews, who made her film debut in the Disney musical box office champion "Mary Poppins." She won the Oscar for best actress and became everybody's fair lady, except Warner Brothers', who had given the plum role of Eliza Doolittle, which Julie Andrews had created on Broadway, to the no less delectable Audrey Hepburn. "My Fair Lady" collected eight Oscars, including best film, best director (George Cukor) and best actor (Rex Harrison). Peter Ustinov received his second supporting Oscar for his role in "Topkapi." French actress Lila Kedrova received her Oscar for the European-made "Zorba the Greek." Other hits with public and critics alike included "Dr. Strangelove (Or How I Learned to Stop Worrying and Love the Bomb)," "Becket," "Love with the Proper Stranger" and "Night of the Iguana." The latest Bond film "Goldfinger" outgrossed all the others and Sean Connery was the top box office star for the year. Another great success was "The Carpetbaggers," from the best-selling novel. The film introduced a surprising new sex symbol in the shape of Carroll Baker, who could also be seen as a Quaker in "Cheyenne Autumn." "Fail Safe" and "The Best Man" were two of the better American films of the year. From England came "The Servant," "The Pumpkin Eater," "Girl with Green Eyes," "Night Must Fall" and the Beatles' hit musical debut, "A Hard Day's Night." From Ingmar Bergman came "The Silence" and from France the very popular "Umbrellas of Cherbourg" and "That Man From Rio." New faces on the scene included George Segal, James Fox, Peter McEnery, Stephan Powers, Jessica Walter and Jean-Paul Belmondo. Death took Gracie Allen, William Bendix, Eddie Cantor, Cedric Hardwicke, Alan Ladd, Peter Lorre, Harpo Marx and Diana Wynyard amongst others.

HONOR BLACKMAN IN "GOLDFINGER" (U.A.)

FREDRIC MARCH

BURT LANCASTER

AVA GARDNER, KIRK DOUGLAS

STEVE McQUEEN, NATALIE WOOD IN "LOVE WITH THE PROPER STRANGER" DIRECTOR, ROBERT MULLIGAN (PARAMOUNT)

"SEVEN DAYS IN MAY" DIRECTED BY JOHN FRANKENHEIMER (PARAMOUNT)

303

PETER O'TOOLE

DAVID WESTON, RICHARD BURTON
Above: SIAN PHILLIPS, RICHARD BURTON

JOHN GIELGUD, RICHARD BURTON

"BECKET" DIRECTED BY PETER GLENVILLE (PARAMOUNT)

SOPHIA LOREN, MARCELLO MASTROIANNI IN
"MARRIAGE—ITALIAN STYLE" DIRECTOR,
VITTORIO DE SICA (PARAMOUNT)

MARLENE DIETRICH IN
"PARIS WHEN IT SIZZLES"
DIRECTOR, RICHARD QUINE (PARAMOUNT)

GENEVIEVE PAGE, SIMONE SIGNORET
IN "TODAY WE LIVE" (M-G-M)

FRANCE NUYEN, ROBERT MITCHUM IN
"MAN IN THE MIDDLE" DIRECTED BY
GUY HAMILTON (20th CENTURY-FOX)

PAULA PRENTISS, ROCK HUDSON IN
"MAN'S FAVORITE SPORT" DIRECTED
BY HOWARD HAWKS (UNIVERSAL)

JEAN-PAUL BELMONDO IN "THAT
MAN FROM RIO" DIRECTED BY
PHILIPPE DE BROCA (LOPERT)

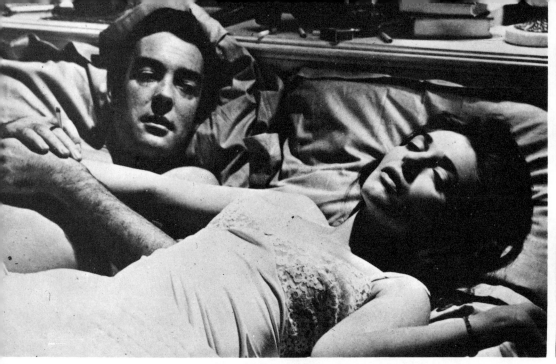

RICHARD JOHNSON, ANNE BANCROFT

ANNE BANCROFT, PETER FINCH

"THE PUMPKIN EATER" DIRECTED BY JACK CLAYTON (COLUMBIA)

CLAUDIA CARDINALE

PETER SELLERS, CAPUCINE

PETER McENERY, HAYLEY MILLS
IN "THE MOONSPINNERS"
(BUENA VISTA) ·

"THE PINK PANTHER" DIRECTED BY BLAKE EDWARDS (UNITED ARTISTS)

Centre: RICHARD BURTON, SUE LYON, DEBORAH KERR,
AVA GARDNER. Left and Right: AVA GARDNER

"THE NIGHT OF THE IGUANA" DIRECTED BY JOHN HUSTON (M-G-M)

BRIGITTE BARDOT, JEAN
TUSCANO IN "LOVE ON
A PILLOW" (ROYAL)

MARGARET LEIGHTON, HENRY FONDA,
ANN SOTHERN IN "THE BEST MAN"
DIRECTOR, FRANKLIN SCHAFFNER (U.A.)

CLIFF ROBERTSON IN
"THE BEST MAN"
(UNITED ARTISTS)

CLIFF ROBERTSON, MARIA PERSCHY
IN "633 SQUADRON" DIRECTED BY
WALTER E. GRAUMAN (U.A.)

TIPPI HEDREN, SEAN CONNERY IN
"MARNIE" DIRECTED BY ALFRED
HITCHCOCK (UNIVERSAL)

CLIFF ROBERTSON, JANE FONDA, ROBERT
CULP IN "SUNDAY IN NEW YORK"
DIRECTED BY PETER TEWKSBURY (M-G-M)

ROD TAYLOR (Centre), GLENN FORD
(Right) IN "FATE IS THE HUNTER"
DIRECTOR, RALPH NELSON (20th CENT. FOX)

MICHAEL CAINE

STANLEY BAKER,
MICHAEL CAINE

NIGEL GREEN

ALAN BATES, MILLICENT MARTIN IN
"NOTHING BUT THE BEST"
DIRECTED BY CLIVE DONNER (ROYAL)

"ZULU" DIRECTED BY CY ENFIELD (EMBASSY)

ANTHONY QUINN

GREGORY PECK

JULIE ANDREWS, JAMES GARNER, JOYCE GRENFELL
IN "THE AMERICANIZATION OF EMILY"
DIRECTED BY ARTHUR HILLER (M-G-M)

"BEHOLD A PALE HORSE" DIRECTED BY FRED ZINNEMANN (COLUMBIA)

JEREMY BRETT, AUDREY HEPBURN,
REX HARRISON, WILFRED HYDE-WHITE

Top: REX HARRISON, AUDREY HEPBURN
Centre: REX HARRISON, AUDREY HEPBURN,
WILFRED HYDE-WHITE
Below: STANLEY HOLLOWAY

AUDREY HEPBURN

AUDREY HEPBURN

SCENES FROM "MY FAIR LADY" DIRECTED BY GEORGE CUKOR (WARNER BROS.)

GINA LOLLOBRIGIDA, SEAN CONNERY
IN "WOMAN OF STRAW"
DIRECTOR, BASIL DEARDEN (U.A.)

JOAN CRAWFORD IN
"STRAIT-JACKET" DIRECTED BY
WILLIAM CASTLE (COLUMBIA)

HENRY FONDA IN
"FAIL SAFE" DIRECTED
BY SIDNEY LUMET (COLUMBIA)

CEDRIC
HARDWICKE

MARTHA HYER

GEORGE RAFT

ROD TAYLOR

MARIA PERSCHY

GEORGE
CHAKIRIS

JACK LE VIEN, SIR WINSTON CHURCHILL
"THE FINEST HOURS" DIRECTED BY
PETER BAYLIS (COLUMBIA)

RITA TUSHINGHAM, PETER FINCH IN
"GIRL WITH GREEN EYES"
(LOPERT)

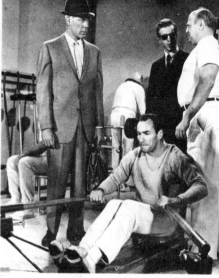

LEE MARVIN, CLU GULAGER
IN "THE KILLERS" DIRECTED
BY DONALD SIEGEL (UNIVERSAL)

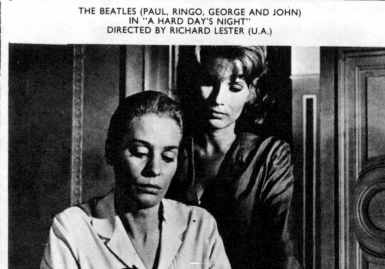

THE BEATLES (PAUL, RINGO, GEORGE AND JOHN)
IN "A HARD DAY'S NIGHT"
DIRECTED BY RICHARD LESTER (U.A.)

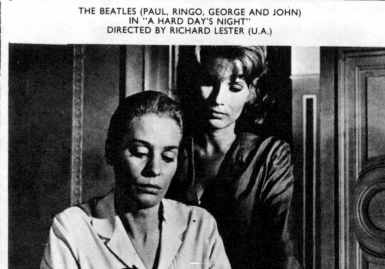

INGRID THULIN, GUNNEL LINDBLOM
IN "THE SILENCE" DIRECTED BY
INGMAR BERGMAN (JANUS)

Above Left: SOPHIA LOREN. Above Right: ALEC GUINNESS, SOPHIA LOREN
Below Left: SOPHIA LOREN, STEPHEN BOYD, GUY ROLFE

"THE FALL OF THE ROMAN EMPIRE" DIRECTED BY ANTHONY MANN (PARAMOUNT)

LYNN REDGRAVE

WALTER SLEZAK

VERA MILES

CATHERINE DENEUVE, MARC MICHEL
IN "THE UMBRELLAS OF CHERBOURG"
DIRECTED BY JACQUES DEMY (LANDAU)

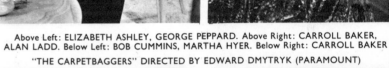

Above Left: ELIZABETH ASHLEY, GEORGE PEPPARD. Above Right: CARROLL BAKER,
ALAN LADD. Below Left: BOB CUMMINS, MARTHA HYER. Below Right: CARROLL BAKER

"THE CARPETBAGGERS" DIRECTED BY EDWARD DMYTRYK (PARAMOUNT)

PAUL NEWMAN

PAUL NEWMAN, LAURENCE HARVEY,
CLAIRE BLOOM

"THE OUTRAGE" DIRECTED BY MARTIN RITT (M-G-M)

SIDNEY POITIER, RICHARD WIDMARK
IN "THE LONG SHIPS" DIRECTED BY
JACK CARDIFF (COLUMBIA)

ANN-MARGRET, ELVIS PRESLEY
ON THE SET OF "VIVA LAS VEGAS"
(M-G-M)

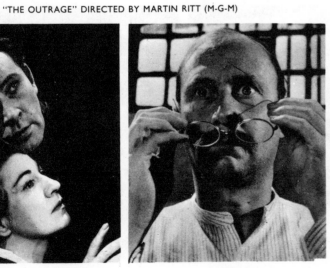

RICHARD BURTON, EILEEN
HERLIHY IN "HAMLET" DIRECTOR, JOHN
GIELGUD (WARNER BROS.)

DONALD PLEASANCE IN
"DR. CRIPPEN"
(WARNER BROS.)

LEE HARVEY OSWALD, JACK RUBY IN
"FOUR DAYS IN NOVEMBER"
DIRECTOR, MEL STUART (U.A.)

JULIE ANDREWS IN "MARY POPPINS"
DIRECTED BY ROBERT STEVENSON (BUENA VISTA)

Above: DICK VAN DYKE, JULIE ANDREWS
Below: KAREN DOTRICE, GLYNIS JOHNS, MATTHEW GARB
DAVID TOMLINSON IN "MARY POPPINS" (BUENA VISTA

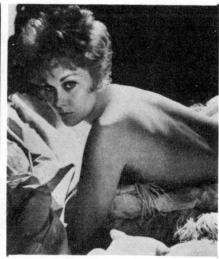

LAURENCE HARVEY, KIM NOVAK

"OF HUMAN BONDAGE" DIRECTED BY KEN HUGHES (M-G-M)

KIM NOVAK

SAMANTHA EGGAR, CURT JURGENS
IN "PSYCHE '59" DIRECTED BY
ALEXANDER SINGER (ROYAL)

OLIVIA DE HAVILLAND IN
"LADY IN A CAGE" DIRECTED
BY WALTER GRAUMAN (PARAMOUNT)

BETTE DAVIS, MICHAEL CONNORS,
SUSAN HAYWARD IN "WHERE LOVE
HAS GONE" (PARAMOUNT)

SUSAN HAMPSHIRE, ALBERT FINNEY
IN "NIGHT MUST FALL"
DIRECTOR, KAREL REISZ (M-G-M)

MELINA MERCOURI

PETER USTINOV

"TOPKAPI" DIRECTED BY JULES DASSIN (U.A.)

INGRID BERGMAN
IN "THE VISIT"
(20th CENTURY-FOX)

SHIRLEY JONES, MARLON BRANDO
IN "BEDTIME STORY" DIRECTED BY
RALPH LEVY (UNIVERSAL)

JOHN MILLS, HAYLEY MILLS, EDITH
EVANS, DEBORAH KERR IN "THE CHALK
GARDEN" (UNIVERSAL)

SOPHIA LOREN, MARCELLO MASTROIANNI
IN "YESTERDAY, TODAY AND TOMORROW"
DIRECTOR, VITTORIO DE SICA (PARAMOUNT)

CARROLL BAKER, PETER VAN EYCK
IN "STATION 6—SAHARA"
(ALLIED ARTISTS)

NATALIE WOOD, MEL FERRER IN
"SEX AND THE SINGLE GIRL"
DIRECTOR, RICHARD QUINE (WARNER BROS.)

GENE TIERNEY CAROL LYNLEY
IN "THE PLEASURE SEEKERS"
(20th CENTURY-FOX)

JAMES STEWART, BILLY MUMMY,
BRIGITTE BARDOT IN "DEAR BRIGITTE"
DIRECTOR, HENRY KOSTER (20th CENTURY-FOX)

CARY GRANT, AUDREY HEPBURN,
JAMES COBURN, NED GLASS

"CHARADE" DIRECTED BY STANLEY DONEN (UNIVERSAL)

CARY GRANT

HARVE PRESNELL, DEBBIE
REYNOLDS IN "THE UNSINKABLE
MOLLY BROWN" (M-G-M)

FRANK SINATRA, BING CROSBY,
DEAN MARTIN IN "ROBIN AND
THE SEVEN HOODS" (WARNER BROS.)

EDMUND PURDOM, JEANNE
MOREAU, REX HARRISON

SHIRLEY MacLAINE

OMAR SHARIF,
INGRID BERGMAN

VIRNA LISI, JACK LEMMON IN
"HOW TO MURDER YOUR WIFE"
DIRECTOR, RICHARD QUINE (U.A.)

"THE YELLOW ROLLS-ROYCE" DIRECTED BY ANTHONY ASQUITH (M-G-M)

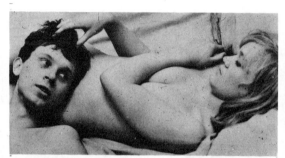

GERALDINE FITZGERALD, ROD STEIGER
IN "THE PAWNBROKER" DIRECTED BY
SIDNEY LUMET (LANDAU)

Above: HANA BREJCHOVA, JANA NOVAKOVA
IN "A BLONDE IN LOVE" (CONTEMPORARY FILMS)
Below: MACHA MERIL IN "UNE FEMME MARIÉE"
DIRECTOR, JEAN-LUC GODARD (GALA)

J. KRONER, IDA KAMINSK IN
"SHOP ON MAIN STREET"
(CONTEMPORARY FILMS)

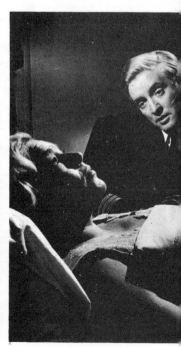

JAMES FOX

SARAH MILES, STUART WHITMAN

VIVIEN LEIGH,
LEE MARVIN

SIMONE SIGNORET,
OSKAR WERNER

'THOSE MAGNIFICENT MEN IN THEIR FLYING MACHINES"
DIRECTED BY KEN ANNAKIN (20th CENTURY-FOX)

"SHIP OF FOOLS" DIRECTED BY STANLEY KRAMER (COLUMBIA)

STEVE McQUEEN

DALIAH LAVI

MICHAEL CAINE
IN "THE IPCRESS FILE"
(RANK)

LEE MARVIN IN "CAT BALLOU"
DIRECTOR, ELLIOT SILVERSTEIN (COLUMBIA)

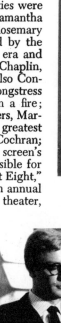

1965 "The Sound of Music," the biggest money-maker of the year and possibly in the history of films, re-established the trend towards musicals, even if most of them came from Broadway successes. It made Julie Andrews one of the biggest draws in films at a time when opinion was that "stars were on their way out," and won most of the year's major Oscars, including best film and best direction (Robert Wise). The Oscar for best actress went to the English discovery, Julie Christie, who appeared in two of the year's big hits, the English-made "Darling" and the American-financed, internationally-cast "Dr. Zhivago." Lee Marvin became a star and won an Oscar for his performance in "Cat Ballou;" Shelley Winters won her second award as best supporting actress for "A Patch of Blue;" Martin Balsam won the best supporting actor award for his role in "A Thousand Clowns," and the Czechoslovakian "The Shop on Main Street" was voted best foreign film. Other excellent films from abroad were Fellini's "Juliet of the Spirits," "Loves of a Blonde," "Une Femme Mariée" and "The Gospel According to St. Matthew." Carroll Baker and Carol Lynley appeared in rival versions of the biography of Hollywood's great glamour goddess of the thirties, "Harlow." Olivier's latest Shakespearian venture was a disappointingly filmed record of his stage success "Othello." Of the year's big successes "What's New Pussycat?" "The Knack," "Repulsion," "The Hill," "The Ipcress File," "The Spy Who Came in from the Cold" and the latest Bond adventure "Thunderball" came from England. American-made films of merit included "The Great Race," "King Rat," "Bunny Lake Is Missing," "Ship of Fools," "The Cincinnati Kid," "The Pawn-broker" and "The War Lord." Promising new personalities were Elizabeth Hartman, David McCallum, Michael Parks, Samantha Eggar, Virna Lisi, Geraldine Chaplin, Barbara Harris, Rosemary Forsythe and Katherine Ross. The year was saddened by the sudden deaths of many Hollywood greats of the silent era and the early years of sound. 'It' girl Clara Bow, Sidney Chaplin, Lars Hanson, and Mae 'Merry Widow' Murray died; also Constance Bennett, Nancy Carroll, Judy Holliday and songstress Jeanette MacDonald; Linda Darnell died tragically in a fire; Dorothy Dandridge; the favorite foil of the Marx Brothers, Margaret Dumont; the English half of one of the screen's greatest comedy teams, Laurel and Hardy, Stan Laurel; Steve Cochran; Mary Boland and Everett Sloane. So too did one of the screen's greatest producers, David O. Selznick, the man responsible for "Gone with the Wind," "Duel in the Sun" and "Dinner at Eight," and Daniel Blum, founder and editor of the popular film annual "Screen World" and writer of many books dealing with theater, television and films.

STEVE McQUEEN, ANN-MARGRET,
KARL MALDEN IN "THE CINCINNATI KID"
DIRECTOR, NORMAN JEWISON (M-G-M)

DORIS DAY, ROD TAYLOR IN
"DO NOT DISTURB" DIRECTED BY
RALPH LEVY (20th CENTURY-FOX)

MICHAEL CAINE, GUY DOLEMAN
IN "THE IPCRESS FILE"
DIRECTOR, SIDNEY FURIE (RANK)

JANE FONDA IN "CAT BALLOU"
(COLUMBIA)

KIM NOVAK IN "THE AMOROUS
ADVENTURES OF MOLL FLANDERS"
DIRECTOR, TERENCE YOUNG (PARA.)

PETER O'TOOLE, DALIAH LAVI

CURT JURGENS, ELI WALLACH

"LORD JIM" DIRECTED BY RICHARD BROOKS (COLUMBIA)

TOM COURTENAY, JOHN
MILLS, GERALD SIM

GEORGE SEGAL, JAMES FOX

JEAN SIMMONS, LAURENCE HARVEY

DONALD WOLFIT

"KING RAT" DIRECTED BY BRYAN FORBES (COLUMBIA)

"LIFE AT THE TOP" DIRECTOR, TED KOTCHEFF (COLUMBIA)

Above: MICHAEL HORDERN, RICHARD
BURTON. Below: RICHARD BURTON, OSKAR
WERNER IN "THE SPY WHO CAME IN FROM
THE COLD" DIRECTOR, MARTIN RITT (PARAMOUNT)

Above: RICHARD BOONE, CHARLTON
HESTON. Below: ROSEMARY FORSYTH,
CHARLTON HESTON IN "THE WAR LORD"
DIRECTOR, FRANKLIN SCHAFFNER (UNIVERSAL)

PAUL SCOFIELD, BURT LANCASTER
IN "THE TRAIN" DIRECTED BY
JOHN FRANKENHEIMER (U.A.)

SANDRO MILO

FREDRICH LEDEBUR

"JULIET OF THE SPIRITS" DIRECTOR, FEDERICO FELLINI (RIZZOLI)

Above: ROBERT SHAW. Below: HENRY FONDA IN "BATTLE OF THE BULGE" DIRECTOR, KEN ANNAKIN (WARNER BROS.)

BRIGITTE BARDOT IN "VIVA MARIA" (UNITED ARTISTS)

"THE GOSPEL ACCORDING TO ST. MATTHEW" DIRECTED BY PIER PAOLO PASOLINI (CONTINENTAL)

MAX VON SYDOW IN "THE GREATEST STORY EVER TOLD" DIRECTOR, GEORGE STEVENS (U.A.)

"KING AND COUNTRY" DIRECTOR, JOSEPH LOSEY (B.H.E. PRODUCTIONS)

Above: MICHAEL CRAWFORD, RITA TUSHINGHAM, DONAL DONNELLY. Below: DONAL DONNELLY, MICHAEL CRAWFORD, RAY BROOKS IN "THE KNACK" (LOPERT)

Above: REX HARRISON. Below: CHARLTON HESTON, REX HARRISON IN "THE AGONY AND THE ECSTASY" DIRECTOR CAROL REED (20th CENTURY-FOX)

Above: CHARLTON HESTON, RICHARD HARRIS. Below: CHARLTON HESTON IN "MAJOR DUNDEE" (COLUMBIA)

OMAR SHARIF, JULIE CHRISTIE

ALEC GUINNESS

OMAR SHARIF

(M-G-M)

DOCTOR ZHIVAGO

Producer, Carlo Ponti; Director, David Lean; Screenplay, Robert Bolt; Based on Book by Boris Pasternak; Music, Maurice Jarre; Director of Photography, Fred A. Young; Costumes, Phyllis Dalton; Production Designer, John Box.

CAST

Yuri Zhivago	Omar Sharif
Lara	Julie Christie
Tonya	Geraldine Chaplin
Pasha	Tom Courtenay
Yevgraf	Alec Guinness
Anna	Siobhan McKenna
Alexander	Ralph Richardson
Komarovsky	Rod Steiger
The Girl	Rita Tushingham
Amelia	Adrienne Corri
Professor Kurt	Geoffrey Keen
Sasha	Jeffrey Rockland
Katya	Lucy Westmore
Razin	Noel Willman
Liberius	Gerard Tichy
Kostoyed	Klaus Kinski
Petya	Jack Mac Gowran
Gentlewoman	Maria Martin
Yuri (at age of 8)	Tarek Sharif
Tonya (at age of 7)	Mercedes Ruiz
Colonel	Roger Maxwell
Major	Inigo Jackson
Captain	Virgilio Texeira
Bolshevik	Bernard Kay
Old Soldier	Eric Chitty
The Priest	Jose Nieto

GERALDINE CHAPLIN

SCENES FROM "DR. ZHIVAGO" DIRECTED BY DAVID LEAN (M-G-M

SEAN CONNERY
IN "THUNDERBALL"
DIRECTOR, TERENCE YOUNG (UNITED ARTISTS)

ROMY SCHNEIDER,
PETER O'TOOLE

PETER SELLERS

"WHAT'S NEW PUSSYCAT" DIRECTED BY CLIVE DONNER (U.A.)

NATALIE WOOD, KEENAN WYNN,
TONY CURTIS
"THE GREAT RACE" DIRECTED BY BLAKE EDWARDS (WARNER BROS.)

JACK LEMMON

LAURENCE OLIVIER, KEIR DULLEA
IN "BUNNY LAKE IS MISSING"
DIRECTOR, OTTO PREMINGER (COLUMBIA)

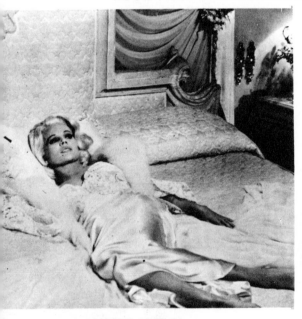

CARROLL BAKER IN
"HARLOW" DIRECTED BY
GORDON DOUGLAS (PARAMOUNT)

JEAN HARLOW

CAROL LYNLEY IN
"HARLOW" DIRECTED BY
ALEX SEGAL (MAGNA PICTURES)

JACK WATSON, OSSIE DAVIS, SEAN
CONNERY, ALFRED LYNCH, ROY KINNEAR
IN "THE HILL" DIRECTOR, SIDNEY LUMET (M-G-M)

LAURENCE OLIVIER

LAURENCE OLIVIER, MAGGIE SMITH

"OTHELLO" DIRECTED BY STUART BURGE (WARNER BROS.)

JULIE ANDREWS,
CHRISTOPHER PLUMMER

JULIE ANDREWS, CHRISTOPHER PLUMMER, CHARMIAN CARR,
THE VON TRAPP CHILDREN

JULIE ANDREWS

(20th Century-Fox)

THE SOUND OF MUSIC

Producer-Director, Robert Wise; Associate Producer, Saul Chaplin; Director of Photography, Ted McCord; Screenplay, Ernest Lehman; From the Musical Play by Richard Rodgers and Oscar Hammerstein II; Lyrics, Oscar Hammerstein II; Music and Additional Lyrics, Richard Rodgers; Choreography, Marc Breaux and Dee Dee Wood; Costumes, Dorothy Jeakins; Puppeteers, Bil and Cora Baird; Assistant Director, Ridgeway Callow; In Todd-AO(R) and DeLuxe Color.

CAST

Maria	Julie Andrews
Captain Von Trapp	Christopher Plummer
The Baroness	Eleanor Parker
Max Detweiler	Richard Haydn
Mother Abbess	Peggy Wood
Liesl	Charmian Carr
Louisa	Heather Menzies
Friedrich	Nicolas Hammond
Kurt	Duane Chase
Brigitta	Angela Cartwright
Marta	Debbie Turner
Gretl	Kym Karath
Sister Margaretta	Anna Lee
Sister Berthe	Portia Nelson
Herr Zeller	Ben Wright
Rolfe	Daniel Truhitte
Frau Schmidt	Norma Varden
Franz	Gil Stuart
Sister Sophia	Marni Nixon
Sister Bernice	Evadne Baker
Baroness Ebberfeld	Doris Lloyd

CHRISTOPHER PLUMMER

JULIE ANDREWS, CHARMIAN CARR AND THE VON TRAPP FAMILY

CHARMIAN CARR, DUANE CHASE

"THE SOUND OF MUSIC" DIRECTED BY ROBERT WISE (20th CENTURY-FOX)

JASON ROBARDS JR., BARBARA
HARRIS IN "A THOUSAND CLOWNS" DIRECTOR,
FRED COE (UNITED ARTISTS)

SIDNEY POITIER, ELIZABETH
HARTMAN IN "A PATCH OF BLUE"
DIRECTOR, GUY GREEN
(M-G-M)

SAMANTHA EGGAR, MAXIMILIAN
SCHELL, INGRID THULIN IN
"RETURN FROM THE ASHES" (U.A.)

JONATHAN WINTER IN
"THE LOVED ONE" DIRECTED
BY TONY RICHARDSON (M-G-M)

Above: LAURENCE HARVEY, JULIE CHRISTIE. Below:
DIRK BOGARDE, JULIE CHRISTIE; JULIE CHRISTIE,
ROLAND CURRAN, JEAN CLAUDIO IN "DARLING"
DIRECTED BY JOHN SCHLESINGER (EMBASSY)

TREVOR HOWARD, JOHN MILLS, RICHARD
TODD IN "OPERATION CROSSBOW"
DIRECTOR, MICHAEL ANDERSON (M-G-M)

RINGO STARR, PAUL McCARTNEY, JOHN
LENNON, GEORGE HARRISON IN "HELP"
DIRECTED BY RICHARD LESTER (U.A.)

CATHERINE DENEUVE IN
"REPULSION" DIRECTED BY ROMAN
POLANSKI (ROYAL FILMS INTERNATIONAL)

RAF VALLONE

TUESDAY WELD

JACK HAWKINS

FLORA ROBSON

DOROTHY PROVINE

319

GEORGE C. SCOTT
"THE BIBLE" DIRECTED BY JOHN HUSTON (20th CENTURY-FOX)

FRANCO NERO, RICHARD HARRIS

JONATHAN WINTERS, BRIAN KEITH,
ALAN ARKIN IN "THE RUSSIANS ARE
COMING, THE RUSSIANS ARE COMING
DIRECTOR, NORMAN JEWISON (U.A.)

JACK GILFORD, BUSTER KEATON,
ZERO MOSTEL IN "A FUNNY THING
HAPPENED ON THE WAY TO THE FORUM"
DIRECTOR, RICHARD LESTER (U.A.)

HARRIET ANDERSSON, JAMES MASON
IN "THE DEADLY AFFAIR"
DIRECTED BY SIDNEY LUMET (COLUMBIA)

JOANNA PETTET, JESSICA WALTER, CANDICE BERG
SHIRLEY KNIGHT, ELIZABETH HARTMAN, JOAN
HACKETT, KATHLEEN WIDDOES, MARY-ROBIN REI
IN "THE GROUP" DIRECTOR, SIDNEY LUMET (U.A.

DIRK BOGARDE, MONICA VITTI, TERENCE STAMP
IN "MODESTY BLAISE"
DIRECTED BY JOSEPH LOSEY (20th CENTURY-FOX)

BAARD OWE, NINA PENS RODE
IN "GERTRUD" DIRECTED BY
CARL TH. DREYER (OMNIA)

JACK LEMMON, WALTER MATTHAU
IN "THE FORTUNE COOKIE"
DIRECTOR, BILLY WILDER (U.A.)

VANESSA REDGRAVE

GUY STOCKWELL

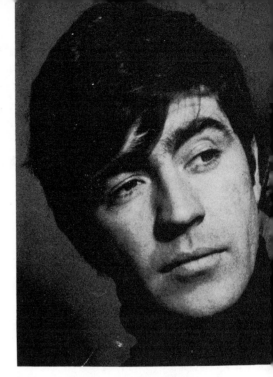

ALAN BATES

RAQUEL WELCH

VICTOR MATURE

1966 Undoubtedly one of the year's most significant moments came with the sale to ABC Television of "The Bridge on the River Kwai" for a record $2,000,000. An estimated audience of 60,000,000 people saw the film, leading most of the other major television networks to pay out a total of $70,000,000 for recent films from Metro, Paramount and Fox. Overnight, TV money became a major source of capital for high-budgeted film production. Oscars this year went mostly to adaptations of stage successes, while the big films continued to make big money, and a remake of a perennial oldie scored again. "A Man for all Seasons" received the Oscars for the year's best film, for its star, Paul Scofield, and director Fred Zinnemann. Broadway's brilliant Mike Nichols directed "Who's Afraid of Virginia Woolf?" gaining Elizabeth Taylor her second Oscar for best actress and a supporting Oscar for Sandy Dennis. Walter Matthau's fine performance in "The Fortune Cookie" won him the best supporting actor award. The foreign award went to the French-made "Un Homme et Une Femme." Quality films from abroad included "Dear John," Carl Th. Dreyer's masterly and deeply-felt "Gertrud," and the Russian "Hamlet," possibly the best film of a Shakespeare play ever made. The year's big films included the racing drama "Grand Prix," "The Blue Max," "Khartoum," "The Bible," "Madame X," "Lord Love a Duck," "Arabesque," "The Naked Prey," "This Property is Condemned," "Harper," "The Group," "Cul-de-Sac," the controversial "War Game," "Morgan," "Georgy Girl" and "Blow-Up." Most of the year's exciting new faces came from these films, including the sisters Lynn and Vanessa Redgrave, David Warner, David Hemmings, Oliver Reed, Camilla Sparv, Salome Jens, Raquel Welch, Richard Crenna and Guy Stockwell. Death took the great Russian actor, Nikolai Cherkassov, and one of the all-time masters of comedy, Buster Keaton. Others to die included silent stars Julia Faye, Natacha Rambova, the first screen lover, Francis X. Bushman; talkies stars Herbert Marshall, Sophie Tucker, Ed Wynn and Clifton Webb; actress and gossip columnist Hedda Hopper; script-writer Jules Furthman; Billy Rose, Herbert J. Yates, Robert Rossen and the great German producer Erich Pommer.

ALAIN DELON, DEAN MARTIN
IN "TEXAS ACROSS THE RIVER"
DIRECTOR, MICHAEL GORDON (UNIVERSAL)

ROBERT FULLER, JORDAN CHRISTOPHER,
YUL BRYNNER IN "RETURN OF THE SEVEN"
DIRECTOR, BURT KENNEDY (U.A.)

PETER SELLERS, TINO BUAZZELLI IN
"AFTER THE FOX" DIRECTED BY
VITTORIO DE SICA (UNITED ARTISTS)

GIOVANNA RALLI

PETER FALK

SARAH MILES

HUGH GRIFFITH

ELKE SOMMER

GUY DOLEMAN

YVES MONTAND,
EVA MARIE SAINT
"GRAND PRIX" DIRECTED BY JOHN FRANKENHEIMER (M-G-M)

CLAUDIA CARDINALE

LEE MARVIN, BURT LANCASTER
"THE PROFESSIONALS" DIRECTED BY RICHARD BROOKS (COLUMBIA)

DORIS DAY, ARTHUR GODFREY IN
"THE GLASS BOTTOM BOAT" DIRECTED
BY FRANK TASHLIN (M-G-M)

MARLON BRANDO, ANJANETTE COMER
IN "SOUTHWEST TO SONORA"
(UNIVERSAL-INTERNATIONAL)

DEBBIE REYNOLDS IN "THE SINGING NUN"
DIRECTOR, HENRY KOSTER (M-G-M)

SHIRLEY EATON

BORIS KARLOFF

KATHERINE ROSS

LUCIANA PALUZZI

JOHN PHILLIP LAW

JEAN SEBERG

(Warner Brothers)

WHO'S AFRAID OF VIRGINIA WOOLF?

Producer, Ernest Lehman; Director, Mike Nichols; Screenplay, Ernest Lehman; From the Play by Edward Albee; Music, Alex North; Director of Photography, Haskell Wexler.

CAST

Martha.................................Elizabeth Taylor
George.................................Richard Burton
Nick.................................George Segal
Connie.................................Sandy Dennis

Above: ELIZABETH TAYLOR, RICHARD BURTON, GEORGE SEGAL. Below: RICHARD BURTON, ELIZABETH TAYLOR, GEORGE SEGAL, SANDY DENNIS

Above:
ELIZABETH TAYLOR, RICHARD BURTON

SCENES FROM "WHO'S AFRAID OF VIRGINIA WOOLF?"

Above: GEORGE SEGAL, SANDY DENNIS.
Below: ELIZABETH TAYLOR

SCENE FROM "THE WAR GAME" DIRECTED BY PETER WATKINS (B.B.C.)

RAQUEL WELCH IN "ONE MILLION YEARS B.C." DIRECTOR, DON CHAFFEY (WARNER BROS.)

STEVE McQUEEN IN "NEVADA SMITH" DIRECTED BY HENRY HATHAWAY (PARAMOUNT)

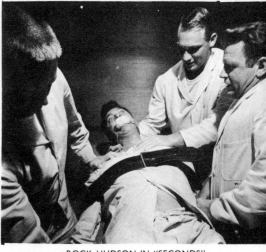

ANNE BANCROFT, BETTY FIELD IN "SEVEN WOMEN" DIRECTED BY JOHN FORD (M-G-M)

SOPHIA LOREN IN "JUDITH" DIRECTED BY DANIEL MANN (PARAMOUNT)

ROCK HUDSON IN "SECONDS" DIRECTOR, JOHN FRANKENHEIMER (PARAMOUNT)

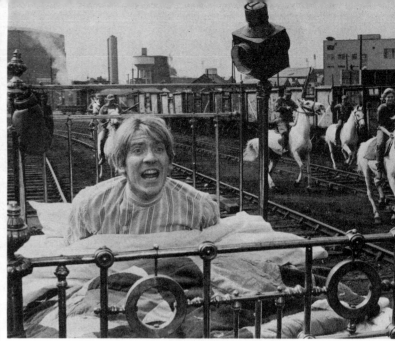

JOANNE WOODWARD, HENRY FONDA
IN "BIG HAND FOR THE LITTLE LADY"
DIRECTOR, FIELDER COOK (WARNER BROS.)

STEVE McQUEEN IN
"THE SAND PEBBLES"
DIRECTOR, ROBERT WISE
(20th CENTURY-FOX)

DAVID WARNER, VANESSA REDGRAVE IN
"MORGAN, A SUITABLE CASE FOR TREATMENT"
DIRECTOR, KAREL REISZ (BRITISH LION)

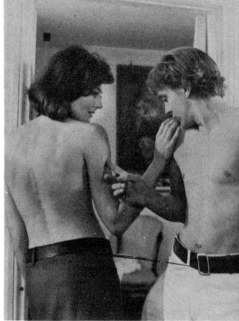

PAUL NEWMAN IN
"HARPER" DIRECTOR, JACK
SMIGHT (WARNER BROS.)

DAVID HEMMINGS

VANESSA REDGRAVE, DAVID HEMMINGS

SCENES FROM "BLOW-UP" DIRECTED BY MICHELANGELO ANTONIONI (M-G-M)

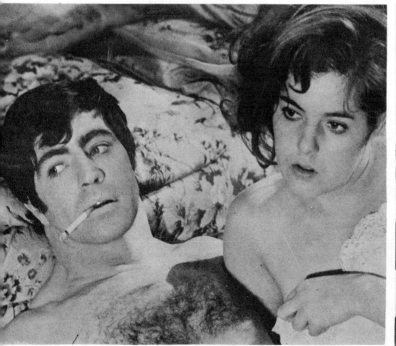

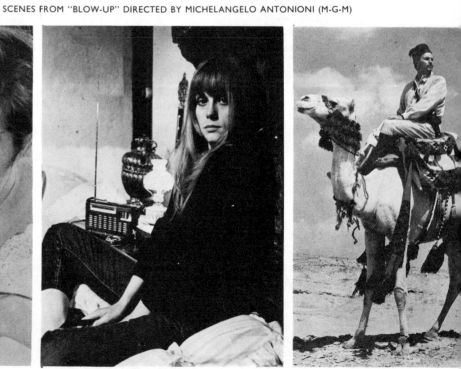

ALAN BATES, LYNN REDGRAVE IN
"GEORGY GIRL" DIRECTED BY
SILVIO NARIZZANO (COLUMBIA)

FRANÇOISE DORLEAC IN
"CUL-DE-SAC" DIRECTED BY
ROMAN POLANSKI (COMPTON)

CHARLTON HESTON IN
"KHARTOUM"
DIRECTOR, BASIL DEARDEN

324

RICHARD HARRIS   JULIE ANDREWS   MAX VON SYDOW   MARLON BRANDO, JANICE RULE IN
"THE CHASE" DIRECTOR, ARTHUR PENN
"HAWAII" DIRECTED BY GEORGE ROY HILL (UNITED ARTISTS)   (COLUMBIA)

BILL TRAVERS, VIRGINIA McKENNA IN
"BORN FREE"
DIRECTED BY CARL FOREMAN (COLUMBIA)   CONSTANCE BENNETT, LANA TURNER IN
"MADAME X" DIRECTED BY DAVID LOWELL RICH
(UNIVERSAL)

LAURENCE OLIVIER
IN "KHARTOUM"
(UNITED ARTISTS)   GEORGE PEPPARD,   URSULA ANDRESS
JAMES MASON   GEORGE PEPPARD
SCENES FROM "THE BLUE MAX" DIRECTOR, JOHN GUILLERMIN (20th CENT. FOX)   325

Above: WENDY HILLER, PAUL SCOFIELD
Below: ROBERT SHAW, VANESSA REDGRAVE

PAUL SCOFIELD

Above: ORSON WELLES.   Below:
PAUL SCOFIELD, ROBERT SHAW

SCENES FROM "A MAN FOR ALL SEASONS" DIRECTED BY FRED ZINNEMANN (COLUMBIA)

DEAN MARTIN IN
"THE SILENCERS"
DIRECTOR, PHIL KARLSON (COLUMBIA)

AUDREY HEPBURN, PETER O'TOOLE IN
"HOW TO STEAL A MILLION" DIRECTED
BY WILLIAM WYLER (20th CENTURY-FOX)

RUDOLF NUREYEV, MARGOT FONTEYN IN
"ROMEO AND JULIET"
DIRECTOR, PAUL CZINNER (RANK)

SIMONE SIGNORET

GERT FROEBE

JANE ASHER, MICHAEL CAINE
IN "ALFIE"
DIRECTOR, LEWIS GILBERT (PARAMOUNT)

"IS PARIS BURNING" DIRECTED BY RENE CLEMENT (PARAMOUNT)

E. RADSIN, INNOKENTY SMOKTUNOVSKY

ANASTASIA VERTINSKAYA

PAUL NEWMAN, JULIE ANDREWS
IN "TORN CURTAIN" DIRECTED
BY ALFRED HITCHCOCK (UNIVERSAL)

"HAMLET" DIRECTED BY GRIGORI KOZINTSEV (U.S.S.R.)

RITA TUSHINGHAM, OLIVER REED
IN "THE TRAP"
(RANK)

JIM HUTTON, CARY GRANT IN
"WALK, DON'T RUN"
DIRECTOR, CHARLES WALTERS (COLUMBIA)

CORNEL WILDE IN "THE NAKED
PREY" DIRECTED BY CORNEL WILDE
(PARAMOUNT)

JOHN WAYNE, ANGIE DICKINSON,
KIRK DOUGLAS IN "CAST A GIANT SHADOW"
DIRECTOR, MELVILLE SHAVELSON (UNITED ARTISTS)

LOLA ALBRIGHT, TUESDAY WELD
IN "LORD LOVE A DUCK"
(UNITED ARTISTS)

SOPHIA LOREN, PAUL NEWMAN IN
"LADY L." DIRECTED BY PETER USTINOV
(M-G-M)

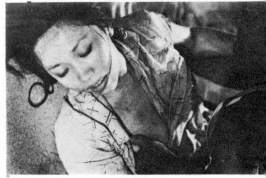

SHIRLEY ANNE FIELD, MICHAEL CAINE
IN "ALFIE"
(PARAMOUNT)

CHARLES BRONSON, NATALIE WOOD
IN "THIS PROPERTY IS CONDEMNED"
DIRECTOR, SIDNEY POLLACK (PARAMOUNT)

KYOKO KISHIDA, EIJI OKADA
IN "WOMAN OF THE DUNES"
(CONTEMPORARY FILMS)

SCENE FROM WALT DISNEY'S FULL LENGTH
CARTOON FEATURE "THE JUNGLE BOOK"
DIRECTED BY WOLFGANG REITHERMAN (BUENA VISTA)

TOMMY STEELE
"THE HAPPIEST MILLIONAIRE"
DIRECTED BY NORMAN TOKAR (BUENA VISTA)

FRED MacMURRAY, GREER GARSON

CHARLIE CHAPLIN IN
"A COUNTESS FROM HONG KONG"
(UNIVERSAL)

JOHN WAYNE, CHARLENE HOLT,
ROBERT MITCHUM IN "EL DORADO"
DIRECTOR, HOWARD HAWKES (PARAMOUNT)

CATHERINE DENEAUVE,
FRANÇOISE DORLEAC IN
"YOUNG GIRLS OF
ROCHEFORT" (WARNERS)

DORIS DAY, RICHARD HARRIS
IN "CAPRICE"
(20th CENTURY-FOX)

TERENCE STAMP, JULIE CHRISTIE

JULIE CHRISTIE, PETER FINCH

ALAN BATES, JULIE CHRISTIE

"FAR FROM THE MADDING CROWD" DIRECTED BY JOHN SCHLESINGER (M-G-M)

JULIE ANDREWS, JOHN GAVIN
"THOROUGHLY MODERN MILLIE" DIRECTED BY GEORGE ROY HILL (UNIVERSAL)

CAROL CHANNING

MARY TYLER MOORE,
JULIE ANDREWS

URSULA ANDRESS

ROBERT REDFORD IN
"BAREFOOT IN THE PARK"
(PARAMOUNT)

1967 This proved to be a year of contrasts. On the one hand there were such lavishly budgeted musicals as the Julie Andrews hit, "Thoroughly Modern Millie," and on the other, the hard-core violence of films like "The Dirty Dozen" and Arthur Penn's brilliant "Bonnie and Clyde," which many thought should have won the major Oscars for direction, film and screenplay. These went to Mike Nichols as director for "The Graduate," while "In the Heat of the Night" was selected best film with Rod Steiger winning his Oscar for his role as a small-town cop. George Kennedy was voted best supporting actor for his part in the allegorical prison drama, "Cool Hand Luke"; Estelle Parsons was voted best supporting actress for "Bonnie and Clyde." For years Katharine Hepburn was due for another Oscar and finally received it for what seemed spurious reasons at best: her sentimental role in the year's big hit, "Guess Who's Coming to Dinner," which sadly was co-star Spencer Tracy's last film. In England film production continued to boom with more new films being made than at any time since the early forties. Julie Andrews' stage musical "Camelot" was a failure for Vanessa Redgrave and Richard Harris. The Disney factory had a happy smash with their vintage-style animation feature, "Jungle Book," but their English musical star Tommy Steele failed to make it with the lavishly mounted "Half-a-Sixpence," while miscasting and an appalling score fatally burdened the otherwise attractive Fox musical "Dr. Doolittle." Shakespeare was big box-office with the Taylor/Burton "Taming of the Shrew" enjoying considerable success, but the same team failed with Marlowe's "Dr Faustus" and Graham Greene's "The Comedians." Everyone was excited by Charlie Chaplin's return to film-making as director of "Countess from Hong Kong" but the result was disappointing. From John Huston came the brilliant "Reflections in a Golden Eye"; John Wayne starred in Howard Hawks' enjoyable western, "El Dorado," and Burt Kennedy's "War Wagon." The year also marked Audrey Hepburn's retirement from films after reminders of her unique personality in "Two for the Road" and the thriller, "Wait Until Dark." In the foreign section there were Ingmar Bergman's masterly "Persona" and the popular French love story, "A Man and A Woman," directed by Claude Lelouch. A pedestrian version of Joyce's "Ulysses" aroused considerable controversy; Losey's "Accident," Schlesinger's slow-moving adaptation of Thomas Hardy's "Far from the Madding Crowd" and Jack Clayton's brooding "Our Mother's House" were notable English entries although the commercial success, "To Sir, With Love," made more money than these three combined. The movie world was saddened by the deaths of two great stars, Spencer Tracy and Vivien Leigh. Death also took Mischa Auer, Basil Rathbone, Jayne Mansfield, Reginald Denny, Charles Bickford, French actress Françoise Dorleac, silent film stars Mary Garden and Geraldine Farrar, English pioneer director Maurice Elvy and the writer Carson McCullers. The crop of new faces included Michael J. Pollard, Gene Hackman, Charlene Holt, Tommy Steele, Mary Tyler Moore, Hywel Bennet, Carol Channing, Sharon Tate, Suzy Kendall, Michael Sarrazin and the versatile Elaine May and Liza Minnelli.

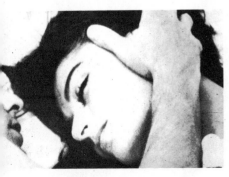

JEAN-LOUIS TRINTIGNANT, ANOUK
AIMEE IN "UN HOMME ET UNE FEMME"
DIRECTOR, CLAUDE LELOUCH (U.A.)

RICHARD HARRIS, VANESSA REDGRAVE

VANESSA REDGRAVE

VANESSA REDGRAVE, RICHARD HARRIS

SCENES FROM "CAMELOT" DIRECTED BY JOSHUA LOGAN (WARNER BROS.)

PAUL JONES IN "PRIVILEGE"
DIRECTED BY PETER WATKINS
(UNIVERSAL)

MICHAEL CAINE, JANE FONDA IN
"HURRY SUNDOWN" DIRECTED BY
OTTO PREMINGER (PARAMOUNT)

BARBARA JEFFORD, MILO O'SHEA IN
"ULYSSES" DIRECTED BY JOSEPH STRICK
(BRITISH LION)

Left: STANLEY BAKER, JACQUELINE SASSARD
Right: JACQUELINE SASSARD, DIRK BOGARDE
IN "ACCIDENT" DIRECTED BY JOSEPH LOSEY

OMAR SHARIF, PETER O'TOOLE IN
"NIGHT OF THE GENERALS"
DIRECTOR, ANATOLE LITVAK (COLUMBIA)

MICHAEL CRAWFORD, OLIVER
REED IN "THE JOKERS" DIRECTED BY
MICHAEL WINNER (UNIVERSAL)

GAYLE HUNNICUTT

JAMES BOOTH

BARBARA RUSH

MICHAEL YORK

CHARLENE HOLT

JAMES WARD

MICHAEL J. POLLARD   FAYE DUNAWAY, WARREN BEATTY   ESTELLE PARSONS, GENE HACKMAN

"BONNIE AND CLYDE" DIRECTED BY ARTHUR PENN (WARNER BROS.)

PAUL NEWMAN, GEORGE KENNEDY IN "COOL HAND LUKE"
DIRECTED BY STUART ROSENBERG
(WARNER BROS.)

KATHARINE HEPBURN, SPENCER TRACY IN
"GUESS WHO'S COMING TO DINNER"
(COLUMBIA)

SIDNEY POITIER, ROD STEIGER IN
"IN THE HEAT OF THE NIGHT"
(UNITED ARTISTS)

ANNE BANCROFT

DUSTIN HOFFMAN

"THE GRADUATE" DIRECTED BY MIKE NICHOLS (AVCO EMBASSY)

ELIZABETH TAYLOR IN "THE TAMING OF THE SHREW"

RICHARD BURTON

Above: ELIZABETH TAYLOR, RICHARD BURTON
Below: CYRIL CUSACK, ELIZABETH TAYLOR,
RICHARD BURTON

ELIZABETH TAYLOR, NATASHA PYNE

"THE TAMING OF THE SHREW" DIRECTED BY FRANCO ZEFFIRELLI (COLUMBIA)

TONY BECKLEY, MARTINE BESWICK,
TERENCE MORGAN, SUZY KENDALL,
NORMAN RODWAY IN "PENTHOUSE"
DIRECTOR, PETER COLLINSON (PARAMOUNT)

RAQUEL WELCH, TONY FRANCIOSA
IN "FATHOM"
(20th CENTURY-FOX)

DEAN MARTIN, JEAN SIMMONS
IN "ROUGH NIGHT IN JERICHO"
DIRECTOR, ARNOLD LAVEN
(UNIVERSAL)

LIV ULLMAN, BIBI ANDERSSON
IN "PERSONA" DIRECTED BY
INGMAR BERGMAN (U.A.)

JOHN WAYNE, ROBERT WALKER, HOWARD
KEEL, KEENAN WYNN, KIRK DOUGLAS IN
"THE WAR WAGON" (UNIVERSAL)

ROCK HUDSON, NIGEL GREEN,
GEORGE PEPPARD IN "TOBRUK"
DIRECTOR, ARTHUR HILLER

ELIZABETH TAYLOR, BRIAN KEITH IN
"REFLECTIONS IN A GOLDEN EYE"
DIRECTED BY JOHN HUSTON (WARNER BROS.)

LEE MARVIN   RICHARD JAECKEL, LEE MARVIN, RALPH MEEK
"THE DIRTY DOZEN" DIRECTED BY ROBERT ALDRICH
(M-G-M)

RICHARD BURTON, JAMES EARL JONES, ALEC GUINNESS,
ELIZABETH TAYLOR, PETER USTINOV IN "THE COMEDIANS"
DIRECTED BY PETER GLENVILLE (M-G-M)

RICHARD BURTON IN "DR FAUSTUS"
DIRECTED BY NEVILLE COGHILL, RICHARD BURTON
(COLUMBIA)

"CLOSELY WATCHED TRAINS"
(CURZON)

TOMMY STEELE IN "HALF-A-SIXPENCE"
(PARAMOUNT)

MICHAEL RENNIE, MERLE OBERON
IN "HOTEL" DIRECTED BY
RICHARD QUINE (WARNER BROS.)

ALBERT FINNEY, AUDREY HEPBURN IN
"TWO FOR THE ROAD" DIRECTED BY
STANLEY DONEN (20th CENTURY-FOX)

MARTIN BALSAM, PAUL NEWMAN IN
"HOMBRE" DIRECTED BY MARTIN RITT
(20th CENTURY-FOX)

WILLIAM DIX, REX HARRISON,
ANTHONY NEWLEY

REX HARRISON

SAMANTHA EGGAR

"DR DOLITTLE" DIRECTED BY RICHARD FLEISCHER (20th CENTURY-FOX)

SHASHI KAPOOR, HAYLEY MILLS IN
"PRETTY POLLY" DIRECTED BY
GUY GREEN (UNIVERSAL)

SANDY DENNIS IN "UP THE DOWN
STAIRCASE" DIRECTOR, ROBERT
MULLIGAN (WARNER BROS.)

DIRK BOGARDE IN "OUR MOTHER'S
HOUSE" DIRECTED BY JACK CLAYTON
(M-G-M)

JOHN WAYNE IN
"THE GREEN BERETS"
(WARNER BROS.)

TONY CURTIS, CAROLYN CONWELL IN
"THE BOSTON STRANGLER"
DIRECTED BY
RICHARD FLEISCHER (20TH CENTURY FOX)

MARTIN SHEEN, PATRICIA NEAL, JACK ALBERTSON IN
"THE SUBJECT WAS ROSES" (M-G-M)

CLIFF ROBERTSON, LILIA SKALA IN
"CHARLY"
(CINERAMA)

TOSHIRO MIFUNE, LEE MARVIN IN
"HELL IN THE PACIFIC"
DIRECTED BY JOHN BOORMAN (CINERAMA)

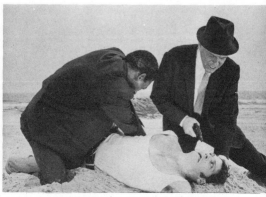

PER OSCARSSON IN "HUNGER"
(SIGMA III)

JOSEF SVET IN "THE FIREMENS' BALL"
DIRECTED BY MILOS FORMAN (GALA)

AL FREEMAN JR, FRANK SINATRA,
TONY MUSANTE IN "THE DETECTIVE"
(20TH CENTURY-FOX)

ALEX CORD IN
"THE PRODIGAL GUN"
(COLUMBIA)

OSKAR WERNER IN
"INTERLUDE"
(COLUMBIA)

THE MONKEES IN
"HEAD"
(SCREEN GEMS)

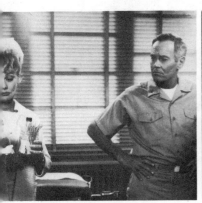

LUCILLE BALL, HENRY FONDA IN
"YOURS, MINE AND OURS"
(UNITED ARTISTS)

JOHN ALDERTON, JAMES FOX,
SUSANNAH YORK IN
"DUFFY" (COLUMBIA)

GEORGE C. SCOTT,
JULIE CHRISTIE IN
"PETULIA" (WARNER BROS.)

GROUCHO MARX IN "SKIDOO"
DIRECTED BY OTTO PREMINGER
(PARAMOUNT)

GINA LOLLOBRIGIDA IN
"THE QUEENS"
(COLUMBIA)

ERIC PORTMAN, CARLOS PIERRE IN
"DEADFALL"
(20TH CENTURY-FOX)

1968 Underground and semi-porno films reached larger audiences than ever, forcing Hollywood to jump on the sex bandwagon. For only the second time in the history of the Academy Award one of its main Oscars was awarded to two performers in the same category. Newcomer Barbra Streisand shared the Oscar with Katharine Hepburn, at her best in the immensely popular "Lion in Winter." Zeffirelli's exuberant "Romeo and Juliet" was a world-wide success and Polish director Roman Polanski's American debut produced a classic piece of Gothic horror in modern style with "Rosemary's Baby." Barbra Streisand repeated her stage triumph in "Funny Girl" on the screen, and the joyful "Finian's Rainbow" starred the ageless Fred Astaire. "Hell in the Pacific," "Bullitt," with its heart-stopping car chase, "Will Penny," "Targets" and "Pretty Poison" remain memorable. John Wayne starred in and directed the hawkish "Green Berets"; Paul Newman directed his wife, Joanne Woodward, in the touching "Rachel, Rachel," and actor Albert Finney's sadly neglected "Charlie Bubbles" was one of the best British films of the year, although it was the elephantine "Oliver!", directed by Carol Reed, that proved a big box-office success. Sex-orientated films like Paul Morrissey's "Flesh" and Russ Meyer's "Vixen" led the challenge to Hollywood, which replied by depicting lesbianism in films like "The Fox" and "The Killing of Sister George." The first signs of the violence soon to dominate films could be seen in two Clint Eastwood vehicles, "Hang 'Em High" and "Coogan's Bluff." A sci-fi story with serious overtones, "Planet of the Apes," was a success and fathered a series. Oscars went to Cliff Robertson for his performance in "Charly," Jack Albertson for his supporting role in "The Subject Was Roses" and Ruth Gordon for her supporting role in "Rosemary's Baby." The gargantuan Russian epic, "War and Peace," won the Oscar as best foreign film over the Canadian "Warrendale," Luis Buñuel's "Belle De Jour," Milos Forman's "Firemens' Ball" and the British film, "Poor Cow." But, towering above all other films of the year was Stanley Kubrick's masterpiece, "2001, A Space Odyssey." The Academy's staggering neglect of this masterwork ranks with the staggering neglect of Chaplin and Garbo. New faces included Jacqueline Bisset, Jim Brown, Beau Bridges, Genevieve Bujold, Marianne Hill, Mia Farrow, James Caan, Katherine Ross, Jon Voight, Michael Sarrazin and Gayle Hunnicut. Death took the legendary Tallulah Bankhead, silent stars Mae Marsh, Ramon Novarro, Dorothy Gish and thirties favorites Kay Francis, Lee Tracey, Fay Bainter, Franchot Tone and Lilian Harvey: directors Anthony Asquith, Robert Z. Leonard, author John Steinbeck and one of the screen's immortals, Carl Theodore Dreyer.

ALBERT FINNEY, COLIN BLAKELY IN
"CHARLIE BUBBLES" DIRECTED BY
ALBERT FINNEY (UNIVERSAL)

HARRY ANDREWS, SIMONE SIGNORET,
VANESSA REDGRAVE IN "THE SEAGULL"
(WARNER BROS.)

CHRISTOPHER JONES IN
"WILD IN THE STREETS"
(AMERICAN INTERNATIONAL)

CLINT EASTWOOD IN
"HANG 'EM HIGH"
(UNITED ARTISTS)

ELVIS PRESLEY IN
"LIVE A LITTLE, LOVE A LITTLE"
(M-G-M)

CANDICE BERGEN IN
"THE MAGUS"
(20th CENTURY-FOX)

TUESDAY WELD, ANTHONY PER...
IN "PRETTY POISON"
(20TH CENTURY-FOX)

JOANNE WOODWARD IN
"RACHEL, RACHEL"
DIRECTED BY PAUL NEWMAN (WARNER BROS.)

INGRID THULIN, MAX VON SYDOW IN
"HOUR OF THE WOLF"
DIRECTED BY INGMAR BERGMAN (SVENSK FILM)

PIERRE CLEMENTI, CATHERINE DENEUVE, MICHELE MORGAN IN
"BENJAMIN"
(PARAMOUNT)

JULIE ANDREWS IN "STAR"
DIRECTED BY ROBERT WISE
(20TH CENTURY-FOX)

SONDRA LOCKE, ALAN ARKIN IN
"THE HEART IS A LONELY HUNTER"
(WARNER BROS.)

ROD STEIGER, JOHN PHILLIP LAW IN
"THE SERGEANT"
(WARNER BROS.)

CLINT EASTWOOD IN
'COOGAN'S BLUFF" DIRECTED BY
DON SIEGEL (UNIVERSAL)

CATHERINE DENEUVE, GENEVIEVE PAGE IN
"BELLE DE JOUR" DIRECTED BY
LUIS BUÑUEL (ALLIED ARTISTS)

JOHN PHILLIP LAW, JANE FONDA IN
"BARBARELLA"
(PARAMOUNT)

CHARLTON HESTON IN
"WILL PENNY" DIRECTED BY
TOM GRIES (PARAMOUNT)

BORIS KARLOFF IN "TARGETS"
DIRECTED BY
PETER BOGDANOVICH
(PARAMOUNT)

NICOL WILLIAMSON IN
"INADMISSIBLE EVIDENCE"
(PARAMOUNT)

TERENCE STAMP,
CAROL WHITE IN "POOR COW"
(WARNER BROS.)

JACK LEMMON, WALTER MATTHAU IN
"THE ODD COUPLE"
(PARAMOUNT)

MOYRA FRASER, BARRY EVANS IN
"HERE WE GO ROUND THE MULBERRY BUSH"
(UNITED ARTISTS)

SUSAN GEORGE, MICHAEL YORK IN
"THE STRANGE AFFAIR"
(PARAMOUNT)

ELIZABETH TAYLOR, MIA FARROW IN
"SECRET CEREMONY" DIRECTED BY
JOSEPH LOSEY (UNIVERSAL)

STEPHANE AUDRAN, JACQUELINE SASSARD IN
"LES BICHES"
DIRECTED BY CLAUDE CHABROL (U.G.C.)

"YELLOW SUBMARINE"
(UNITED ARTISTS)

ALAN BATES IN
"THE FIXER"
DIRECTED BY JOHN FRANKENHEIMER (M-G-M)

ALAIN COHEN, MICHEL SIMON IN
"THE TWO OF US"
(P.A.C.)

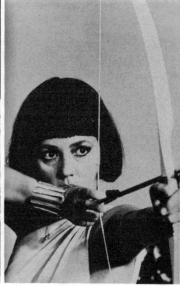

JEANNE MOREAU IN
"THE BRIDE WORE BLACK"
DIRECTED BY
FRANÇOIS TRUFFAUT (UNITED ARTISTS)

LEONARD WHITING, OLIVIA HUSSEY IN
"ROMEO AND JULIET" DIRECTED BY
FRANCO ZEFFIRELLI (PARAMOUNT)

MIA FARROW, RUTH GORDON IN
"ROSEMARY'S BABY" DIRECTED BY
ROMAN POLANSKI (PARAMOUNT)

"WARRENDALE"
DIRECTED BY ALLAN KING
(GROVE PRESS)

BURT LANCASTER IN
"THE SCALPHUNTERS"
DIRECTED BY SYDNEY POLLACK
(UNITED ARTISTS)

MIA FARROW, JOHN CASSAVETES IN
"ROSEMARY'S BABY"

CAROL WHITE

BEAU BRIDGES

LIZA MINNELLI

JAMES CAAN

JACQUELINE BISSETT

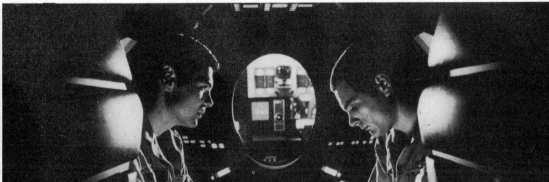

KEIR DULLEA

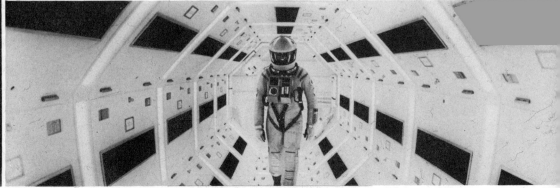

GARY LOCKWOOD, KEIR DULLEA

"2001, A SPACE ODYSSEY"
DIRECTED BY STANLEY KUBRICK (M-G-M)

341

BARBRA STREISAND

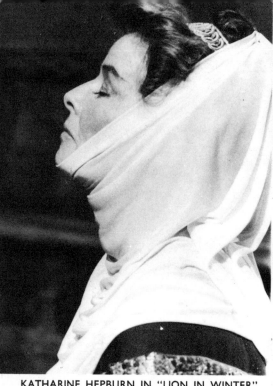

KATHARINE HEPBURN IN "LION IN WINTER"
DIRECTED BY ANTHONY HARVEY
(AVCO EMBASSY)

OMAR SHARIF, BARBRA STREISAND IN
"FUNNY GIRL" DIRECTED BY
WILLIAM WYLER (COLUMBIA)

ROSEMARY HARRIS, RACHEL ROBERTS IN
"A FLEA IN HER EAR"
(20TH CENTURY-FOX)

FRED ASTAIRE IN "FINIAN'S RAINBOW"
DIRECTED BY FRANCIS FORD COPPOLA
(WARNER BROS.)

ARLTON HESTON, RODDY MCDOWALL, LOU WAGNER

WOODROW PARFREY, JAMES WHITMORE, MAURICE EVANS

"PLANET OF THE APES" (20TH CENTURY-FOX)

SOPHIA LOREN
"CINDERELLA, ITALIAN STYLE" (M-G-M)

DOLORES DEL RIO

"LA CHINOISE" DIRECTED BY
JEAN-LUC GODARD
(LEACOCK-PENNEBAKER)

MARIANNE HILL

STEVE MCQUEEN, FAYE DUNAWAY IN
"THE THOMAS CROWN AFFAIR"
(UNITED ARTISTS)

STEVE MCQUEEN IN "BULLITT"
DIRECTED BY PETER YATES
(UNITED ARTISTS)

TREVOR HOWARD IN
"THE CHARGE OF THE LIGHT BRIGADE"
DIRECTED BY TONY RICHARDSON
(UNITED ARTISTS)

JACKIE CURTIS, CANDY DARLING,
JOE DALLESANDRO IN "FLESH"
DIRECTED BY PAUL MORRISSEY (WARHOL)

ANNE HEYWOOD, SANDY DENNIS IN
"THE FOX" DIRECTED BY
MARK RYDELL (WARNER BROS.)

KIM NOVAK IN
"THE LEGEND OF LYLAH CLARE"
DIRECTED BY ROBERT ALDRICH
(M-G-M)

SUSANNAH YORK, BERYL REID, CORAL BROWN IN
"THE KILLING OF SISTER GEORGE"
(CINERAMA)

"VIXEN"
DIRECTED BY RUSS MEYER
(EVE)

"WAR AND PEACE"
DIRECTED BY SERGEI BONDARCHUK
(CONTINENTAL)

MARK LESTER IN
"OLIVER!"
DIRECTED BY CAROL REED (COLUMBIA)

CLAUDE JADE, JEAN-PIERRE LEAUD IN
STOLEN KISSES" DIRECTED BY FRANÇOIS TRUFFAUT
(LOPERT)

JOHN MCMARTIN, SHIRLEY MACLAINE IN
"SWEET CHARITY"
(UNIVERSAL)

DUSTIN HOFFMAN, MIA FARROW IN
"JOHN AND MARY"
DIRECTED BY PETER YATES (20TH CENTURY-FO

ROBERT REDFORD, PAUL NEWMAN IN
"BUTCH CASSIDY AND THE SUNDANCE KID"
DIRECTED BY GEORGE ROY HILL (20TH CENTURY-FOX)

GENE HACKMAN, ROBERT REDFORD IN
"DOWNHILL RACER"
DIRECTED BY MICHAEL RITCHIE (PARAMOUNT)

JIM BROWN, RAQUEL WELCH IN
"100 RIFLES"
(20TH CENTURY-FOX)

ROBERT REDFORD, ROBERT BLAKE IN
"TELL THEM WILLIE BOY IS HERE"
(UNIVERSAL)

"FUTZ" DIRECTED BY TOM O'HORGAN
(COMMONWEALTH UNITED)

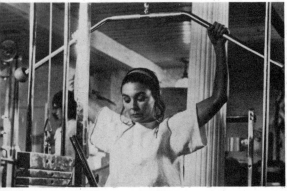
JEAN SIMMONS IN
"HAPPY ENDING"
(UNITED ARTISTS)

ANNE WIAZEMSKY, SILVANA MANGANO, TERENCE STAMP,
ANDRES JOSE CRUZ IN "THEOREM"
DIRECTED BY PIER PAOLO PASOLINI (EAGLE)

LIZA MINNELLI, WENDELL BURTON IN
"THE STERILE CUCKOO"
(U.K. TITLE "POOKIE") (PARAMOUNT)

"PUTNEY SWOPE"
(CINEMA V)

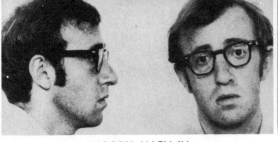

WOODY ALLEN IN
"TAKE THE MONEY AND RUN"
(CINERAMA)

ALFRED HITCHCOCK IN
"TOPAZ"
(UNIVERSAL)

DEBORAH KERR

1969 The year of the youth-made, youth-orientated "Easy Rider"; the year of Sam Peckinpah's "The Wild Bunch"; the year of the politically-motivated and popular French-made "Z," which won an Oscar for best foreign film; the year of John Wayne's Oscar for his performance in Henry Hathaway's "True Grit"; the year which saw a growing number of Black Films like "Cotton Comes to Harlem"; in short, there was something for everyone. Robert Redford emerged as a star with "Downhill Racer," "Tell Them Willie Boy Is Here" and the runaway success, "Butch Cassidy and the Sundance Kid." Ali MacGraw attracted attention in "Goodbye Columbus," as did Liza Minnelli in "The Sterile Cuckoo." Two lavish musicals, "Sweet Charity," with Shirley Maclaine and "Hello Dolly," with Barbra Streisand were flops. Wife-swapping in "Bob and Carol and Ted and Alice" and the explicit sex in "I Am Curious, Yellow" proved to be big box-office draws; so did escapist films like the World War Two adventure, "Where Eagles Dare," the excellent western thriller, "The Stalking Moon" and the comedy, "Cactus Flower," with Ingrid Bergman. John Schlesinger's story of two losers in New York, "Midnight Cowboy," won an Oscar and made a star of Jon Voight, while Sidney Pollack's "They Shoot Horses, Don't They?" harrowingly depicted the horrors of the Depression. Notable foreign films were Sergio Leone's homage to the western, "Once Upon A Time In The West," Pier Paolo Pasolini's compelling "Theorem" and the prolific Truffaut's "Stolen Kisses." Visconti made a gloomy and portentous study of Nazi Germany in the Thirties with "The Damned"; Richard Attenborough scored a success with the musical version of the First World War, "Oh What A Lovely War," while "The Battle of Britain" seemed to feature more guest stars than airplanes. Unjustly neglected films included "Happy Ending," with a glowing performance from Jean Simmons, George Cukor's silky adaptation of the Alexandria Quartet into "Justine" and Tom O'Horgan's first film "Futz." Oscars went to veteran Gig Young and newcomer Goldie Hawn for their supporting performances in "They Shoot Horses, Don't They?" and "Cactus Flower." Maggie Smith was voted best actress for her role as a school teacher in "The Prime of Miss Jean Brodie," and a special Oscar was given to Cary Grant. New faces on the scene included Bonnie Bedelia, Richard Benjamin, Robert Blake, Dyan Cannon, Goldie Hawn, Elliott Gould, Jack Nicholson and Brenda Vaccaro. The year was saddened by the brutal killing of Sharon Tate and the death of all-time greats Robert Taylor and Judy Garland and the great director Josef von Sternberg: others included Enid Bennett, George "Gabby" Hayes, John Boles, Rudolf Forster, Sigrid Gurie, Boris Karloff, Jeffrey Hunter, Gladys Swarthout, studio executive Nicholas M. Schenk, writer and producer Charles Brackett, photographer Karl Freund and director Leo McCarey.

DAVID HEMMINGS, JOANNA PETTET IN
"THE BEST HOUSE IN LONDON"
(M-G-M)

PATTY DUKE IN
"ME NATALIE"
(NATIONAL GENERAL)

STEVE McQUEEN, MITCH VOGEL,
RUPERT CROSSE IN "THE REIVERS"
DIRECTED BY MARK RYDELL
(NATIONAL GENERAL)

IRENE PAPAS IN "Z"
(CINEMA V)

CHRISTINE NOONAN, MALCOLM MCDOWELL IN "IF" DIRECTED BY LINDSAY ANDERSON (PARAMOUNT)

WILLIAM HOLDEN

"THE WILD BUNCH" DIRECTED BY SAM PECKINPAH (WARNER BROS.)

NICOL WILLIAMSON IN "HAMLET" DIRECTED BY TONY RICHARDSON (COLUMBIA)

MICHAEL CAINE, NIGEL DAVENPORT IN "PLAY DIRTY" (UNITED ARTISTS)

RICHARD BURTON, GENEVIEVE BUJOLD IN "ANNE OF THE THOUSAND DAYS" (UNIVERSAL)

SILVANA MANGANO IN "THE WITCHES" (LOPERT)

RICHARD THOMAS, CATHY BURNS, BRUCE DAVISON, BARBARA HERSHEY IN "LAST SUMMER" (20TH CENTURY-FOX)

ROBERT SHAW, CHRISTOPHER PLUMMER IN "THE ROYAL HUNT OF THE SUN" (NATIONAL GENERAL)

ARLO GUTHRIE IN "ALICE'S RESTAURANT" DIRECTED BY ARTHUR PENN (UNITED ARTIS

SUSANNAH YORK

AL LEWIS, GIG YOUNG
"THEY SHOOT HORSES, DON'T THEY?"
DIRECTED BY SYDNEY POLLACK (ABC)

MICHAEL SARRAZIN, JANE FONDA

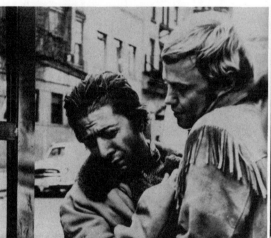

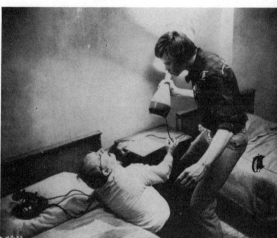

JON VOIGHT, SYLVIA MILES

DUSTIN HOFFMAN, JON VOIGHT
"MIDNIGHT COWBOY"
DIRECTED BY JOHN SCHLESINGER
(UNITED ARTISTS)

BARNARD HUGHES, JON VOIGHT

DYAN CANNON

JUDY GEESON, ROD STEIGER,
CLAIRE BLOOM IN
"THREE INTO TWO WON'T GO" (UNIVERSAL)

PETER O'TOOLE IN
"GOODBYE, MR CHIPS" (M-G-M)

JACK NICHOLSON

SHARON TATE

MICHELE LEE, BUDDY HACKETT,
DEAN JONES IN "THE LOVE BUG"
DIRECTED BY ROBERT STEVENSON (DISNEY)

"A BOY NAMED CHARLIE BROWN"
(20TH CENTURY-FOX)

ANOUK AIMEE

347

VERNA BLOOM, ROBERT FORSTER IN
"MEDIUM COOL"
DIRECTED BY HASKELL WEXLER (PARAMOUNT)

CLINT EASTWOOD, JEAN SEBERG IN
"PAINT YOUR WAGON"
DIRECTED BY JOSHUA LOGAN (PARAMOUNT)

MAGGIE SMITH, ROBERT STEPHENS IN
"THE PRIME OF MISS JEAN BRODIE"
DIRECTED BY RONALD NEAME
(20TH CENTURY-FOX)

"ONCE UPON A TIME IN THE WEST"
DIRECTED BY SERGIO LEONE
(PARAMOUNT)

"I AM CURIOUS, YELLOW"
(GROVE PRESS)

GODFREY CAMBRIDGE, RAYMOND ST JACQUES IN
"COTTON COMES TO HARLEM"
(UNITED ARTISTS)

CHIEF DAN GEORGE,
GLENN FORD, CHRISTOPHER SHEA IN
"SMITH!" (BUENA VISTA)

REX HARRISON, RICHARD BURTON IN
"STAIRCASE" DIRECTED BY STANLEY DONEN
(20TH CENTURY-FOX)

BEBE LONCAR

IAN HENDRY

BRENDA VACCARO

RICHARD BENJAMIN

SIR LAURENCE OLIVIER

MAGGIE SMITH
"OH, WHAT A LOVELY WAR!"
DIRECTED BY RICHARD ATTENBOROUGH
(PARAMOUNT)

SIR RALPH RICHARDSON,
KENNETH MORE, IAN HOLM

DEBORAH KERR, KIRK DOUGLAS IN
"THE ARRANGEMENT"
DIRECTED BY ELIA KAZAN (WARNER BROS.)

JACK NICHOLSON, PETER FONDA IN
"EASY RIDER"
DIRECTED BY DENNIS HOPPER
(COLUMBIA)

RICHARD BENJAMIN,
ALI MACGRAW IN
"GOODBYE COLUMBUS" (PARAMOUNT)

INGRID PITT, CLINT EASTWOOD,
MARY URE, RICHARD BURTON IN
"WHERE EAGLES DARE" (PARAMOUNT)

ELLIOTT GOULD, NATALIE WOOD, ROBERT CULP,
DYAN CANNON IN
"BOB AND CAROL AND TED AND ALICE" (COLUMBIA)

TOMMY TUNE, BARBRA STREISAND IN
"HELLO DOLLY" DIRECTED BY GENE KELLY
(20TH CENTURY-FOX)

GOLDIE HAWN IN
"CACTUS FLOWER" (COLUMBIA)

JOHN WAYNE, KIM DARBY IN
"TRUE GRIT" DIRECTED BY
HENRY HATHAWAY (PARAMOUNT)

INGRID THULIN

"THE DAMNED"
DIRECTED BY LUCHINO VISCONTI
(WARNER BROS.)

HELMUT BERGER

JOHN WAYNE

VANESSA REDGRAVE IN
"ISADORA"
(UNIVERSAL)

CHRISTOPHER JONES

AVA GARDNER IN
"MAYERLING"
(WARNER BROS.)

ROD STEIGER IN
"THE ILLUSTRATED MAN"
DIRECTED BY JACK SMIGHT
(WARNER BROS.)

SIR MICHAEL REDGRAVE,
SIR LAURENCE OLIVIER
"THE BATTLE OF BRITAIN" (UNITED ARTISTS)

GENEVIEVE PAGE IN
"DECLINE AND FALL OF A BIRDWATCHER"
(20TH CENTURY-FOX)

BRUCE CABOT, JOHN WAYNE,
ROCK HUDSON IN "THE UNDEFEATED"
(20TH CENTURY-FOX)

ANNA MASSEY, KEIR DULLEA IN
"DE SADE" (AMERICAN INTERNATIONAL)

CHRISTOPHER PLUMMER, PETER BULL IN
"LOCK UP YOUR DAUGHTERS"
(COLUMBIA)

ANNE HEYWOOD, GREGORY PECK IN
"THE CHAIRMAN"
(20TH CENTURY-FOX)

BURT LANCASTER IN "GYPSY MOTHS"
DIRECTED BY JOHN FRANKENHEIMER
(M-G-M)

MARLON BRANDO IN
"THE NIGHT OF THE FOLLOWING DAY"
(UNIVERSAL)

TOM COURTENAY,
ROMY SCHNEIDER IN "OTLEY"
(COLUMBIA)

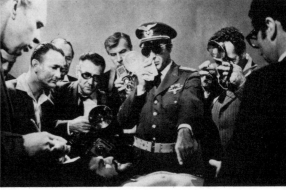

"CHE!"
DIRECTED BY RICHARD FLEISCHER
(20TH CENTURY-FOX)

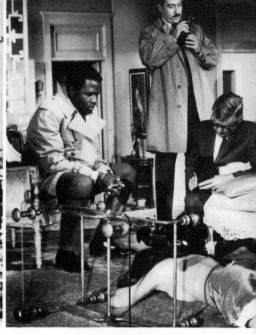

JAMES EARL JONES, JANE ALEXANDER
"THE GREAT WHITE HOPE" DIRECTED BY MARTIN RITT (20TH CENTURY-FOX)

LARRY PENNELL, JAMES EARL JONES

SIDNEY POITIER IN
"THEY CALL ME MR TIBBS"
(UNITED ARTISTS)

"TORA! TORA! TORA!"
(20TH CENTURY-FOX)

MELINA MERCOURI, DESPO IN
"PROMISE AT DAWN"
(AVCO EMBASSY)

KAREN BLACK, JACK NICHOLSON IN
"FIVE EASY PIECES" DIRECTED BY
BOB RAFELSON (COLUMBIA)

ZERO MOSTEL IN
"THE ANGEL LEVINE"
(UNITED ARTISTS)

PEARL BAILEY IN
"THE LANDLORD"
(UNITED ARTISTS)

ESTELLE PARSONS, GODFREY CAMBRIDGE
IN "WATERMELON MAN" DIRECTED BY
MELVIN VAN PEEBLES (COLUMBIA)

ROBERT STEPHENS, COLIN BLAKE
"THE PRIVATE LIFE OF
SHERLOCK HOLMES"
DIRECTED BY BILLY WILDER
(UNITED ARTISTS)

THE BEATLES, YOKO ONO IN
"LET IT BE"
(UNITED ARTISTS)

ELLIOTT GOULD IN
"GETTING STRAIGHT"
(COLUMBIA)

TONY LO BIANCO, SHIRLEY STOLER IN
"THE HONEYMOON KILLERS"
(CINERAMA)

MAE WEST IN
"MYRA BRECKINRIDGE"
DIRECTED BY MIKE SARNE
(20TH CENTURY-FOX)

1970 That symbol of Hollywood's world dominance, M-G-M, sold off 70 years of screen memorabilia to the highest bidder in an attempt to meet the studio's staggering overheads and closed an era in the history of the film industry. Negro-orientated films like Martin Ritt's "The Great White Hope" and "They Call Me Mr Tibbs," with Sidney Poitier, found a vast audience who were prepared to sit through banal films provided they were "black." It was a year of enormous hits and catastrophic flops. The mawkish "Love Story" became so popular it was positively embarrassing and the topical hi-jacking drama of "Airport," with its all-star cast, appealed to the same audiences. Yet war films also proved to be big box-office successes. The screwball satire "M★A★S★H" brought Elliott Gould, Donald Sutherland and director Robert Altman to the fore and the blood and guts saga of "Patton" earned its star, George C. Scott, a well-deserved Oscar as well as six other Oscars for best film, Franklin Schaffner's direction and the screenplay. The Ken Russell film "Women in Love" won actress Glenda Jackson an Oscar, while "Investigation of A Citizen Above Suspicion" was voted the best foreign film of the year. John Mills won the supporting award in David Lean's "Ryan's Daughter"; Helen Hayes became the first actress to win an Oscar for best actress and supporting actress, gaining the latter for her role in "Airport." Other successful films were Arthur Penn's wry look at the western saga in "Little Big Man," the celebration of rock culture in Mike Wadleigh's "Woodstock," Minnelli's "On A Clear Day You Can See Forever," with Barbra Streisand and Yves Montand, and another Martin Ritt film, "The Molly Maguires." Excellent small-budget films were "Joe" and "Five Easy Pieces." Veteran directors John Huston and Howard Hawks scored with "The Kremlin Letter" and "Rio Lobo" but George Stevens' "The Only Game In Town," with Elizabeth Taylor and Warren Beatty, was sadly underrated. The colossal flops included M-G-M's "Zabriskie Point," 20th Century-Fox's "Tora! Tora! Tora!" and "Myra Breckinridge," distinguished only by Mae West's return to the screen. Otto Preminger continued his unbroken string of indifferent films with "Tell Me That You Love Me, Junie Moon." European films were easily holding their own against their American rivals and while those that made the most money were not always the best, the pick of the year included "My Night At Maud's," "Borsalino," "The Things of Life" and Bresson's "Au Hasard Balthazar." The Canadian film, "Goin' Down The Road" attracted attention, and it was impossible to ignore Fellini's visually stunning "Satyricon." From Ingmar Bergman came "The Passion of Anna" and from Luis Buñuel, "The Milky Way" and "Tristana." English films included another D. H. Lawrence story, "The Virgin and The Gypsy" and the controversial "Performance," starring the rock'n'roll idol Mick Jagger. Death took Ed Begley, Bourvil, Billie Burke, Frances Farmer, silent vamp Louise Glaum, Edward Everett Horton, Chester Morris, Charles Ruggles, Inger Stevens and Sonny Tufts. The new faces included Jane Alexander, Stacy Keach, Karen Black, Sally Kellerman, Ryan O'Neal and Carrie Snodgrass.

ANGELA LANSBURY IN
"SOMETHING FOR EVERYONE"
(NATIONAL GENERAL)

GENE HACKMAN, MELVYN DOUGLAS IN
"I NEVER SANG FOR MY FATHER"
(COLUMBIA)

ELLEN BURSTYN IN
"TROPIC OF CANCER"
(PARAMOUNT)

MARCELLO MASTROIANNI IN
"LEO THE LAST" DIRECTED BY
JOHN BOORMAN (UNITED ARTISTS)

DUSTIN HOFFMAN

DUSTIN HOFFMAN, CHIEF DAN GEORGE
"LITTLE BIG MAN" DIRECTED BY ARTHUR PENN (NATIONAL GENERAL)

CHIEF DAN GEORGE

DONALD SUTHERLAND, ELLIOTT GOULD IN "M*A*S*H" DIRECTED BY ROBERT ALTMAN (20TH CENTURY-FOX)

YVES MONTAND, BARBRA STREISAND IN "ON A CLEAR DAY YOU CAN SEE FOREVER" (PARAMOUNT)

LEE MARVIN, JACK PALANCE IN
"MONTE WALSH"
(NATIONAL GENERAL)

SALLY KELLERMAN IN
"M*A*S*H"

RICHARD HARRIS IN
"CROMWELL"
(COLUMBIA)

CARRIE SNODGRASS IN
"RABBIT RUN"
(WARNER BROS.)

MICK JAGGER IN
"PERFORMANCE"
(WARNER BROS.)

FLORINDA BOLKAN IN
"INVESTIGATION OF A
CITIZEN ABOVE SUSPICION"
(COLUMBIA)

BEN GAZZARA, PETER FALK,
JOHN CASSAVETES IN "HUSBANDS"
DIRECTED BY JOHN CASSAVETES
(COLUMBIA)

JENNIE LINDEN, GLENDA JACKSON IN
"WOMEN IN LOVE" DIRECTED BY
KEN RUSSELL (UNITED ARTISTS)

MARIO ROMAGNOLI IN
"SATYRICON" DIRECTED BY FEDERICO FELLINI
(UNITED ARTISTS)

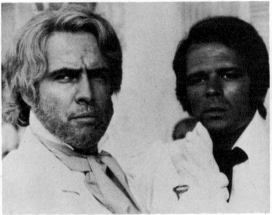

LIV ULLMAN, MAX VON SYDOW IN
"THE PASSION OF ANNA" DIRECTED BY
INGMAR BERGMAN (SVENSK FILM)

MARLON BRANDO, RENATO SALVATORI IN
"QUEIMADA"
(UNITED ARTISTS)

"THE RISE OF LOUIS XIV"
DIRECTED BY ROBERTO ROSSELLINI
(BRANDON)

ALAIN DELON,
JEAN-PAUL BELMONDO IN
"BORSALINO" (PARAMOUNT)

JEAN-PAUL BELMONDO, CATHERINE DENEUVE IN
"MISSISSIPPI MERMAID" DIRECTED BY
FRANÇOIS TRUFFAUT (UNITED ARTISTS)

ALAN BADEL IN
"THE ADVENTURERS"
(PARAMOUNT)

PAUL FRANKEUR, DELPHINE SEYRIG IN
"THE MILKY WAY" DIRECTED BY
LUIS BUÑUEL (U.M.)

FRANCO NERO, JOANNA SHIMKUSS IN
"THE VIRGIN AND THE GYPSY"
(CHEVRON)

"AU HASARD BALTHAZAR"
DIRECTED BY ROBERT BRESSON
(ARGOS)

355

GREGORY PECK, TUESDAY WELD IN
"I WALK THE LINE" DIRECTED BY
JOHN FRANKENHEIMER (COLUMBIA)

THE ARISTOCATS
(BUENA VISTA)

ELVIS PRESLEY IN
"ELVIS — THAT'S THE WAY IT IS"
(M-G-M)

JOHN MILLS

SARAH MILES, CHRISTOPHER JONES
"RYAN'S DAUGHTER" DIRECTED BY DAVID LEAN (M-G-M)

ALI MACGRAW, RYAN O'NEAL IN
"LOVE STORY" DIRECTED BY
ARTHUR HILLER (PARAMOUNT)

JOE DALLESANDRO,
GERI MILLER IN "TRASH"
DIRECTED BY PAUL MORRISSEY
(WARHOL)

LEE VAN CLEEF,
WILLIAM BERGER IN "SABATA"
(UNITED ARTISTS)

CANDICE BERGEN, PETER STRAUSS IN
"SOLDIER BLUE"
(AVCO EMBASSY)

PAUL NEWMAN, JOANNE WOODWARD
"WUSA"
DIRECTED BY STUART ROSENBERG
(PARAMOUNT)

356

GEORGE C. SCOTT IN "PATTON" DIRECTED BY FRANKLIN J. SCHAFFNER
(20TH CENTURY-FOX)

SIR JOHN GIELGUD, ALBERT FINNEY IN
"SCROOGE" DIRECTED BY
RONALD NEAME (NATIONAL GENERAL)

BUD CORT IN
"BREWSTER MCLOUD" DIRECTED BY
ROBERT ALTMAN (M-G-M)

GOLDIE HAWN IN
"THERE'S A GIRL IN MY SOUP"
(COLUMBIA)

GEORGE SEGAL, BARBRA STREISAND IN
"THE OWL AND THE PUSSYCAT"
(COLUMBIA)

DARIA HALPRIN, MARK FRECHETTE IN
"ZABRISKIE POINT" DIRECTED BY
MICHELANGELO ANTONIONI (M-G-M)

JULIE ANDREWS IN
"DARLING LILI" DIRECTED BY
BLAKE EDWARDS (PARAMOUNT)

RONALD FRASER, DENHOLM ELLIOT,
MICHAEL CAINE IN
"TOO LATE THE HERO"
(CINERAMA)

RYAN O'NEAL IN "THE GAMES"
DIRECTED BY MICHAEL WINNER
(20TH CENTURY-FOX)

MARLENE JOBERT IN
"RIDER ON THE RAIN"
(AVCO EMBASSY)

357

RICHARD HARRIS, SAMANTHA EGGAR
"THE MOLLY MAGUIRES" DIRECTED BY
MARTIN RITT (PARAMOUNT)

SEAN CONNERY

JOHN WAYNE IN
"RIO LOBO" DIRECTED BY
HOWARD HAWKS
(NATIONAL GENERAL)

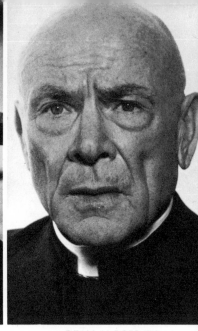

DEAN JAGGER IN
"THE KREMLIN LETTER"
DIRECTED BY JOHN HUSTON
(20TH CENTURY-FOX)

YVES MONTAND IN
"L'AVEU"
(WARNER BROS.)

"WOODSTOCK" (WARNER BROS.)

GIG YOUNG, CLORIS LEACHMAN IN
"LOVERS AND OTHER STRANGERS"
(CINERAMA)

"THE BOYS IN THE BAND"
DIRECTED BY WILLIAM FRIEDKIN
(NATIONAL GENERAL)

"KING LEAR" (RUSSIA)

ALAN ARKIN IN
"CATCH 22" DIRECTED BY
MIKE NICHOLS (PARAMOUNT)

RICHARD HARRIS IN
"A MAN CALLED HORSE"
(WARNER BROS.)

FRANÇOISE FABIAN,
JEAN-LOUIS TRINTIGNANT IN
"MY NIGHT AT MAUD'S" DIRECTED BY
ERIC ROHMER (PATHE)

DAVID BRADLEY IN
"KES"
(UNITED ARTISTS)

DENNIS PATRICK, PETER BOYLE IN
"JOE"
(CANNON)

HELEN HAYES, JEAN SEBERG IN
"AIRPORT"
(UNIVERSAL)

"WATERLOO"
DIRECTED BY SERGEI BONDARCHUK
(DE LAURENTIIS—MOSFILM)

KIRK DOUGLAS, HENRY FONDA IN
"THERE WAS A CROOKED MAN"
(WARNER BROS.)

ELIZABETH TAYLOR, WARREN BEATTY IN
"THE ONLY GAME IN TOWN" DIRECTED BY
GEORGE STEVENS (20TH CENTURY-FOX)

"BENEATH THE PLANET OF THE APES"
(20TH CENTURY-FOX)

ROBERT DE NIRO, DIANE VARSI,
DON STROUD IN "BLOODY MAMA"
DIRECTED BY ROGER CORMAN
(AMERICAN INTERNATIONAL)

STACY
KEACH

KAY THOMPSON IN
"TELL ME THAT YOU LOVE ME,
JUNIE MOON" DIRECTED
BY OTTO PREMINGER
(PARAMOUNT)

NOEL COWARD IN
"THE ITALIAN JOB"
DIRECTED BY PETER COLLINSON
(PARAMOUNT)

MONICA
VITTI

GLENDA
JACKSON

INGRID PITT, SANDOR ELES,
IN "COUNTESS DRACULA" (HAMMER)

VINCENT PRICE IN
"THE ABOMINABLE DR PHIBES"
(AMERICAN INTERNATIONAL)

BRUCE DAVISON IN
"WILLARD" (CINERAMA)

JANET SUZMAN, MICHAEL JAYSTON
IN "NICHOLAS AND ALEXANDRA" (COLUMBIA)

"BLUE WATER, WHITE DEATH"
(20TH CENTURY-FOX)

WOODY STRODE, BEKIM FEHMIU IN
"THE DESERTER" DIRECTED BY
BURT KENNEDY (PARAMOUNT)

DOMINIC GUARD, MARGARET LEIGHTON,
JULIE CHRISTIE IN "THE GO-BETWEEN"
DIRECTED BY JOSEPH LOSEY (M-G-M)

MILENA DRAVIC IN
"W. R. MYSTERIES OF THE ORGANISM"
DIRECTED BY DUSAN MAKAVEJEV
(CONNOISSEUR FILMS)

JANE ASHER, JOHN MOULDER-BROWN IN
"DEEP END" DIRECTED BY JERZY SKOLIMOWSKI (PARAMOUNT)

BARBARA PARKINS IN
"THE MEPHISTO WALTZ" (20TH CENTURY-F

KATHARINE HEPBURN IN "THE TROJAN WOMEN" (CINERAMA)

BURT LANCASTER IN "VALDEZ IS COMING" (UNITED ARTISTS)

JAMES OLSON, ARTHUR HILL, KATE REID, DAVID WAYNE IN "THE ANDROMEDA STRAIN" DIRECTED BY ROBERT WISE (UNIVERSAL)

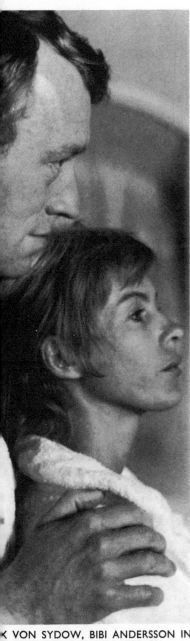

1971 Towering over the year's releases was Stanley Kubrick's "A Clockwork Orange." When the time for the Academy awards rolled round, an enjoyable cops and robbers thriller, "The French Connection," garnered five of the major Oscars including that for best film, best director (William Friedkin) and best actor (Gene Hackman). The omission of any major awards for the Kubrick film ranks with the staggering ignorance that neglected "2001, A Space Odyssey," Chaplin and Garbo. That aside, another widely acclaimed film at the year's end was "The Last Picture Show," which won for actress Cloris Leachman and actor Ben Johnson the best supporting awards. Jane Fonda won her Oscar playing a prostitute in "Klute" and the Italian "Garden of the Finzi-Continis" was best foreign film. Mike Nichols' study of sexual relationships in "Carnal Knowledge" was a considerable success, as was "Willard," a horror film about rats. Vincent Price starred in high camp style in another successful horror film, "The Abominable Dr Phibes." The annual John Wayne western, "Big Jake," and the annual Neil Simon comedy, "Plaza Suite," also proved very popular. "The $1,000,000 Duck," "The Barefoot Executive" and the animation feature "The Aristocats" showed the appeal and durability of the Disney branch of comedy, while the more sophisticated "A New Leaf" marked a promising directorial debut for its co-star Elaine May. The Black Film's answer to James Bond arrived in the person of Richard Roundtree in "Shaft"; other interesting films included "Two Lane Blacktop," Robert Altman's "McCabe and Mrs Miller," "Summer of '42," a persuasive exercise in nostalgia and Milos Forman's witty "Taking Off." Notable foreign films included Visconti's "Death in Venice," Pasolini's lusty "Decameron," the brilliantly funny Yugoslavian film, "W.R. The Mysteries of the Organism" and Ingmar Bergman's first English-language film, "The Touch." English films like "The Devils" and "Get Carter" attracted attention but it was left to Schlesinger's "Sunday, Bloody Sunday" and Joseph Losey's effective screen adaptation of L.P. Hartley's novel, "The Go-Between," to receive both the honours and popular success. The year's new faces included Richard Roundtree, Ellen Burstyn, Al Pacino, Dominique Sanda, Malcolm McDowell, Barry Newman, Trish Van De Vere, and the latest of actor Lloyd Bridges' sons to make good in films, Jeff Bridges. Death took the "first" cowboy star of the screen, "Bronco Billy" Anderson, silent favourites Betty Bronson, Bebe Daniels, Chester Conklin and one of the great silent comedians, Harold Lloyd. Others included Edmund Lowe, Audie Murphy, Michael Rennie, Van Heflin, Glenda Farrell, Paul Lukas, Pier Angeli, Bella Darvi, Spring Byington, France's Fernandel, Italian matinee idol Tullio Carminati, Hollywood mogul Spyros P. Skouras and the father of the Terrytoons, Paul Terry. Further signs that an epoch in film history was over came with the auctioning off of most of the goods and chattels of the once prestigious 20th Century-Fox.

VON SYDOW, BIBI ANDERSSON IN "THE TOUCH" DIRECTED BY INGMAR BERGMAN (ABC)

CATHERINE DENEUVE IN "PEAU D'ANE" ("THE MAGIC DONKEY") DIRECTED BY JACQUES DEMY (TARGET INTERNATIONAL)

ANICEE ALVINA, SEAN BURY IN "FRIENDS" DIRECTED BY LEWIS GILBERT (PARAMOUNT)

RICHARD ROUNDTREE IN "SHAFT" DIRECTED BY GORDON PARKS (M-G-M)

SUE LYON, GEORGE HAMILTON IN "EVEL KNIEVEL" (FANFARE)

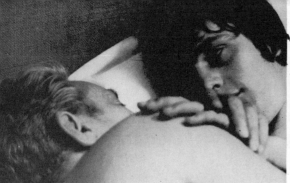

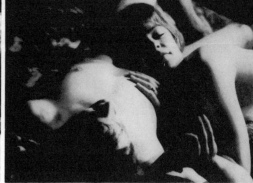

PETER FINCH, MURRAY HEAD

MURRAY HEAD, PETER FINCH,
GLENDA JACKSON

MURRAY HEAD, GLENDA JACKSON

"SUNDAY, BLOODY SUNDAY" DIRECTED BY JOHN SCHLESINGER (UNITED ARTISTS)

MICHAEL GREER, WENDELL BURTON IN
"FORTUNE AND MENS' EYES" (M-G-M)

SIDNEY POITIER, HARRY BELAFONTE IN
"BUCK AND THE PREACHER"
(COLUMBIA)

DEBBIE REYNOLDS, SHELLEY WINTERS
IN "WHAT'S THE MATTER WITH HELEN?"
(UNITED ARTISTS)

"VANISHING POINT" (CUPID)

TOM LAUGHLIN IN
"BILLY JACK"
(WARNER BROS.)

JOHN PHILLIP LAW IN
"THE RED BARON"
DIRECTED BY ROGER CORMAN (UNITED ARTISTS)

ANGELA LANSBURY IN
"BEDKNOBS AND BROOMSTICKS"
(BUENA VISTA)

CLORIS LEACHMAN,
TIMOTHY BOTTOMS

SAM BOTTOMS, BEN JOHNSON
"THE LAST PICTURE SHOW"
DIRECTED BY PETER BOGDANOVICH (COLUMBIA)

GARY GRIMES, JENNIFER O'NEILL IN
"SUMMER OF '42" DIRECTED BY
ROBERT MULLIGAN (WARNER BROS.)

GEORGE C. SCOTT, DIANA RIGG IN
"THE HOSPITAL" (UNITED ARTISTS)

LAURENCE DE MONAGHAN,
JEAN-CLAUDE BRIALY IN "CLAIRE'S KNEE"
DIRECTED BY ERIC ROHMER (COLUMBIA)

HELMUT BERGER, DOMINIQUE SANDA IN
"THE GARDEN OF THE FINZI-CONTINIS"
DIRECTED BY VITTORIO DE SICA
(WALTER READE)

JACK PALANCE IN
"THE HORSEMEN"
ECTED BY JOHN FRANKENHEIMER
(COLUMBIA)

CLINT EASTWOOD IN
"BEGUILED"
DIRECTED BY DON SIEGEL
(UNIVERSAL)

CLINT EASTWOOD IN
"KELLY'S HEROES" (M-G-M)

MICK JAGGER IN
"GIMME SHELTER"
(20TH CENTURY-FOX)

363

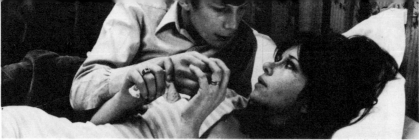

"MURMUR OF THE HEART" (U.K. TITLE "DEAREST LOVE")
DIRECTED BY LOUIS MALLE (GALA)

OLIVER REED IN
"THE DEVILS"
DIRECTED BY KEN RUSSELL
(WARNER)

RICHARD CHAMBERLAIN IN "THE MUSIC LOVERS"
DIRECTED BY KEN RUSSELL (UNITED ARTISTS)

KRIS KRISTOFFERSEN,
KAREN BLACK IN "CISCO PIKE"
(COLUMBIA)

BUCK HENRY, LYNN CARLIN IN
"TAKING OFF" DIRECTED BY MILOS FORMAN (UNIVERSAL)

"TALES OF BEATRIX POTTER"
(M-G-M)

WARREN BEATTY IN
"McCABE AND MRS MILLER"
DIRECTED BY ROBERT ALTMAN (WARNER BRO

LINDA HAYDEN IN
"BABY LOVE" (CINERAMA)

SAL MINEO, KIM HUNTER,
RODDY MCDOWALL IN
"ESCAPE FROM THE PLANET OF THE APES"
(20TH CENTURY FOX)

WOODY ALLEN IN
"BANANAS" (UNITED ARTISTS)

JOAN PLOWRIGHT, JEANNE WAT
LOUISE PURNELL IN
"THE THREE SISTERS" DIRECTED
SIR LAURENCE OLIVIER (BRITISH

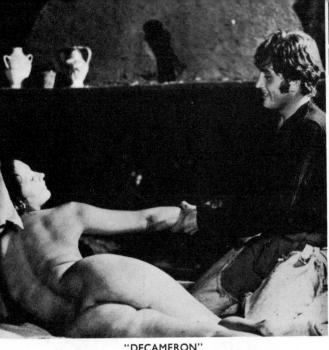

"PRETTY MAIDS ALL IN A ROW"
(M-G-M)

"DECAMERON"
DIRECTED BY PIER PAOLO PASOLINI
(UNITED ARTISTS)

GENE HACKMAN, MARCEL BOZZUFFI
"THE FRENCH CONNECTION"
DIRECTED BY WILLIAM FRIEDKIN
(20TH CENTURY-FOX)

MICHAEL CAINE,
OMAR SHARIF IN
"THE LAST VALLEY" (CINERAMA)

ART GARFUNKEL, CANDICE BERGEN IN
"CARNAL KNOWLEDGE" DIRECTED
BY MIKE NICHOLS (AVCO EMBASSY)

GENE HACKMAN

PAT QUINN, JOHN RUBINSTEIN IN
"ZACHARIAH" (CINERAMA)

DAVID GUMPILIL, JENNY AGUTTER,
LUCIEN JOHN IN "WALKABOUT"
(20TH CENTURY-FOX)

"JOE HILL"
DIRECTED BY BO WIDERBERG
(PARAMOUNT)

JACQUES TATI IN
"TRAFFIC" (COLUMBIA)

TOPOL IN
"FIDDLER ON THE ROOF"
DIRECTED BY NORMAN JEWISON
(UNITED ARTISTS)

"THE RAILWAY CHILDREN"
DIRECTED BY LIONEL JEFFRIES (M-G-M)

MALCOLM MCDOWELL,
MICHAEL BATES,
ANTHONY SHARP

MALCOLM MCDOWELL
"CLOCKWORK ORANGE"
DIRECTED BY STANLEY KUBRICK
(WARNER BROS.)

SILVANA MANGANO,
BJORN ANDERSSON

DIRK BOGARDE
"DEATH IN VENICE"
DIRECTED BY LUCHINO VISCONTI
(COLUMBIA)

BJORN ANDERSSON

JANE FONDA IN
"KLUTE" DIRECTED BY
ALAN J. PAKULA (WARNER BROS.)

ELAINE MAY, WALTER MATTHAU IN
"A NEW LEAF" DIRECTED BY ELAINE
MAY (PARAMOUNT)

JOHN WAYNE IN "BIG JAKE"
(20TH CENTURY-FOX)

BARRY NEWMAN

TRISH VAN DE VERE

JON VOIGHT

CAROL LYNLEY

LEE GRANT, WALTER MATTHAU IN
"PLAZA SUITE" DIRECTED BY
ARTHUR HILLER (CINEMA-INTERNATIONAL)

JAMES TAYLOR, DENNIS WILSON, LAURIE BIRD IN
"TWO LANE BLACKTOP"
DIRECTED BY MONTE HELLMAN (UNIVERSAL)

BRITT EKLAND IN
"GET CARTER"
DIRECTED BY MIKE HODGES (M-G-M)

WARREN OATES, PETER FONDA IN
"THE HIRED HAND" DIRECTED BY
PETER FONDA (UNIVERSAL)

TONY ROBERTS, DEAN JONES,
SANDY DUNCAN IN "$1,000,000 DUCK"
(BUENA VISTA)

ROBERT RYAN IN "LAWMAN"
DIRECTED BY MICHAEL WINNER
(UNITED ARTISTS)

"THE CONFORMIST"
DIRECTED BY BERNARDO BERTOLUCCI (CURZON)

SHIRLEY MACLAINE, CLINT EASTWOOD
IN "TWO MULES FOR SISTER SARA"
DIRECTED BY DON SIEGEL
(UNIVERSAL)

JACK LEMMON, SANDY DENNIS IN
"THE OUT OF TOWNERS"

ALI MACGRAW

BILLIE WHITELAW, GENE WILDER IN
"START THE REVOLUTION WITHOUT ME"
(COLUMBIA)

"A SEPARATE PEACE"
(PARAMOUNT)

BARBRA STREISAND, RYAN O'NEAL IN
"WHAT'S UP DOC?" DIRECTED BY
PETER BOGDANOVICH (WARNER BROS.)

GEORGE C. SCOTT IN
"THEY MIGHT BE GIANTS"
DIRECTED BY ANTHONY HARVEY (UNIVERSAL)

CHARLES BRONSON IN "CHATO'S LAND"
DIRECTED BY MICHAEL WINNER
(UNITED ARTISTS)

RICHARD VAN VLEET IN
"BEN" (CINERAMA)

SYLVIA MILES, ANDREA FELDMAN IN
"HEAT" DIRECTED BY PAUL MORRISSEY (WARHOL)

ALBERT FINNEY,
FULTON MCKAY

"GUMSHOE" (COLUMBIA)

BILLIE WHITELAW,
JANICE RULE

STEVE MCQUEEN IN "JUNIOR BONNER"
DIRECTED BY SAM PECKINPAH
(CINERAMA)

RICHARD WIDMARK, FREDERIC FORREST IN
"WHEN LEGENDS DIE"
(20TH CENTURY-FOX)

CLIFF ROBERTSON, GERALDINE PAGE IN
"J. W. COOP" DIRECTED BY CLIFF ROBERTSON
(COLUMBIA)

PETER CUSHING IN
"TALES FROM THE CRYPT"
(CINERAMA)

TOM COURTENAY IN
"ONE DAY IN THE LIFE
OF IVAN DENISOVICH"
(CINERAMA)

MICKEY ROONEY IN "PULP"
DIRECTED MY MIKE HODGES
(UNITED ARTISTS)

1972 The most explicit sex this side of your bedroom flooded the screen with films like "Such Good Friends," "Portnoy's Complaint" and "Fritz the Cat," the first cartoon feature to be awarded an X certificate. By the end of the year it seemed that a puritan backlash might be on the way although it did little to affect the other current obsession, the glorification of sadistic violence. This was seen in films like Peckinpah's "Straw Dogs," Don Siegel's "Dirty Harry" and in the biggest box-office success in film history, "The Godfather," with a performance by Brando in the title role that won him an Oscar for best actor, which he refused. A new film genre emerged with the crop of so-called Black Films in which black stars re-created the classic exploits of the former white cinema heroes. "Shaft's Big Score" was a popular sequel to the hit of the previous year; other Black Films included "The Legend of Nigger Charlie," "Melinda" and "Superfly." Alongside these trends ran a varied selection of popular films including Bob Fosse's "Cabaret," which gained Liza Minnelli the Oscar for best actress, and Peter Bogdanovich's screwball comedy "What's up Doc?" with Barbra Streisand and Ryan O'Neal. Alfred Hitchcock and John Huston were both on form with "Frenzy" and "Fat City," and Sean Connery returned as the true-blue James Bond in "Diamonds Are Forever." Robert Redford, the star of the year, was in the excellent political satire "The Candidate" as well as "Jeremiah Johnson" and "Hot Rocks." Underrated films included "A Separate Peace," "Junior Bonner" and the Conrad Rooks screen adaptation of Herman Hesse's novel "Siddhartha." From Europe came a stream of quality films including Polanski's "Macbeth" and Pasolini's bawdy "Canterbury Tales." Among the British films were "The Ruling Class," Robert Bolt's "Lady Caroline Lamb," in which he directed his wife, Sarah Miles, and two Ken Russell films, the musical "The Boyfriend" and the biopic "Savage Messiah." Triumphant above all however were Bunuel's masterly "The Discreet Charm of the Bourgeoisie" and Fellini's exultant "Roma." The many new faces included Joe Dallesandro, Jon Finch, Edward Albert, Carolyn Seymour, Tommy Tune, Diane Keaton and Joel Grey, who deservedly won an Oscar for his role in "Cabaret." Death took screen giants Maurice Chevalier and Miriam Hopkins and the urbane character actor George Sanders, as well as silent "Duse" Asta Nielsen, Jessie Royce Landis, Marilyn Maxwell, Marie Wilson, Isabel Jewell, Gia Scala, Bruce Cabot, Brandon de Wilde, Oscar Levant, Akim Tamiroff, Betty Blythe and Claire Windsor; directors Walter Lang, Frank Tashlin, John Grierson, Sidney Franklin, Dr. Paul Czinner, Mitchell Leisen and the operetta composer Rudolf Friml.

KIKA MARKHAM, STACY TENDETER IN
"ANNE AND MURIEL" DIRECTED BY
FRANÇOIS TRUFFAUT (CINETEL)

CLIFF ROBERTSON IN
"THE GREAT NORTHFIELD, MINNESOTA RAID"
(UNIVERSAL)

RAQUEL WELCH IN
"KANSAS CITY BOMBER" (M-G-M)

"RED PSALM" DIRECTED BY
MIKLOS JANSCO (HUNGAROFILM)

EILEEN HECKART, GOLDIE HAWN,
EDWARD ALBERT IN
"BUTTERFLIES ARE FREE" (COLUMBIA)

RON O'NEAL IN "SUPERFLY"
DIRECTED BY GORDON PARKS JR.
(WARNER BROS.)

RICHARD ROUNDTREE

MOSES GUNN

"SHAFT'S BIG SCORE"
DIRECTED BY GORDON PARKS (M-G-M)

GODFREY CAMBRIDGE, RAYMOND ST. JACQUES
IN "COME BACK, CHARLESTON BLUE"
(WARNER BROS.)

CALVIN LOCKHART IN
"MELINDA" (M-G-M)

"THE LEGEND OF NIGGER CHARLIE"
(M-G-M)

BARRY NEWMAN IN
"FEAR IS THE KEY" (M-G-M)

SEAN CONNERY IN
"DIAMONDS ARE FOREVER"
(UNITED ARTISTS)

JON VOIGHT IN "DELIVERANCE"
DIRECTED BY JOHN BOORMAN
(COLUMBIA)

PAULA PRENTISS

ROSALIND CASH

RICHARD ROUNDTREE, KATHY IMRIE,
ROSALIND MILES

LANA WOOD

JAMES COBURN, ROD STEIGER IN
"A FISTFUL OF DYNAMITE"
DIRECTED BY SERGIO LEONE (UNITED ARTISTS)

SIMON WARD IN "YOUNG WINSTON"
DIRECTED BY RICHARD ATTENBOROUGH
(COLUMBIA)

DOTT JOHNSON, KIM DARBY, TONY MUSANTE
IN "THE GRISSOM GANG"
DIRECTED BY ROBERT ALDRICH (CINERAMA)

GENE HACKMAN IN
'THE POSEIDON ADVENTURE'
(20TH CENTURY-FOX)

TWIGGY, CHRISTOPHER GABLE
"THE BOYFRIEND"
DIRECTED BY KEN RUSSELL (M-G-M)

TOMMY TUNE

PAUL NEWMAN, LEE MARVIN IN
"POCKET MONEY"
DIRECTED BY STUART ROSENBERG
(CINERAMA)

ALAIN DELON IN
"THE ASSASSINATION OF
TROTSKY" DIRECTED BY
JOSEPH LOSEY (M-G-M)

MARGARET LEIGHTON, ELIZABETH TAYLOR,
SUSANNAH YORK IN
"ZEE AND CO" (COLUMBIA)

GEORGE HARRISON, BOB DYLAN IN
"CONCERT FOR BANGLA DESH"
(20TH CENTURY-FOX)

KAREN BLACK, RICHARD BENJAMIN IN
"PORTNOY'S COMPLAINT"
(WARNER BROS.)

SCOTT ANTONY IN
"SAVAGE MESSIAH"
DIRECTED BY KEN RUSSELL (M-G-M)

FRANCO NERO, LIV ULLMAN IN
"POPE JOAN" (COLUMBIA)

"FRITZ THE CAT"
(BLACK INK)

RICHARD CONTE, MARLON BRANDO

JAMES CAAN

AL PACINO
"THE GODFATHER"
DIRECTED BY FRANCIS FORD COPPOLA (PARAMOUNT)

MARLON BRANDO, AL PACINO

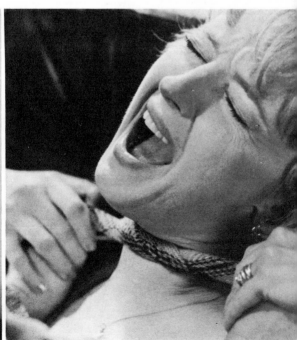

"ROMA"
DIRECTED BY FEDERICO FELLINI
(UNITED ARTISTS)

FERNANDO REY IN
"THE DISCREET CHARM OF THE BOURGEOISIE"
DIRECTED BY LUIS BUÑUEL (20TH CENTURY-FOX

STACY KEACH, JEFF BRIDGES IN
"FAT CITY" DIRECTED BY JOHN HUSTON
(WARNER BROS.)

WOODY ALLEN, DIANE KEATON IN
"PLAY IT AGAIN, SAM"
(PARAMOUNT)

BARBARA LEIGH-HUNT IN "FRENZY"
DIRECTED BY ALFRED HITCHCOCK
(UNIVERSAL)

LIZA MINNELLI

JOEL GREY
"CABARET"
DIRECTED BY BOB FOSSE
(CINERAMA)

HELMUT GRIEM, MICHAEL YORK,
LIZA MINNELLI

GEORGE SEGAL, ROBERT REDFORD, PAUL SAND IN
"HOT ROCKS" (U.K. TITLE "HOW TO STEAL A
DIAMOND IN FOUR UNEASY LESSONS")
DIRECTED BY PETER YATES (20TH CENTURY-FOX)

ROBERT REDFORD IN "THE CANDIDATE"
DIRECTED BY MICHAEL RITCHIE (WARNER BROS.)

ROBERT REDFORD, WILL GEER IN
"JEREMIAH JOHNSON" DIRECTED BY
SYDNEY POLLACK (WARNER BROS.)

JAN MICHAEL VINCENT IN
"THE MECHANIC" DIRECTED BY MICHAEL WINNER
(UNITED ARTISTS)

RICHARD CHAMBERLAIN, SARAH MILES IN
"LADY CAROLINE LAMB"
DIRECTED BY ROBERT BOLT (M-G-M)

PETER O'TOOLE, JAMES COCO IN
"MAN OF LA MANCHA"
DIRECTED BY ARTHUR HILLER
(UNITED ARTISTS)

ALAN BATES, JANET SUZMAN IN
"A DAY IN THE DEATH OF JOE EGG"
(COLUMBIA)

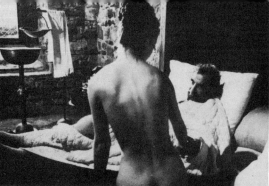

HUGH GRIFFITH IN "THE CANTERBURY TALES"
DIRECTED BY PIER PAOLO PASOLINI (UNITED ARTISTS)

SUSAN GEORGE, DUSTIN HOFFMAN IN
"STRAW DOGS"
DIRECTED BY SAM PECKINPAH (CINERAMA)

MICHELINE LANCTOT IN
"LA VRAIE NATURE DE BERNADETTE"
(CANADA)

BARBARA HARRIS, JACK LEMMON IN
"THE WAR BETWEEN MEN AND WOMEN"
(20TH CENTURY-FOX)

CLINT EASTWOOD IN
"DIRTY HARRY"
DIRECTED BY DON SIEGEL (COLUMBIA)

GENE ROCHE, MICHAEL SACKS IN
"SLAUGHTERHOUSE FIVE"
DIRECTED BY GEORGE ROY HILL
(UNIVERSAL)

DALIAH LAVI IN
"CATLOW" (M-G-M)

EDY WILLIAMS IN "THE SEVEN MINUTES"
DIRECTED BY RUSS MEYER
(20TH CENTURY-FOX)

CLINT EASTWOOD, JESSICA WALTER IN
"PLAY MISTY FOR ME"
DIRECTED BY CLINT EASTWOOD
(UNIVERSAL)

JEFF BRIDGES IN
"BAD COMPANY"
(PARAMOUNT)

GAYLE HUNNICUT

CAROLYN SEYMOUR

PETER BOYLE

"ALICE IN WONDERLAND"
(20TH CENTURY-FOX)

JON FINCH IN "MACBETH"
DIRECTED BY ROMAN POLANSKI
(COLUMBIA)

WALTER MATTHAU IN
"KOTCH" (CINERAMA)

CHARLES BRONSON IN
"THE VALACHI PAPERS"
(CINEMA INTERNATIONAL)

SIMI GAREWAL IN
"SIDDHARTHA"
DIRECTED BY CONRAD ROOKS

JAMES COCO, DYAN CANNON IN
"SUCH GOOD FRIENDS"
DIRECTED BY OTTO PREMINGER
(PARAMOUNT)

PETER O'TOOLE IN
"THE RULING CLASS"
(UNITED ARTISTS)

JOHN WAYNE, NICHOLAS BEAUVY IN
"THE COWBOYS" DIRECTED BY MARK RYDELL
(COLUMBIA)

GOLDIE HAWN, WARREN BEATTY IN
"THE HEIST" DIRECTED BY RICHARD BROOKS
(COLUMBIA)

AVA GARDNER IN
"THE LIFE AND TIMES OF JUDGE ROY BEAN"
DIRECTED BY JOHN HUSTON
(CINERAMA)

RITA HAYWORTH IN
"THE WRATH OF GOD" (M-G-M)

MARLON BRANDO, STEPHANIE BEACHAM IN
"THE NIGHTCOMERS" DIRECTED BY MICHAEL WINN
(AVCO EMBASSY)

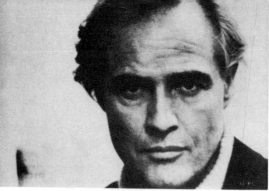

MARLON BRANDO, MARIA SCHNEIDER
"LAST TANGO IN PARIS"
DIRECTED BY BERNARDO BERTOLUCCI
(UNITED ARTISTS)

MARLON BRANDO

VERNA BLOOM, CLINT EASTWOOD IN
"HIGH PLAINS DRIFTER"
(UNIVERSAL)

PETER FINCH, GLENDA JACKSON IN
"BEQUEST TO THE NATION"
(UNIVERSAL)

ALI MACGRAW, STEVE MCQUEEN IN
"THE GETAWAY" DIRECTED BY
SAM PECKINPAH (CINERAMA)

ALAIN DELON IN
"SCORPIO"
(UNITED ARTISTS)

MAGGIE SMITH, ALEC MACOWEN IN
"TRAVELS WITH MY AUNT"
(M-G-M)

ROGER MOORE IN
"LIVE AND LET DIE"
(UNITED ARTISTS)

ELIZABETH TAYLOR, BILLIE WHITELAW IN
"NIGHTWATCH"
DIRECTED BY BRIAN HUTTON (M-G-M)

GLENDA JACKSON, GEORGE SEGAL IN
"A TOUCH OF CLASS"
DIRECTED BY MELVIN FRANK
(AVCO EMBASSY)

RYAN O'NEAL, JACQUELINE BISSETT IN
"THE THIEF WHO CAME TO DINNER"
(WARNER BROS.)

SIR LAURENCE OLIVIER, MICHAEL CAINE IN
"SLEUTH" DIRECTED BY
JOE MANKIEWICZ (20TH CENTURY-FOX)

"BROTHER SUN, SISTER MOON"
DIRECTED BY FRANCO ZEFFIRELLI
(PARAMOUNT)

JULIET MILLS, JACK LEMMON IN
"AVANTI"
DIRECTED BY BILLY WILDER
(UNITED ARTISTS)

EDWARD FOX IN
"THE DAY OF THE JACKAL"
DIRECTED BY FRED ZINNEMAN
(C.I.C.)

RACHEL ROBERTS,
ALBERT FINNEY IN
"ALPHA BETA"

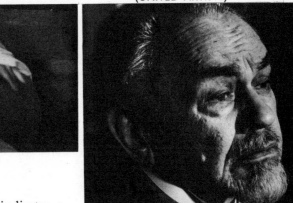

EDWARD G. ROBINSON
WHO DIED 26 JANUARY 1973

TED NEELY IN
"JESUS CHRIST, SUPERSTAR"
DIRECTED BY NORMAN JEWISON
(UNIVERSAL)

1973 A review of the 1973 releases indicates a continuance of the trends of recent years in film-making, namely a growth in the number of independent productions, and the increasing strength of the European cinema in both the British and the American markets. The start of the year saw a major sensation, with the release of "Last Tango In Paris," directed by Bernardo Bertolucci and starring Marlon Brando. Sam Peckinpah directed a taut and violent thriller, "The Getaway," with Steve McQueen and Ali MacGraw, and George Cukor brought Graham Greene's "Travels with My Aunt" to the screen, winning Maggie Smith an Oscar nomination for best actress. Films from distinguished directors included Luchino Visconti's "Ludwig," Billy Wilder's "Avanti," Lindsay Anderson's "Oh, Lucky Man," Fred Zinneman's "Day of the Jackal," and Joe Mankiewicz's "Sleuth," with the intriguing combination of Sir Laurence Olivier and Michael Caine. Also scheduled for release were Franco Zeffirelli's "Brother Sun, Sister Moon," and Norman Jewison's screen version of the smash musical "Jesus Christ, Superstar." Also awaited were Sir Alec Guinness' portrayal of Adolf Hitler in "Hitler – The Last Ten Days," and "Live and Let Die," the new James Bond adventure, with Roger Moore as Bond. An interesting battle awaited the two film versions of "A Doll's House," the first with Claire Bloom re-creating her stage success, and the second directed by Joseph Losey and starring the irrepressible Jane Fonda. Promising new faces included Maria Schneider, Edward Fox, Ted Neely, "Superfly" Ron O'Neal, Paul Winfield and Cicely Tyson. The beginning of the year also saw the death of one of cinema's all-time greats, Edward G. Robinson.

SIR ALEC GUINNESS IN
"HITLER—THE LAST TEN DAYS"
(M-G-M)

RALPH RICHARDSON, MALCOLM MCDOWELL IN
"OH, LUCKY MAN" DIRECTED BY
LINDSAY ANDERSON (WARNER BROS.)

ROMY SCHNEIDER, HELMUT BERGER IN
"LUDWIG"
DIRECTED BY LUCHINO VISCONTI (M-G-M)

JANE FONDA IN
"STEELYARD BLUES"
(WARNER BROS.)

CLAIRE BLOOM, ANTHONY HOPKINS IN
"A DOLL'S HOUSE"
DIRECTED BY PATRICK GARLAND

TREVOR HOWARD, JANE FONDA, DAVID WARNER IN
"A DOLL'S HOUSE"
DIRECTED BY JOSEPH LOSEY (WORLD FILMS)

PETER SELLERS IN
"BLOCKHOUSE"
(HEMDALE)

CHARLES BOYER

SALLY KELLERMAN

JAMES MASON, BEAU BRIDGES IN
"CHILD'S PLAY" DIRECTED BY
SIDNEY LUMET (PARAMOUNT)

MICHAEL YORK, PETER FINCH
"LOST HORIZON" (COLUMBIA)

WALTER MATTHAU, CAROL BURNET IN
"PETE 'N' TILLIE" DIRECTED BY
MARTIN RITT (UNIVERSAL)

SEAN CONNERY IN
"THE OFFENCE"
DIRECTED BY
SIDNEY LUMET (UNITED ARTISTS)

CICELY TYSON

PAUL WINFIELD

ROBERT REDFORD

INDEX